Professing Sociology

Professing Sociology:

Studies in the Life Cycle

of Social Science

IRVING LOUIS HOROWITZ
WASHINGTON UNIVERSITY

ALDINE PUBLISHING COMPANY
CHICAGO

First published 1968 by
Aldine Publishing Company
320 West Adams Street
Chicago, Illinois 60606

Library of Congress Catalog Card Number 68-8151
Designed by Chestnut House
Printed in the United States of America

To my teachers at the City College of New York, especially Abraham Edel, Samuel Hendel, and Edward Rosen, who, in the words of Spinoza, taught me to "make a ceaseless effort not to ridicule, not to bewail, nor to scorn human actions, but to understand them."

Contents

I. THE INNER LIFE OF SOCIOLOGY

1. *Consensus, Conflict, and Cooperation, 3*
2. *Scientific Criticism and the Sociology of Knowledge, 17*
3. *Social Science Objectivity and Value Neutrality, 30*
4. *Crime, Custom, and Culture, 46*
5. *A Formalization of the Sociology of Knowledge, 65*
6. *The Sociology of Social Problems, 80*
7. *On Alienation and the Social Order, 101*
8. *Social Deviance and Political Marginality, 108*

II. THE ACADEMIC LIFE OF SOCIOLOGY

9. *On Learning and Teaching Sociology, 129*
10. *Establishment Sociology, 159*
11. *Sociology for Sale, 167*
12. *Anthropology for Sociologists, 174*
13. *Max Weber and the Spirit of American Sociology, 186*
14. *Mainliners and Marginals, 195*
15. *From Social Psychology to Social Performance, 221*

III. THE POLITICAL LIFE OF SOCIOLOGY

16. *Functionalist Sociology and Political Ideologies, 235*
17. *International Social Science Research, 250*
18. *Social Science and Public Policy, 262*

19. *The Life and Death of Project Camelot, 287*

20. *Federally Sponsored Overseas Research, 305*

21. *Social Science "Fiction" and the Americanization of Conflict, 314*

22. *Social Indicators and Social Policies, 328*

23. *Social Science Yogis and Military Commissars, 340*

NAME INDEX, *355*

SUBJECT INDEX,

Preface

ONE CURIOUS TASK faced by anyone assembling his papers in any given field is to tease out the "design," the *telos*, as it were, linking disparate work together. Of course, in some sense, such a chore is clearly arbitrary and idiosyncratic: arbitrary in that these papers were obviously done on different occasions and for different purposes; and idiosyncratic in that the selection and arrangement process may be just as much a response to external "marketing" needs as to internal "scientific" needs.

In point of fact, the arrangement I finally arrived at represents not just a categorical division of labor, but an historical evolution in my thought on the nature of sociology.

In the main, the papers grouped in the section headed "The Inner Life of Sociology" were done earlier than the other two sections. They reflected my concern with issues in functionalism, conflict theory, problems of objectivity, relativity, and finally, the sociology of knowledge. In those virginal years, it seemed to me that the structural renovation of sociology along the lines of an increasing awareness of the big problems, the classic tradition, the relevant stance, the historically and philosophically self-aware, etc., necessarily preceded all other issues. Indeed, this view is summed up in the paper with which I introduced *The New Sociology*. I was taken with a Baconian enterprise that the need of the moment was a New Organon, if not a New Instauration.

But theory, even sociological theory, requires an institutional framework, a source from which the struggle of ideas can be nourished by ideas of struggle. Without an appreciation for the institutional setting of sociology—the place where, after all, most sociologists make their living and legitimize their careers— the analysis of theory appears a formalistic exercise in the passage of novel ideas from great man to great man. But it would be ludicrous to reduce the history of sociological ideas to a simple transmission belt from mind to mind. It is more nearly the case that sociological history is embedded in the educational agencies and research bureaucracies from which sociologists issue forth their proclamations and projections.

But this, too, is only a portion of the pie. The institutional fiber of educational life is itself far from autonomous. The myth of academic insularity, with its notions of *noblesse oblige*, might be preferable to the Veblenesque way things academic are actually structured. But it confuses the desirable with the actual to assume that the educational fortress from which sociology ventures forth now structures the character or concerns of sociology. Clearly, the whole political life of the nation, and of the world, for that matter, has a pervasive effect, an effect that has transformed the problems of sociology from a classic struggle between analysis and advocacy into problems over choices in application. The old daemon lurking in the minds of most sociologists was: Is sociology really a science? The new daemon looming just as prominently is: Now that sociology is a science, what will be its effects on the lives of men and nations?

I do not wish to imply that these three broad reference points simply supersede one another; problems of principles, pedagogy, and politics coexist in space and time. What I am saying is that my personal priorities have shifted over time, and that I believe this personal shift has been tempered in the crucible of some hard looking at the social world.

For me at least there is no longer any doubt that the threats posed to sociological autonomy by Defense Department requirements are far more perilous than any posed by old-fashioned functionalists. And I take it to be a mark of wisdom and not just age that I can make such a distinction in my work life no less than in my private life. Sociology, whatever its variants or vagaries, or however I may express myself in criticism or defense of a particular school, is, after all, the discipline dedicated to rationalizing modern perceptions of the social world to creating a body of "languages" and measures to serve individual goals, not to bolster any number of collective madnesses.

These papers are presented essentially as they first appeared, with only minor editorial changes. I wish to acknowledge with thanks the original publishers' permissions to reprint them here.

PART I. *The Inner Life of Sociology*

1. *Consensus, Conflict, and Cooperation*

FEW WORDS IN THE vocabulary of contemporary sociology appear as soothing or as reassuring as *consensus*. The chain of agreeable associations of the term symbolizes the final mating of the science of sociology and a theory of social equilibrium. What stands in need of investigation is the price paid for this essentially recent turn in sociological theory. Specifically it must be asked whether the movement away from traditional theories of conflict and conflict resolution represents a genuinely new stage in the secularization of social science or is in fact a narrowing down of the field, brought about by social pressures.

Whatever its meaning, the notion of consensus is an impressively stated, although inadequately explored, reference point in present-day sociology. The resilient strength of consensus theories stems in part from some vague sense that they are connected to functionalism. For those skeptical of this fusion of consensus and function, analysis of the issues is blunted by the plethora of definitions that greet the unwary examiner. The fact is that there is an absence of consensus in sociological theory as to just what does and does not constitute consensus or a consensual matrix.

First presented as the presidential address to the New York State Sociological Society in 1961. The theme of the meetings was the same as the title of the address. The paper was first published in *Social Forces*, 41, no. 2 (December, 1962). The version herein printed is from the slightly changed version that appeared in *System, Change and Conflict*, edited by N. J. Demerath III and Richard A. Peterson (New York: Free Press, 1967).

3

There are at least seven shadings of meaning currently attached to the term "consensus" beyond the common-sense usage of the word as a proper synonym for "agreement between people." First and perhaps most commonly, sociologists define consensus as "adjustment of social dissension." This usage is borrowed from the present psychoanalytic definition of normality as social adjustment and neurosis as the absence of adjustment.[1] The second view has its point of departure in role theory. Consensus is seen as an accord between role behavior and role expectation.[2] The third position, while having a point of contact with an adjustment approach to consensus, lifts it out of the individual realm into a cultural framework. "Where an opinion is very widely held and cuts across all groups in society" there you must have consensus.[3] The fourth theory sees our term as affiliated with hedonistic impulse, as "possible only when two or more parties want to maintain a relationship which each regards as in its own interest."[4] A cognate definition is offered by the same writer in terms of game theory. "Two parties or groups are playing to gain a maximum, but they are prepared to settle for less within the recognized limits."[5] The sixth account identifies consensus with the curbing of hedonistic impulse and instinct, and with the Durkheim notion of solidarity and social cohesion generally.[6] The last author sees consensus in its barest atomic terms as a sharing of perspectives, as "nothing more or less than the existence on the part of two or more persons, of similar orientations toward something."[7]

Examining these definitions dispassionately, and leaving aside the truth content of each, it is difficult to understand why the concept of consensus has aroused such intense sociological interest. No logical unraveling of the above definitions will explain why consensus, barely a meaningful word in the sociological lexicon of previous decades, is now viewed as a fully matured theory. An accounting of the term is therefore required on extra-philological grounds. The expanding uses and abuses of consensus theory overshadow the existing definitional ambiguities.

Consensus theory is now employed to settle a wide range of sociological problems. What is most frequently encountered is the identification of consensus with functional efficiency, and no less with the social requisites of political

1. J. O. Hertzler, *American Social Institutions: A Sociological Analysis* (Boston: Allyn and Bacon, 1961), p. 63.

2. Neal Gross, "The Sociology of Education," in *Sociology Today: Problems and Prospects*, ed. by R. K. Merton, L. Broom, L. S. Cottrell, Jr. (New York: Basic Books, 1959), p. 140.

3. Leonard Broom and Philip Selznick, *Sociology: A Test with Adapted Readings*, 2nd ed. (Evanston, Ill.: Row, Peterson & Co., 1958), p. 278.

4. Arnold W. Green, *Sociology: An Analysis of Life in Modern Society*, 3rd. ed. (New York: McGraw-Hill Book Co., 1960), p. 65.

5. *Ibid.*, p. 67.

6. Ely Chinoy, *Society, An Introduction to Sociology* (New York: Random House, 1961), pp. 344–346.

7. Theodore Newcomb, "The Study of Consensus," in Merton, Broom, and Cottrell, *Sociology Today*, p. 279.

democracy.[8] In its simplest form, the bivariate equation is that increase in the amount of social consensus yields an increase in functional efficacy and democratic polity; while inversely, decrease in the amount of social consensus creates social disorganization and dysfunction. On a broader front, advocates of consensus theory see this as a new turn in sociology—away from the knotty issue of how conflicts arise and are settled toward the spatially and temporally more durable issue of how men cooperate with one another. By defining the core of social action in terms of two functional references: (a) the maintenance of a pattern of orientation, and (b) the definition of the meaning of one or more situational objects, consensus comes to be equated with social equilibrium.[9]

Before proceeding to the substance of my remarks, an historical observation is in order. It is clear that the early development of sociology from Marx to Simmel took as its point of departure the idea that society is best understood as a selective and collective response to the needs of social interaction in a nonequilibrated world. This involved a rejection, conscious or otherwise, of the idea that society is best understood as a contractual or informal agreement made between equals to secure common goals. As such, the Roman Empire for Simmel is not a union of the general will with particularized wills, but rather an illustration of the efficiency, the functionality of political superordination, of what he terms Caesaristic types of rule. Thus, what consensus exists is for Simmel the "tendency of domination by means of leveling." This apparent consensual apparatus is but *disguised* superordination. In discussing Philip the Good of Burgundy, he notes that "legal differences were created exclusively by the arbitrary pleasure of the ruler. They thus marked all the more distinctly the common, unalterable subordination of his subject."[10]

Similarly, for Marx, the economic system called capitalism does not come into existence as a consequence of the clamor of public opinion or to express the general will (although those who do come to power exercise such rationalizations), but simply to satisfy the historical process that brings a social class to power. The welding of such power to a new social class is the purpose of the state, which in turn enters the historical picture as the central agency of coercion while posing as the agency of social consensus.

The *practical* struggle of these particular interests, which constantly *really* run counter to the communal and illusory communal interests, makes *practical* intervention and control necessary through the illusory "general interest" in the form of the state. The social

8. Seymour M. Lipset, "Political Sociology," in Merton, Broom, and Cottrell, *Sociology Today*, p. 114.

9. Talcott Parsons, *The Social System* (Glencoe, Ill.: Free Press, 1951), p. 507. This same view is even more forcefully developed in "The Point of View of the Author," in *The Social Theories of Talcott Parsons*, ed. by Max Black (Englewood Cliffs, N.J.: Prentice-Hall, 1961), p. 327.

10. Georg Simmel, "Subordination under an Individual," *The Sociology of Georg Simmel*, ed. and trans. by K. H. Wolff (Glencoe: Free Press, 1950), pp. 201–207.

power, *i.e.*, the multiplied productive force, which arises through the cooperation of different individuals as it is determined within the division of labor, appears to these individuals, since their cooperation is not voluntary but natural, not as their own united power, but as an alien force existing outside them, of the origins and end of which they are ignorant, which they thus cannot control.[11]

Consensus is thus the idealization of coercion.

The roots of conflict theory reach back in time to Hobbes and the formation of the modern nation-state, Marsilius of Padua in the medieval world, and Thrasymachus, Socrates, and Plato in ancient Greek society. In essence, the position holds that social organization does not flow from the consensus of *vox populi*, but from the contradictory yet interrelated needs and designs of men. It is interesting to note that the debate between Thrasymachus and Socrates in *The Republic* concerning the nature of justice (the dialogue on power versus virtue) at no point assumes society to be the consequence of popular will or common agreement. Nonetheless, it cannot be said that the history of social and political theory has been a one-sided acceptance of conflict theory and its underlying power thesis as the only explanation of social structure and social action. Such an assertion would have to discount the bulk of writings from Aristotle's "golden mean" to Dewey's "common faith." Thus the history of conflict and consensus has been a dialogue between exclusive frames of reference seeking to explain the same phenomenon—human cooperation.

From the point of view of sociological history, however, it is pertinent to bear in mind its close affiliation with conflict theorists: Marx on *Klassenkampf*, Gumplowicz on *Rassenkampf*, Mosca's ruling and ruled classes, and Simmel on *Superordnung* and *Unterordnung*. Only now, with sociology in the full passion of its empiricist revolt against European systems of sociology and social philosophy, has a strenuous effort been made to overcome theories of conflict—what have come to be termed "crisis ideologies." Part of this cleansing process has been the promotion of consensus theory. With this promotion has come the inevitable search for new sociological hero images. The brilliant social historian de Tocqueville in particular has been elevated in current estimates.[12]

The rallying point in de Tocqueville is the comment that "a society can exist only when a great number of men consider a great number of things from the same point of view; when they hold the same opinions upon many subjects,

11. Karl Marx and Friedrich Engels, "The German Ideology," in *Basic Writings on Politics and Philosophy: Marx and Engels*, ed. by L. S. Feuer (Garden City, N.Y.: Doubleday and Co., 1959), pp. 255–256, also p. 253.

12. Seymour M. Lipset, *Political Man: The Social Bases of Politics* (Garden City, N.Y.: Doubleday and Co., 1960), pp. 26–28, 65–66. Lipset's continual juxtaposition of de Tocqueville and Marx is a strong indication that the differences between consensus and conflict theories involve something more than scientific requirements. Indeed, he has made them ideological poles: consensus representing democracy and conflict representing authoritarianism.

when the same occurrences suggest the same thoughts and impressions to their minds."[13] Here then seems to be the historical progenitor of the new theory of consensus, and the repudiation of those political sociologies which seek to define social structure in terms of holders and seekers of power, of the ability to command and to coerce. We must now focus attention on current efforts to convert de Tocqueville's insight into a theory.

Perhaps the most widespread axiom of consensus theory holds that it is a necessary condition for social structure.[14] The social structure has come to be defined as excluding those patterns of human action which are spontaneous and unstructured. Social structure is said to consist in a "set of statuses" defined by relatively stable relationships between people. What follows is a mechanical notion of the relation of consensus and conflict as structured and unstructured modes of behavior, respectively. Consensus involves objectification of position, group cohesion, collective representations, common traditions, and rules for inducting and indoctrinating new members; while conflict is seen as external to social structure, as spontaneity, impulsive action, lack of organization, and intuitive response to immediate situations. In short, consensus differs from conflict as organization differs from deviance.[15] Thus to discuss social structure is by definition not to examine conflict situations, and of course, the pernicious *vice versa*, to examine conflict situations is to discuss something extraneous to social structure.

To place conflict outside the framework of social structure, or to go beyond that and see conflict as necessarily destructive of the social organism, is to place a definite premium on social equilibrium. It strongly implies that a society can be changed only by apocalyptic or spontaneous methods. The identification of consensus with social structure reinforces the stereotyped view that change does not emanate from the Establishment and, keeping within the boundaries it informally sets, is deviant in relation to social order as such. Consensus theory thus tends to become a metaphysical representation of the dominant ideological matrix. It rests on a principle of "general interests" that every member of society is supposed to imbibe if he wishes to avoid the onus of being a deviant or an unconnected isolate. The sociology of small groups has been especially active in pushing this view; the implication being that a condition of social conflict necessarily is a world of deviants and isolates quite incapable of attending to problems of functional survival.[16] The possibility that differing goal orientations are consonant with a single functional agency is too rarely

13. Alexis de Tocqueville, *Democracy in America*, trans. by H. Reeve (New York: Century and Co., 1899), vol. I, p. 398.

14. Cf. Robert E. Park, "Reflections on Communication and Culture," *American Journal of Sociology*, XLIV (1939): 191–205.

15. Kurt Lang and Gladys E. Lang, *Collective Dynamics* (New York: Thomas Y. Crowell Co., 1961), pp. 13–14.

16. Theodore Newcomb, "The Study of Consensus," in Merton, Broom, and Cottrell, *Sociology Today*, p. 284.

entertained.[17] Briefly then, only when social function is narrowly defined as social equilibrium can a sociological theory of conflict be viewed as an overt or hidden menace to the social system.

A series of considerations that are increasingly being adduced to demonstrate the singular advantages of consensus theory over conflict theory relates to the difficulties of a social examination of unstable relations. Three factors in particular are pointed out: (a) the transitory nature of conflict situations, that is, the actual behavior of a mass in an extreme situation, such as civil war or revolution, is so short-lived and capricious that predicting conclusions or consequences of conflict situations is impossible; (b) the necessity for dealing with conflict situations in their natural social environment has as its corollary the absence of controlled experiments such as one finds in strictly delineated types of research; (c) the consequent necessity of presenting evaluations in terms of second- and thirdhand materials such as newspaper reports, autobiographical sketches, and historical studies of unique events—all of which clearly involve the sociological researcher in commitments beyond the empirical confines of the sampling situation.[18]

Scrutiny of this series of objections reveals a transparency and shallowness that pose a serious threat to sociological research as such. The criteria of scientific analysis have never been reducible to the simplicity of an investigatory context. What the above objections fail to take account of is the need for a criterion of significance, the importance of contextual variables to the general growth of sociological knowledge. While it is correct that conflict situations, even of major proportions, are generally of "short" duration (at least in relation to the consequences), this is not a serious objection either to the empirical study of conflict situations or, more to the point, to a causal analysis of the genesis and sources of such situations. Sheer brevity of the conflict situation in relation to the consensual consolidation that may follow indicates only that certain sampling devices are ineffectual to resolve certain kinds of social events. To reason that any step beyond the borders of current methodological safeguards is to step beyond sociology as such is sheer casuistry, justifying the deep fears of many scholars in cognate social sciences that sociologists are too interested in domination and too little interested in cooperation.

The objection to the study of conflict situations because such situations have no well-defined contours or boundaries is equally transparent. This is very nearly always the case of the anthropologist in relation to a given culture. Would it seriously be contended that the "natural" setting of anthropological research makes it a lesser social science? The surest guarantee against provincialism and ethnocentrism would be a greater effort by sociologists to develop

---

17. Gideon Sjoberg, "Contradictory Functional Requirements and Social Systems," *Journal of Conflict Resolution*, IV (1960): 198–208; see also Eugene Litwak, "Models of Bureaucracy Which Permit Conflict," *American Journal of Sociology*, LXVII (1961): 177–184.

18. A fuller catalog of objections to the study of conflict situations is contained in Lang and Lang, *Collective Dynamics*, pp. 545–553.

techniques of study suitable to this "natural" social setting. The failure to do so has too frequently placed the sociologist in the position of offering question-naires devised for particular situations as uniformly (if not universally) valid in other cultural and social settings. The natural setting within which conflict arises, far from being an obstacle, should provide a powerful incentive to move beyond the highly structured, but hardly universal, world of the small group. That this opportunity has not been seized is more a reflection of the limits of the "opinion leaders" among sociologists than a true delimiting of the legitimate boundaries of sociology.

The pernicious notion that the sociologist somehow has a unique tool of investigation that entitles him to ignore or downgrade the value of journalistic reports or historical surveys is insupportable on scientific grounds. Criteria for sound analysis are fairly constant throughout the spectrum of the social and historical sciences. The same questions can be asked about newspaper clippings as about questionnaires. Lasswell has done just that in his *Language of Politics*:

Can we assume that a scholar read his sources with the same degree of care throughout this research? Did he allow his eye to travel over the thousands upon thousands of pages of parliamentary debates, newspapers, magazines, and other sources listed in his biblio-graphy or notes? Or did he use a sampling system, scanning some pages superficially, though concentrating upon certain periods? Was the sampling system for the *Frankfurter Zeitung*, if one was employed, comparable with the one for the *Manchester Guardian?* Were the leaflets chosen simply because they were conveniently available to the scholar, or were they genuinely representative of the most widely circulated propaganda leaflets?[19]

These are, to be sure, correctly framed sociological questions. But they carry no implication that results are inferior if they are gathered from one source and not another. There is a difference between *resolving* a case for a position on the basis of news reports and *employing* such reports in attempting to arrive at some position.

To equate the worth of a theory (such as consensus theory *or* conflict theory) with ease of study is a sophistical device that leads to a situation in which only those things are studied for which data already exists—which may help to account for that fantastic sameness and duplication of research efforts in present-day small-group sociology. The greatest sociological requirement is precisely to fashion methods adequate to the tasks of studying problems of social order in a world of conflicting interests, standards, and values. Social order must itself be defined, and, no less, define the larger universe of social change. The sociolo-gist can hardly run the risk of being surprised by events of common currency in consequence of a theory of society bewitched by order and befuddled by change.

The faith in consensus theory as operationally more worthwhile than conflict

19. Harold D. Lasswell, "Why be Quantitative," in *Reader in Public Opinion and Com-munication*, enlarged ed., ed. by Bernard Berelson and Morris Janowitz (Glencoe, Ill.: Free Press, 1953), p. 267.

theory often takes the form of a deep respect for the amazing complexity of social organization in industrial economies: the automation of production, the automation of human responsibilities, the precision of "chain of command" and "line" matrices, and the autoregulative capacities of man in mass society to continually adjust to (and make adjustments in) bureaucratic procedures. The Parsonian school of sociology in particular seems impressed with the regularities that obtain between organization and society as such. Here the dilemma lies in equating organization with consensus. The stress and strain of organizational life give rise to a definition of social action as that autoregulative mechanism which adjusts for such "alienative" factors.

Such a view suffers from the master problem in traditional laissez-faire economics; namely, the assumption that automatic marketing "laws" somehow operate over and above the actual desires and ends of men. To meet the laissez-faire implications in the theory of social consensus, certain functionalists have developed a theory of the "safety valve," such that organizations "provide substitute objects upon which to displace hostile sentiments as well as means of abreaction of aggressive tendencies."[20] But this subtheory only reinforces the "metaphysical pathos" surrounding the theory of social organization since, far from being challenged, the assumption of institutional omnipotence and omniscience is reinforced. One is forced to conclude that the "clever" organization can even program small-scale conflict situations in order to guarantee the consensual apparatus as a whole.

The wide uses of consensus theory, particularly as a replacement for conflict theory, shows a close historical and analytical connection to the displacement of the language of social class by an alternate language of social status. It is a shift from viewing industrial society as susceptible to many and varied forms to seeing the industrial complex as growing omnipotent with time. Essentially, the Weberian theory of bureaucracy is a pessimistic vision, a view of organization as once and for all superseding production as the master social agency. In the theory of bureaucracy, the question of which class or group of classes holds the reins of power is secondary, since the "basic" bureaucratic factor continues to grow whatever economic organization obtains. Bureaucracy comes to be viewed as omnipotent, subject to temporary setbacks but never to any real or sizable defeat. If such is the case, then consensus theory is indeed no less omnipotent than the organization procedures from which it derives its originating impulse.

Consensus theory has led to such a stress on continuities and similarities in the life of an industrial complex that all real differences between democracy and autocracy, ruling and being ruled, exploiting and being exploited, are eliminated—in theory at least. The "natural history of society" technique, which sees everything in terms of functional identities, has made a universe in which only

---

20. Lewis A. Coser, *The Functions of Social Conflict* (Glencoe, Ill.: The Free Press, 1956), pp. 155–156.

grey cats and clever hounds exist. Political systems are reduced to "quantifiable" terms of how decisions are arrived at in system A or system B. The fusion of Michels and Weber being urged upon us, a fusion between "iron laws" of oligarchy and bureaucracy respectively, is not a resolution of the crisis in consensus theory, but a symptom of that crisis.[21] Since everything is reduced to administrative techniques, goals of any specific organization vanish into functional identifications, and the individual is left with an impotence that derives from being a part of an association that has a consensual life over and above the person. Consensus becomes the ideological celebration of the corporate personality, possessing a reality that transcends human society as such.

The mystique of consensus theory is evident in the work of many students of complex organization. Here we are met with the impermeable and impenetrable sovereignty of total specialization: the narcotizing effect of role-sets, the functional value of constraint and persuasion, decision-making machinery, etc. The paradox is that consensus theory, far from acting as a bulwark of democratic social theory (as it starts out to be), is the very reverse. It is not a theory for reaching agreements, but one which states that harmony is intrinsic in the organization of the bureaucratic life: a harmony that exists over and above the actual accords reached by men. And such must consensus theory remain, since any serious theory of agreements and decisions must at the same time be a theory of disagreements and the conditions under which decisions cannot be reached. Yet consensus theorists, starting from the metaphysical "need" for consensus as universal, can only talk about absolute and relative consensus, complete or partial integration, but never about conflict as a means of expressing genuine social needs and aspirations.[22]

On this point, Gouldner has put matters rightly by pointing out:

Instead of telling men how bureaucracy might be mitigated, they insist that it is inevitable. Instead of explaining how democratic patterns may, to some extent, be fortified and extended, they warn us that democracy cannot be perfect. Instead of controlling the disease, they suggest that we are deluded, or more politely, incurably romantic for hoping to control it. Instead of assuming responsibilities as realistic clinicians, striving to further democratic potentialities wherever they can, many social scientists have become morticians, all too eager to bury men's hopes.[23]

In this connection it is interesting to note Parsons' restructuring of Merton's

---

21. Lipset, "Political Sociology," pp. 89–91.

22. See, in particular, Chester I. Barnard, *The Functions of the Executive* (Cambridge: Harvard University Press, 1938); James D. Mooney and Alan C. Reiley, *The Principles of Organization* (New York: Harper & Bros., 1939); Talcott Parsons, "Suggestions for a Sociological Approach to the Theory of Organizations," *Administrative Science Quarterly*, 1 (1956): 63–85; Philip Selznick, "Foundations of the Theory of Organization," *American Sociological Review*, XIII (1948): 25–35.

23. Alvin W. Gouldner, "Metaphysical Pathos and the Theory of Bureaucracy," *American Political Science Review*, 49 (1955): 506–507.

paper on "Social Structure and Anomie." Parsons writes that "what Merton calls 'conformity' is clearly what we here mean by the equilibrated condition of the interactive system without conflict on either side or alienative motivations."[24] But if we employ a pattern-variable scheme which admits of an equation between "rebellion" and "alienation," and between "conformity" and "equilibrium," we are a priori ruling out the possibility that a condition of rebellion is consonant with equilibrium at any level and, correspondingly, that extreme states of consensus might create social or personal disequilibrium. If this formula is seriously entertained, I find it hard to fathom Parsons' sensitivity to the charge that his is a conservative doctrine that sees social change as deviant to social order and as a phenomenon that is possible only when the "control mechanisms of the social system" break down. Paradoxically, these remarks by Parsons are made in connection with the necessity for theory of change.[25]

The entire concept of deviant behavior itself rests on a faith that consensus is in every situation observable and functionally relevant—a statement that cannot pass inspection. From the point of view of established consensus as to the sanctity of private property, an act of juvenile vandalism might be measured in the same way as an act of political rebellion, e.g., the physical damage involved in the "Freedom Riders" actions. But from the point of view of the goals sought, what is meant by consensus needs to be spatially and temporally stipulated; and no less, the difference between means and ends must itself be considered as a factor existing over and beyond the supposed functional damage the social order sustains. Too often, deviance is ambiguously formulated so as to cover extremely different situations; i.e., a departure from the rules on the part of an isolated member of a group, as well as defiance of group rules by those external to the specific referential set.

It cannot be stated as a theoretical first principle that consensus carries an implication of social equilibrium or, for that matter, that conflict entails disequilibrium. There is a distinction to be made between types and levels of conflict, especially between those conflicts *over* the basis of consensus, and those conflicts arising *within* the consensual apparatus. There are, to draw an analogy from game theory, conflicts programmed for continuation of the game (such as parliamentary debates), and there are those programmed to end the game through a change of the rules as such (such as coups d'etat). In neither case is a theory of conflict tied to social disorganization or to deviance from norms. This is not to say that conflict situations do not contain possibilities of social disorganization. Of course they do. For example, the absence of a formal constitution over an extended period of time can create political chaos and turmoil. But likewise, a perfect constitution, preparing the ground for every sort of contingency, can have a boomerang effect and heighten the stress situation by a failure to arrive at common standards of belief and action. In short, both consensus and conflict

24. Talcott Parsons, The Social System, pp. 257–259.
25. Ibid., pp. 320–321.

are phenomena that may promote or retard social cooperation or political cohesion.

Simmel caught the authentic spirit of the relation of conflict to social cooperation when he noted that

If a fight simply aims at annihilation, it does approach the marginal case of assassination in which the admixture of unifying elements is almost zero. If, however, there is any consideration, any limit to violence, there already exists a socializing factor, even though only as the qualification of violence. One unites in order to fight, and one fights under the mutually recognized control of norms and rules.[26]

It must therefore be noted that conflict no less than consensus operates within the social structure, within the system of mutually established laws, norms, and values.

If consensus and conflict occupy the same social universe and logically imply one another, what is the basis for suggesting the empirical superiority of conflict theory as an analytical tool? Fundamentally, it is the impossibility of describing any but the most permissive and tolerant communities in terms of consensus matrices. On the other hand, conflict theory, with its openness to problems of coercion, pressure groups, social classes, political myths, cultural clashes, racial strife, etc., more nearly approximates the going issues in *Gesellschaft* relationships. In short, from a descriptive point of view, conflict theory covers a wider and more profound range of questions. From a prescriptivist position, it is, to be sure, better for men to settle their differences on the basis of free agreement rather than external pressures. But this is an entirely different level of sociological analysis, the level of what kind of decisions make for human cooperation. In any event, consensus theorists cut themselves off from this avenue of thought because of their uniform faith in a descriptivist sociology. They are thus reduced to platitudinous statements that not enough attention has been given to the consensus apparatus in group relations. However, even admitting the validity of this claim, it does not carry a mandate to consider consensus as either a more virtuous—or what is more significant, a more practiced—form of arranging social affairs than custom, myth, or even coercion.

Why, then, has the great shift from conflict theory to consensus theory taken place at this juncture in American sociology? Several hypotheses suggest themselves. First, that as American society becomes more democratic, more easygoing, the search for the consensual basis becomes more pronounced. This seems to be the viewpoint adopted by Lipset. However, his view of the end of ideology seems not so much a consequence of an expanding democratic temper as it is simply a reflection of domestic affluence and the large share of the United States inhabitants who benefit from the affluent society.[27]

26. Georg Simmel, *Conflict*, pp. 25–26. Quoted in Coser, *The Functions of Social Conflict*, p. 121.

27. Lipset, *Political Man*, pp. 403–417; see also in this connection, Daniel Bell, *The End of Ideology* (Glencoe, Ill.: Free Press, 1960).

A much more powerful line of reasoning has been suggested by Morris Janowitz, when he indicates that technical bureaucracies and team-member proficiency have tended to usurp the older power of formal authority as distinct from science—which is to say that the older situation of science as isolated from policy-making has disintegrated. With this, authority shifts from outright reliance on domination to a wider utilization of manipulation, on demonstrated managerial skills, operational proficiencies, and the capacity to develop positive organizational loyalties. Therefore, in such a context, consensus comes to be the decisive pivot upon which the success or failure of the manipulative society hangs.[28]

But perhaps the most powerful reason for the shift to consensus theory is the "enlightened" recognition that mass terror is not as powerful an instrument for extracting economic and political loyalties as mass persuasion. The entire theoretical edifice of small-group theory comes to rest on the idea that the formal sanctioning of force is less potent a factor in individual or group motivation than the informal sanctions of the immediately involved reference-set. The belief in consensus as a stratagem is well articulated by Frank when he writes:

The idea has spread that employers were wasting human energy by the traditional authoritarian ways of imposing their decisions on their employees. Psychologists—collaborating with engineers and economists and, more recently, anthropologists—have made many studies concerned with the impact of physical aspects of the workplace, such as lighting, color of walls and machines, temperature and humidity; with working conditions, such as hours, shifts, rest periods, piece rates, and especially relations of foremen and supervisors to their groups. Such studies helped to articulate a new view of corporate life.[29]

But what, it must be asked, is the content of this new view of corporate life? Is it a theory of the corporation or simply a technique of mass persuasion and manipulation? Is it a sociological statement of the nature of the corporate structure, or the uses by the corporate structure of sociological statements? The promotion of consensus as a theory has had as its asking price the conversion of sociology from a science to a tool policy—a policy which, moreover, fails to reach the goal of harmony.[30] As White recently indicated, "There is nothing new in manipulated opinion and engineered consent. . . . Even the sheer bulk of

28. Morris Janowitz, *Sociology and the Military Establishment* (New York: Russell Sage Foundation, 1959), pp. 27–38. Janowitz' remarks are confined to the military. Responsibility for enlarging the scope and context of his argument is mine.

29. Lawrence K. Frank, "Psychology and the Social Order," in *The Human Meaning of the Social Sciences*, ed. by Daniel Lerner (New York: Meridian Books, Inc., 1959), p. 230.

30. David Riesman, Nathan Glazer, Reuel Denney, *The Lonely Crowd: A Study of the Changing American Character* (Garden City, N.Y.: Doubleday Anchor Books, 1954,) pp. 306–307.

distortion is not altogether new, merely more refined. What is new is the acceptability, the mere taken-for-grantedness of these things."[31]

I want to terminate my remarks with a plea for sharper logical and linguistic distinctions, and specifically to point out that the issue of human cooperation, while related to consensus and conflict, has a quite unique dimension and operational range. It must be pointed out that a decision in favor of consensus theory is not automatically a decision on behalf of cooperation. It is simply a decision to examine social structure to the partial or total exclusion of social dynamics; a decision to act as if breaks with tradition, shifts in the culture complex, disruption of moral patterns, can be described as marginal in character. There is indeed a kind of safety in the continuing, the prolonged, the enduring. But this safety gratuitously cloaking itself in the mantle of the secularization of science is nothing but the abdication of the field of social change, and hence an abandonment of the ongoing problems confronting those most directly concerned with achieving human cooperation at group, regional, national, or international levels.

The functional successes of any given social structure should not define the limits of sociological discourse. For we may find ourselves celebrating one social order one day and another the next—and in precisely the same "functional-structural" terms. The central task of sociology is explanation and prediction, each in terms of the other, and no theory that identifies consensus with the social order as such can fail to come upon hard times.

What then is the difference between consensus and cooperation? There seem to be three distinguishable factors to be identified. First: consensus stands for agreement internally, i.e., in terms of shared perspectives, agreements on the rules of association and action, a common set of norms and values. Cooperation for its part makes no demands on role uniformity but only upon procedural rules. Cooperation concerns the settlement of problems in terms that make possible the continuation of differences and even fundamental disagreements. Thus one can legitimately speak of cooperation between labor and management, while one speaks on the degree of consensus each side brings to bear at the bargaining table. Second: consensus is agreement on the content of behavior, while cooperation necessitates agreement only on the form of behavior. We speak of "consensus" if all members of the Women's Christian Temperance Union agree to abstain from drinking alcoholic beverages. But we speak of "cooperation" when agreement is reached on the forms allowed for drinking and the forms allowed for curbing the intake of liquor. As the "Prohibition Era" dramatically showed, the substitution of consensus for cooperation did not lead to a new morality but simply to chaos. Third: cooperation concerns toleration of differences, while consensus demands abolition of these same differences. If a game-theory analogy is preferred, the distinction between cooperation and

31. Howard B. White, "The Processed Voter and the New Political Science," *Social Research*, XXVIII (1961): 150.

consensus might be stated in the following terms: consensus programs the termination of the game by insisting on the principle of unity and unilateral victory, whereas cooperation is pluralistic because it programs the continuation of the game by maintaining and insisting upon the legitimacy of differences.

What is required at this juncture is a more adequate sociological theory of cooperation; a stipulation of the conditions of that minimum set of beliefs about man and his social universe that is consonant with continued survival and growth. Such a theory of cooperation would insist on the need for maintaining life although leaving open the question of what to do with it; insist on the need to secure the material and cultural needs of men although differing on the sort of social system best able to meet such needs. Beyond this, there is a need for a theory of conflict, a programming of conflict, that would allow people to shift and choose their conceptions of what constitutes progress, pleasure, etc., and the institutionalization of avenues of action to implement these conceptions. Consensus theory has done nothing to melt the present freezing of attitudes on either a national or international scale. Nor will it, unless sociologists show a willingness to expand their collective vision of the social universe beyond the confines of a dormitory or a hospital ward.

The unity required to evolve such a sociological theory of cooperation is methodological rather than systematic. It requires us to approach ideas and attitudes concerning cooperation as hypotheses whose truth content must be measured by the degree with which they can be correlated to objective circumstances. This is something quite different than placing men in a Procrustean bed of pattern variables that may or may not hold for previous or future generations —or, for that matter, for the present one. The methods of sociology do not exclude decisive choices in favor of specific objectives. However, they do caution us against ignoring alternative conceptual frameworks on the basis of their unpopularity or marginality. The concept of cooperation is essentially the programming of common standards in a world of conflicting interests, and even of different notions as to what constitutes interests. Precisely because a general theory of cooperation would offer no transcendental commitments to the eternal righteousness of any existing social order, it can place itself in the service of men. It would be well for sociology to perform a decisive role in the structuring of a theory of cooperation, both for the general values it would help establish and for a way to settle some long-standing ambiguities in sociological research.

2. *Scientific Criticism and the Sociology of Knowledge*

I

A science must have a specified content and definite if fluid limits, but a scientific enterprise must also have unrealized goals. What makes goals scientific rather than speculative is the availability of a methodology for realizing them in future practice. It can be said that the initial aim of the sociology of knowledge is its separation from purely or even partially ideological concepts. Much past criticism of *wissenssoziologie* has centered about the impossibility of taking a nonideological position on ideological issues. This highly respected criticism is transparently thin in that its guarded assumption really amounts to the assertion that social science is an impossibility. I am not attempting a defense of the notion of the socially unbound intellectual put forth by Alfred Weber and Karl Mannheim (which itself involves a series of unverifiable assumptions about social mobility and class characteristics). What is being noted is simply the common sense fact that the social scientist, like the natural scientist, is not prevented from formulating hypotheses and law statements. Social bounds are a factor, not a barrier, in scientific work.

This paper was intended to show how leading conceptual variables in many of the social sciences represent particularistic responses to general sociopolitical problems. It was stimulated by a general concern to indicate where the sociology of knowledge "fits" in relation to the hierarchy of social and humanistic disciplines. The paper was first published in *Philosophy and Phenomenological Research*, 21, no. 2 (December, 1960); reprinted by permission.

What seems to be confused in the critical literature is the question of whether the empirical structuring of religious, scientific, and ideological ideas is possible as a separate question from the value judgments rendered on the basis of such findings. A convention of physicists might offer many contradictory statements on what use men should make of atomic power, but this does not mean that no common ground concerning the formalization of the principles of atomic energy is possible.

Science is a practical and direct response to goals sought. The existence of different types of goals creates the need for different sciences.

This is not to deny that the sociology of knowledge might be a "dangerous science" to socially backward and oppressive elements. The very attempt to weed out false but politically operative propositions from the true is latent with dangers for ideologically sanctioned institutions and movements. Again, if we take an anology from the early history of science, we see a like situation in the Copernicus-Galileo presentation of the heliocentric theory of the universe. It may be recalled that as long as this astronomical theory was offered as just another "opinion," no social or religious repercussions occurred. Indeed, the scientists themselves were very often equally concerned with supporting religious orthodoxies. It was only when the heliocentric theory was offered as truth, *i.e.*, as scientifically established rather than esthetically desirable, that the persecutions began. The established authorities realized, even earlier than the proponents of the new cosmology, that there was indeed a distinction between objective truth and subjectively held opinions, between reason judging the truths of revelation and revelation judging the truths of reason. The sociology of knowledge is dangerous in the same way because its ultimate aim is to discover what is objectively true *about* these subjectively held opinions.

To say this implies that the sociology of knowledge has as a fundamental goal the discovery of *both* the social roots of error and of truth; scientifically verified beliefs as well as political truisms.[1]

The burden of the work of Edgar Zilsel, for example, was to examine the sociological conditions for the rise of science: the root factors in the economy, polity, and philosophy of capitalism that made possible the rapid rise of science. The work of Mannheim, on the other hand, was concerned primarily with those factors in modern industrial society that promoted and intensified the use of ideology, of nonempirical thinking, to gain specific social ends—irrespective of the value of these ends. Thus we can see that, even within the sociology of know-

---

1. One of the few books which has asserted that the sociology of knowledge is not limited to a search for ideological influences arising from social life, but that it is a science which can cast light on the origins of truth as on the origins of error, is Werner Stark's *The Sociology of Knowledge* (Glencoe, Ill.: Free Press, 1958). However, with Stark this only remains an assertion, since truth is conceived of as related to historical origins and not to conceptual validity. Conceptual truth in Stark's approach is the province of the transcendental. His attack on the naturalistic ontology is really a defense of traditional metaphysics of the Kantian variety. See especially Ch. 4, "The Consequences of the Sociology of Knowledge."

ledge, the object under study largely determines the mechanisms and tool of study. Those concerned with scientific history will more often be drawn to the social roots of truth; whereas those concerned with social history will more often be drawn to the seeds of ideological error.

Our discussion of the sociology of knowledge has thus far centered on general and external aims. It has, in addition to these, a significant contribution to make to the internal growth of science. The critical function of the sociology of knowledge enables it to act as a catalytic agent in the integration of social science disciplines into a common interlocked network of analysis.

If we take as our overall criteria the interconnection of social action and human survival, we can see how the various sciences, such as economics, psychology, and political science, might be employed to uncover the mainsprings of social action. Max Weber and Thorstein Veblen illustrated the potency of bringing to the foreground the interrelationship of social to economic action. The question of the nature of production is properly a question determined by economic theory.

However, the question of consumer satisfaction and demand is a social question. Thus Weber and Veblen could inquire into the larger consequences of an exchange economy: contractual relationships; distribution of industrial wealth; the utilities of goods; the uses of money for power, philanthropy, prestige, and the mystification of the economic "market"; the concept and forms of profit-making; the aesthetics of a moral economy; and the economic control of the idea market. In this way sociology as a discipline does two things: it reveals its distinctive operational level, and it employs the findings of economic science.

Bukharin, Plekhanov, and Russian Marxists generally miss the point quite thoroughly when they assert that sociology is simply a myth, a capitalist device to disparage the "real" science of society, Marxian economics.[2] The nature of sociology is not to undermine respect for other social science disciplines, and certainly not economics, but to reveal the social implications and ramifications in all human contacts. In a sense, *Das Kapital* illustrates this wider use of economics; it is constantly drawing the wider social implications of the production of economic values. Marx's discussion of the relation of man to machine in capitalist industry well illustrates this thesis.[3]

One of the qualities that sets Marx apart from the older classical economists is just this acute sense of socioeconomic interrelatedness. Only the potential dangers, real or imagined, to a monolithic state can account for either the absence or arrest of such areas of investigation as sociology, anthropology, and ethnology.

2. See on this subject L. Labedz, "The Soviet Attitude to Sociology," in *The Soviet Cultural Scene: 1956–1957*, ed. by W. Z. Laquer and George Lichtheim (New York: Praeger, 1958).

3. Cf. Karl Marx, "Machinery and Modern Industry," in *Das Kapital* (Hamburg: O. Meissner, 1872), vol. I.

The field of political science, which is probably that discipline bearing the closest operational kinship to the sociology of knowledge (although there are significant differences arising from the institutional emphasis of the former and the ideational preeminence in the latter), offers an enormous fund of information to draw upon. Even if we restrict ourselves to the modern period, ignoring the large contributions made to classical political theory by Hobbes, Rousseau, Hegel, and Marx, it will be seen that the broad political anchor points of the sociology of knowledge would be only a head without hands were the empirical findings of political science to be ignored. The changing juridical commitments of political institutions examined by Hans Kelsen and Rudolf Schlesinger, the study of the oligarchic tendencies of political party organizations made by Roberto Michels, the mass-class relationships in the galvanization of political action made by Vilfredo Pareto and Georges Sorel—these serve to illustrate some points of convergence between the two social sciences.

There are also the more microscopic types of studies which have been particularly fruitful for those concerned with problems of knowledge and their social distortion. One can mention the empirical typology of elites, made from such different vantage points by C. Wright Mills, G. D. H. Cole, and Harold Lasswell; specialized discussions on mass communication, authoritarian types, popular taste, and organized political action, made by empiricists like Paul Lazarsfeld and rationalists like T. W. Adorno; and the work on organizational structure of church, state, and the military made by Robert K. Merton and Talcott Parsons. The purpose in presenting a few of the political science areas that intersect the sociology of knowledge in techniques and methodology is not to supply an arid bibliography, but to show the ways in which the sociology of knowledge can avoid spinning theories out of daydreams—to avoid the reduction of scientific sociology into what Kelsen has called "an ocean of psychic happenings."

What distinguishes classic political theory from its modern counterpart parallels the general shift from a synthetic to an analytic social science. In the sociology of knowledge it involves a shift from the recognition of ideology as a social force to the structural investigation of the true and false elements of these ideologies. Political science has in like manner shifted from a reformulation of the big issues of state and society, civilization and the individual, authority and freedom, into an analysis of the structural components of these institutional entities. The refinement of techniques does not necessarily symbolize an abandonment of these larger issues, but the casting of them in a framework which takes into account the microscopic no less than the macroscopic. This is a process that avoids the reification of general hypothesis. That political analysis sometimes lapses into formalism, i.e., into a form of quantitative analysis that becomes socially trivial and intellectually sterile, is a fault which only an increased sharpening of logical tools and political courage can correct—not a return to older forms of rationalism and rationalizing.

The political scientist has come to offer social science not simply an external description of the structure of political parties and leaders, but to attempt, in addition, a broad sort of correlation of structure to motivation. To the question of what are the essential catalytic agents of political action, we may receive a diverse set of answers: the release from political responsibility offered by placing all hopes on an unrealizable myth, the instinctual search for power, the belief that economic problems first and foremost require political solutions. Again, we may find it useful to consider more directly psychological elements in political power by examining Laswell's characterological types; for example, the possible connection between a pacifist and his acute castration complex, an anarchist leader who reveals an intense father-hatred and thus antistate orientations, the religious zealot who turns to politics to compensate for a guilt complex underlying an apparently noble struggle for the purification of politics.[4] Lasswell clearly offers an exaggerated and one-sided picture, made in the first flush of the Freudian impact in the United States. It may nonetheless offer a basis from which we can broaden a valuational framework. What is important in both the classic and contemporary literature of political science is not so much the selection of a single figure or idea upon which to anchor the sociology of knowledge, but the realization that the external or internal, the large-scale or middle-range studies of political science provide, along with economics, the factual base for an understanding of the determinants of knowledge, scientific and ideological.

Such an approach, far from leading to a sort of Jamesian "wide-open universe," moves in a quite reverse direction. It increases the degree of social determination, reveals hitherto unknown aspects of the character of social laws, and for this reason moves closer to a scientific solution of problems.

The formerly special preserve of philosophic epistemology has cleaved itself in such a way that the sociology of knowledge has largely taken possession of the analysis of the social determinants of knowledge, while psychology and psychoanalysis have more and more to do with the subjective and physiological aspects of the knowing process. The interplay of the sociology of knowledge and psychology has become as significant in terms of the social constellation of the individual as the relation of economics is to political science at the institutional level of social interaction. Particularly useful up to this point has been the discovery of broad psychic types, behaviorally conditioned.

No less significant is the discovery of certain causal relations that exist between the various contexts in which the mind is required to function. Neurosis, whether it is conceived of in Pavlovian terms as necessarily involving a breakdown in both the physical and psychic functions of the individual, or in a Freudian context as an emotional inability to cope functionally with the demands and restraints of society, certainly implies at the minimum a distortion in the processes of learning and belief, and in the forms in which the human mind represents its social and biological relations.

This necessarily takes into account the functional role of sexual restrictions

4. Harold D. Lasswell; see especially his short study, "Psychopathology and Politics," in *Political Writings* (Glencoe, Ill.: Free Press, 1951).

and idols that civilization creates as a necessary condition for suvival and advancement. The solution of a primary level of economic needs, the transparent realization of economic freedom through the creation of a stratum of society absolved from pure scarcity, commences the production of psychic types that play a critical role in the formulation of both science and ideology. Aristotle may have been correct in noting that in leisure begins the production of ideologies geared to justify the bifurcation of society into leisure groups and laboring groups.

Large-scale consequences flow from a recognition of the psychological dimension in social activities. This may be illustrated at a primary level by the application of the Freudian concepts of Id, Ego, and Superego. To what extent is the Id the psychic reflection of instinctual biological desires moving counter to established culture patterns? To what degree do the Ego and Superego reflect a conformist impulse of the individual to acquiesce in social controls? It might now even be asked to what extent does the self-consciousness of unconscious factors effect the action-knowledge-action chain?

For the sociology of knowledge, "subjective" information presents a crucial challenge concerning the types of ideological rationalizations made by individuals and cultures to protect various sorts and sets of interests. It may raise issues as to the most useful type of psychological attitude for the production of scientific work, on one side, and authoritarian modes of domination, at the other extreme.

The sociology of knowledge is not required to supply ultimate and immutable answers to such questions, for such attempts fall outside the scope of scientific possibility. What is noted is the relative interconnectedness of the human sciences, particularly those which have for their primary concern the sources of knowledge and the sources of the distortion of knowledge because of either real or imagined biosocial requirements.

Interconnectedness is crucial in the study of knowledge since, unlike a discipline like physics, every social event is unique and nonrepeatable. The absence of controlled experimentation in the analytic situation requires the widest employment of all areas involved in the study of the relation of society to human understanding.[5] It has been pointed out in this connection that "the reconstructive sociology, especially guided by the concept of the field situation, requires the collaboration of the different social sciences which treat, at various spheres and levels of generalization, the different facts and processes which occur in society. This collaboration must not be a mere juxtaposition of performances, but a real functional union, and has to be carried out on the basis of a cognitive frame of reference defined by the necessities of rational insight."[6]

5. Cf. Victor F. Lenzen, *Procedures of Empirical Science* (Chicago, Ill.: University of Chicago Press, 1938).

6. Gino Germani, "Sociología y acción social," in *La Sociología Científica* (Mexico City: Instituto de Investigaciones Sociales, Universidad Nacional, 1956).

What this conscious, integrational approach to the sociology of knowledge entails is a thorough belief in the supremacy of science in the comprehension and solution of human problems and predicaments. Even if one were to accept the metaphysical gambit of maintaining that no ontic demonstration of the superiority of one axiomatic system over another can be adequately formulated, this is not sufficient reason on operational grounds to reject the employment of scientific knowledge. For it is in the consequences of science, in the rational determination of future events and future actions, that we measure the superiority of science over intuition, rationality over irrationality.[7]

The sociology of knowledge, in taking the sphere of the social determinants of knowledge as a problem rather than as a given, offers a distinctive dimension for the purification of the social sciences. It separates, in the initial constellation, factual, hypothetical, emotive, and evaluative elements. In the next place, it offers an analysis of the roots of these elements in society. Finally, in separating the constitutive factors in the social sciences, what is presupposed is a deep-seated connection with such sciences—an identification with the aims and results of social science as a whole.

II

The sociology of knowledge has a value that transcends the utilization of contributions from other social sciences. At the core of the discipline is its role as a methodological filter for the social sciences and a critical attitude toward its own level of development. A deplorable element in the history of social science has been the pseudoscientific language utilized by political power elements to justify narrow political ambitions and still narrower political credos. The method of authority and the method of tenacity, Peirce's two options to a scientific appraisal of events, have grown powerful; but not as independent methods as Peirce had thought. Rather they come disguised as racial or regional science of a higher

7. See, in particular, Karl R. Popper, *The Open Society and Its Enemies* (Princeton, New Jersey: Princeton University Press, 1956), especially Chs. 24 and 25. For other studies bearing on the nature of the social sciences, especially for its potential application to research in the sociology of knowledge, the following could be profitably consulted: Warner Muensterberger and Sidney Axelrod, eds., *Psychoanalysis and the Social Sciences* (New York: International Universities Press, 1947–58), vols. I–V. For essays bearing on communication, anthropology, and religion: Ruth Benedict, "Continuities and Discontinuities in Cultural Conditioning," in *Personality in Nature, Society and Culture*, 2nd ed. (revised and enlarged), ed. by Kluckhohn, Murray, and Schneider (New York: Knopf, 1953); J. B. Gittler, "Possibilities of a Sociology of Science," in *Social Forces*, vol. XVIII (1940); Abram Kardiner, "Psychodynamics and the Social Sciences," in *Culture and Personality*, ed. by S. Stansfeld Sargent and Marian W. Smith (New York: Viking Fund, 1949); Otto Neurath, "Foundations of the Social Sciences," in *International Encyclopedia of Unified Science*, vol. II, no. 1; Jerome F. Scott and R. P. Lynton, "Developing the Systematic Knowledge of Social Understanding," in *The Community Factor in Modern Technology* (Paris: UNESCO, 1960); Edgar Zilsel, "Physics and the Problem of Historico-Sociological Laws," in *Readings in the Philosophy of Science*, ed. by H. Feigl and M. Brodbeck (New York: Appleton-Century-Crofts, 1953).

type. The suppression of social science rarely proceeds candidly in our sophisticated epoch. Philistinism comes as mental philanthropy. It may even come as a
defense of science against newfangled revisions and alterations. Doctrinal conformity rather than empirical testing becomes the hallmark of validating propositions as true or false. Ideas are seen as true to the degree to which they represent
entrenched ideas with fidelity. This is the standard form of the "scientific"
ideological argument. The antiseptic role performed by the sociology of knowledge can perhaps best be illustrated by reference to a critical analysis of those
figures and tendencies in social science from which it has learned most.

To start with, it might be said of men like Max Weber and Thorstein Veblen
that their emphasis upon the consuming aspects of economy, rather than upon
production as such, and upon bureaucratic or democratic *forms* of rule, rather
than upon the *control* of the political machinery, represented the shifting interests
of capitalist economy more than the shifting needs of political economy.

The products of a machine technology rather than technology itself become
central. The solution of the problem of mass production generated problems in
ways of stimulating mass consumption. Retail marketing, distribution, and adver-
tising become central in value as well as fact. It is this response to the needs and
ambitions of these new echelons of a bourgeois world to which Weber and
Veblen were unconsciously responding. The degree to which their respective
visions of socialism were a challenge to big industrialism from the perspective
of these middle strata can be gauged by the emphasis given to problems that can
only exist in an advanced capitalism where social fluidity and gradation are the
rule rather than the exception.

Historically, the dominant emphasis in political science has been upon questions of power and authority, rather than upon issues relating to the genesis of
such power. This is clear even in the efforts of Roberto Michels and Harold
Lasswell. It might be asked to what degree this reflects a shift in the actual relations of economy to politics, or to what degree it is simply a verbal shift from
the more clearly defined area of economic exploitation to the ambiguous and
value-nebulous problem of political domination. On the other hand, might it
not be the case that actual relations between economics and politics have changed
in the contemporary era? To what degree does the centralization of authority in
the state overthrow the preeminence of economic considerations? Admitted that
in a "free" market and laissez faire context, economic laws work themselves out
mysteriously, as a fetish; however, does not the central agency of state authority
play a role of economic regulation and rehabilitation (if needed) that modifies
the normal operations of a market exchange economy?[8]

The power theses of political science seem in some measure to be an unconscious motor response to such objective shifts. But just as clearly, the power
theses perform an ideological function by focusing exclusive attention on who

8. Cf. Franz L. Neumann, "Economics and Politics in the Twentieth Century," in *The
Democratic and the Authoritarian State*, ed. by Herbert Marcuse (Glencoe, Ill.: Free Press, 1957).

gets what, rather than upon the more pregnant theme of who gets what under what sociocultural conditions. The outlook of pure egoism underlies more in current political science thinking than most might be willing to admit. The orientation toward egoism and the abstract union of egos in a "free" society is part and parcel of the traditional defense of capitalism as an economic organization. The refinement of utilitarianism, of notions of self-interest and monetary value, is perhaps not the least significant ideological element in the widespread promulgation of power theories.

Nor can the psychoanalytical movement escape the consequences of its origins and roots in the petty bourgeois atmosphere of Vienna at the beginning of the century. This is a fact quite apart from the economic privations suffered by the founders of psychoanalysis. The social and economic milieu of the patients, no less than of the physician-analysts, was distinctly oriented toward middle class comforts and standards. This gives a measure of substance to the acrimonious claims of Catholic and Socialist spokesmen that psychoanalysis was framed as a secular response to bourgeois religious and spiritual needs. The trend of analysis reflected a distinctly individualist concern with character factors, such as infantile experiences, which tended to suppress the biosocial character of mental disorders. The mind was separated from the brain, psychiatry separated from neurology, and sexuality separated from sociality. Reification of abstract precepts became a psychoanalytic commonplace, without any apparent awareness that analysis in this way merely reproduced the bifurcation of reality made in former ages by the great system-building philosophers.

It is a tribute to Freud that toward the close of his career he came to realize that a definite ambiguity resided in an individualist treatment of what is essentially a widespread social dilemma. To what degree did psychoanalysis attempt to supply a personalistic solution to the essentially objective fact that persons of professional and business backgrounds had more leisure time than they were capable of utilizing in nonsexual ways? This is by no means intended as a facetious commentary on the social origins of the psychoanalytic movement, nor is a rejection of its achievements intended; quite the reverse. Genuine and urgent problems issue from the relation of leisure and labor to normality and abnormality, without pontificating over the origins of psychoanalysis.[9]

For instance, it must be asked to what degree the solution of economic problems and technological problems, *i.e.*, the achievement of relative social abundance, tends to maximize, instead of alleviate, pressures upon human thought processes. However, the dominant trends in psychoanalytic theory, with some notable exceptions, tend to ask the more trivial question of how a repressed individual can adjust best to the needs of a repressive social organism. This would seem to be particularly the issue upon which neo-Freudian tendencies are

9. See, for example, *Mass Leisure*, ed. by Eric Larrabee and Rolf Meyersohn (Glencoe, Ill.: Free Press, 1958); and *Mass Culture*, ed. by Bernard Rosenberg and David Manning White (Glencoe, Ill.: Free Press, 1957).

hinged; for, despite its tendencies to emphasize the worth of the freely developing personality, neo-Freudianism too often assumes a disguised moral stance conducive to the needs of a society standing above men, rather than a functioning entity created by men.

We may take as typical of this pathway Fromm's *Escape From Freedom*. Here we are greeted with an expanded pragmatic theory of belief. Methods for fixing belief replace a causal analysis of how beliefs, taboos, and illusions arise. Illustrative methods of fixing belief are carefully expounded. "Authority," "Destruction and Self-Destruction," "Automatic Conformity," are all viewed as the principle modes of the escape from freedom. As in Charles Peirce (who, it might be mentioned, wrote eighty years earlier than Fromm), the machinery of social domination used to impose absolute repression and oppression is reversed. In Fromm's hands, mechanisms of social oppression become transformed into mechanisms of personal evasion.[10] Every political question thus becomes a moral issue.

By subjectivizing the relation between repression and belief on one hand, while yet honestly seeking to reinforce "progression" against "reactionary" social forces on the other, Fromm turns psychoanalysis into an adjustment orientation.

Man does not "escape" from freedom, for the simple reason that the nature of freedom is itself definable and quantifiable in terms of the root elements in social coercion, toleration, and liberty. The concept of the integration of the personality into polity rather than the emancipation of the person from certain concrete elements in social repression is what underlies much neo-Freudian thought. The analyst is himself in need of analysis—just as in the last century it was ably pointed out that the doctrine of progress through knowledge and self-knowledge forgets that the educator himself requires education.

The standpoint of adjustment in psychology and psychiatry, like the standpoint of reconstruction in social philosophy, tends to reinforce the status quo against those who advocate emancipation or those who take the standpoint of "marginal" or "deviant" individuals. "The Superego and the Censor" of the psychoanalytic movement seems to rest upon an unwillingness to recognize that its sexual categories are in no small part a microcosmic representation of the formal categories of economics. To what degree, for example, is the concept of repression simply the internalization of the concept of oppression? Facing this squarely, what is to be the position of psychoanalysis on the resolution of repression? Likewise, if the concept of adjustment is really related to the social attitudes of conformism, in what way is it possible to have a healthy, emancipated civilization rather than an alienated and frustrated society? Given the

10. Cf. Erich Fromm, "Mechanisms of Evasion," in *Escape from Freedom* (New York: Rinehart & Co., 1960); and *The Sane Society* (London: Routledge & Kegan Paul, Ltd., 1956), Ch. 7. For a critique of his position see the final chapter in Herbert Marcuse's *Eros and Civilization* (London: Routledge & Kegan Paul, Ltd., 1956).

unwritten compact of the analyst with his society, to what extent is the "resolution" an intensification of human alienation? The very fact that such questions can be asked—indeed, are being asked—is indicative of the conflicting ideological elements still forming the cushion for psychiatry and psychoanalysis.

Nor can the sociology of knowledge be less ruthless in respect of its own historical perspectives. The type of solution offered by Mannheim to the pendulum of ideology (controlling interests) and utopia (outside interests), for example, is in no small part a distended reproduction of elitist currents under capitalism. For the whole notion of the socially unbound intellectual involves a special interest attitude of the thinker vis-à-vis the doer on the one hand and the owner on the other. It is the speculative notion of the social scientist inherited from Hegelian philosophy. Mannheim's intellectual is a man who is steadily rinsing his brain with ideas, but never gets to wash his hands with soap. Elitism underlies such a position because the assumption is that truth is the special preserve of a tiny segment of the population, a preserve that becomes profaned by genuine social involvements.

This underscores a more profound shortcoming of Mannheim, namely that his sociology of knowledge is a theory of social roots of error. Taking his theory that the interest situation of a particular social group necessarily represents an ideological position, no nonideological standpoint can be developed by any socioeconomic force committed to the activities of the natural world. Thus with Mannheim we can only choose between false ideological alternatives, or else search out the truth by separating ourselves from the social life of man.[11] This approach simply yields false options, for it involves the permanent separation of head and hand, political policies and political theories. It sanctifies and defies the structural conditions of present-day Western society by reinforcing the notion that the functional divisions between men, classes, and nations is not primarily a feature of economic history but of scientific knowledge itself.

The operations of the sociology of knowledge do not yield uniform results. The fact that its analysis of other social sciences and of itself offers the possibility of constant verification and modification renders it capable of gaining at least its proximate goals. In its ability to separate and segregate reality from fantasy, science from ideology, the sociology of knowledge is able to avoid the capriciousness of individual genius and collective blindness alike.

Science is connected to the material functioning of society as a whole. It is not restricted to some and mysteriously opened for others. This is not to deny that social systems may retard scientific advancement. It is to deny that such retardation is a class element rather than a social element. In *refining* its examination

11. Mannheim's view of science in relativistic. Even quantitative and analytic sciences are "discoverable on the basis of a definite *Weltanschauung*." And while a world view may not necessarily be a source of error (only usually), it gives rise only to "spheres of knowledge," not to truth as such. Science is thus viewed by him as "a style of thinking" only quantitatively different from other "styles." Cf. *Ideology and Utopia* (New York: Harcourt, Brace, 1959), Ch. 3, part 5.

of the social roots of error, the sociology of knowledge may help to *define* the conditions presupposed in the production of social truths. In this enterprise, all who share the scientific attitude can make substantial contributions; not because the social scientist is liberated from class attitudes, racial prejudices, or sexual restrictions; but because they are part of the calculations possible, indeed necessary, to frame any scientific discipline objectively.[12]

If it is important to calculate the degree of interference in microphysics, it is even more urgently required in a science directly linked to human interference in sociopolitical judgments. The economic or moral element present in a social science experiment is not anathema, not a proof that objective verification is impossible. It becomes impossible only when economic and moral conditioning is suppressed or, what is worse, talked out of existence.

The relation of the sociology of knowledge to a definite valuational standpoint might be summed up by noting frankly that the future of social science as a whole, as well as in its parts, is intimately connected to the development of a science of ethical judgment. This is a necessary complement to the sociology of knowledge—a sociology of ethics that would render information about why men value what they value under given life conditions. The development of a firm set of hypotheses for the purpose of placing valuation itself upon a non-ideological footing is a joint enterprise of the social sciences. The reciprocity of ethics and sociology is rooted in the common desire to distinguish factual elements in thought and judgments about morals from the emotive, normative, and interest-bound elements.[13]

The unity of the social sciences is not a subtle device for returning to pure empiricism, or a formal physicalist analysis lacking any prescriptive or directional value. It is, rather, a search for the forms in which it might be possible to realize a humanized moral standpoint without resorting to either tautologies or platitudes. The function of the sociology of knowledge in this joint enterprise is not merely to be a participant sharing the fruits, but to be a critic making certain that the fruits ripen.

12. On various aspects of social conditioning and scientific criticism, see Robert S. Cohen, "Alternative Interpretations of the History of Science," in *The Validation of Scientific Theories*, ed. by Philipp G. Frank (Boston: Beacon Press, 1957); Gerard L. DeGre, "The Pluralistic Basis of Knowledge," in *Society and Ideology: An Inquiry into the Sociology of Knowledge* (New York: Columbia University, Ph.D. thesis, 1943); Karl Mannheim, "The Problem of the Intelligentsia: An Enquiry into Its Past and Present," in *Essays on the Sociology of Culture*, ed. by Ernest Manheim in cooperation with Paul Kecskemeti (London: Routledge & Kegan Paul, Ltd., 1956); Hans Reichenbach, "The Functional Conception of Knowledge," in *The Rise of Scientific Philosophy* (Berkeley: University of California Press, 1958).

13. On the interrelations between ethics and social science, compare Maurice Mandelbaum, "The Resolution of Moral Controversies," in *The Phenomenology of Moral Experience* (Glencoe, Ill.: Free Press, 1955); Abraham Edel, "Cultural and Social Perspectives," in *Ethical Judgment: The Uses of Science in Ethics* (Glencoe, Ill.: Free Press, 1955); Morris Ginsberg, "The Individualist Basis of International Law and Morals," in *Reason and Unreason in Society: Essays in Sociology and Social Philosophy* (London: Heinemann, 1956).

The ultimate aim of the sociology of knowledge corresponds to the historic quest of philosophy. It has as a goal that kind of information distinguishing man from his natural environment, and the ways in which this distinction can be scientifically telescoped. This is not a plea for the divorce of theory from action—far from it. It is an assertion that the aim of theory is to measure the actual distance men have traversed from their "original state of nature." Diderot once remarked that, from the sheer physical standpoint, we live in a cold and barren universe. It is man, the social animal, the transforming animal, that alone renders the world we inhabit meaningful and productive. The distance man puts between himself and the physical surroundings is measured by consciousness. The aim of the sociology of knowledge is to reveal the gap between the distance thus far traversed and what we imagine we have traversed—in brief, to help men distinguish between consciousness and false consciousness.

3. *Social Science Objectivity and Value Neutrality: Historical Problems and Projections*

FOR THE MOST PART, American sociology has accepted the appealing formula of neutrality with regard to political and ideological values, a formula put forward especially by the functionalist school. It has the golden merit of posing issues in a seemingly natural science manner. The sociologist can adopt the physicist's pose toward his work. We provide society with carefully sifted information, comparative analyses of social structures, and, at the upper range, the likely consequences of performing or not performing an action in terms of the given diagnosis. The social scientist using a functionalist *philosophy* can feel free of responsibility at a decision-making level. Whether society decides to employ or ignore the provided data is held to be a matter of indifference, a situation requiring moral wisdom rather than social theory. Without minimizing the sound contributions of the function-structure approach, particularly in overcoming the provincialism and conceit of the prefunctionalist schools

First presented at the Sixth Inter-American Congress of Philosophy held in Buenos Aires during September, 1959. The paper examined the dual traditions of uncovery and discovery which existed in classical sociological theory. It was first published in *Diogenes: International Review of the Human Sciences*, Whole Number 39 (September–December, 1962).

of anthropology,[1] there is a sure moral undercurrent in a method that sees the social scientist as diagnostician and society as a patient. It has the appearance of satisfying the historic identification of social theory with social welfare, and no less an emotional identification with a neutral-objective image culled from physics. Social history becomes a variable in the preparation of trend reports and is thereby trivialized into a moment in the functionalist scheme.[2]

There is a significant logical shortcoming in the identification of function-alism and neutralism. To infer the value neutrality of functionalism from the fact that conservatives claim functionalism as liberal, while liberals claim the reverse, is a specious form of logic. Upon inspection, the claims of various critics of different persuasion might add up to the same substantive charge, e.g., the pragmatic criterion of success employed. Also to be considered is that the claims of one sector of critics might turn out on inspection to be quite right at any given moment in space. In any event, it is small consolation for functionalism to claim that its results are a consequence of its purge of conjecture and hypo-theses from social investigations. It is similarly untenable to deny to those holding distinct and examined existential perspectives the capacity to develop comparable techniques yielding similar results. Yet, this seems very much the prevailing attitude toward nonfunctionalist modes of analysis, even though it rests on the false assumption that a scientific explanation can be arrived at only by one type of method.[3]

This critical prolegomenon given, it is time to state my thesis: that the history of social science is internally and organically bound at its upper and lower levels by ethical perspectives, by what Nadel has well termed "ideas about worth-whileness."[4] It is my further contention that the suppression of this commitment of social science to ethical perspectives leads not to better scientific work, but on the contrary, to a series of disastrous consequences: (a) indifference to problem solving; (b) unconscious ideological distortions in theory construction; (c) a neglect of the scientific evaluation of value theory; (d) an identification of objectivity in social research with indifference to ethical judgments.

The problem of defining the interior relationships between social science and values is obviously more complex than the simple assertion that a relationship exists. On the other hand, the problem is insoluble only if we enter the oracular universe of Scheler and the phenomenalist, irrationalist tradition. To assert the

1. Cf. Bronislaw Malinowski, "Functionalism in Anthropology," in *Sociological Theory: A Book of Readings*, ed. by L. A. Coser and B. Rosenberg (New York: Macmillan Co. 1957), esp. pp. 519–521.

2. Cf. Irving L. Horowitz, "Laws and Levels in the Sociology of Knowledge," in *Philosophy, Science and the Sociology of Knowledge* (Springfield, Ill.: Charles C Thomas, 1961), pp. 112–119.

3. R. B. Braithwaite, *Scientific Explanation* (Cambridge: Cambridge University Press, 1953), esp. pp. 342–368.

4. S. F. Nadel, *The Foundations of Social Anthropology* (London: Cohen & West, 1951), p. 264.

functional role of values in social science hypotheses does not entail the assumption that social position and stratification make scientific objectivity impossible; and it certainly does not imply that our only recourse is in seeking Providential aid.[5] To insist that facts have no meaning apart from values is as fruitless as to claim that fact and value are in separate realms. These are the false alternatives that have frustrated the sound development of a social accounting of value functions.[6]

In order to get beyond the present muddle of having to choose between the reified poles of an empirically bound or a value-laden sociology, we must first reconsider the nineteenth-century question as to the objectivity of social science, and then consider the twentieth-century question as to the character of social science objectivity as contingent on this older issue for its solution. This is not an iconoclastic desire to resort to a regressive chain of problems, but rather an assertion that the "bad faith" of contemporary researches on the place of values in social science issues from a failure to make clear any options for either narrow empiricism or a far too broad phenomenalism.

I. Social Science and Value Perspectives: An Historical Briefing

Efforts to create a social science along natural science lines, free of subjective commitments, are hardly novel. To be sure, there is a taken-for-granted view among classical economists that physics provides the perfect model for constructing a political economy. The "naturalness" of an economic system was said to flow from the objective necessity of labor, industry, value, and profit; just as the "naturalness" of Newtonian physics flowed from the perfect harmony of matter and its "universal" laws of attraction and repulsion. Adam Smith offers this sort of model. "In every part of the universe we observe means adjusted with the nicest artifice to the ends which they are intended to produce; and in the mechanism of a plant or animal body, admire how everything is contrived for advancing the two great purposes of nature, the support of the individual and the propagation of the species."[7] Smith's idea of the cosmic destiny of physical order carrying over into human affairs served economic theory very well in its formative stages. So well did it work that Comte made the *telos* a part of society in general by classifying nature into a hierarchy moving from mathematics to physics, chemistry, biology, and then, sociology.[8] Comte's belief in sociology as the optimal science was infectious, reflecting as it did the

5. Cf. Marvin Farber, "Max Scheler and the Spiritual Elevation of Man," in *Naturalism and Subjectivism* (Springfield, Ill.: Charles C Thomas, 1959), pp. 297–329.

6. Cf. Robert S. Lynd, *Knowledge For What? The Place of Social Science in American Culture* (Princeton: Princeton University Press, 1939), esp. p. 187f.

7. Adam Smith, *The Theory of Moral Sentiments*, ed. by H. W. Schneider (New York: Hafner Publishing Co., 1948), Section 3:3, p. 125.

8. Auguste Comte, *The Positive Philosophy of Auguste Comte*, ed. by. H. Martineau (London: Kegan Paul, Ltd.), vol. I, p. 24.

positivist urge to get on with the task of studying society independent of metaphysical considerations, and yet claiming for sociology "a higher position of rationality than the present state of the human mind seems to promise." This apex is guaranteed by the past successes of the "anterior sciences."[9]

Although Smith and Comte believed in the essentially value-free character of their respective sciences, they differed with modern empiricist trends in accepting the notion of the socially curative powers of social science. Smith, for example, concludes his *Wealth of Nations* with a plea for England to revitalize its notion of Empire along reciprocally beneficial fiscal lines or surrender the "imagination" of Empire altogether.[10] Comte, for his part, went a good deal further, conceiving of positive sociology as the religion of humanity, to be considered primarily in terms of principles of Love, Order, and Progress.[11] This would indicate that social theory from 1750–1850 considered the dualism between scientific theory and social decisions to be entirely illegitimate.

Nonetheless, the neatness of utilitarian and positivist doctrines, founded as they were on the "lawful" and "objective" nature of human behavior, possessing built-in conclusions of self-evident value open to all men of reason, good-will, or simply self-interest, crashed with the growth of a radical critique of existing society as such. The detection of flaws in the laissez-faire *telos* brought in its wake a new, nonrationalistic vision of human nature and conduct. Marx's criticisms of Proudhon, the Comte of French economic theory, betray the growing impatience of the age with neat Enlightenment formulas of education and legislation, the value of which depended on a series of axioms about "the ideal image of man" inherited from St. Augustine.

The basis of Marx's claims against the philanthropic school of social science, of which Comte and Proudhon were prime examples, is that social theory advances to the extent that social classes mature both politically and ideologically, and not as a consequence of the divine light of reason. The true intellectuals "no longer need to seek science in their minds; they have only to take note of what is happening before their eyes and to become the mouthpiece of this." Marx was convinced that the identification of social science with the historical causes of the oppressed would have a salutary effect on science as such, making it "revolutionary" instead of "doctrinaire." Marx's argument against Proudhon was the failure of the latter to get behind philanthropy into the hidden unconscious class interests motivating social men. For this reason, Proudhon is a "composite error" rather than the "synthesis" he wishes to be.[12] It is not the rationality of scientific discovery that is particularly novel in Marx, but rather the scientific

9. *Ibid.*, vol. II, p. 104.

10. Adam Smith, *An Inquiry into the Nature and Causes of the Wealth of Nations*, ed. by Edwin Cannan (New York: Random House, 1937), pp. 898–899.

11. Cf. Rollin Chambliss, *Social Thought from Hammurabi to Comte* (New York: Henry Holt & Co., 1954), p. 400.

12. Karl Marx, *The Poverty of Philosophy* (New York: International Publishers, n.d.), pp. 106–107.

discovery that interests—hidden or overt, irrational or rational—are subject to empirical scrutiny. Given a disequilibrium of economic wealth, interests (of which values are a central part) determine the character of scientific invention more profoundly than the other way around. That is why a scientific gain is not automatically translated into a social benefit.[13]

Freud, for his part, reinforces the Marxian view of science as interest-bound in his efforts to develop a scientific typology of irrational behavior. For Freud, the very systematization of knowledge about the irrational is itself the proving-grounds rather than the negation of science.[14] Upon learning that Marx did not deny the functional role of ideational and superego factors in human change, Freud was ready to grant that the contrast he had believed to exist between Marxism and psychoanalysis was groundless. We need not explore the varied efforts to "reconcile" the writings of Freud and Marx.[15] What is important for our inquiry is the functional similarity of Marx's "ideological disguise" and Freud's "mechanism of repression." Both operate unconsciously, behind men's backs, shaping the process and the contents of scientific as well as social activity. The latent, hidden facets of human interests, ambitions, and impulses, and not the supposed "common-sense" rational motivations represented for both men the crucible in which science as well as superstition is formed. The stance toward values determines the essence of social theory, just as the stance toward facts determines the essence of physical science theory. The division between *Geistes-wissenschaften* and *Naturwissenschaften* that crystallized later in the century was a natural consequence of the disintegration of the earlier positivist orientation.[16]

Freud provided an explanation into the function of reason as a disguise and censor of "reality." Rationalism came to be viewed as rationalization, and the process of science became one of "unmasking" individual behavior, much as Marx sought to "unmask" large group behavior. Science is therefore not akin to common-sense observation; to the contrary, social sciences are primarily responsible for considering the function of values as intrinsic to the structure of human activity. We are not here concerned with the special place Marx assigned to the professional politician or Freud to the psychoanalytically trained

13. Karl Marx, *Capital: A Critique of Political Economy* (Chicago: Charles H. Kerr, 1909), vol. 3, Ch. 5, pp. 92–105.

14. Cf. Else Frenkel-Brunswik, "Confirmation of Psychoanalytic Theories," in *The Validation of Scientific Ideas*, ed. by Philipp G. Frank (Boston: Beacon Press, 1956), pp. 112–114.

15. Cf. among others, F. H. Bartlett, *Sigmund Freud: A Marxian Essay* (London: Victor Gollancz, 1938); R. Osborne, *Freud and Marx* (London: Victor Gollancz, 1937); N. O. Brown, *Life Against Death: The Psychoanalytical Meaning of History* (Middletown, Conn.: Wesleyan University Press, 1959); and H. Marcuse, *Eros and Civilization: A Philosophical Inquiry into Freud* (Boston: Beacon Press, 1955).

16. Cf. Wilhelm Dilthey, *Einleitung in die Geisteswissenschaften*, in *Gesammelte Schriften*, vol. I (Leipzig-Berlin: B. G. Teubner, 1921; reprinted 1959). As later efforts demonstrated, this study did not have the intended effect of settling the question of the natural or socio-historical "essence" of human studies.

physician. The values of the scientist for these essentially nineteenth-century men were exempted and extrapolated from the main currents of society. The exploration of this hidden assumption of the scientist *qua* scientist as value-free was the work of a later stage in social science.

If, for the earlier positivist tradition, reality is identified with progress, in the unmasking tradition, we have the identification of reality with process. And if in Marx this process is an admixture of progressive and regressive elements with the progressive elements winning out in the long run, in Freud, process is completely severed from progress. The conflict between "civilization" and the "ego impulse" has no finite determination; it is simply a set of polarities: "love and death trends" which display the "innate conflict of ambivalence." Values are intrinsic to social science because progress, unlike process, is a humanly defined concept and not a universal law of nature.[17]

Nineteenth-century social science bequeathed to us antithetical views of the relation of science to values: the Smith-Comte tradition which held that all problems in social science are removable once we segregate factual and valuative elements; and the Marx-Freud tradition of unmasking, holding that social science is interest- and attitude-bound. There can be little doubt that, coming into the new century, positivism and empiricism in social science were at a disadvantage. Every empirical explanation of social events seemed tinged, if not entirely reducible, with the point of view or ideological mooring of the investigator. Thus, when Spencer, the last persuasive nineteenth-century advocate of an evolutionary functional view, offered an "empirical" typology of society, it was plain that "militant" and "industrial" (the two principle types he distinguished) were collective euphemisms representing Kaiserism for the former and English constitutionalism for the latter. Indeed his use of the word "industrial" made no reference to an economic entity at all, but only to the qualities of any English squire of the past: "independence, resistance to coercion, honesty, truthfulness, forgivingness, kindness."[18] Objectivity, at least of such an evolutionary type, seemed less able to explain than be explained. Gurvitch insists that even now empiricism in social theory has not gotten beyond the Spencerian stage.[19]

We may sum up the unmasking, *i.e.*, the critical rather than empirical tradition, in the following broad terms: (a) objectivity in social science differs from objectivity in the physical sciences by virtue of an essential and organic value dimension; (b) social science is purposive in the sense that men seek to establish goals not present in nature as such; (c) purposive behavior is not capricious, and hence not inconsistent with the truth-revealing potential of

17. Sigmund Freud, *Civilization and Its Discontents* (1930) (New York: Doubleday and Co., 1958), p. 89.

18. Herbert Spencer, *The Principles of Sociology* (New York: D. Appleton & Co., 1896), vol. II, part V, pp. 568–640.

19. George Gurvitch, *Trois Chapitres d'Histoire de la Sociologie: Comte, Marx et Spencer* (Paris: Centre de Documentation Universitaire, 1955). See especially the ninth conference on Spencer.

science; (d) the acquisition of truths in social science is not open to all equally, since social stratification and class differentiation act to prevent a disinterested appraisal of events; (e) the presence of moral components does not prevent a scientific view of society, but, to the contrary, is its necessary (if not sufficient) condition.

The unmasking tradition, with its newly established bastions capable of showing the ideological basis of the social science that preceded it, itself came on hard times. The Marxian accounting for values became transformed into the dogma of partisanship; the Nietzschean concern for values in a world of historical law became a signal for constructing mythological theories of the *übermensch*; the Freudian analysis of the properties of the unconscious soon became transformed into philosophies justifying the cult of irrationalism. The unmasking tradition in the hands of lesser individuals was transformed into an oracular, antiscientific tradition, tied to the desired or anticipated fortunes of petty political considerations. This is, to be sure, not a unique by-product of inherited social theories. Justifications for the established order are just as possible on functionalist as on historicist grounds.

In the social context existing between the *fin de siècle* and World War I, sociology was once more driven to establish itself as an autonomous science by freeing itself from the moral purpose which, on inspection, was simply political purpose. A return to the Smith-Comte tradition was indicated, but with a firm realization that the early positivism's "ghost in the machine" had to be eradicated. This was the outstanding achievement of Durkheim and Weber. Durkheim sought to move beyond oracular writers like Stahl in Germany and Cousin in France, who had conceived of social science as an aid and adjunct to patriotism and the moral authority of the state.[20] The famous *Rules of Sociological Method* is an attack by Durkheim upon the right of metaphysical doctrine of any variety to exercise an intellectual tyranny over sociology, and an insistence on the ultimate knowability of human action and belief.[21] Weber carried on precisely the same struggle in Germany against the moralism of Schmoller and the politicalization of social science carried on by Marxians. Weber's rediscovery of the Kantian disjunction of fact and value was a direct consequence of framing a response to a practical question: what should the attitude of the scholar-teacher be towards his materials, and towards the recipients of these materials, the students?[22]

20. Cf. Emile Durkheim, *L'Education morale* (Paris: Alcan, 1925), pp. 3–5.

21. Cf. Emile Durkheim, *The Rules of Sociological Method* (Chicago: University of Chicago Press, 1938), esp. pp. 141–146.

22. Max Weber's two most famous statements on the relationship of fact to value are contained in the *Gesammelte Aufsätze zur Wissenschaftslehre* (Tübingen, 1922). They have been separately translated. See "The Meaning of 'Ethical Neutrality' in Sociology and Economics," in *The Methodology of the Social Sciences*, ed. and trans. by E. A. Shils and H. A. Finch (Glencoe, Ill.: Free Press, 1949), esp. pp. 3–8; and "Science as a Vocation," in *From Max Weber: Essays in Sociology.* ed. and trans. by H. H. Gerth and C. W. Mills (New York: Oxford University Press, 1946), pp. 143–147.

It is precisely the practical nature of the response to the unmasking tradition turned oracular that linked Weber and Durkheim. They were united in the common enterprise of placing social science back on the road to empirical discovery by making sociology an autonomous, independent force. The impact of these two men on the evolution of sociology has been immense, so that it is important yet difficult to state their contributions synthetically.

The first point in the methodological counterattack is that social science cannot be tied to either religious or political ambitions. Restorationism and socialism were equally castigated for failing to distinguish between description and prescription. Durkheim first asserts the independence of sociology from other disciplines, and goes on to assert that it "will be neither individualist, communistic, nor socialistic in the sense commonly given these words." Such emotive concepts are to be ignored since they "tend not to describe or interpret, but to reform, social organization."[23] Weber is no less emphatic in describing the degeneration of German philosophy and religion into a pawn of "fanatical office-holding patriots." Precisely this bureaucratization of society creates the seeds for extremist demands for an ordering of society along totalitarian lines. Vision and prevision are muddled.[24]

The second assault upon the unmasking tradition was the assertion that social events, in contrast to political decisions, are not purposive, at least not in the teleological sense. The anticipation of future events can only be in the form of presenting existential options, not in determining which option is morally superior. Weber is most emphatic on this point, indicating that "purpose is the conception of an *effect* which becomes a *cause* of an action. Since we take into account every cause which produces or can produce a significant effect, we also consider this one. Its specific significance consists only in the fact that we not only *observe* human conduct but can and desire to understand it."[25] Durkheim is equally explicit in rejecting any but an empiricist attitude toward social causation. "All that we can observe experimentally in the species is a series of changes among which a causal bond does not exist." Continuing in the same Humean vein, he adds that all we can say is that "certain conditions have succeeded one another up to the present, but not in what order they will henceforth succeed one another, since the cause on which they are supposed to depend is not scientifically determined or determinable."[26] This noncausal view, which underlies much of the functional-structural literature, operated satisfactorily with Trobriand Islanders, but caused no end of anguish to men like Malinowski, whose ingrained hatred for totalitarianism was frustrated by a categorical denial that such a political phenomenon as Nazism could be condemned on moral grounds.[27]

23. Durkheim, *Rules of Sociological Method*, p. 142.
24. Weber, *Methodology of the Social Sciences*, p. 47.
25. *Ibid.*, p. 83.
26. Durkheim, *Rules of Sociological Method*, p. 118.
27. Bronislaw Malinowski, "An Analysis of War," *Magic, Science and Religion and Other Essays* (Glencoe, Ill.: Free Press, 1948), pp. 306–307.

The relativist basis of this comparative, acausal method, which, acting as a brake on the presumptions and fallacies that passed for anthropology from Bachoffen to Lévy-Bruhl, itself became a sterile defense mechanism against the use of historical criteria in social science research.

The third point in the arsenal of those arguing against a union of the scientific and valuative was the rehabilitation of the philosophic distinction between the "is" and the "ought." Weber was emphatic in viewing the Kantian distinction of the phenomenal and the noumenal as a rigid rule of social science. "Even such simple questions as the extent to which an end should sanction unavoidable means, or the extent to which undesired repercussions should be taken into consideration, or how conflicts between several concretely conflicting ends are to be arbitrated, are entirely matters of choice or compromise. There is no (rational or empirical) scientific procedure of any kind whatsoever which can provide us with a decision here."[28] For his part, Durkheim moved from the disjunction of fact and value to the formulation of three rules of observation; the essence of which is that the further removed we are from moral criteria, equated by Durkheim with the subjective, the stronger the possibilities are for a non-psychological social science.[29] Here, the notion of the sociologist as the physician and society as the patient received its earliest formulation. Neither Durkheim nor Weber denied the value-relevance (*Wertbeziehung*) of social science, but rather the value-content of social science. This distinction made, Durkheim did not hesitate to call sociology a natural science.[30] Weber was too influenced by the *Zeitgeist* tradition to go so far, and contended only that sociology was an empirical science.

The fourth and final axiom in method sociology noted the importance of social science as an instrument or set of rules that opens objective investigation to all who abide by its canons, without regard to the class, status, or power of the investigator. Scientific organization is based on commonly adhered-to rules, which alone guarantee the worth of social science data. Weber and Durkheim saw in methodology the precondition for expertise—what Weber called "technical criticism."

The method of sociology lifted the investigator out of all ideological pitfalls. Sociological training prepares the investigator for his elevation from "utilitarian calculation and syllogistic reasonings." The novitiate may still be bound by moral considerations, the finished Durkheimian product is illusion-free and bias-clear.[31] As Ginsberg recently pointed out, Durkheim's "work suffers from a failure to distinguish clearly between problems of origin and problems of validity and from too great a readiness to identify the impersonal with the

28. Weber, *Methodology of the Social Sciences*, pp. 18–19; also pp. 13, 54.

29. Durkheim, *Rules of Sociological Method*, pp. 31–44.

30. *Ibid.*, p. 1 and *passim*. See, on this, Harry Alpert, *Emile Durkheim and His Sociology* (New York: Columbia University Press, 1939), pp. 80–111.

31. Durkheim, *Rules of Sociological Method*, p. 144.

collective, the pressure of society with objective validity."[32] Weber is no less subject to this line of criticism. His idea that the best way to stay clear of illusions and biases is to lay them bare at all times assumes that this sort of self-revelation is itself free of rationalization and a value perspective.[33]

I have dwelt at length on Durkheim and Weber not only to recall the debt modern social science owes to them, but rather to show that even if we accept everything in these four axioms, we are not out of the woods in which Marx and Freud placed the social sciences. One can hardly overlook the profoundly moral attitude of Durkheim to society, his attempt to establish a "science of morality." As Catlin notes, "the positivist obsession takes charge, which denies the distinction of science and ethics, logic based on anthropological fact and values conditioning judgments."[34] In Weber's case, the moral grounds are only slightly less easy to dissect. There is his famous description of "charismatic authority," so heavily stamped with a youthful absorption in Prussian militarism that it is difficult to avoid a psychological explanation for the form as well as the content of this concept.[35] Similarly, liberalist values are stamped throughout the editorial comments of the *Archiv für Sozialwissenschaft*.[36] Nor did the shift from factory to marketing orientation fail to leave its impression on Weber. His concern with the social basis of contracts, status factors in the distribution of industrial privileges, and the bureaucratization of the political process all derived in part from an acceptance of the major premise of the liberal ideology of the twentieth century—that sociology has replaced economics as the central frame of human reference.[37]

Even Weber's most sympathetic and least critical commentator took note of the moral dominion from which Weber commenced his studies. "Weber was preoccupied with the problem of individual autonomy in a world that was increasingly subjected to the inexorable machinery of bureaucratic administration." Surely, if bureaucracy is inexorable, the scientist in Weber should have been content with a description of how this process unfolds. Clearly he was not because of the very values which led him to study bureaucracies in the first place. As we learn, "Weber's perspective for the future was a direct product of his personal position as a liberal critic of bureaucratic absolutism in imperial Germany, and today we sympathize readily with this early formulation of George Orwell's *1984*."[38]

32. Morris Ginsberg, *Essays in Sociology and Social Philosophy: On the Diversity of Morals* (New York: Macmillan Co., 1957), pp. 52–53.

33. Weber, "Science as a Vocation," Gerth and Mills, *From Max Weber*, pp. 145–146.

34. G. E. G. Catlin, "Introduction" to Durkheim, *The Rules of Sociological Method*, pp. xxix–xxx.

35. Weber, "The Meaning of Discipline," Gerth and Mills, *From Max Weber*, pp. 253–264.

36. Weber, *Methodology of the Social Sciences*, esp. pp. 59–63.

37. Cf. Horowitz, *Philosophy, Science and the Sociology of Knowledge*, p. 64.

38. Reinhard Bendix, *Max Weber: An Intellectual Portrait* (New York: Doubleday & Co., 1960), pp. 455–456.

To conclude, we may say that Weber and Durkheim and their innumerable followers succeeded in raising the level of craftmanship in social research to new heights by forging heuristic precepts and rules of procedure. However, they did not succeed, any more than Kant or Hume, in settling the place of values in social studies. The distinction between value-free and value-relevance proved to be only a ploy and not a solution. The main point in the Marx-Freud line of reasoning remained curiously unexamined, namely that ideologies operate unconsciously (or subconsciously) and are therefore not subject to autoregulation by the investigator. Indeed, the very "exposure" of an ideology tends to render it impotent and inoperative. Weber and Durkheim improperly assumed that methodology—procedural rules—can replace motivations. The recognition of a valuational dimension to social research is not a sign of dishonest pedagogy, but is a consequence of interest factors and action orientations which are situationally determined rather than methodologically deleted. The unmasking tradition could adopt the axiological position of Weber and Durkheim without feeling pinched as to its fundamental convictions.

To illustrate the above point, I should like now to contrast the work of Mannheim and Scheler with the methodological school of sociology. Certain conclusions of the Durkheim-Weber school appear in the work of the early sociologists of knowledge, e.g., the treatment of ideas as facts for analysis, the relativist view of truth, an awareness that the meaning of propositions is related to the functional uses of these propositions, and an antipathy towards the materialist philosophy underlying much of the unmasking tradition. But when we examine what Mannheim and Scheler stood for, we can see that the main threat is considered to stem from the methodological, positivist tradition. Indeed, it has been noted that the work of Mannheim and Scheler was in good measure understandable as a desiccated, academically respectable type of Marxism.[39] It was not simply against the idea of social science as a natural science, but against science as a sufficient and inclusive instrument of analysis, that the main energies of the two were directed.[40]

Scheler and Mannheim represent essentially similar lines in social theory. This is not an arbitrary lumping together since Mannheim himself categorically says that "we completely agree with Scheler, then, that metaphysics has not been and cannot be eliminated from our world conception, and that metaphysical categories are indispensable for the interpretation of the historical and intellectual world."[41] If anything, Mannheim was a "purer" metaphysician than Scheler,

39. Cf. Farber, *Naturalism and Subjectivism*, pp. 297–329. See also Howard Becker and H. Otto Dahlke, "Max Scheler's Sociology of Knowledge," in *Philosophy and Phenomenological Research*, vol. II (1940), pp. 310–322.

40. Max Scheler, *Die Stellung des Menschen im Kosmos* (Darmstadt: O. Reichl, 1928), p. 112; *Der Formalismus in der Ethik und die Materiale Wertethik* (Halle: M. Niemeyer, 1927), p. 412.

41. Karl Mannheim, *Essays on the Sociology of Knowledge* (London: Routledge & Kegan Paul, Ltd., 1952), p. 175.

since "according to our view [Mannheim always liked to speak of himself in the plural], God's eye is upon the historic, *i.e.*, it is not meaningless, whereas Scheler must imply that he looks upon the world with God's eyes."[42] And lest we imagine that this is intended simply as a pun, Mannheim elsewhere admits that "we are somehow guided by a 'plan,' and 'intelligible framework' of history whenever we put the seemingly most isolated particular fact into a context."[43] Mannheim's contextualism, like Scheler's phenomenalism, is brought into play as a direct attempt to transcend empirical sociology. This truncated Hegelianism is resuscitated for the purpose of once again throwing social research back on the mercy of a *deus ex machina*.

The Scheler-Mannheim style of thought adds an additional element to this restoration of social metaphysics, namely, the rejection of the naturalistic distinction between science and ideology,[44] and the rejection of a methodology offering but partial results and pragmatic solutions.[45] The principle of social engineering in Mannheim and divine engineering in Scheler disguised an anti-scientific quest for certainty. In the name of preserving values, this line of thought managed to recreate the gap between facts and values. Durkheim's sacredness of facts is magically transformed into Scheler's sacredness of values. One is left with the prospect of choosing between the false alternatives of narrow empiricism and grand-scale metaphysics.

II. SOCIAL SCIENCE AND VALUE PERSPECTIVES: AN AMERICAN BRIEFING

The tendency in American sociology during earlier generations of this century was to bypass rather than move beyond these various European currents. This might be put more exactly by saying that we tended to reproduce the various lines of argument between a value-oriented and a value-free sociology at a lower level of sophistication. The efforts of Parsons, Gerth, Mills, and Knight to make the work of Weber available in English, and the parallel efforts of Wirth, Shils, Keckesmeti, and Lowie to do the same for Mannheim, quickened the pace of our discussions of value theory in the social sciences. With the possible exception of Ward and Cooley (who maintained close ties with continental currents), analysis of this problem in the formative period of American sociology, 1900 to 1930, was virtually nonexistent. The decade between 1930 and 1940 was fateful for American studies in sociological theory in several ways: (a) it initiated the use of sociological studies and briefs in governmental and private business institutes; (b) it was the period of widespread dissemination of European trends in academic sociology; (c) it was the age in which honest social research was subverted by totalitarian regimes, and thus a time of migration for intellectuals in particular.

42. *Ibid.*, p. 178.
43. *Ibid.*, p. 175.
44. *Ibid.*, p. 184.
45. Max Scheler, *Die Wissensformen und die Gessellschaft: Probleme einer Soziologie des Wissens* (Leipzig: Verlag Der Neue Geist, 1926), pp. 48, 64.

American sociology during this decade digested and disseminated a hundred years of European intellectual experience. In order to fully understand the current status of discussions of value theory in sociology, it might prove helpful to briefly review the main lines of thought distinguishing this earlier period.

The entrance of Marxism into academic life coincided with the Depression period and the consequent search for an alternative to the "reform" sociology of Giddings, Ogburn, and Sumner. A good example of how this functioned in relation to the problem of values in anthropology is provided by Calverton.

The existence of cultural compulsives makes objectivity in the social sciences impossible. . . . No mind can be objective in its interpretation and evaluation of social phenomena. One can be objective only in the observation of detail or the collection of facts—but one cannot be objective in their interpretation. Interpretation necessitates a mind-set, a purpose, an end. Such mind-sets, such purposes, such ends, are controlled by cultural compulsives. Any man living in any society imbibes his very consciousness from that society, his way of thought, his prejudice of vision. The class he belongs to in that society in turn gives direction to his thought and vision.[46]

The unmasking tradition, however, never served as more than a peripheral reminder that there exists more than one way to treat the problem of fact and value in social theory. The dominant view, perhaps best expressed by MacIver, amounted to a positive assessment of the Durkheim-Weber tradition. Since the present crop of sociologists were weaned on his *Society*, it is perhaps useful to recount the conclusions offered:

(1) Science is concerned not with the establishment of ultimate ends or values, but only with the relation between means and ends; the ends can never be demonstrated, but only the relevance or adequacy of means to postulated ends. (2) Science is concerned with what *is*, not with what in the last resort *ought* to be; and it must always avoid the confusion of the *is* and the *ought*, of the fact and the ideal. (3) Social science has *as part of its subject matter* the valuations operative in social institutions and organizations but not the valuations of these valuations on the part of those who investigate them. (4) Social science in investigating the instrumental character of institutions and organizations, that is, their services and disservices as means to postulated ends, must always guard against the danger that the bias of the investigator will magnify those aspects of service or disservice which give support to his own valuations.[47]

46. V. F. Calverton, ed., "Introduction," *The Making of Man: An Outline of Anthropology* (New York: Modern Library, Random House, 1931), p. 29. For a sociological statement akin to Calverton's see Behice Boran, "Sociology in Retrospect," *American Journal of Sociology*, 52 (January, 1947): 312 and *passim*. The Freudian side of the unmasking tradition has also received noticeable attention; see C. C. Bowman, "Hidden Valuations in the Interpretation of Sexual and Family Relationship," *American Sociological Review*, 11 (October, 1946): 536–544; and also "Cultural Ideology and Heterosexual Reality," *American Sociological Review*, 14 (October, 1949): 624–633.

47. Robert M. MacIver, *Society: A Textbook of Sociology* (New York: Rinehart & Co., 1937), p. 520.

MacIver's statement of the functional-methodological school of social thought, and the discussion preceding his conclusions, are far less dogmatic than the European version. Altogether new influences had settled in: Dewey in philosophy, Mead in social psychology, and Hobhouse in moral theory. American pragmatism in particular felt its keen social role, and took the idea of moral mandates far more seriously than continental positivism. Indeed, English and American pluralism distinguishes itself precisely in its ultimate faith in the morality of rational men.

If there is a strong moral impulse felt even by "neutralists" like MacIver, this impulse realized itself among those sociologists more directly involved in community studies, propaganda analysis, and studies in crime and social disorganization. The most coherent expression of this came from the "Chicago School" of which Louis Wirth is a brilliant example. The firmness of the distinction between fact and value, aimed as it was against revolutionary and reactionary social doctrines, nonetheless effectively stifled reform theories as well. The problem became how to bring values back into social science without again conjuring up the daemons of Marx or Sorel. The work of Mannheim was eminently suited to this enterprise.

The fact that in the realm of the social the observer is part of the observed and hence has a personal stake in the subject of observation is one of the chief factors in the acuteness of the problem of objectivity in the social sciences. In addition, we must consider the fact that social life and hence social science is to an overwhelming extent concerned with beliefs about the ends of actions. It would be naive to suppose that our ideas are entirely shaped by the objects of our contemplation which exist outside us or that our wishes and our fears have nothing whatever to do with what we perceive or with what will happen. It would be nearer the truth to admit that those basic impulses which have been generally designated as "interests" actually are the forces which at the same time generate the ends of our practical activity and focus our intellectual attention.[48]

Wirth hoped that by making explicit the valuational elements in social science, we would be better able to cope with the elemental needs of men. The purpose is not the unmasking of opponents, but rather the revelation of our own interests, attitudes, and ambitions, which might raise us out of the abyss of ideological boundaries. The same sort of viewpoint was expressed in anthropology by Benedict in her strong plea for cultural relativism as a position making possible that social tolerance and political pluralism which is the hallmark of the liberal inheritance.[49] Values are thus viewed as a practical handmaiden to social science activities. But in the hands of the relativism and pluralism of Wirth and

48. Louis Wirth, "Preface" to Mannheim's *Ideology and Utopia* (London: Routledge & Kegan Paul Ltd., 1936; New York: Harcourt, Brace Harvest Books edition, 1955), p. xxii.
49. Ruth Benedict, *Patterns of Culture* (Boston: Houghton Mifflin Co., 1934; London: Penguin edition, 1946), pp. 256–257.

Benedict, values remained a philosophic preference rather than a social scientific necessity—and philosophic tastes are fickle.

For the postwar, post-Depression generation of American sociology, all talk of the valuational implications of social science research seemed part of a watershed long since crossed. There came into focus a strong current that identified social science not only with value neutrality, but with scholarly aloofness from moral issues. Whereas MacIver tempered and qualified his acceptance of the disjunction of fact and values, we now find Bierstedt turning his disjunction into a veritable law of sociology. His position "considers sociology 'value-free' in general and politically neutral in particular, and one finally that emphasizes, rather than erases, the distinction between sociology on the one hand and social and political philosophy on the other."[50] Goode and Hatt give vigorous assent to this, informing us that we cannot, even in principle, provide an accounting of value alternatives. "Science can only tell us *how* to achieve goals; it can never tell us *what* goals should be sought."[51] This, of course, marks a profound retreat even from Weber's disclaimers. Methodology, instead of being considered as a heuristic device informing value theory, comes to be a substitute for values as such.

With Lundberg we reach the epitome of current efforts to make sociology a natural and pure science. He exhibits not just indifference to values, but an open hostility to the existence of a plurality of values. He succeeds in making Ogburn's unfortunate culture-lag doctrine conform to his own reductionist image of society. He says: "The fact that there are differences of opinion in a large society as to what these [present-day] values are itself represents an unnecessary social lag. For in such recent developments as scientific public opinion polling, the values of a population and the unanimity and relative intensity with which they are held can also be determined."[52] The confusion between consensus and conformism is made complete. We are left with the impression that we ought not to be laggards, that resistance to a social consensus is tantamount to being backward, if not deviant. This "natural science" approach reduces morality to making sure that the number of police does not lag behind population shifts.[53] Berelson, in an otherwise useful monograph on higher education in the United States, seems to equate objectivity in matters of degree requirements with what administrative deans believe to be necessary. Discontent with certain standardization procedures recommended, *e.g.*, the transformation of the doctorate into a "technical degree," becomes an aspect of academic deviance.[54] The echoes of this

50. Robert Bierstedt, ed., *The Making of Society: An Outline of Sociology*, rev. ed. (New York: Random House, Modern Library, 1949), Preface, p. v.

51. William J. Goode and Paul K. Hatt, *Methods in Social Research* (New York: McGraw-Hill Book Co., 1952), p. 27.

52. George A. Lundberg, C. C. Schrag, and O. N. Larsen, *Sociology*, rev. ed. (New York: Harper & Bros., 1958), pp. 722–723.

53. *Ibid.*, p. 72.

54. Bernard Berelson, *Graduate Education in the United States* (New York: McGraw-Hill Book Co., 1960), esp. pp. 233–260.

neutralist posture are well illustrated in recent RAND studies of nuclear war. The question of moment, it seems, is not the feasibility, desirability, or necessity of nuclear conflict, but rather how rapidly it will take the survivors of such a war to reconstruct their former social patterns. The cupidity of this view is so complete that the possibility that people might actually have learned something from a total hydrogen war (aside from ways of preventing it) is not raised.[55] As Von Wiese prophesied: "Value judgments, adieu."[56] The truth, of course, is not that values have actually dissolved into game theory, but rather that the social scientist has become so identified with the going values of the Establishment that it *seems* as if values have disappeared.

55. Cf. in particular, Herman Kahn, *On Thermonuclear War* (Princeton: Princeton University Press, 1960); and Thomas C. Schelling, *The Strategy of Conflict* (Cambridge: Harvard University Press, 1960). In this connection see *Daedalus: Journal of the American Academy of Arts and Sciences*, 89, no. 4 (Fall, 1960).

56. Leopold von Wiese, *Systematic Sociology*, ed. by Becker (New York, 1932), p. 8, also pp. 64–68.

4. *Crime, Custom, and Culture: The Functionalist Theory of Bronislaw Malinowski*

PRECIOUS FEW FIGURES in contemporary social science have been able to transcend their own disciplinary provinces and make an impact on social theory and research as a whole. The tendencies to specialization, to what has pithily been termed the secularization process,[1] have led to a deepening insularity of scholarly pursuits. One of the few anthropologists who escaped this fate of expertise and reached into every aspect of the social sciences without compromising the integrity of his own area was the late Bronislaw Malinowski. The achievement of Malinowski can perhaps be best appreciated in the light of subsequent changes in anthropology itself, which at this point is bureaucratically departmentalized into five parts: ethnology, linguistics, physical anthropology, archeology, and social anthropology.[2] At the jurisdictional level alone, the

This paper traces out the anthropological uses of functionalist theory, in order to show how its early democratic aspects dwindle as functionalism as a research strategy hardens into a methodology. It was first published in the *International Journal of Comparative Sociology*, III, no. 2 (December, 1962).

1. Seymour Martin Lipset and Neil J. Smelser, "Change and Controversy in Recent American Sociology," *British Journal of Sociology*, 12 (1961): 41–51.

2. Walter A. Fairservis, Jr., "Foreword," in Raymond Firth, *Human Types: An Introduction to Social Anthropology*, rev. ed. (New York: Mentor Books, New American Library, 1958).

fracturing of the field has created a new set of inner conflicts and hostilities that would make the appearance of a new Tylor, Boas, or Malinowski quite improbable. And whether this secularization process has produced a more formidable body of work, even in the much vaunted middle-range problems, is clearly subject to doubt.[3] A new overview of Malinowski's work in thus proper, not only or even primarily on historical grounds (for after all, a posthumous *festschrift* often has a ghostly quality of sealing the lid on the intellectually departed[4]), but more vitally as a method for placing current tensions and tendencies in their proper intellectual settings.

Perhaps the main reason Malinowski succeeded so well in gaining a wide-spread hearing was less his pragmatic and empiricist mistrust of grand theories, than his almost inadvertent creation of an operational set of anthropological "first principles." Paradoxical as this may appear, it is clear that while Malinowski emphasized the role of the anthropologist as an objective reporter, he nonetheless did his reportage with a deep, direct, and passionate confrontation with man as a cultural configuration having private and public parts, individual and social needs. The qualities of manliness—and this could signify unreason as well as reason, cowardice no less than heroism, custom in addition to law—are present in some degree in all men, whether they be Trobriand fishermen or Polish noblemen. The character and worth of men is defined and not destroyed by the roles, functions, and positions performed in the act of social creation. To take this simple "humanistic" standpoint on the essential unity of man as a social and psychological animal required Malinowski to reject hoary ethnocentric doctrines emanating from European citadels of learning earlier in the century. It meant a break with the polarization of primitives and moderns, prelogical and logical, profane and sacred. It meant further a rejection of a simplistic pre-determinism which viewed the behavior of primitive peoples as some sort of proving grounds for a general theory of *future* developments within *advanced* cultures. That Malinowski was equal to the task is an ineluctable fact that no amount of criticism of his supposed or actual theoretical limits can overcome.[5]

3. Cf. Robert Redfield, "Relations of Anthropology to the Social Sciences and to the Humanities," in *Anthropology Today*, ed. by A. L. Kroeber (Chicago: University of Chicago Press, 1953), pp. 728–738.

4. Should this be construed too literally, I hasten to add that this is not the case with the recent commemorative volume on Malinowski. See Raymond Firth, *Man and Culture: An Evaluation of the Work of Bronislaw Malinowski* (London: Routledge & Kegan Paul Ltd., 1957).

5. In an unfortunate essay, Malinowski has been reproached for not developing a universal account of social systems; see Talcott Parsons, "Malinowski and the Theory of Social Systems," in Firth, *Man and Culture*, pp. 53–70. However, since Malinowski made no pretenses at being the grand theorist of the social sciences, this charge is rather inept. Further, this essay makes the important factual error of claiming that Malinowski was unaware of the writings of Max Weber. This is clearly not the case. Cf. Bronislaw Malinowski, "Labour and Primitive Economics," *Nature*, Whole No. 116 (1925), pp. 926–930; *A Scientific Theory of Culture and Other Essays* (Chapel Hill: University of North Carolina Press, 1944), p. 20; and *Magic, Science and Religion and Other Essays*, selected by Robert Redfield (Glencoe, Ill.: Free Press, 1948), p. 25f.

Turning to our main purpose: how does *Crime and Custom* illustrate the principle aspects of Malinowski's strategy and theory? Further, how have these strategies and theories become the common currency of modern anthropology and sociology? In order to provide meaningful answers to these related questions, Malinowski's work will be considered under five headings: (I) the meaning of culture; (II) functionalism as the theory and method of culture; (III) the nature of human institutions; (IV) the nature of social and cultural change; (V) the scope and method of anthropology. We will then be in a position to see how *Crime and Custom* fits into Malinowski's total contribution.

I. The Meaning of Culture

Central to all of Malinowski's work is a multivariate analysis of culture. If the earlier stages in anthropological theory defined culture idealistically, in terms of consciousness,[6] further developments produced a reaction to this so that culture was defined much more decisively in terms of material artifacts.[7] Malinowski faithfully sought to avoid a reductionist choice as to the "ultimate" component in culture. Thus culture is seen as comprised of "inherited artifacts, goods, technical processes, ideas, habits and values." Malinowski further adds that "social organization cannot be really understood except as a part of culture; and all special lines of inquiry referring to human activities, human groupings and human ideas and beliefs can meet and become cross-fertilized in the comparative study of cultures."[8]

Such a view avoids several inherited metaphysical issues Malinowski held to be destructive of a scientific theory of society: the view of culture as a symbolic *Geistesmensch* in which culture is identified with some particular advanced form of civilization; and, no less, the biological view of culture as bound to a *Naturmensch*. Artifact and custom are for Malinowski indispensable, since they mutually produce, effect, and even define each other.[9] He did not always remain faithful to this dualistic formulation. At times he speaks of culture as comprising four irreducible and cross-fertilizing variables: a body of material possessions, a type of social organization, communication by means of a language system, a system of "spiritual" values.[10] The difficulty with this latter definition is that it defines culture by its affective capacities rather than by its specific properties. Perhaps this is why Malinowski chose to simplify his definition in later writings.

The truly controversial and novel element which Malinowski introduced into

6. Edward Tylor, *Primitive Culture* (London: John Murray, 1891), pp. 1–6.

7. Franz Boas, *Primitive Art* (New York: Dover Publications, 1927; reprinted 1955), pp. 4–5; and Kenneth P. Oakley, *Man the Tool-Maker* (London: British Museum of Natural History, 1950), pp. 1–3.

8. Bronislaw Malinowski, "Culture," in *Encyclopedia of the Social Sciences* (New York: Macmillan Co., 1931), vol. 4, p. 621.

9. *Ibid.*, p. 625.

10. Bronislaw Malinowski, *Sex and Repression in Savage Society* (1927) (New York: Meridian Books, 1959), pp. 161–162.

discussions on the meaning of culture is the idea of its being *sui generis*, and to be understood must be studied in terms of the given functional interrelations of customs and artifacts, and never in *statu nascendi*.[11] This position well illustrates Malinowski's profoundly hostile attitude towards any kind of "philosophical" anthropology. Idealism and Historicism are contemptuously referred to as "Hearsay Anthropology," to be rejected as such.[12] The most adequate statement Malinowski offered of his position is in *Sex and Repression in Savage Society*, which for its lucidity no less than its content, bears careful reading.

The main categories of culture must from the very outset have been intertwined and simultaneously at work. They could not have originated one after the other, and they cannot be placed in any scheme of temporal sequence. Material culture, for instance, could not have come into being before man was able to use his implements in traditional technique which, as we know, implies the existence of knowledge. Knowledge again and tradition are impossible without conceptual thought and language. Language, thought, and material culture are thus correlated, and must have been so at any stage of development, hence also at the beginnings of culture. . . . Morals, again, constitute a force without which man could not battle against his impulses or even go beyond his instinctive endowment, and that he had to do constantly under culture even in his simplest technical activities.[13]

Malinowski worked tirelessly and, it must be admitted, tendentiously and with a jaundiced eye cocked on the work of associates and others in the field. Nonetheless, he managed to establish what have become the preconditions for functionalist theory: the liquidations of a priori notions of preliterate peoples— either for the purpose of sanctioning certain lines of changes in advanced civilizations,[14] or of pampering the European self-image as somehow superior to and more logical than that of savages.[15] "The savage," writes Malinowski, "is neither an extreme 'collectivist' nor an intransigent 'individualist'—he is, like man in general, a mixture of both."[16]

Unfortunately, Malinowski's "man in general" was no less ideologically bound, in his case to a notion of an "ideal type" man of commerce who existed only in Europe and North America. But even within this ideologically bound view of culture, Malinowski succeeded in annihilating anti-democratic and colonialist pretensions. Functional anthropology had to develop a broad view

11. Malinowski, "Culture," in *Encyclopedia of Social Sciences*, p. 624.

12. Bronislaw Malinowski, *Crime and Custom in Savage Society* (London: Routledge & Kegan Paul Ltd., 1926), p. 121.

13. Malinowski, *Sex and Repression*, p. 163.

14. Lewis H. Morgan, *Ancient Society, or Researches in the Lines of Human Progress from Savagery through Barbarism to Civilization* (New York and London: Macmillan Co., 1877); and Frederick Engels, *The Origin of the Family, Private Property and the State, in the Light of the Researches of Lewis H. Morgan* (Moscow: Foreign Languages Publishing House, 1884; reprinted 1948).

15. Lucien Lévy-Bruhl, *La Mentalité Primitive* (Paris: Presses Universitaires de France, 1921).

16. Malinowski, *Crime and Custom*, p. 56.

of culture, not only to solve research and field problems, but, in an overriding sense, to solve social and political problems as well. "Culture as a way of life, as a national type of pursuit, taste and interest, cannot be dictated, controlled or legislated. It ought to be given the best conditions for development and cross-fertilization with outside influences, but left to maintain its own balance and its own development under conditions of full autonomy."[17]

II. FUNCTIONALISM AS THE THEORY AND METHOD OF CULTURE

The literature on functionalism has, from the time of Herbert Spencer, held a central place in the analysis and comparison of social systems. It cannot be said that Malinowski's discussion of this subject ever reached the theoretical sagacity achieved in the present period by Merton[18] and Radcliffe-Brown.[19] This notwithstanding, to Malinowski belongs the distinction of establishing functionalism as the methodological partner of a general scientific view of human culture; and no less, of developing an applied theory of functionalism as a style of field research in primitive societies.

Interestingly enough, Malinowski's rare venture into a general summation of functionalist principles is made in a most perfunctory manner. The telling problems in the theory are omitted, while functionalism as a practical guide to the perplexed working on problems of the middle range, from family organization, marriage, polity, economy, and religion to knowledge and culture in general, is thoroughly emphasized. This imbalance between general theory and field research is characteristic of Malinowski's empiricist impatience with theoretical issues that might possibly have the effect of transforming anthropology back into an armchair enterprise belonging to gifted amateurs and literati. Malinowski alludes steadily to the field researcher and to his direct observations. Since this problem no longer obtains, since the most urgent set of problems for contemporary anthropology is a clear statement of its theoretical horizons, it is not without value to extrapolate and paraphrase the principles of functionalism as Malinowski envisioned these principles.[20]

a. Functionalism aims to understand the ongoing nature of culture, rather than offer speculative conjectures as to its evolution or past historical events.

b. Functionalism is a theory that completely banishes conjectural hypotheses, preconceived assumptions, or particularized ethnocentric interests.

c. Functionalism insists upon considering every custom, material artifact, or set of beliefs as fulfilling some vital need, having a definite task to accomplish within a working social whole.

17. Malinowski, *A Scientific Theory of Culture*, pp. 220–221.

18. Robert K. Merton, "Manifest and Latent Functions," in *Social Theory and Social Structure*, rev. ed. (Glencoe, Ill.: Free Press, 1957), pp. 19–84.

19. A. R. Radcliffe-Brown, "On the Concept of Function in Social Science," in *Structure and Function in Primitive Society* (New York and London: Oxford University Press, 1952), pp. 178–187.

20. Bronislaw Malinowski, "Functionalism in Anthropology," in *Encyclopædia Britannica* (first supplementary volume, 1936), pp. 132–139.

d. Functionalism is a view of culture as something over and above the biological components in human activity. Knowledge supplies man with responses beyond animal instinct, while artifact supplies man with implements beyond his anatomical endowment.

e. Functionalism considers the development of culture to consist in the development of well-defined, specialized institutions out of amorphous and non-specialized behavioral patterns.

f. Functionalism takes an evolutionary view of man, the essence of which is the progressive adaptation of institutions to their functions.

g. Functionalism reveals what a culture does for any specific community. This intrinsic criterion is an antiseptic to ethnocentric judgments and imperial actions.

h. Functionalism is not only a theory, but also a method, concerning itself with the actual workings and machinery of a culture, supplying the correct foundations for the practical applications of social science.

The task of this survey of Malinowski's contribution does not entail an expansive critique of functionalist *theory*. This task has been ably performed by Nagel,[21] Dahrendorf,[22] and Hempel.[23] What remains is to examine Malinowski's approach as a *method* of research distinguishing the anthropologist or sociologist from the missionary or tourist. This point is particularly evident throughout *Crime and Custom*.

Whereas in most advanced cultures, suicide is viewed as dysfunctional to the social structure, and even to the established moral codes in the case of European civilization, Malinowski carefully observed that this was not the case in every primitive culture. Suicide "looms large in the psychology of the natives, is a permanent damper on any violence of language or behaviour, on any deviation from custom, or tradition, which might hurt or offend another. Thus suicide, like sorcery, is a means of keeping the natives to the strict observance of the law, a means of preventing people from extreme and unusual types of behaviour. Both are pronounced conservative influences and as such are strong supports of law and order."[24] The ease with which Malinowski made such statements, and our view of such statements as commonplaces of a functionalist position, should not blind us to the fact that his orientation upset much of the sociological and theological pronouncements of the earlier part of this century.

Another popularly misunderstood aspect of primitive life, which the functionalist account helped clear up, is the purpose of so-called "black magic." Even for the majority of Malinowski's contemporaries, this was viewed as a typical

21. Ernest Nagel, "A Formalization of Functionalism," in *Logic Without Metaphysics* (Glencoe, Ill.: Free Press, 1956), pp. 247–283.

22. Ralf Dahrendorf, "Struktur und Funktion," *Kölner Zeitschrift für Soziologie und Sozialpsychologie*, 7 (1955): 492–519.

23. Carl G. Hempel, "The Logic of Functional Analysis," in *Symposium on Sociological Theory*, ed. by Llewellyn Gross (Evanston, Ill.: Row, Peterson & Co., 1959), pp. 271–307.

24. Malinowski, *Crime and Custom*, p. 98.

example of savage myth and illogicality. Malinowski's position, since amply demonstrated, is that black magic "acts as a genuine legal force, for it is used in carrying out the rules of tribal law, it prevents the use of violence and restores equilibrium."[25] As such, this corresponds to the usage of magic in primitive life, to enable "man to carry out with confidence his important tasks, to maintain his poise and his mental integrity in fits of anger, in the throes of hate, of unrequited love, of despair and anxiety."[26] In sum, magic, with black magic as a special subsystem, gives to primitive man what transcendental faiths provide for his modern counterpart: confidence, steadfastness and optimism.

The overall functionality of primitive culture is established by Malinowski on grounds not unlike those used by democratic political theorists to justify advanced modern culture: the symbolic regulation of conflict through legal agencies rather than through direct force; an established system of mutual obligations involving the recognition that social consensus is intertwined with self-interest; and finally, the existence of an established system of rewards and punishments.[27]

The study of preliterate cultures must therefore proceed in the same way and with the same system of valuation as the analysis of a contemporary Western European society. Differences between anthropology and sociology are therefore neither methodological nor morphological, but simply a difference in the groups being investigated. Functionalism cuts across disciplinary barriers, showing lines of academic division to be based on useful conventions and not on universal contracts. In an epic statement to this effect, Malinowski emphasizes the essential unity of human life. "The true problem is not to study how human life submits to rules—it simply does not; the real problem is how the rules become adapted to life."[28]

III. The Nature of Human Institutions

The most complex aspect of Malinowski's theoretical system is his highly refined view of institutions. Here precision is of the utmost importance, since what is at stake for Malinowski is the logical inclusiveness and empirical coefficients of such terms as "culture," "society," and "the individual." Extensive confusion has been generated by the failure to carefully consider the way in which Malinowski weights these pivotal terms. Some of the heavier charges against his approach: the careless and confused use of concepts like science and magic; the "casuistic" insistence on the indispensability of religion in human affairs; the pragmatic faith in an abstracted psychologism; the crude juxtaposition of person against society; the philosophically restrictive notion of truth. While they may

25. *Ibid.*, p. 86.

26. Malinowski, *Magic, Science and Religion*, p. 70.

27. Malinowski, *Crime and Custom in Savage Society*, p. 20; and *Magic, Science and Religion*, pp. 50–71.

28. Malinowski, *Crime and Custom*, p. 127.

indeed withstand any patched-up recasting as Nadel suggests,[29] they do not emerge as quite so glaring in the light of Malinowski's overall culturalist strategy.

The primary and most inclusive unit in human relations is culture. The basic method for the study of this unit is functional and structural. Malinowski fused theory and method by considering culture as the whole integral system. The functionality of culture is therefore a phenomena connected to the entire organic system, and not to every particularized unit or subsystem.[30] The practical immediate claim of such a view is that the social scientist is in a position to inform policy-makers how not to tamper needlessly with any part of a cultural edifice under penalty of seeing the whole system cease functioning.

Culture is said to yield two major derivatives: the social heritage of man and the individual life-style. The natural history of man is an anthropological undertaking, since culture exists over and above societal or individual expressions of itself. Given institutional patterns may shift, *i.e.*, derivative subsystems might be classified as profane (societal) and/or sacred (individual), but the essential trinitarianism, with culture as custodian as well as creator of all individual or social *forms*, remains a constant motif throughout Malinowski's work. Social institutions, no less than individual emotive responses to the world at large, are defined, and in their turn define the cultural process. This emerges forcefully in Malinowski's discussion of instincts, institutions, and culture, where he indicates that "the essential foundation of culture lies in a deep modification of innate endowment in which most instincts disappear, and are replaced by plastic though directed tendencies which can be moulded into cultural responses."[31] Social integration of these instinctual responses is a factor in its own right, but both integration and response are made possible by the existence of a cultural base. To reinforce this position, Malinowski speaks of human sociality as an "acquired habit" derived from a "dovetailing of legal, political, and cultural functions."[32]

While it is broadly correct that Malinowski exhibited a profound preference for "concrete" individuals over "abstract" society, what spared him from the crudities of the early pragmatist form of relativism was his specification of culture as the unifying agent which is larger than the totality of individuals or even the sum of existing social systems. There is a powerful organicism in this position, which was largely responsible for Malinowski's hostile view toward possibilities of assigning historical and causal priorities in social research. It was this cultural organicism rather than individualism that led him to stubbornly maintain, in contradistinction to the evidence, the universal need for both social and personal expressions of culture—particularly science and religion.

Despite a powerful animus for dialectical formulations, Malinowski had a way

29. Siegfried F. Nadel, "Malinowski on Magic and Religion," in Firth, *Man and Culture*, pp. 189–208.
30. Malinowski, "Functionalism in Anthropology," pp. 134–135.
31. Malinowski, *Sex and Repression*, p. 170.
32. *Ibid.*

of returning to reified polarities to explain problems of culture. Paradoxically, his search for the middle way, the judicious formulation, compelled him to push his conceptual framework into extreme poles, the better to strike the supposed balance. The very definition of culture as a delicate harmony of sociality and individuality involved an appeal to a mechanical principle of equilibrium as the necessary resultant of dialectical forces. This is the main driving force of Malinowski's theory of reciprocity, in which society is the "keeper of the lay tradition" and the individual is the keeper of the "religious principle or Divinity."[33] The collective conscious of Durkheim and the individual habits of Tarde were seen by Malinowski as isolates of the subsystems sociality and individuality, whose meaning could be made plain only by a "wholist" or culturalist view. The fact that culture alone must be taken *sui generis*, while every other phenomenal sub-system can be explained in *statu nascendi*, suggests that Malinowski considered culture (and not personality as is frequently suggested)[34] to be the master key opening up every other door in human affairs. In short, no amount of empiricist display in favor of specificity spared him a bias in favor of treating personality and society as parts of a total cultural system.

In Malinowski's scheme there exist cultural institutions as well as social insti-tutions. What distinguishes them is that the former have an extended duration of life, surviving the vicissitudes of political and economic rearrangements. Furthermore, unlike psychological phenomena as such, cultural institutions have a public character. The importance of religion for Malinowski is not just that "there are no peoples, however primitive, without religion and magic."[35] This is, after all, an anthropological commonplace that can be cogently argued either way. The fundamental importance of religion inheres in its role as a primary agent of culture, its capacity to channelize individual emotive responses into elements of social and legal cohesion.[36] Correspondingly, the importance of science, or better, technology, also lies in its universality, in its cultural perfor-mance. Science, the profane counterpart of magic and religion, is also larger in scope than the individual or the social order in which it is nurtured. Like religion, science is an agency that defines and is defined by the content and aims of culture. While cultural institutions are modified by social and individual factors, such institutions reveal distinctively unique rates and patterns of growth, change, or decay. The elements of culture thus exist at a logically more inclusive level of

33. Malinowski, *Magic, Science and Religion*, p. 40.

34. Franz Boas, in reviewing *Crime and Custom in Savage Society*, drew attention to Malinowski's abstract search for psychological laws as the necessary consequence of his nonhistorical dialectic. Boas is quoted as saying that since "the very complexity of historical development contradicts the assumption that supposedly existing 'laws' of psychology, no matter how much we may value the study of social behaviour, can ever replace the necessity of an historical approach to ethnic phenomena." Cf. Melville J. Herskovits, *Franz Boas: The Science of Man in the Making* (New York: Charles Scribner's Sons, 1953), p. 67.

35. Malinowski, *Magic, Science and Religion*, p. 1.

36. Malinowski, *Crime and Custom*, p. 44.

human reality than those elements that go into making a personality or a community.

This is not to imply that Malinowski offered satisfactory explanations of either science or religion. He defined these cardinal concepts from a "common-sense" rule of thumb perspective, with all the porosity such definitions hold in store. Malinowski himself, for example, could rarely distinguish handicrafts from science, or any private act of contrition or dedication from religion as such. Nonetheless, to the extent that science and religion are sources of human stability, or at least are not subject to direct alteration with the rise of every new economic or political system, Malinowski placed his finger on a special set of institutions that must be examined from an overall social science position, and not from the bastions of any single technique of investigation.

Malinowski's contributions to a theory of cultural institutions had contradictory effects for the rest of his empiricist anthropology: It strengthened his conservatism in relation to concrete social and psychological issues, as witnessed by his hostility towards doctrines of social change, like socialism, and doctrines of personal emancipation such as psychoanalysis. Malinowski's polemical streak compelled him to see in both doctrines foils for developing his own position. This severely restricted him from employing possible sources for a broader picture of cultural institutions. On the other hand, Malinowski's trinitarian picture of culture had the effect of aiding his escape from the false alternatives represented by an extreme sociologism such as that evolved by the Durkheim school, and the no less pernicious exclusivity of most varieties of psychological behaviorism.

If anthropology emerged in Malinowski's position as the most inclusive and, at the same time, the least well-defined area of social science, this was not due to any efforts to enshrine anthropology as the crown jewel of social science, but rather to the herculean effort to place the study of man on an empiricist basis without doing violence to a humanistic attitude toward cultural diversities. Whether the culturalist standpoint is quite as distinct from the strictly social and individual phenomena remains a conjectural sore point between the social sciences. Nonetheless, Malinowski's formulation of cultural institutions has a clear value in the study of science, religion, and the values attendant to each.

IV. The Nature of Social and Cultural Change

It has become increasingly clear that a major weakness in classic formulations of the functionalist methodology is the heavy premium which is placed on the locale of those mechanisms in a total social system. In consequence of this operationalist emphasis, a heavy penalty is imposed upon research methods inquiring into mechanisms in a social order which are dysfunctional and at variance to the system as such. Beyond this, early functionalist techniques failed to account for the internal reasons for the decomposition of social systems as such, even though particular parts might be nicely adjusted to the whole. The assumption of symmetry in human relations has justifiably been challenged by recent sociological theory; as yet the properties of an asymmetrical system have not received adequate attention by social anthropology.[37]

What tended to work against a full appreciation of the problem of functional asymmetry, and conversely, dysfunctional symmetry, is that from an empiricist and nonhistorical viewpoint, every society "works" to some degree. There is a strong impulse in Malinowski particularly to enshrine a tautology—whatever functions is a society, and whatever is a society must function—into an empirical fact. Those less content with formulas, those concerned with genetic problems of social disintegration and alteration, were subject to a heavy burden of proof. Consideration of the preconditions for changes in a given social system, the causal basis for such changes, and the values and premium attached to change by respective groups, all tend to move beyond empiricist confines. The prescriptive nature of such problems appeared both insurmountable and not worth the effort in the face of available techniques for describing ongoing social systems. The "brute" fact standpoint in sociology and anthropology thus tended to eschew problems connected with both internal and external forms of social change.

Whatever the high motives behind Malinowski's functionalism, he contributed greatly to the stagnation of the general theory of change. His work did little to advance the scientific understanding of conflict situations between primitive tribes, of antagonisms between groups within the same tribal order, and of value distinctions between different generations of a particular culture. Malinowski interpreted "the rule of law" so broadly that every phenomenal event from suicide to incest was placed under its imperial dominion. If he developed a keen insight into the psychological dimensions of consensus in primitive law, he did so at the price of an adequate sociological account of conflict in primitive life. The paucity of his work on the sources of conflict situations is ample evidence of a serious theoretical imbalance.

Murdock well sums up the current anthropology attitude to this failing in traditional functionalist theory. And while he himself offers only a fragmentary solution, he does pointedly indicate that change, since it is a fact of all cultural and social systems, is also a problem for social research.

Certain anthropologists have erroneously assumed that the elements of any culture are in a state of nearly perfect integration, or equilibrium, at all times. Actually, however, perfect equilibrium is never achieved or even approached. The adjustment of other elements of culture to an innovation, and of it to them, requires time—often years or even generations. In the meantime other innovations have appeared and set in motion new processes of integration. At any given time, therefore, a culture exhibits numerous instances of uncompleted integrative processes as well as examples of others which have been carried through to relatively satisfactory completion.[38]

37. Irving L. Horowitz, *Philosophy, Science and the Sociology of Knowledge* (Springfield, Ill.: Charles C Thomas, 1961), pp. 106–192.

38. George Peter Murdock, "How Culture Changes," in *Man, Culture and Society*, ed. by H. L. Shapiro (New York: Oxford University Press, 1956), p. 260.

Murdock's account has unfortunately been subjected to an extremely narrow construction. "Change" is interpreted to mean trend reports. Thus, in recent years there have been a great number of "returnees" to the scene of the original investigation, comparing social structures now with what they were ten or twenty years ago.[39] However important such descriptive reexaminations are, they have in the main failed to address themselves to the main issues in the study of social change: what are the causes and conditions for specific sorts of change, and what measures can be developed to predict and explain change? Because these revisitations have not been addressed to such questions, they have generally been less satisfactory than the original field reports.

While Malinowski tended sharply to adopt the "ideological standpoint" of the natives and their culture against all foreign importations, he recognized the difference in substance between social and cultural changes. His analysis, limited as it was by an inherited fear of historicism, nevertheless had a germinal positive content. The major distinctions he posited were that changes in *culture* (a) are adaptive, (b) arise out of contact with other cultures, (c) are gradual and evolutionary in nature; whereas changes in *social structure* (a) are internal, (b) arise out of mutually exclusive patterns of rules and laws within a single organized group, (c) may take place suddenly and spontaneously. This view of the differences between social and cultural change, although sharply challenged recently,[40] continues to be the prevalent view in anthropological theory.

Crime and Custom affords the opportunity to construct a picture of Malinowski's position on social and cultural change via his discussion of conflicting laws and morals in Melanesian society. Employing the principles of Mother-right and Father-love as pivotal, he unfolds a drama of social change brought about by the contest between "the powerful legal system of Mother-right," which is associated with a weak sentiment, and Father-love, which is legally less significant but supported "by a strong personal feeling."[41] This section of the book illustrates Malinowski's fondness for the concrete, and while he offers no general theory of change, it is clear that in the structural maladjustment of law and emotion we have an example of manifest law (Mother-rule) and latent law (Father-love), thus underscoring the mechanism of changing social forms.

In discussing the concept of kinship and clan unity, Malinowski touches (almost accidentally) upon a critical aspect of a sound theory of change, *i.e.*, the imbalance of reality and ideality; or as Malinowski puts it, "the play of the Ideal and its actualization, to the imperfect adjustment between the spontaneous human tendencies and rigid law."[42] Nonetheless, his view was seriously handicapped by a vision of "seething mixture of conflicting principles," more often

---

39. Margaret Mead, *Cultural Patterns and Technical Change* (Paris: UNESCO, 1953).

40. Siegfried F. Nadel, *The Foundations of Social Anthropology* (London: Cohen & West, 1951).

41. Malinowski, *Crime and Custom*, p. 101.

42. *Ibid.*, p. 119.

than not as a clash of theories, laws, and rules, and not of people, clans, and classes—a strange outcome to the empiricist search for the concrete.

The later work of Malinowski did little to round out a picture of the nature of social change. Malinowski indicates that he is little concerned with laws of change as such, but rather with the preconditions for ecological adaptation to new fields of reference.[43] He did, however, reinforce his earlier statements distinguishing cultural from social change by indicating that changes in cultural institutions "obey a specific determinism of their own."[44] But again, Malinowski placed such a premium on adaption, on the adjustment of cultural responses to assumed basic drives, that no necessity arose within his theoretical framework to deal with the clash of cultures on more than a superficial level, a level at which evil Occidentals insinuate themselves and their diseases upon the righteous Savages.[45] The fundamental ambiguity in his defense of cultural relativism is that although a profound and abiding ethical regard for the varieties of human organization is displayed, his empiricist posture prevented the development of a rounded, satisfactory view of social and cultural change.

V. THE SCOPE AND METHOD OF ANTHROPOLOGY

It might be reasoned that a separate discussion of Malinowski's position on the scope and method of anthropology has been obviated by the foregoing remarks. While this is in part correct, such a discussion has the value of underscoring Malinowski's specific challenge and response context. There is a need to see his work as arising out of a rough and underdeveloped theory of evolution in which anthropology was encased at the start of the century in ministerial and messianic wisdom. Malinowski's view of culture as an integrated whole to be evaluated in terms of human adequacies rather than the value preferences of investigators from Berlin and London is an indelible contribution that will always connect his name with the highest aspirations of a meaningful anthropology. There remains the need to show how the scope of anthropology for Malinowski necessarily includes a discussion of its place in practical human affairs.

What are the minimal requirements for sound anthropological research? Certainly for Malinowski the first prerequisite is immersion in the specific milieu of that cultural complex being studied—its language, customs and aspirations. He tells us that "while engaged in my field work in the Trobriands, I used always to live right among the natives, pitching my tent in the village, and being thus forcibly present at all that happened, trivial or solemn, hum-drum or dramatic."[46] Nonetheless, Malinowski did not confuse presence with participation, interest with involvement. While the anthropologists have learned this lesson very well,

43. Bronislaw Malinowski, *The Dynamics of Culture Change: An Inquiry into Race Relations in Africa* (New Haven: Yale University Press, 1945), p. 56.
44. *Ibid.*, p. 12.
45. Malinowski, *A Scientific Theory of Culture*, pp. 91–119.
46. Malinowski, *Crime and Custom*, pp. 76–77.

it remains an unreached ideal for too many sociologists, for whom "functional detachment" from the object of study is still very much the rule.[47]

The other major point made by Malinowski is the need to banish ethnocentricism from anthropological research, the ability to emphatically engage in role transference, the nasty "operation called *Verstehen*" that has been so widely condemned and "disproven." In an amusing footnote on the incongruities between the preachings of missionaries on peace and love, amidst government politicians declarations of loyalty to the Crown in its war effort, Malinowski records the following reaction among his informants. "They were really puzzled at hearing that in one day white men were wiping out as many of their kind as would make up several of the biggest Melanesian tribes. They forcibly concluded that the White Man was a tremendous liar, but they were not certain at which end the lie lay—whether in the moral pretence or in his bragging about war achievements."[48]

Malinowski wrote with particular vigor on the political consequences of employing ethnocentric standards. Only by recalling how widespread this attitude was in European professional circles in the decades immediately preceding and following World War I can his fervor on this question be appreciated.[49] Speaking of the problem of genocidal depopulation, Malinowski wrote:

All that would appear to the convention-bound, parochial, middle-class mind as "disgusting," "silly," "immoral," was simply destroyed with the stroke of the pen, and, worse, with rifles and bayonets. And yet to a deeper knowledge based on real human sympathy and on conscientious scientific research, many of these "savage" customs are revealed as containing the very essence of the tribal life to a people as something indispensable to their existence as a race. Imagine well meaning, perhaps, but rigid and conceited bureaucrats sitting in judgment over British civilization. They would see thousands of youths and men "wasting their time" over "silly"games like golf, cricket, and football, in "immoral" betting, in "disgusting" boxing and fox-hunting. "These forms of sport are *streng verboten*" would be their verdict. Yet anyone looking from an ethnological point of view on this problem would soon see that to wipe out sport, or even undermine its influence, would be a crime.[50]

This position had nothing in common with the sentimental, absurd notion that to know the savage is to love him. It simply states that the acquisition of knowledge calls into play fundamental social and political values of the investigator. The relativity of such values should be faced squarely. In speaking of the anthropological contribution to the study of international conflict, Malinowski

47. Melvin Tumin, "Some Social Requirements for Effective Community Development," *Community Development Review*, II (1958): 27.

48. Malinowski, *Crime and Custom*, p. 83f.

49. Cf. H. Ian Hogbin, "Anthropology as Public Service and Malinowski's Contribution to It," in Firth, *Man and Culture*, pp. 245–264.

50. Bronislaw Malinowski, "Ethnology and the Study of Society," *Economica*, 2 (1922): 214.

raises the value premises of the field directly. His judgment was that the integral organization and total bureaucratization of Occidental life are the true enemy of culture, as well as the most powerful stimulant to hostilities.[51] In this, his position is similar to Weber's fears that the bureaucratization of the economy is the true enemy of civilized existence.[52] There are indeed "values" in manifesting discontent over the tendencies in modern organizational patterns, but it is precisely such values that underlie the scope of social science research. Between the "savagery of civilization" and the "civilization of the savages" Malinowski would say we have no need to make a choice. Social scientists must avoid any imputation of moral virtue or vice to what is simply a case of superordination and subordination on a cultural scale.[53]

The third central component in defining the minimal role and function of anthropology is a continuous and careful weighing of the evidence. The study of man should not find itself reduced to the study of formal rule systems as stipulated by informants, but, quite the contrary, should be an analysis of how rules are adopted, overhauled, abandoned, and even winked at, in real life situations. "In actual life rules are never entirely conformed to, and it remains, as the most difficult but indispensable part of the ethnographer's work, to ascertain the extent and mechanism of the deviations."[54] The caution and circumspection with which Malinowski urged field researchers to view statements made by informants seems particularly significant at a time in social science research when a premium is placed on the interview situation and its techniques. The methodology of social science is thus no license for the liquidation of objective standards and personal insights on the part of the researcher himself. The treatment of informants' data objectively is not equivalent to objectivity as such.

What are the maximum limits beyond which anthropology cannot be effective or legitimate? How does Malinowski see the upper range of research problems? Here Malinowski begins with a correlation between the limits of empirical study and the purpose of anthropology. Ambitious theories of the historical evolution of primitive peoples, and abstract doctrines of the collective conscience or individual unconscious, should be employed with circumspection and with a regard for sound canons of evidence. The first stage is to distinguish between objective facts and psychological feelings. "After all, neither group-marriage nor totemisms, neither avoidance of mother-in-law nor magic happen in the 'unconscious'; they are all solid sociological and cultural facts, and to deal with them theoretically requires a type of experience which cannot be acquired in the consulting room."[55]

51. Malinowski, *Magic, Science and Religion*, pp. 306–307.

52. Max Weber, "The Three Types of Legitimate Rule," in *Complex Organizations: A Sociological Reader*, ed. by Amitai Etzioni (New York: Holt, Rinehart and Winston, 1962), pp. 1–12.

53. Malinowski, *Magic, Science and Religion*, p. 302.

54. Bronislaw Malinowski, *The Sexual Life of Savages* (London: Routledge & Kegan Paul Ltd., 1932), p. 429.

55. Malinowski, *Magic, Science and Religion*, p. 7.

The second point is a clear differentiation on the part of the anthropologist between those recommendations based on the organic and intrinsic needs of the given society or culture, and policy-making decisions extrinsic to the given society. Anthropologists are neither missionaries nor militarists, and should conduct themselves accordingly. In a prophetic statement to this effect, Malinowski shows himself a firm opponent of colonialism and an opponent of the use of science to foster antidemocratic aims.

Nationalism in the sense of a conservative reaction and the recognition of the integral value of its own culture by each nation, is spreading like wild fire all over the world. We, the members of the white race, are primarily responsible for that, and we have been giving our religion, our education, and many other spiritual boons to other races and other peoples, with an implied promise that once they accept our civilization they will become our equals. This promise has not been redeemed. We are beginning now to see how dangerous it is to speak about the white man's burden, and to make others shoulder it and carry it for us. We give all the promises implied in our concept of human brotherhood and of equality through education, but when it comes to wealth, power and self-determination we refuse this to other people.[56]

In brief, anthropology is a scientific enterprise that can only be compromised by the injection of extraneous political standards of the good and the right. Science has a value perspective of its own: objectivity in reporting data, integrity and honesty in field studies, accuracy of findings as verified (or verifiable) by other researchers; if such procedures conflict with political practices or policies, so much the worse for political considerations.

This is not to imply that Makinowski viewed anthropology as *anti-politique*. It is to say that political, economic, or educational applications of social science are best when they are founded on sound evidence of peoples—primitive and modern, preliterate and literate, Africans and Europeans—going about their business of surviving. The focus is on how people variously settle questions of land tenure, financial and taxation arrangements, comparative systems of formal and informal educations, the wider problems of regulating population, hygienic methods in each culture complex, and differences in ideological thought styles.

Crime and Custom illustrates Malinowski's notion of the limits of practical anthropology. The very exploration of primitive law and custom itself acts on the premise that law is not something the white race brings to the savages, but an aspect of culture germane to the conduct of all known societies. The entire development of cultural anthropology since Malinowski has shown a profound turn in the directions he outlined. The works of Lewis,[57] Radcliffe-Brown,[58]

---

56. Malinowski, *A Scientific Theory of Culture*, p. 219.

57. Oscar Lewis, *Tepoztlán: Village in Mexico* (New York: Holt, Rinehart & Winston, 1960).

58. A. R. Radcliffe-Brown, "On the Concept of Function in Social Science."

and Redfield[59] are particularly good examples of the keen awareness which now exists of the upper and lower reaches, the maximal as well as minimal requirements of a sound science of human culture.

While Malinowski eschewed the prejudices of politicians and missionaries, he welcomed the replacement of prejudices with humanistic *and* scientific alternatives in forming policies. He may have exaggerated the scientific claims of his form of world federalism, which, it must be frankly admitted, came perilously close to contradicting his belief in the self-determination of peoples and cultures. But his was an exaggeration intended as an antiseptic to dogmatic politics and totalitarian claims. And if he opposed those fully developed, and sometimes overdeveloped, nationalisms rampant throughout Europe, he yet saw anthropology as a support for national, social, cultural, and individual autonomy. "In a humanity still divided by races, cultures, customs, and languages, a full tolerance in racial relations, and in the respect for the individual, is the very mainspring of all progress and the foundation of all stability."[60]

VI. PURPOSES AND PROBLEMS IN *Crime and Custom*

Malinowski's classic work has already reached the age where its reappearance is as much a reflection of the period in which it was written as it is of the information therein contained. As such, it is useful to indicate how *Crime and Custom* was used to settle accounts with past ethnographic positions.[61]

The work in general is an assault upon a view of law extending from Hobbes to Hegel to the effect that the essential variable in a definition of law is the fact and principle of coercion, the "theory of negative sanctions," as Malinowski calls it. In opposition to this, Malinowski seeks to investigate the subject of primitive jurisprudence in such a way that law would be defined as a series of binding obligations, reciprocally agreed upon, while legal sanctions in turn are defined in terms of the principle of reciprocity and parity. While Malinowski insists that the Trobrianders are examples of a theory of law founded on consensus rather than coercion, the actual evidence is itself still subject to a Hobbesian alternative. The legal practices of savage society do not in themselves constitute a theory of law. Malinowski not infrequently confuses the pragmatic employment of a legal code with generalizations as to its theoretical foundation. Thus, the pragmatic approach of Malinowski cannot properly be said to have eliminated the classic theory of law as a set of rules based upon socially sanctioned uses of force.

Malinowski's objections to the work done by *le cercle Durkheim* of Mauss and Lévy-Bruhl are on firmer ground, since both the notions of the collective conscience and the sharp divisions between savagery and civilization based on the

59. Robert Redfield, *The Primitive World and Its Transformations* (Ithaca, N.Y.: Cornell University Press, 1953).

60. Malinowski, *Magic, Science and Religion*, pp. 308–309.

61. E. Adamson Hoebel, "Law and Anthropology," *Virginia Law Review*, 32 (1946): 836–854.

respective logical capacities of each clearly reflected the metaphysical and ethno-centric biases of the proponents of the theories. The *conscience collective* struck Malinowski as perilously like the modern European's belief in a *Weltanschauung* as a necessary component in securing social solidarity; a faith Malinowski found no evidence for among the native peoples he studied. The division between Malinowski and Durkheim also reflects an ongoing discussion in anthropological circles concerning a sociological or psychological interpretation of religious phenomena. Malinowski clearly stood with those who saw the essence of religious belief as private and personal in character. Religion as an institution was indeed social in character; but Malinowski held that such institutions define social structures and not universal cultural qualities. The rivalries between the "empirical" school of Malinowski and the "rationalist" school of Durkheim by now have something of an arid quality, since what seems to be at issue are philosophical postures and not sociological realities.

The third main purpose of *Crime and Custom* is to develop a theory of primitive law that would avoid a view of primitive man as the apotheosis of either pure good (communism) or pure evil (cannibalism). In the main, Malinowski sees himself as overthrowing the scaffold erected by Morgan, Bachoffen, Engels, and Rivers, to the effect that primitive man viewed law as purely regulative in nature (when present at all), since the only reason for calling law into practice is to punish transgressors of communal order. *Crime and Custom* is further an argument against the idea that law comes into existence only when social classes arise to build a coercive mechanism called the State. Here Malinowski sought mightily to show that primitive man is psychologically much like his modern compatriot in terms of a shared system of human needs, wants, and aims, and hence he like the modern civilized man expects roughly the same thing from law—the regulation and rationalization of reciprocally agreed-upon rules.

While there can be no doubt that Malinowski called attention to serious shortcomings in early ethnography and its amateurish attempt to prove either evolutionary or dialectical theories of change, his own position reveals a power-ful prejudice of still another type. Malinowski's discussion of law proceeds in terms of a hedonist-utilitarian model. The primitive mind emerges as something of a proper Benthamite, always calculating his self interests such that present virtuous acts have as their consequence a full complement of future material awards. Perhaps it is the case that the primitive like the modern is a composite of virtues and vices, rewards and punishments, but it is surely not so that he conducts his affairs and arranges his legal system so as not to do violence to a shopkeeper notion of values and norms. This is perhaps the most serious single shortcoming in *Crime and Custom* (and indeed, of all Malinowski's work during this period), namely, its continuous reference to a "model" modern, an abstraction culled from the urban petty bourgeoisie that was a London commonplace. The attempt to fit the Trobriander so that he would become readily identifiable to the "typical" trader or tailor raised on Adam Smith as someone just like himself led to just those sorts of scientific vulgarizations that Malinowski deplored in others.

In the last resort, the merit of *Crime and Custom* does not reside in any particular statement made, but rather in the observation that crime exists among all people, that custom is not the exclusive regulative mechanism in primitive societies, and that law functions apart from custom to punish criminality, however crime be defined in penal statutes.

Why such an obvious existence of legal codes among primitives could for so long remain outside the focus of social science studies is a sociological question of capital importance. While Malinowski himself offers some clues as to why this was so, they remain intuitive stabs. What is needed still is some sort of sociology of anthropology that could tell us why the anthropologists compile the sort of information on primitive man they do, and why they leave other types of information out of account. The concept of ethnocentricity is, after all, a euphemism, covering up a multitude of investigatory issues such as the ideological bias of the researchers, the respective valuational standpoint of investigators and informants, the extrascientific purposes of any given anthropological enterprise. This is the sort of knowledge which the sociologists of knowledge might profitably place before the prospective anthropological researcher. Malinowski's herculean efforts to overcome national and political biases in social sciences research, and his firm insistence on the essential integrity and unity of the human race, must certainly be included as landmarks in the study of both primitive and civilized man, of both the investigated and the investigators.

5. A Formalization of
the Sociology of Knowledge

THERE IS A WIDESPREAD belief that the sociology of knowledge is neither sociology nor knowledge. The claim is made that to qualify as sociology, some branch of sociocultural interaction must be studied, while to qualify as a study of knowledge would presuppose definitive information or expertise in the field being examined—something particularly rare in the annals of the sociology of knowledge. An additional factor that has made the reception of the sociology of knowledge something less than complete is its origins in the metaphysical tradition of *Geisteswissenschaft*. Given the current animus for products of this "oracular tradition," the sociology of knowledge has been contemptuously designated as romantic prose.

The customary reason for expressing impatience with the sociology of knowledge is its failure to come up with "concrete studies." While this is not an entirely just charge, it is my contention that the relative paucity of empirical studies in this area is directly connected to a confusion over its boundaries as well as its contents. Nonetheless, it is with trepidation that this return to "funda-

This paper utilized my previous work, *Philosophy, Science and the Sociology of Knowledge*, to develop a systematic and condensed formalization procedure to explain the interrelations of the component parts to the sociology of knowledge. It was published simultaneously in *Behavioral Science*, 9, no. 1 (January, 1964), and in a volume I edited on *Historia y elementos de la sociología del conocimiento* (Buenos Aires: University of Buenos Aires Press, 1964), which, to the best of my knowledge, still remains the only reader in the sociology of knowledge. (Reprinted by permission of *Behavioral Science*.)

mentals" is offered, precisely because of the calculated risk entailed in offering a programmatic statement when the need is for specific applications. While such applications have not been completely lacking, I share in the general belief that the sociology of knowledge cannot be accepted by fiat. On the other hand, while no thorough inventory of materials in use by sociologists of knowledge has yet been undertaken, it is not too much to hope that the area will not be rejected *ex cathedra* by the same sort of fiat.

The burgeoning of materials in the sociology of knowledge, particularly in its theoretical aspects, has made possible and feasible efforts toward a systematic evaluation of the field and its various parts. A number of major advances in this direction have already been registered. We might single out for special notice Merton's paradigm for the study of Mannheim's sociology of knowledge, and also his tabulation of Znaniecki's work on the social role of the man of knowledge; Wolff's careful restructuring of Merton's examination of continental European and American thought styles; Nettler's striking efforts to establish quantitative criteria for measuring the sociology of knowledge; and Johnson's diagrams of the types of functions of religious beliefs.[1] Mills's recent articulation of Marxism[2] in terms of ideology (institutions and attitudes justified), ethics (a worked-out body of ideals and beliefs), agencies of change (reform, restoration, revolution, etc.), and theory (the assumptions about how man in society functions) is yet another entry in the joint effort to put some methodological rigor into the sociological study of the cognitive aspects of social life. These efforts represent more than a genealogy. They supply a firm base for further study of ideological and utopian systems.

IDEOLOGY AND UTOPIA

What has hampered attempts at formalization up to now has been the seeming insurmountability of structuring the theory of ideology in such a way that psychological and social components are brought into a single accounting scheme. This has not been correlated with ideological and utopian systems of thought. With the assistance of the pattern-variable technique it is now possible to systematize the interrelation between ideological and utopian systems at both personal and group levels of reality.[3] In so doing, I will limit my comments to

1. Robert K. Merton, *Social Theory and Social Structure*, rev. ed. (Glencoe, Ill.: Free Press, 1957), pp. 456–488, and "The Social Role of the Man of Knowledge," *American Sociological Review*, 6 (1941): 111–155. Also K. H. Wolff, "The Sociology of Knowledge and Sociological Theory," in *Symposium on Sociological Theory*, ed. by L. Gross (Evanston, Ill.: Row, Peterson & Co., 1959), pp. 567–592; Gwynn Nettler, "A Test for the Sociology of Knowledge," *American Sociological Review*, 10 (1945): 393–399, and "A Measure of Alienation," *American Sociological Review*, 22 (1957): 670–677; H. M. Johnson, *Sociology: A Systematic Introduction* (New York: Harcourt, Brace, 1960), pp. 402–403, 462–463.

2. C. Wright Mills, *The Marxists* (New York: Dell Publishing Co., 1962), pp. 12–14.

3. Talcott Parsons, "General Theory in Sociology," in *Sociology Today: Problems and Prospects*, ed. by R. K. Merton, L. Broom, and L. S. Cottrell, Jr. (New York: Basic Books, 1959), pp. 3–38.

an explication of the tables, since a more elaborate analysis has already been presented elsewhere.[4] The purpose of developing a formal scheme, beyond the obvious pedagogic attraction of symmetry and isomorphism, is to assist those working in the sociology of knowledge to locate with greater precision the specific aspects of the ideological-utopian spectrum under analysis and, no less, the logical levels at which such issues are being tested. In this way, some of the oracular wooliness which has in the past marred surveys and studies of the sociology of knowledge can be overcome.[5]

Individual and Social Ideologies

The use herein made of Parsons' "double interchange" paradigm stems from a belief that the sociology of knowledge must sharply distinguish the subideologies of primary-group interaction from the ideological constellations projected to defend institutions as such. This does not mean that a decision must be reached as to which is more "basic," the social group or the political institution. There must, however, be an awareness of the different roles performed by each in thought as well as in action. Indeed, in terms of problems treated by the sociology of knowledge, large-scale institutions tend to be more central, in that they function to promote techniques of persuasion and to integrate group norms.

The aggregate of individual ideas, or public opinion as such, is generally less responsible than responsive to ideological formations. The advantage of differentiating the decision-making from the action-taking processes is that we are able to distinguish *ideas* about the social system in general from ideological moorings in particular. Both institutions and individuals can "behave" ideologically—that is, responding to the felt needs of particular social interests—without leading to the distintegration of the sociology of knowledge into the miasmic study of such aberrations as "private ideologies" on one side and "universal ideologies" on the other. In Tables 1 and 2 these distinctions are expressed in terms of a modified "stimulus-response" situation; with social institutions projecting ideologies which individuals adopt, and, similarly, social agencies integrating and intersecting with individual goals.

To pursue this matter further, adoption of ideas is considered an individual act, while projection of ideas is considered social because ideology is an eminently sociological phenomenon. It is an entity that satisfies group requisites and is then refracted onto the individual members of the group. Admittedly, this position tends to consider the individual as the bearer rather than the originator of ideological commitments. But although from a historical viewpoint this perhaps represents a return to the sociologism of the *collective conscience*, the alternatives

4. Irving L. Horowitz, *Philosophy, Science and the Sociology of Knowledge* (Springfield, Ill.: Charles C Thomas, 1961), pp. 79–105.

5. I have in mind here particularly the work of Scheler. With the publication of his *Vom Ewigen im Menschen* in English translation (1960) the full extent of the transcendental metaphysics which colored the origins of the sociology of knowledge can be gauged. See M. Farber, *Naturalism and Subjectivism* (Springfield, Ill.: Charles C Thomas, 1961), pp. 297–329.

appear far less satisfactory. To speak of ideology in a language of interaction is to avoid coming to terms with the causal problem—the problem of the social sources of ideological thinking. And to speak of private or universalistic ideologies is to atomize the issues on one hand, and confuse ideology with science and religion on the other. Thus, imperfect though the tables may be, they have the advantage of distinguishing between the self-image of the psyche and the collective self-image of society. The latter is the specific ideological pivot of social institutions.

No assumption need be made on the basis of Tables 1 and 2 that a society is necessarily conservative or that individuals are necessarily radical (or vice versa). It is assumed that designations of social systems and individual action are subject to different pressures and counterpressures. The purpose of ideology has generally been recognized as being to bring about a social consensus where none exists, and to maintain such consensus in times of stress, such as war, revolution, or rebellion. The reason the sociology of knowledge is particularly concerned with problems of political organization and disorganization is that the organs of political power are frequently, if not invariably, charged with the responsibility of seeing to it that the "dominant ideology" is in some sense held by the citizenry as the "common ideology."[6] If this blurs the line between unconscious defense of the state interests and propagandistic manipulation of public opinion for the defense of these same interests, it is because in concrete social life the line between ideology and propaganda is indeed quite indistinct. Nonetheless, the "double interchange" technique makes fewer presuppositions than alternative models for the sociology of knowledge. It does not, for example, demand a settlement of the philosophical issues of relativism, or the commitments of the investigator, in order to examine the main features in ideological or utopian systems.

Ideological and Counterutopian Systems

The purpose of Table 1 is to illustrate the *logical* relationships that exist between (1) ideology as an adoptive process to the dominant ideas of a given society and (2) the framing of goals within the social structure in which the individual operates. Often, the counterutopian syndrome is framed more as a critique of and a pessimistic response to utopian constellations than as a positive description of future standards and norms of conduct. Such efforts as those made by Zamyatin, Huxley, Orwell, and Young illustrate this negative reaction to those utopists who frame goals outside the standard ideological poles within which society operates.[7] The future state is described as one in which happiness and

---

6. Cf. Karl Mannheim, *Essays on Sociology and Social Psychology* (New York: Oxford University Press, 1953), pp. 231–242.

7. Evgenii Zamyatin, *We* (New York: E. P. Dutton, 1959); Aldous Huxley, *Brave New World* (Garden City, N.Y.: Sun Dial Press, 1926); George Orwell, *1984* (New York: Harcourt, 1949); and Michael Young, *The Rise of the Meritocracy* (New York: Random House, 1959).

Table 1: Pattern-Variable for the Study of Conservative Constellations of Thought

	Ideology	Counterutopian
Psychological	*Adoption* of popularly accepted or dominant ideas about the structure, processes, and aims of the political and economic system of which the individual is a member.	*Goal-attainment* seen to reside within the operative values of government or other agencies of the social structure.
Sociological	*Projection* of techniques of persuasion and delimitation of the ground rules of permissible range of organized action.	*Integration* of social functions within established system of norms, values, and goals of the political-economic structure.

freedom are incompatible. The fear of the future thus engendered serves to reinforce acceptance of the values of the present. Deutscher,[8] in discussing Orwell's work, vividly shows how the transvaluation of utopian values forms a counterutopian syndrome. The counterutopian projection causes the individual to adhere more affectively to the major ideological system, whether in consequence of intellectual commitment or as a result of an unconscious emotional catharsis.

As the pattern-variable shows, there is a distinction to be drawn between individual and organizational forms of reacting to either an ideological or a counterutopian framework. It should be noted that projections of techniques of persuasion do not carry within themselves any implication of being conscious manipulations of individual egos. In general, the opposite is more nearly the case; that is, such techniques are projected out of the certain belief in the righteousness and legality of established rules of conduct and styles of thought. To push ideas beyond the consensual base is held to be tantamount to promoting illegality and subversion. Similarly, the wide penetration into mass culture of counterutopian works of "fiction," or the more academic form such a literature assumes in the work of Hayek and von Mises,[9] for example, is not due to conspiratorial efforts of the state. These writings are *not* essentially propagandistic, but are symbolic representations of a determinate scale of presently available social goods as against an amorphous scale of future social evils. Thus the conservative spectrum of ideology and counterutopia seeks the positive utilization of individual members of a society along established lines; *e.g.*, free-enterprise economy in a monopolistic or oligopolistic context; communist society in a

8. Isaac Deutscher, *Heretics and Renegades and Other Essays* (London: Hamish Hamilton, 1955), pp. 35–50.

9. F. A. Hayek, *The Road to Serfdom* (Chicago: University of Chicago Press, 1944); and Ludwig von Mises, *Theory and History* (New Haven: Yale University Press, 1957).

Table 2: Pattern-Variable for the Study of Radical Constellations of Thought

	Utopian	*Counterideology*
Psychological	*Adoption* of system of moral perfection from which to examine and judge the political and economic system.	*Goal attainment* seen to reside outside the operative values of government or other agencies of the social structure, whence is derived justification of change.
Sociological	*Projection* of techniques of persuasion (prophetism, proselytism, messianism) grounded in the desire to revise thoroughly the ground rules of permissible range of organized action.	*Integration* of social functions outside and against the established system of norms, values, and goals, but not without the substitution of another set of norms, values, and goals.

strongly centralized state polity; and welfare state in a mixed industrial complex. These are not simply social myths, they are sacred values that the ideology and the counterutopian projection enshrine in different ways at different times, but within a single frame of sociopolitical interaction.

The specific advantage of Table 2 as a model for the study of utopian constellations is the "looking-glass self" aspect of utopias. They are nothing but inversions of ideologies, with the particular change being in the dimension of time. The utopian system is a projection into the future from the present. It is teleological in nature. It is an urging against ideology from the viewpoint of what might be, whereas ideology issues into a defense of interests which are already entrenched. It might be suggested that the present makes stronger claims of allegiance on the individual than the amorphous future. But this is so only in times and places of relative affluence. This is not the case in so-called "underdeveloped" areas, where ideological loyalties are noticeably weak and impotent, while utopian images have a much greater attractive force. This being the case, it makes little sense to speak of an "exhaustion of ideology," while at the same time urging a need for more and better utopian thought. Such differentiations between ideological and utopian systems of thought are emotive. They reflect the particular judgments of history made by adherents, and not the actual relationship that exists between ideology and utopia.[10]

10. This artificial division between ideology (bad) and utopia (good) dates back to Mannheim himself, who made a plea for the latter at the expense of the former; see Karl Mannheim, *Ideology and Utopia* (New York: Harcourt, Brace, 1936), pp. 262–263. More recently, Daniel Bell has offered a similar analysis urging greater effort at manufacturing utopias, since in the West at least, ideologies seem to have "exhausted" themselves. See Daniel Bell, *The End of Ideology: On the Exhaustion of Political Ideas in the Fifties* (New York: Collier Books, 1961), pp. 393–402.

Utopian and Counterideological Systems

If there exists a fair amount of agreement as to the description of ideological and counterutopian systems, this same consensus vanishes in discussions of utopian and counterideological systems. This has largely been the result of failing to stipulate the logical status of the "systems" under analysis. From a modal point of view, and no less in consequence of empirical facts, Table 2 is a direct inversion of Table 1; that is, utopian thought is *formally* similar to ideological thought. However, this is yet to be reflected in the literature. Utopian thought is still vaguely defined as "any attempt to make the possibilities of the future imaginatively concrete,"[11] thus ignoring its central function as a critique of existing relationships by calling forth positive moral alternatives. Similarly, counterideology should be defined as the framing of goals outside presently accepted dominant values and norms (while yet sharing with ideology similar psychological properties). Instead, it is loosely considered to be a truncated and localized form of ideology, a phenomenon that "justifies the patterns of a deviant group but without seeking to change the society as a whole."[12]

In both instances, customary definitions are deficient empirically as well as logically. What the analyst of classical utopian systems such as those of Campanella, More, and Bacon[13] is immediately confronted with is the value-centered nature of the societies projected. The future society is seen not just as a predetermined item on a historical agenda, but a positive good (as such goods are defined by nascent tendencies in the present society) that *ought to be* brought about by human agencies. The phenomena about which counterutopians are most pessimistic—technology, science, industry, and personality growth—are held as supremely valuable by utopians.

For counterideology to be defined only in terms of social deviance places a premium on conventional norms, leading to the implausible conclusion that a counterideology is without roots in large-scale social movements that do indeed seek the radical reorientation of society as a whole. From the viewpoint of the sociology of knowledge, particular doctrines such as democracy, liberalism, communism, fascism, republicanism, etc., may function either as ideology or as counterideology. The actual determinants are historical and empirical. A sociological inventory would disclose what is being defended or attacked, praised or criticized, at a given point in social evolution. Thus Marxism, the state ideology of the Soviet Union, is in a Western European context still a liberal heresy, a counterideology. In the same way, monarchism, the state ideology of a number of European states, is in an American context a conservative heresy, a counterutopia.

---

11. Kenneth Keniston, "Alienation and the Decline of Utopia," *American Scholar*, 29 (1960): 182.

12. Johnson, *Sociology: a Systematic Introduction*, p. 589.

13. Cf. F. R. White, ed., *Famous Utopias of the Renaissance* (New York: Packard & Co., 1946.)

This type of logical patterning requires a view of utopian and counter-ideological clusters as being something more than an exaggerated use of imagination. Likewise, ideologies are not to be found in "ideal-type" molds labeled conservatism, historicism, liberal-democratic bourgeois thought, socialism, communism, and fascism.[14] Ideologies are better seen as a crystallized set of attitudes that may serve different political functions at different periods in history. To adopt a view of ideology strictly in terms of particularistic political orientations is to run the risk of changing definitions with each successive stage of social process. This is a consequence of Mannheim's typology that seriously hampers its utilization.

The force of utopianism derives ideally from its impulse to moral regeneration, while politically it derives from its positive formulation of new rules for the governing instruction of men. Deviance is not disorganization; neither is utopianism a synonym for alienation. This indicates that the challenge of one set of rules to another is a violation of the consensual apparatus, but is yet in strict accord with the needs of society continually to rationalize and redefine the social system within legally stipulated limits. The integrative role of counter-ideology likewise stems ideally from its rejection of ideological patterns of thought, but politically from its function of "unmasking" established ideologies. The pattern-variables herein devised for structuring conservative and radical constellations of thought are not simply a formal isomorphism but constitute an essential phase in the social psychology of mass movements for revolution, reform, and restoration. Whether we choose to see these pattern-variables as operative within a "natural model" on the order of Sorel or Michels, or a "rational model" on the order of Simmel or Weber, does not alter the relational constitution of the paired concepts in the sociology of knowledge: ideology/counterutopia, and utopia/counterideology.

Definition of Ideology

The term "ideology" is suffering under the weight of its present absorption into the popular culture. And as is often the case when this happens, the term has taken on all sorts of meaning about society in general: from a pejorative word signifying everything that is unscientific to a praiseworthy word meaning the political perspective that cements social cohesion of the group.[15] As a result, the word "ideology" has in common-sense jargon become a synonym for "secular" thought as such; that is, an effort "to explain injustice, suffering, death, and the

14. Karl Mannheim, *Ideology and Utopia: An Introduction to the Sociology of Knowledge* (New York: Harcourt, Brace–Harvest Books, 1954), pp. 117–146.

15. A grave defect in the typology for authoritarian ideologies developed by Shils is that it considers only the "right" and the "left" as ideology-bound; see E. A. Shils, "Authoritarianism—'Right' and 'Left,'" in *Studies in the Scope and Method of "The Authoritarian Personality*," ed. by R. Christie and Marie Jahoda (Glencoe, Ill.: Free Press, 1954), pp. 24–49. Now why a theory of consensus should be less "authoritarian" than a theory of conflict remains unexamined. Likewise, why a doctrine of "art for the people's sake" is more

meaning of Life."[16] It is suggested that a functional account of what an ideology does may clear up a considerable amount of confusion by explicitly stating the essential aspects of an ideological system. This is at any rate the purpose of Table 3.

Here our purpose is to define ideology and, by a process of logical entailment, counterideology as well. To do this meaningfully is to explain what functions are serviced by what factors in an ideological complex. By expanding our definition of the functions of ideology to make room not only for justification (Marx) and rationalization (Weber), but also for the role of ideology in organizing and institutionalizing social drives, one can more readily understand the binding force of an ideological complex upon a social structure. Such a tabulation enables the investigator to establish those elements which are genuinely ideological in character, while also putting the sociologist on notice as to those factors of information and knowledge requiring a different sort of analysis. Not to consider ideologies from a sociological viewpoint leads to an evaluation based on false alternatives: (a) to the Marxian position which considers ideologies as *partial*, that is, limited to specific social classes having an interest in the maintenance of the established social order (which in turn leads to the strange postulate that in the modern world only the oppressed proletarian class are the true carriers of science and knowledge;[17] (b) to Mannheim's position of seeing ideologies as *total*, that is, as unlimited to any given social class (which in turn leads to the equally peculiar paradox of turning over the task of truth-making to a "socially unattached intelligentsia");[18] and finally (c) to Scheler's view of ideologies as *transcendental*, that is, as inspired by problems of the soul (which in turn leads Scheler to assign the task of truth-making to truth-seekers, the "fourth estate" of Christian educators).[19]

These remarks are not intended as an overall critical evaluation of the founders of the sociology of knowledge, but simply to point up that the absence of a *sociological* explanation of ideologies has led to dogmatism and absurdities. Left unchecked, the social study of systems of knowledge takes flight into becoming a branch of speculative metaphysics, as critics of the sociology of knowledge maintain, rather than being a branch of social science, as its advocates wish.

authoritarian than one which asserts "art for art's sake" is also unexplained. To equate ideology with extremism is once more to fall back into a pejorative definition of ideology as something "alien" to a democratic culture. A recent attempt to overcome this "centrist" bias by distinguishing six ideological bases and their inner political polarities is to be found in Seymour M. Lipset, *Political Man: The Social Bases of Politics* (Garden City, N.Y.: Doubleday & Co., 1960), pp. 131–176.

16. Cf. H. C. Bredemeir and R. M. Stephenson, *The Analysis of Social Systems* (New York: Holt, Rinehart & Winston, 1962), pp. 317–319.

17. Karl Marx, *The Poverty of Philosophy* (New York: International Publishers, 1935), pp. 106–107.

18. Mannheim, *Ideology and Utopia* (1936), pp. 155–162; and *Essays on the Sociology of Knowledge* (London: Routledge, 1952), pp. 134–190.

19. Max Scheler, *On the Eternal in Man* (New York: Harper & Bros., 1960), pp. 405–448.

Table 3: Factorial-Functional Definition of Ideology

Material Factors in Ideology	*Social Functions of Ideology*
1. A theoretical amalgamation, a collective representation, of the activities and ambitions of the state and its agencies.	1. *Justification* of established State authority.
2. Presentation in a coherent and relevant framework of the current values, norms, and actions of the state and its agencies.	2. *Rationalization* of established principles of political and economic organization.
3. Directing the members of a social organization into selective (and selected) channels of social action.	3. *Organization* of public support for elective and/or nonelective elites.
4. Stipulation of acceptable and nonacceptable forms of social action, and selection of appropriate channels and agencies of such action.	4. *Institutionalization* of social needs and aims of government power at national, regional, and local levels.

Ideology and Propaganda

There is a manifest sense in which propaganda statements are distinguishable from ideological statements. In the former there is some recognition by the propagandist that his remarks are not the "whole truth." The myth-maker distinguishes himself from the myth as such. It is different with the ideologist, mainly because the barrier between ideology and reality still does not separate him from his statements. The ideologist is not a myth-maker or a myth-purveyor in the Sorelian sense because he has a total commitment to his institutional allegiances. He is in effect a "true believer." However, the difficulty with the common-sense view of ideology is that there is an absence of recognition of the degree to which *belief* in ideology can be distinguished on objective grounds from *nonbelief* in propaganda. The purpose of Table 4 is to sharply differentiate ideology from propaganda without sacrificing the realization that there is a good deal of shading off in practice between the two "styles" or "systems" of ideas.

If the integrity of both public opinion research and the sociology of knowledge is to be kept, it serves no purpose to reduce the latter to the former as has been suggested.[20] It bears noting that the formative, pioneering efforts of Mannheim have been so closely allied to the social study of *ideological* systems that not a few critics have assumed that the philosophic errors of the man *eo ipso* condemn the sociology of knowledge as such.[21] Table 4 is therefore offered as an antidote to reductionistic alternatives to the study of ideology in its own terms, and as a distinctive aspect of social interaction.

20. See C. Frankel, *The Case for Modern Man* (New York: Harper & Bros., 1955), pp. 119-120.
21. R. Aron, *German Sociology* (Glencoe, Ill.: Free Press, 1957), pp. 55-66.

Table 4: Social-Psychological Characteristics Distinguishing Ideology from Propaganda

Social-Psychological Characteristics of Ideology	Social-Psychological Characteristics of Propaganda
1. Unconscious adherence to patriotic symbols, norms, and values. A singular set of beliefs, eliciting strong loyalties.	1. Conscious manipulation of patriotic symbols, norms, and values. Multiple sets of beliefs subject to rapid and radical alteration.
2. Collectively established by the group over an extended period of time. Its purpose is defined by its content or message.	2. Individually or corporately established over short period of time. Its purpose is to satisfy more basic needs external to itself.
3. Technique of persuasion in which persuaders are not intellectually distinguishable from persuaded.	3. Technique of persuasion in which persuaders are intellectually distinguished from persuaded—as myth-creator is distinguished from myth-follower.
4. Arises out of existing social conditions and relations in which the community finds itself.	4. Arises out of need to stimulate and revise artificially standards of social cohesion and conflict.
5. Shaping of "knowledge" and general theories of science and religion.	5. Shaping of "opinion" and mass culture, and generally confined to the "profane" levels of social interaction.
6. Concerned with justification and rationalization of already accepted social behavior patterns.	6. Concerned with multiplying stimuli best calculated to evoke desired behavioral responses.
7. Establishes systematic connections between theories; *i.e.*, laws of historical change; a demand for "rational" motives of action.	7. Establishes fixation of belief in relation to specific issues; willingness to defend or attack social structures in terms of "irrational" motives.

This chart owes a great deal to the work of Merton and Lasswell.[22] However, it should not be misunderstood as a simple juxtaposition of their writings.[23] Taking inventory of the meanings attached to ideology and propaganda serves as a possible guide to the further empirical study of these distinctive sociological levels of mental production. The findings represented by Table 4 may best be summed up by noting that ideology is operative over a relatively large social

22. Robert K. Merton, *Mass Persuasion* (New York: Harper & Bros., 1947); and *Social Theory and Social Structure*, pp. 439–528; Harold D. Lasswell, "The Theory of Political Propaganda," in *Reader in Public Opinion and Communication*, ed. by B. Berelson and M. Janowitz (Glencoe, Ill.: Free Press, 1953), pp. 176–180; and Harold D. Lasswell *et al.*, *Propaganda, Communication, and Public Opinion* (Princeton: Princeton University Press, 1946).

23. Items 3 and 4 of the table are derived primarily from my work on Sorel: Irving L. Horowitz, *Radicalism and the Revolt against Reason: The Social Theories of Georges Sorel* (London: Routledge, 1961), pp. 127–140.

Table 5: Basic Systems of Utopian Constellations

(Underlying Theme: Human life has meaning only in the contemplation and actions undertaken in pursuit of social perfection.)

	Coercive (Caesaristic)	*Permissive (Hedonistic)*	*Libertarian (Economistic)*
Source of Social Evil	Conflicting national and social interests; discord between political parties and economic classes.	Identification of social conformism (evil) with social consensus (good). Ethnic, racial, and religious inequalities.	Conflicting economic and social interests; discord between masses and elites.
Nature of Good Society	Charismatic leader as absolute sovereign; consequent centralization of economic and social functions into political organization.	Solidarity derived from popular consensus and allowing for free expression and communication of dissenting ideas.	Bureaucratic organization; total liquidation of state authority in favor of direct public authority.
Instruments Sanctioned	Military aggrandizement of foreign territories. Legality established by *military* power and administrative fiat.	Parliamentary and popular drive toward salvation. Legality by *political* power and judicial consensus.	Civil (internal) overthrow of established state agencies by either or both legal and extralegal methods. Legality by *economic* power.
Individual Values Sanctioned	Well-defined system of social stratification with each person integrated into the group in terms of well-defined work objectives.	Maximization of mobility and fluidity of the individual, so that social interests are nothing but the sum total of individual ambitions.	Integration of individual and social interests in terms of common symbols. Ego-gratification through recognition of the justifiable claims of society on the individual.
Ultimate Goals Sought	*Social harmony:* Total regulation from elite to the mass.	*Social happiness:* Voluntary regulation through interaction of delegated elites.	*Social equality:* Replacement of external regulation by auto-regulation. Self-destruction of elites.

"space" and develops over an extensive period of historical "time," whereas, by comparison, propaganda is operative within a relatively small and well-defined spatial context and is developed to satisfy short-run demands of a society, a community, or a commercial enterprise.

Utopian Constellations

Table 5 is not an effort to reproduce Spranger's "types of men," nor to insist that the magic number of utopian constellations is three rather than five. What is being claimed is that the literature of utopianism tends to fall into these three operational types. The lines of demarcation between them are fluid but by no means shallow. Powerful loyalties are involved in the struggle to preserve the "integrity" of utopias. This parallels the fact that those who take their ideology seriously have not been found wanting in its defense. Nonetheless, the value of such a tripartite division, aside from its relative analytic simplicity, is its capacity to account for a large number of factors that actually go into the creation of utopian systems. The chart does this by sacrificing specific utopian titles, *i.e.*, "The New Atlantis," "The Republic," "The City of the Sun," etc., but it does not preclude the possibility of new utopian forms, or different combinations fashioned out of materials already accounted for in the diagram.

This final table is developed along lines that differ in format from the others, partly as a consequence of the nature of utopian constellations, but more directly because there is a much greater need to distinguish and classify the forms of utopian thought than to define its characteristics by metahistorical criteria. We can assume that the pattern-variables offered earlier in the paper have resolved certain difficulties in establishing the relation of ideological to utopian systems. In the study of utopian constellations, the main trouble has been with the historicist propensity to confuse *basic* utopian configurations with the historical forms they have taken. Thus Mannheim[24] piles up a series of utopian variates in the modern world (such as Orgiastic Chiliasm of the Anabaptists, and less exotic types such as Liberal-Humanitarian Idea, Conservative Idea, and the Socialist-Communist Utopia), in which a certain confusion inheres between an accounting of religious and political phenomena as such, and between sacred, mythic, and profane activities having only a religious gloss.

The solid aspect in Mannheim's contribution was in taking an approach that accounted for changing varieties of the utopian configuration. Nonetheless, his underlying attachment for the Hegelian *Zeitgeist*—the notion that historical categories nullify the need for a logical ordering of materials—tended to make his presentation confusing as to levels of meaning. Mannheim's valuational preference for utopian judgments over "complacent" empirical judgments, and his further insistence on utopianism as a necessary frame of reference, conflict sharply with his scientific impulse to describe a utopian cluster as a state of mind that is incongruous with the state of authority within which it occurs. Here, as in the study of ideologies, Mannheim makes the existence of utopian "wish-fulfillment" a reason for doubting the possibility that social science can escape the cycle of ideology and utopia. Plagued as he was by a value-preference for utopian configurations and by the scientific need to explore objectively the

24. Mannheim, *Ideology and Utopia* (1936), pp. 211–247.

"other-worldly" basis of utopianism, Mannheim was forced to settle for a verbal ruse, "relationism," as a way out of historicist and relativist labyrinths.[25]

The final attempt, then, is to develop a logical formalization that does not do violence to the empirical situation. The value of such a formalization is that further historical changes in the form of utopian thought can be adopted within the framework devised by a recombination of the individual "elements." That certain reconstructions would have to be made to satisfy the contents of any one variety of utopianism is undoubtedly correct. Nonetheless, as a working model, this model of utopianism based upon a comparative scale of constitutive elements, factors, and types is preferable to general speculation as to the "nature" of utopian modes of thought.

It should be emphasized that Table 5 is but a typification of the facts. No known society, either in practice or in theory, can be placed in a Procrustean bed. Combinations moving from one utopian cluster to another are to be found in every sort of projection made by ongoing societies. Nonetheless, the instrumental worth of such a distribution of elements as is presented in this chart is evident when it is approached as a "periodic table." Given any complex of like elements as those offered, minus one, the tendency of that missing factor (or element) to conform to the given variate is most striking. A survey of the utopian literature would further confirm the predictive worth of the general characterizations provided in the table.[26]

Utopian Constructs

Peculiar to utopian constellations is a positive and optimistic reading of events. Harmony, happiness, and equality are not goals which are mutually exclusive, nor do the prospects of achieving a society in which such goals are realized raise the demons of pessimism. What differentiates utopian constructs, therefore, is not only optimism versus pessimism (as Orwell and Huxley implicitly maintain), but an order of priorities in defining the good society. Thus the Roman Empire was not unaware of either the pleasure principle or the principle of social equity, but in terms of the devices of government available (mainly military), it simply seemed most logical to hold social harmony as an ultimate goal. The same can be said of Germany during the era of National Socialism— where again, the goals of harmony were considered to transcend all others,

---

25. *Ibid.*, pp. 253–256, 261–263.

26. As a recent effort to construct a utopian *Pax Romana*, see George Santayana, *Dominations and Powers: Reflections on Liberty, Society and Government* (New York: Charles Scribner's Sons, 1951). Edward Bellamy's *Looking Backwards: 2007–1887* (New York: Grosset & Dunlap, 1887) remains the classic example of a *Pax Liberalis* in American society. Despite the Bolshevik disavowal of utopianism, a consequential example of Libertarian Utopia is found in V. I. Lenin, "Transition from Capitalism to Communism," in *Marx-Engels-Marxism* (New York: International Publishers, 1935). To appreciate how a reworking of the elements in Table 5 would still yield a fruitful line of analysis, see such an "Orgaistic Chiliasm" as in W. C. Weitling, *Die Menscheit, wie sie ist und wie sie sein sollte* (Munich: M. Ernst, 1895).

irrespective of the means used. While we tend to be able to see the utopianism inherent in *Pax Romana*, or a thousand years of peace, we find it more difficult to realize that less extreme forms of governmental intervention also give rise to utopian beliefs. Only egalitarian and utilitarian ambitions such as *Pax Britannica* are fashioned out of different social materials. While utopian systems carry either an implicit or explicit criticism of the existing society, they too fashion their ideas and ideals out of materials immediately available in the environment. A paramount interest of science fiction literature is thus not only to grasp the shape of the future as a whole, but also to see how the materials of the present will be used in the projected society. The "realism" in utopian systems stems precisely from their capacity to extract and extrapolate elements of social reality that are already common social currency. For this reason, the equation of "utopian" with "illusory" is improper. It misses the central thread running through all utopian thought, *i.e.*, the projection of a future fashioned from materials taken from the here and now.

What I have attempted in these exploratory remarks and tables is to explain what the sociology of knowledge can perform operationally; namely, the promotion of empirical studies in the sociology of knowledge based on some firm logical distinctions and minus the awkward baggage of obscure phraseology and inherited metaphysical credos that identify logical truths with historical events. The history of the sociology of knowledge has been a progressive intellectual emancipation from its metaphysical inheritance. To the furtherance of this task these tables and remarks are addressed.

6. *The Sociology of Social Problems:*
A Study in the Americanization
of Ideas

I. Social Problems and Social Theory

The study of social problsm is marred by intellectual timidity and mired in moral ambiguity. Of all areas and aspects of sociology as it is currently practiced, none seems at one and the same time more pervasive and parochial— pervasive in the sense that all sociologists acknowledge that there are indeed social problems and these ought to be removed; parochial in the sense that this concern for the importance of social problems seems so confined to the United States. Even when issues normally covered by a social problems orientation in the United States are handled by European scholars, they are cast in different terms—as anything from social welfare to social policy. The concept of a social problem is therefore far from self-evident. All that can be said for certain is that the social problems approach is a challenge to the sanitized world of value-suspending social science approaches.

This is a previously unpublished paper, written to show how the field of social problems arose as a practical response to American conditions, and hence tending to leave unanswered some basic questions as to the relation of social problems to sociology on one side and personal therapy on the other. It was written in 1966.

80

1

One big reason for pervasive categorizing of social problems in American sociology is that few, if any, writers attempt to stipulate what is *not* a social problem. Universal and all-pervasive definitions of social problems in most textbooks virtually inhibit all but the most daring from making serious inquiries into the exact nature and meaning of a social problem. In one recent text, that of Horton and Leslie, it is simply stated that "Whenever people begin to say, 'Isn't it awful? Why don't they do something about it?' we have a social problem." The authors go on to state that a formal definition of social problems could be reduced to the following formula: "A social problem is a condition affecting a significant number of people in ways considered undesirable about which it is felt something can be done through collective social action."

While definitions provided by other sociologists are perhaps less extensive or inclusive, few of them offer satisfying, usable alternatives to universalistic definition of social problems. In some measure the definition of social problems does not simply reflect ambiguity, but also a search for extension of disciplinary domains. Sociologists often try to draw from psychology those interested in basic problems of human organization and human life, and this accounts for the highly personality-oriented definitions so often encountered.[1]

Ironically enough, in contrast to the universalistic definition of what constitutes a *theory* of social problems stands a remarkable parochialism as to the *practical limits* of American problems. Generally speaking, sociologists writing on social problems have simply taken for granted an American context for the study of social problems. Some even assume that the Americanization of sociology is nothing but the focus on problems rather than on principles. McDonagh and Simpson in their recent text offer some remarkable explanations as to why social problems are generally discussed in an American context. It is at any rate the only explanation I have come upon, and therefore worth noting: "The national government has developed the technology of economic regulation to such a degree that a depression of the scope experienced in the thirties is highly improbable. Too, nations have joined together politically through the media of the hot lines and the United Nations in order to limit the possibility of a thermonuclear holocaust."[2]

These writers have made social problems into a domestic specialty and assume that *political* problems are a distinct category. Relationships between nations are thus taken care of by such international agencies as the United Nations and by multilateral agreements. Concern may then turn to problems of the nation, to the "core problems," social problems in contrast to resolved political problems. That such a naive assumption would be made concerning the state of the world

1. William E. Cole and Charles H. Miller, *Social Problems: A Sociological Interpretation* (New York: David McKay Co., 1965).

2. Edward C. McDonagh and Jon E. Simpson, eds., *Social Problems: Persistent Challenges* (New York: Holt, Rinehart & Winston, 1965).

indicates more than a pervasive parochialism—as in the case of the universalistic claims for social problems, it reveals the desire to "overcome" the "limits" of political science as a discipline. Thus, by a technique of displacement, social problems become "fundamental" while political problems become derivative. The study of sociology then becomes an essential task of modern times. It becomes the central or general discipline of all the social sciences. The needs, or rather the overweening demands of a profession, combine with the under-developed level of the ideology of social problems to produce rather startling effects. Internally, those concerned with "problems" can appear to challenge the sociological establishment, while externally—that is, with respect to the other social sciences—they appear as the "applied" wing of the sociological empire.

2

In the main, there are four different types of theories concerning social problems.

First, it is said that social problems basically derive from social disorganization, which in turn is the outcome of the processes of change and development. The organization of society comes to be disrupted by demands of the moment. The various institutional agencies of society likewise fall into disuse or disrepute, creating a wide base of social disorganization. The difficulty with this kind of theory is connected with the general problems of social change and revolution. Against its own desires, it often takes social institutions to be social norms.[3]

The second basic view concerning social problems is the personal deviation approach. Social problems are the products of individuals who are deficient, who are norm violators, and who manifest an inability either to learn or to accept normative patterns of society. These inabilities may themselves be learned patterns of behavior reinforced by deviant subcultures. But the main point is that the study of social problems focuses on the behavior of deviant aggregates or individuals who violate the collective norm. In this sense the resolution of social problems in the personal deviance approach is sought at the level of inter-personal relationships.[4]

The third approach rests upon values in conflict. A social problem is said to arise at that point where wide sectors of the population exhibit contrasting atti-tudes and demand contradictory solutions to problems. One group's problem will be considered another group's asset. The conflict or intensity of the conflict has to do with numbers of people who hold one set of values in contradiction to those who hold another set of values. An extension of the values-in-conflict approach is the idea that the first and basic ingredient of a social problem is any substantial discrepancy between socially shared standards and actual conditions of social life. This view is an attempted resolution of the values approach and the

3. Alfred McClung Lee and Elizabeth Briant Lee, eds., *Social Problems in America: A Sourcebook* (New York: Henry Holt & Co., 1949).

4. Paul B. Horton and Gerald R. Leslie, *The Sociology of Social Problems*, 3rd ed. (New York: Appleton-Century-Crofts, 1965).

institutional disorganization approach. Thus, in some measure the existence of a social problem is a response, not simply to a conflict of values between social groups, but to a conflict between social groups and actual organizational barriers to wealth, power, or status.[5]

The fourth view, and one which became particularly pronounced during the 1950's, is the position taken by Dynes, Clark, Dinitz, and Ishino. They deal with social problems as a necessary consequence of conflicting patterns in a society. Where integrating or equilibrating formulas break down, there you have social problems exceeding the general management capabilities of a system. In this sense, the definition of social problems is related to a notion of normative dissensus or disagreement among the members of a society on norms rather than on values. It is instructive that the authors of this approach consider normative dissensus in almost Machiavellian diabolical terms, as attempts to gain adhesion and adherence through propaganda, public relations, and means which are in some sense somehow less than democratic. Underlying this view of social problems is the notion that the cause of social problems is social change. The difficulty with this line of analysis is not that social change does not indeed cause social problems, but rather that resolution of the question of social change brings about new sorts of problems, indeed problems which may be more difficult to resolve than the originating problem. For example, at a macroscopic level, the substitution of a totalitarian system for a mildly authoritarian one may resolve certain problems of production but may do so at a prohibitive cost in personal liberties. Thus, a command society may create increased tension leading to far more difficult social problems.[6]

Broadly, these four approaches largely characterize the present state of what is called "the theory of social problems."

3

What Merton has called the duality of science is in many ways at the core of the problem of social problems. Since the essential question is whether sociologists study social problems (presuming we know exactly what a social problem is) by evaluating and analyzing the situation on the basis of scientific considerations first, foremost, and exclusively, or do they make the evaluation on the basis of therapeutic devices or organizational demands? There are two ways of viewing the practice, or it can be viewed as a dualism between science and therapy.

As presently constituted, the essential dilemma seems to be as follows: those who are concerned with social problems at the heuristic or practical level are sociologists concerned with therapeutic resolutions. But since a therapeutic resolution may be a resolution of social problems only as they are defined by the

5. Robert K. Merton and Robert A. Nisbet, eds., *Contemporary Social Problems* (New York: Harcourt, Brace & World, Inc., 1961).

6. See Russell R. Dynes, Alfred C. Clarke, Simon Dinitz, and Iwao Ishino, *Social Problems: Dissensus and Deviation in an Industrial Society* (New York and London: Oxford University Press, 1964).

social order, such an approach gives rise to yet another form of therapeutics: the definition of problems from the standpoint of the deviant subculture. It is significant that whether the definition of the situation is made from the standpoint of the normative culture or the deviant subculture, the basis remains therapeutic and remedial. Those who are engaged in studying the subculture of drug addiction have defenders among the social science ranks who claim that drug addiction, compared with almost all other forms of drug and alcoholic devices for personal stimulus, (a) is nontoxic, (b) does not violate any biological norms of survival, and (c) can actually serve as a stimulant to social integration in the absence of other means of developing social integration. As "evidence" one finds cited certain church groups who have developed positive attitudes and positive responses to drug-taking and drug addiction.

The duality of science as it affects the study of social problems is a duality that more properly involves the "applied" activities of the professional social scientist. Does he make an essential commitment to the person designated as having the social problem, or does he make the essential commitment to the society that demands a resolution of the social problem? At this level the agony of social problems becomes an agony for the social scientist.[7] What has to be measured is the intensity of sociological commitment, no less than the extent of social ailments.

Nowhere is the gap wider between theory and practice than in the field of social problems. In nearly every standard work on the subject the theoretical portions are neatly disengaged from the body of the text. Those interested in science, or in the scientific resolution of social problems, often find their concerns confined to theoretical speculations about the nature of social problems. Serious problems relating to the scientific verification of social problems stand in marked contrast to the bulk of the work. In sections on deviant behavior, the "real" issues of social problems are raised. The practitioners take over: the study of crime, delinquency, mental disorder, drug addiction, suicide, prostitution, population problems, race and ethnic relations, family disorganization, traffic and transportation problems, and problems of disaster.

In this division of labor one finds most clearly the true state of affairs in the study of social problems—the therapists versus the scientists. There can be no doubt that those who sustain the area of social problems are the therapists. This is because they in turn are sustained by funding agencies at various levels of society who, in effect, are in search of amelioration of problems and who in turn define the nature of the social problem. That they "tolerate" scientific speculation is a tribute to the demands of professionalism, rather than to any integrated vision of sociology.

The area of social problems sharply raises the question of basic sociological theory, particularly as it challenges the nature of functional analysis. There can

7. See Howard S. Becker, ed., *Social Problems* (New York: John Wiley, 1967).

be little doubt that the root equation made is between the *social system* and *social function*. Conversely, the root equation has been between the *social problem* and *social dysfunction*. While it is well and good to say that both function and dysfunction are relative terms, and that what is functional for one part of the system may be dysfunctional for the other, the fact is that such a formula, by placing sociological analyses of function and dysfunction in a different universe of discourse from that of moral judgment, cannot stand the test of critical examination. Sociological examination of function may indeed differ from a moral judgment about a social unit, but the very notion of dysfunction inevitably raises moral judgments. It is implausible to go on asserting that a concept of dysfunction or malfunction at the level of the social system can be held to be without an underlying moral imperative equating social function with social order.

The question of functional analysis has been taken up in very appropriate ways elsewhere and by others. However, it is significant that the commonsensical use of the notion of dysfunction is little else than a latter-day terminological substitute for "immorality" or "unethical practice," or for that which is socially undesirable. The assertion that dysfunction is an objective concept and is not morally evaluative would be hard to demonstrate. Dysfunction for whom? Dysfunction at what period? Dysfunction in terms of what normative standpoint? Such questions, in revealing the relativity of judgments, imply powerful political and moral mandates in the area of social problems research. The hope of some functionalists that one could save the area of social problems as a pure objective science rests very heavily on the ability to preserve the notion of social dysfunction as an objective concept. Since no evidence for this concept as being objective has been forthcoming, it must be held that the area of social problems is subject to extreme scrutiny from the standpoint of therapeutics, if its claims are to be upheld.

The dilemma for those who consider social problems as obstacles to be overcome is that any true overcoming of social problems implies a perfect social system. And this entails several goals: first, the total institutionalization of all people; second, the thoroughgoing equilibrium between the parts of a system with respect to their functioning and the functioning of other sectors; and third, the elimination of social change as either a fact or value. Thus, the resolution of social problems from the point of view of the social system would signify the totalitarian resolution of social life. For example, it is true that under the Stalin period in the Soviet Union there was a minimal amount of crime, and under the present Soviet regime there is a much greater increase in all the basic indices of crime. But does this mean, therefore, that the Stalin period represented that which is good in social life as opposed to the present era? I doubt that anyone interested in therapeutic democracy could sustain such a point of view. Indeed, the increase in so-called social problems may in fact mean an increase in social development. Therefore, the existence of social problems may be good. Those who are labeled as problem children or problem people may be the essential agencies of the process of change and development so highly prized in most parts of the world, though of course less valued by those who have reached a mature state of modern development.[8]

Perhaps we should not separate definition of a social problem from what constitutes a social resolution. As far as can be made out, there are no attempts at serious resolution of social problems in a way that would maximize a concept of the problem rather than maximize the concept of rehabilitation to the existing norm. All therapeutic notions of the resolution of social problems invariably end up in terms of a restitution of the normative pattern, when, as a matter of fact, the scientific study of social problems may generate the exacerbation and stimulate an increase in the number of problem areas.

Once social change and social development are held to be ultimate social values, the maximization or the design of a social system that would increase social problems would then have to be seriously considered from that point of view. As the matter now stands, the contradiction is that the society demands rapid escalation of social change and at the same time demands integration of its deviant parts or its deviant members. This simply is no way to deal plausibly with the study of social problems. What perhaps is required is not so much a Society for the Study of Social Problems, but a Society for the Study of Social Designs, designs that in some measure include as part of their overall orientation the stimulation of deviant patterns of behavior.

If it is true. as Lawrence K. Frank long ago pointed out, that the rise of a social problem is an augury of something better, or of at least a more effective way of doing things, and that the bigger and more complicated the problem, the greater the change it portends, what may be required from the point of view of science is precisely the stimulation of social problems. Until now, the drive has been in a reverse direction: the attempted direct assault upon social problems from the point of view of the ameliorative possibilities of a social system.

One of the most conservative voices ever to speak on the issue of social problems (and at the same time the most acute), William Graham Sumner, pointed out that it would be hard to find a single instance of a direct assault of positive effort upon poverty, vice, and misery that has not either failed or, if it has not failed directly and entirely, entailed other evils greater than those that were removed. If this is the case, and in the history of the study of social problems there is little evidence to contradict Sumner's remarks, then perhaps what is required is an indirect assault. Instead of an assault upon the so-called vices of poverty and misery, perhaps there is first a need to recognize the legitimacy of the cultures of poverty and then an appreciation not just of their legitimacy, but of their role in fashioning a society and a social system of greater value and greater worth for all of mankind. But here, too, caution is in order, since an appreciation of the culture of poverty ought not to spill over into a celebration

---

8. See S. N. Eisenstadt, ed., *Comparative Social Problems* (New York: Free Press, 1964); and Herbert C. Kelman, ed., *International Behavior: A Social-Psychological Analysis* (New York: Holt, Rinehart & Winston, 1965).

of the poverty of culture. To strike a balance between therapeutics and science becomes the chief aim of the social problems approach to sociology.

II. Social Problems and Social Practice

If you take the words "social problems" and try to isolate them, it is obvious that these two words should represent "social" in contrast to something else. But the difficulty is that few social scientists seem to know quite what that something else represents. Everyone talks about social problems, and with more official sanction than ever before, but not everybody is aware of the implications of social problems.

1

From the analytic and the historical points of view, the concept of "social" is usually contrasted with "economic" on one hand and "psychological" on the other. The notion of the distinctly social base came in response to uni-causal doctrines of behavior. Criminology, which in many ways was a forerunner for present views of social problems, was especially guilty of uni-causal economic or "cranial" theories of criminal behavior. The whole area of social problems was given initial impetus "in contrasts." The resolution to crime and social problems was seen to lie in rationalizing and equalizing law. Gradually economic explanations of history and law arose. Throughout the formative period of sociology, crime and criminality were seen to have economic or biological sources. Why do people steal? People steal because they need money. Why do people break the law? The law is iniquitous. It is disenfranchising. Why do people do "irrational" things? They do so because they are driven to loss of control. Manipulation of law and the material environment held resolutions to crime and discontent. The definition of society was often one-sided, and problem resolution was thus uni-causal.

The world of social problems raises a host of "modernizing" issues. There are many nonutilitarian crimes—crimes that do not have any direct correlation to the object or person being assaulted. When the windows of schoolrooms are broken during long hot summers by students or ex-students, the object is clearly not to make money. One explanation given by a sociologist is that breaking windows is illustrative of nonutilitarian crime. It represents a revolt against middle class education or middle class educators. In short, crime, particularly that of youthful offenders, may be conscious and yet symbolic.

This explanation of criminal behavior is different from economic explanation. The suggestion that, in the twentieth century at least, there were problems that were noneconomic in character gave rise to the study of social problems as a symbolic phenomenon no less than a pragmatic one. The men who did the most work in this respect, what has come to be called the Chicago School, did more than make imaginative uses of symbolic spheres. They made use of all sorts of "objective" factors—from urbanism to industrialism. They developed a host of supplementary notions concerning the character of problems. It was held, for example, that the closer one lives to the industrial center of a city the higher the rates of crime, and that this held true irrespective of the economic levels involved in the central city. While the data upon which this ecological theory was built has been challenged, the underlying theme of both *plural* and *social* explanation became entrenched.[9]

Along the same lines, a theory of differential punishment was fused to a theory of differential association to explain certain types of criminality. Crime between Negro and Negro was less punished than between white and white, and therefore the statistical loadings are social rather than economic. Another finding of this problems approach was that racial competition is greater at the perimeter of the city and least at the center of the city. In an all-Negro area, a relatively lower rate of crime exists than where there is a black-white struggle at the geographical perimeter. These observations linked the concepts of ethnicity and environment to economic conditions. These linkages had a profound effect on the whole development and structure of sociology. It accounted in good measure for the characteristically American stamp to sociology. Men like Ernest Burgess, Robert Park, Herbert Blumer, Louis Wirth, Walter Reckless, and many others of the Chicago School were certainly instrumental in changing the thinking of a generation of community planners and policy makers. The notion of the social problem in contrast to the idea of economic revolution shaped American local politics from the New Deal in the thirties to the New Frontier in the sixties.

The economic problems approach was not followed directly by the social problems approach but rather by the psychological problems orientation. The reaction to economic determinism was psychological determinism—a far less sophisticated perspective. Problems were held to be basically individual in character. Underlying criminal patterns were said to be individual dislocations. Interestingly, it was the social workers and social welfare people who generally gravitated to this position, *i.e.*, those who had face-to-face contact with the problem people. Since the individual is the person who is the primary agent of crime, or the primary agent of deviance, he must also be the primary focus of power. Thus human will or intention must be at the basis of a solution to crime. The strongly voluntaristic aspects involved in the psychological study of social problems involved an appreciation of the qualities peculiar to many crimes. The theoretical intention involved a recognition that crime is committed by a person, not a society. It also had as a very strong empirical base the fact that many crimes tend to be nonrepetitive in character. Homicide is a nonrepetitive act in nearly every case. The reasons for murder generally have to do with high tension but highly transitory situations. These peaks are unusual and at the same time rarely occur more than once. The troughs are normal and quiescent. That being the case, the maximum degrees of crimes that were noted to be noneconomic in character pose the interesting possibility of explaining all criminality as illus-

9. See Herbert Blumer, "Social Disorganization and Individual Disorganization," *American Journal of Sociology*, 42, no. 1 (May 1937): 871–877.

trative of deviance and personality disorganization, whether permanent or temporary.

This kind of orientation was reinforced by the rise of an Americanized Freudianism. Symbolic killing was said to be taking place daily, or at least nightly. Social leaders were converted into symbolic fathers, and even the most powerful illustrations of social problems were seen to have as their base the dislocation of personality. This lent additional weight to the idea of the psychological character of social problems. The language of shame and guilt, like the language of exploitation and oppression before it, served to stifle the evolution of a social problems approach precisely by the elegant simplicity of one-dimensional analysis.[10]

The sociological theory of social problems raised all kinds of novel considerations. It could do so because of having the advantage of coming last. Advocates of social problems admitted that there are economic problems and economic crimes, psychological problems and psychological crimes. It even pointed out that there are even political crimes: graft, bribery, price-fixing, and vote payments. Then it noted that there are class crimes and/or blue-collar crimes. The more that social problems granted, the more it served to crack open uni-causal explanations. The social problems approach played off one form of determinism against another.

There are obvious class bases, ethnic bases, and status bases to the question of crime. The social problems approach advocated focus on the notion of crime because it was intimately linked with the practical problems of the administration of cities, states, and nations. This is why the approach is characteristically American. It enabled the sociologist for the first time to engage in an act of social reconstruction or social regeneration. Later on this was followed by bureaucratic styles of work connected with federal programs. But the first real impact at a pragmatic level, the first sense of being a profession rather than a teaching vocation (despite loud denials to the contrary), occurred with respect to the urban setting—Chicago, Baltimore, Houston—and the industrial setting—Western Electric, Bell Telephone, etc. Administrators started hiring sociologists not to teach but to solve problems of delinquency, absenteeism, crime.

This then is what really broke the traditional European style in sociology. It was doing sociology rather than thinking sociologically. The Chicago School, for example, did not have a theory when it started. It had a commission from the city of Chicago, a contract to find out how to reduce the urban crime rate. It could engage in new forms of theorizing by virtue of unprecedented involvement in the highest echelons of local political policy, without incurring the high risks of politicians.

When turning to the word "problems," we have another ambiguous term. The problem of problems is what is *not* a problem. How do you define a

---

10. T. W. Adorno, Else Frenkel-Brunswik, D. J. Levinson, and N. Sanford, eds., *The Authoritarian Personality* (New York: Harper & Row, 1950).

situation which is not problematic? What constitutes a resolved problem? How do we know we have resolved a problem? The word itself has enough ambiguity to raise doubts as to its utility. This notwithstanding, it has survived the test of use.

In the sociological literature there are two contrasting uses of the concept of problems. First, the concept of problems is contrasted with that of functions. Normal behavior is said to be different from problem behavior. Those who break rules and upset functional equilibria are engaged in creating social problems. Social problems texts sometimes discuss the functional norms in terms of consensus, and deviance in terms of dissensus. Second, the notion of problems is contrasted with that of forces. There is a vast gulf distinguishing between the "Negro problem" in Chicago and the "Negro forces" in North Carolina. One *acts* on problems; one *examines* forces. It is no accident that the title of the journal emanating from North Carolina is *Social Forces*, while the name of the journal of the Society for the Study of Social Problems is *Social Problems*. This may just be fortuitous timing: a group of men sit around and pick out a name. But obviously behind the act of naming journals and behind the choice of editors is an organizing principle.

The organizing principle of social forces is the concept of depersonalized dynamics. The push and pull of human acts are performed in an agglomerate form that is considered to be beyond the control of any one person or group— irrespective of his or its power or position. The notion of a force is physical. Objects are set in motion, displaying contrary tendencies and trajectories, involving different parameters, that are resolved in the "natural" course of events. This is quite different from the character of social problems. A social problem implies a social solution. Its perspective opposes the hidden hand of physicalism, operating behind the backs of men in the style of a field or force.

Given such a distinction, one would expect to find, and does find, differences in the treatment of the Negro issue. The social forces approach tends to be closer to the general systems view. It studies Negroes "objectively" rather than therapeutically. The examination of demographic patterns among Negroes, their migration and marital patterns, takes precedence over the problem of large families or the problem of homes without husbands. The ease with which the social forces approach can drift into abstract attitudes is reflected in the separation of the forces of social change from the human agencies making such changes.

2

These contrasts made, the chore is now to see what "social problems" has come to mean as an operational phrase. The dilemma arises that in nearly every text on social problems the theoretical statement of the problem is made in open-ended terms, while the contents, the "guts" of social problems texts, are very much the same. What exists is a highly open-ended theory, combined with a notion of problems that is dried up and ossified.

There is a schizophrenic property within the area of social problems. The theorists are open and willing to redefine what they mean by social problems.

The practitioners, to the contrary, are closed, seemingly knowing about what they are doing and what social problems are about. Why should the theorists be so open and the practitioners so closed as to the meaning of social problems? The answer has to do in large part with differences in institutional attachments. The theorist is tied to the academic community. He is paid for a scientific posture. The practitioners are tied essentially to the sociopolitical community, and not primarily to academic institutions. The social problems practitioner defines his role strictly in terms of therapeutic values or the resolution of the problem. The understanding of the problem is taken for granted rather than explicated. They are the pragmatists of the sociological field. They have a job to do, whereas the people who are theorizing about social problems do not have a therapeutic obligation and therefore can raise theoretical questions.

Stated in more professional terms, sociologists concerned with the theory of social problems are concerned with the relationship between social problems and the social sciences in terms of where a problems approach "fits" the model of scientific exactitude. People concerned with practice center their interests on making peace in the community. Their interests, orientations, and objectives are guided by the fact that they have to create a place for themselves in the general society. This means, in effect, that their conception of science will itself be an applied notion.

The most elusive problem of social problems as social practice relates to connections established between analysts and patients. Vested interests are concerned with resolving some problems but not others. And the pressures to validate positions because of societal "demands" are great. For example, if the FBI statistics on crime continue in an upward spiral year in and year out, then the demand for more police is somehow legitimated. And among "men of action," the gulf between legitimation and verification is hardly distinct. But were crime statistics to show a steady decline, there would be no reason to increase the size of the police force. The question then arises: What is the chicken and what is the egg? Does the police force increase its size and then expand its definition of what it considers to be crime, or does crime increase and thus create a need for a larger police force?

Depending upon our perception of such a problem as the connection between police force size and criminal behavior, we are led to radically different conclusions. Even if we can make up our minds on such problems, which I am not sure we can; even if we can do that, another problem greets the practitioner. At what point is the solution worse than the problem? When confronted with concrete decisions, at what point is it worse to have "x" amount of crime than it is to have "y" number of policemen? There is surely a saturation point in police forces as there is a tolerance point for criminal behavior.

A number of sociologists have pointed out that the higher the control mechanism of a social system, the lower is its crime rate. Naturally, if some poor soul in Slobbovia steals a sack of potatoes and is executed for this misdeed, not many people will be tempted to steal potatoes. But the question arises: To what extent can a society better tolerate thefts than legal executions? An international congress of criminologists was held in 1965. The Chinese delegate reportedly arose and said that the reason he had no data was that in his country there was no crime. He is perhaps correct in the sense that there was no officially registered crime. The society itself is criminal. If a citizen who devises a paper weapon as a symbolic reflection of his attitudes toward the social system is going to be shot for it (this actually happened), then the amount of crime will decrease. But what has been achieved is a decrease in unofficial crime and a rapid acceleration in official crime.

The reduction of a problem by increasing social controls extensively may entail a decline in free mobility. Seen in this way, the solutions are worse than the problem, which is not an unreasonable assumption; and the sociologist is faced with a serious crisis affecting the lives of those who live in terms of the practical implementation of reducing social problems. Nor is it plausible to adopt a "practical" eye-winking standpoint of treating social problems.

There is no doubt that most people concerned with social problems would rather have more doctors than police. But this response does not come to terms with the problem I am raising. Suppose we inundate an urban region with 10,000 social workers rather than police officers? The problem remains the same: At what point does the solution become worse than the problem itself? Vested interest groups may be "good" or "bad," but they have a common premise: the more problems there are, the more people are needed to deal with them. Thus the social problems approach may subsitute one interest group for another, but it does not resolve the problematic friction of interest groups as such.

No doctrine can survive if it cannot legitimate itself intellectually. On the surface the social problems approach seemed a clear option to the social systems approach—more liberal both politically and methodologically. However, a probe into the soft underbelly of the language of social problems yields an intellectual debacle, rather than a happy resolution. It leads us to examine the costs of dissensus, while tending to ignore the equal or greater costs of consensus.

III. The Metaphysical Predispositions of Sociologists of Social Problems

In discussing the principles of sociology it is important to recognize that we are not discussing a solid phalanx of truth—of intellectual troops marching arm in arm in the battle for knowledge and against ignorance. Sociology is a serious business. And a characteristic hallmark of serious activities is that the beliefs that divide often are as significant as those that unite.

The first characteristic on which sociologists divide is whether sociology should be important or whether sociology should be impeccable. An appreciation of the division between the social problems and the social systems approaches can be gained by posing the issues in terms of two words—*important* sociology or *impeccable* sociology. The number of sociologists who want important findings and are willing to sacrifice the perfection that goes with systems analysis define the problems approach. The "problems people" are often high risk-takers and tend to be opportunist in their professional behavior. People who are concerned with the sources of welfare and the manipulation of power are not always able to withstand the blandishments of power. The social psychology underlying their interest is not always motivated by the needs of the problem-ridden, but, just as frequently, by the compelling force of elitist persuasions.

On the other hand, there are the impeccable sociologists, the systematic analysts. They are concerned with formal elegance, perfection of design, and data collecting. Everything they write has to be established by antecedent findings. In terms of romantic criteria or humanistic appraisals they are often unattractive. But the social systems approach has the advantage of not being easily ensnared by political opportunism. People concerned with formal elegance and antecedent evidence can rarely even get the chance to be opportunistic within the larger political culture. People who are concerned with the minutiae, however unappealing they may be to the "big-range" sociologists, have the asset of any artist. They want the perfect research design rather than practical results. The aesthetic vision of the impeccable sociologist thus preserves him from the worst infections of "helping" people.

A second basic divide is between sociologists who believe that the world is problematic and those who consider the world to be systematic. Those who are concerned with social problems have a pragmatic vision of the world as being open and "up for grabs." Sociologists concerned with social problems have a belief in a problematic world as a philosophical precondition, no less than as a therapeutic device. No one seriously concerned with social problems can assert the possibility or the desirability of a resolution to all problems. On the contrary, every solution to a social problem carries within itself the risk that the postulated solution may be worse than the original social problem.

One typical, if not invariable, solution to the problem of juvenile delinquency is to hire more police. Yet there seems to be a direct rather than an inverse correlation involved, since the more police there are, the more the crime rate rises. Peculiar statistical correlations begin to appear: an announced increase in the size of the police force often *anticipates* the rise of crime (like Parkinson's Law, where work expands to fulfill the amount of personnel on hand). Where "law enforcement" officers increase, there you are going to find ample "new" sources of crime "discovered." Social problems are not necessarily resolved by those who are hired to resolve them. There have to be more crimes because more police are hired to find crime. The dilemma in a social problems approach is that problems often generate more problems rather than resolutions.

This fact creates a vested interest in locating the sources of new problems, or in redefining old facts as new issues to maintain the professional role of the social problems experts. Those who start with the notion of a social system are concerned with filling in its parts with resolutions. They know the contours of society. They know society is reasonable. How else can one develop a system? There is no place for "sloppiness" in a systematic society. The milkman is always there in the morning because people need milk. By virtue of such a *telos*, the world must be right because it can be explained functionally.

Totalitarian social systems extend this approach: the trains run on time; therefore the world is reasonable. The faith underlying the social systems approach starts from observations of regularity in the world and often ends up by a demand that the whole world be *regulated*. The assumption is not that of the pragmatic wide-open world, but rather the absolute adjustment of the parts of the world so that the rational whole is not disturbed. If the world is reasonable, those elements in it that are out of tune with its reasonableness must be changed. And if the norms of society are reasonable, then deviant types must be processed.

In contrast to this are those who argue the problematic character of the world and who state that the world rather than its parts must be made reasonable. Sociological decisions depend heavily on metaphysical presuppositions, and no less on methodological predispositions. The universes of discourse in the problem and in the system are different. The problems-oriented sociologist lives in the world where drug addiction, alcoholism, prostitution, and other marginal ways of performing for a living are widespread if not normative. The systems-oriented sociologist lives in a world of milkmen who deliver the milk on time and of families who drink the milk and pay their bills on time. The people that they investigate are presumed to be normal no less than normative in their patterns.

The distinction between problems and systems approaches is sometimes made, valuationally, as being between "value-free" sociology and "value-linked" sociology. Other times this difference is registered ecologically and academically, *i.e.*, "Chicago Style" versus "Columbia Style." Yet at other times, the distinction is made organizationally: the role of the Society for the Psychological Study of Social Issues in relation to the American Psychological Association; or of the Society for the Study of Social Problems in relation to the American Sociological Association; or of the Society for Applied Anthropology in relation to the American Anthropological Association. But in each case it is evident that the "stitch" in the side of the parent organization is more akin to a mortal thrust. The rise of policy demands has only heightened the strain between pure sociologists interested in universal truth and applied sociologists interested in current issues.

A third parameter of social problems approaches distinguishes the conception of social change held by problems-oriented and systems-oriented sociologists. The concept of social change is the reverse side of the concept of social order. If social problems and social systems are concerned with maintaining social order, the question of conflict and consensus is concerned with stimulating social change. Nevertheless, to ask the question: "How is change stimulated?" is not quite the same as to ask how social order is maintained.

There are two different visions of changing society. One, that peers communicate and share notes. They have a rational discourse. Then they debate an issue and arrive at a settlement. This is a parliamentary (and incidentally elitist) vision of social change. The progress of man does not so much occur, as it is said to be legislated. Customarily, scholars who are concerned with parliamentary orientations at the same time develop consensual notions of how change is legislated into being. On the other hand, characteristic of the problems approach is an assumption that change is often spontaneous, unregulated, even apolitical. Change is held to be an unanticipated consequence of wars, the rise and fall of empires, or the innovation of marginal social groups. There is a combative notion of change, that is, change as extralegal. Conflict is viewed as generating a doctrine of social problems; correspondingly, a notion of social problems as enveloped by social change comes to dominate the problems approach.

The image of social change as being a segment of the social order is radically at variance with social order as a temporary equilibrium of the forces making for change. In a sense, the paradox of sociologists concerned with order being "political" in contrast to sociologists who believe that change is "nonpolitical" is but a reflex of those sociologists who consider "reality" as problematic rather than systematic.

The vision of the problems approach is often that politics is in its essence "square," i.e., predicated on the supposed need for order. Hence the apolitical side of the problems approach is a demand for transcendence—for getting beyond the square world of the political deal or policy-rooted bargaining table. At the same time, this apolitical vision contains an agonizing contradiction in that social problems imply an applied sociology—and such a sociology can only exist in the murky, and sometimes square, world of politics, domestic and international.

IV. SOCIAL PROBLEMS AS AN APPLIED SOCIOLOGY

There is an increasing tendency in sociology to talk in terms of problems of applied research. There is also an assumption, often implicit, that useful people can do useful things for humanity whether or not there is an adequate scientific warrant. In general, the social problems orientation leans more heavily in the policy direction than any other perspective because it is often connected with social welfare programs having political rather than scientific sanctions. It is hard to claim for social welfare workers, or people performing such roles, any autonomous scientific warrant, although it is relatively simple to speak of their utility.

The social welfare extension of social problems is a therapy rather than a theory. Society insists that the fortunate classes have to help poor people get the necessary medical attention they require. This is held as a task for society, rather than one dictated by scientific norms or modalities. The sociologist thus has the responsibility of resolving this newly evolved relationship between science and welfare. Applied sociology functions as an answer to the question: What is a meaningful sociology?

The difficulty with this rubric, as with all rubrics, is that behind the felicitous phrasing of the words "applied social research" or "applied sociology" stands a host of demoniacal pitfalls. Applied science means different things to different people. In one sense an applied sociology has to do with the notion of inter- ference or intervention on the part of the investigator. Of course, the mere act of intervention or interference itself is changing the social system.

The act of helping a person or resolving a problem is at the same time a creation of a new social order in which there is a new-found place in the world for the intervener. The investigator begins to have a vested interest in the pro- mulgation of the problem. When this takes place, a possible consequence is what might be called a "God-like" effect. The investigator, operating like a *deus ex machina*, manipulates the overall situation. This type of problems-rooted socio- logist considers his role scientific rather than practical, based on the rationale of science. He has to think that the study of social problems is more than instru- mental, just as those who work for the government must be convinced in the scientific no less than the policy aspects of their efforts. He has to control the situation in such a manner as to justify his sociological performance in the light of scientific or nonoperational criteria. Once this sociological type controls the outcomes and not merely the data, he is not only an intervener but a god. He manipulates the situation, or else he will not be controlling for the variants. That is one of the leading contradictions that arises in a theory of applied socio- logy. There is always a tendency for the scientific challenge to be suppressed at the expense of the social problem.

If God is a scientist and if the scientist is a God, then no methodological prob- lem need remain. The dilemma occurs in the assumptions made by the practicing sociologist—assumptions that his standpoint is a priori better than those of his client. If a mother and father have a fifteen-year-old son whom they place under the care of a psychoanalyst because he masturbates, and the analyst takes on that case, he is making an assumption that masturbation requires correction, or at least explanation. From a medical point of view, this is certainly debatable. Masturbation may be considered normal in puberty stages. The analyst who does not point this out to parents at the outset is making assumptions about the nature of the situation that transcend any scientific warrant. The question becomes: What then is the relation of therapy to science?

The same issue arises about sending a team of sociologists to study the problem of petty theft. It may well be that petty theft is a function of unemployment inequities and serves to regulate the cultural norms of a minority group by creating a certain balance between excessive inequities of wealth and poverty. These are radical assumptions, but no more outrageous than their conservative counterparts. To transcend the parochialism of therapy, which underwrites the God-like effect, sociology must clearly distinguish between science and policy. If the sociologist at all times had a set of values, knowledge, and wisdom superior to those he is dedicated to study, there would be no problem. The rub is that the hardest thing to establish is a claim to superiority. In the interlocking character of the financial order, the therapy structure, and the science machine, only the bravest of sociologists would lay claim to a clear understanding of his own motivation.

There is another type of applied sociology in which the notion of application is relatively marginal. That is to say, the applied sociologist, recognizing the contradictions in the "God-like" role, contents himself with a marginal role in the social situation. For example, if he studies the local power elites, he tries to stand outside that vortex of power. If he studies drug addiction, he himself avoids buying or selling drugs. If he studies homosexuality, he avoids becoming a homosexual. However, this kind of nonparticipatory observation creates its own set of problems. What is called into question is not the scientific warranty but the applied warranty. While it may not be necessary to be an elephant to study elephants, it is dubious whether marginal subcultures, in which the basic text of allegiance is precisely participation, can be adequately dealt with by "outsiders" or "nonparticipants."

What are the empirics of emotionally and structurally fluid situations? How can one genuinely study a system of community power without having access to that power structure? How can one describe drug addiction without taking drugs? It is conceivable that the effects of drugs can be sociologically explained by a nonparticipant? Might it not be that the nonparticipant is also playing at God? When a sociologist studies men claiming to be the second reincarnation of Christ, he assumes the falsity of such claims a priori. There is an arrogance of nonbelief involved. How do we really know that one of the claimants to the Christian throne is not Jesus? As long as the investigator assumes that nonparticipation, or even nonbelief in Christian theology, is true beyond issue, he is not calling into account his God-like ways. Thus, the marginal effect, the posture of nonintervention in the name of avoiding God-like manipulation, may end up in the same God-like pose. It makes the assumption of the superiority of the investigator over those investigated, without demonstrating wherein lies this superiority.

A basic modification, made in the theory and practice of applied social research, is the idea of the applied sociologist as the reinforcer of new lines of action. He does not so much intervene to make decisions as reinforce decisions made by others. Some social problems experts claim that the reinforcer role should be the sociologist's role, since in this role he can participate without pontificating. He can be critical of management decisions in industry, or critical of what the local power structure announces, without becoming negative. He can make recommendations freely, but in a way which is gentle enough so that if there is a boomerang effect, he can claim to be detached from the decision-making process as such. It is the equivalent of a standard psychoanalytic ploy. This kind of sociologist claims only a mastery of helping others make their own decisions. He is not like the intervener because the intervener takes tremendous risks.

Yet it is doubtful that this reinforcer role is any less a way of assuming a divine role than the previous two, for it also asserts the superiority of the investigator over the object being investigated. Because of this, a final ploy is tried, a desperate pragmatism in social research, which announces a parity of the investigator and the investigated. Here there is, in effect, a psychoanalytic relationship without any superordinate role. In short, the attempt is made to avoid the anathema of being God-like by assuming the client to be equal to the researcher. On the surface, the liquidation of superordinate roles seems a perfectly reasonable solution to a perplexing dilemma. The only difficulty is that such assumptions of scientific parity between researcher and researched may lead to utter and complete nonsense. If in a poll 90 per cent of the informants either deny the existence of social classes, or at least their membership in a social class, tdis in itself does not prove or disprove the existence of a social class.

To assume a complete ethnographic standpoint in which the information of all informants is equally weighted is to abandon the area of social problems to that of false illusions. In an advanced industrial society, the position of its citizens may be conditioned by the demands of the dominant social sectors and not by a response to one's own circumstances. The problem is one of ethnography coming full force up against the real world. The dilemma of the egalitarian methodology is that it assumes that people always know what they are doing, what they desire, and what their interests are. Further, it assumes that people always tell the truth. The investigator-created relationship always operates within a vortex of truth telling. There are, in short, severe limits to the investigatory role.

These types of social investigators raise issues that the science of sociology must confront if it wants a satisfactory approach to social problems. Any discussion of the character of sociology that attempts to arrange for its legitimation not on the basis of its scientific theory, but on the basis of what it does for humanity, is subject to dissolution once "humanity" declares the problem resolved. This is a fear that haunts the sociologists of social problems. They are really not sure whether they are in the business of saving souls or advancing science. Their warrant is unclear. The commission for the field is unclear. The fact that the city of Chicago may give $4 million a year to the University of Chicago Department of Sociology to work on urban problems may be very attractive, but it does not prove that the sociologist is any less a hired employee than if he were to receive a contract from the federal government to show how the doctrine of counterinsurgency can be applied. Neither gives the sociologist the right of criticism. He is not in a position to question the warrant under which he works. It raises further technical considerations. What are the relationships between contracts and grants? Work under contract does not provide any great distinction from work under salary. A contract is a guaranteed salary, not a scientific commission. No matter how much funding is provided for the social problems expert, no matter how practical his worth, the necessity for the field remains unproven. For unlike sociology in general, the value of a social problems approach is not intrinsic to the object under investigation, because the object of investigation itself determines the character of study.

One may study butterflies and atoms independent of one's interest in either of them, but not so the study of human problems. To study man independent of the consequence to men raises a whole specter of problems. The study of a woman racing about a shopping plaza may be functionally similar to the study of a rat running around a maze. But there is a *prima facie* difference. The idea of a pure or experimental side of sociology becomes transformed into a science based on control or manipulation—and ultimately a science based on terror. The difference between a Pavlovian science and an Orwellian nightmare is measured by the distinctions between dogs and man. The polarities, when considered in this way, deserve to be met squarely. Pragmatic decisions do not resolve dilemmas between experimental and applied sociologies. Whether or not there is a scientific basis for a sociology of social problems raises a powerful problem of a strategic decision. It seems imcomprehensible how one can reconcile pure and applied branches of sociology in a facile manner. To the contrary, the likely possibility is that sociology will cleave along many lines. In its broadest outlines, one branch will become social welfare and the other will move into a kind of social physics. A synthetic figure may emerge to reconcile these presently apparent schisms. But in the immediately foreseeable future, sharp differences are likely. The gap between pure and applied sociology is a far more profound schism than that between sociology and political science, or that between sociology and anthropology, because it is a generic issue which cuts across classificatory boundaries. And like all problems of a generic nature, it demands a specific decision on the part of scholars and researchers as to where they will place their intellectual bets: on scientific autonomy or on social relevance.

Politeness and economic advantage often combine to explain why departments of sociology hang together: *noblesse oblige*, the feudal code of honor, a faith in the network of personal associations, a Luddite belief that if one "rocks the boat" jobs will be forfeited. Sociologists of all intellectual persuasions seem to be prospering along with most professional groups. And times of prosperity are not noticeably coincidental with deep personal or professional reflection. However, let some of the "soft money" which floats the bulk of researches in social science vanish, and assuredly these issues will be debated with a fury that will prove once more that science flourishes best in an environment of doubt, ferment, and reconstruction.

Science, unlike many policy decisions, is not based on manipulation but on clarification. Science is another word for consciousness, enabling one to avoid being manipulated. Applied science ideally is the level at which one understands reality enough to control reality. The question of manipulation always assumes a disequilibrium between the scientific and applied—an assumption too painfully evident in the everyday work of sociology. The main immediate common chore is to better distinguish when sociology is seeking clarification and when it seeks control.

The most promising aspect of the field of social problems, evidence that it is coming of age scientifically and not just therapeutically, is the work done by men such as Howard Becker, Lee Rainwater, Anselm Strauss, Erving Goffman, and a host of other scholars of the younger generation. They have a shared value not so much in social problems or in advocating social solutions, but rather in the therapy of science as such, in the act of self-consciousness which enables the field of sociology to become something other than policy or polemics.

7. On Alienation and the Social Order

I

Despite the incredible degree of confusion which exists about the term "alienation"—a confusion that has caused many influentials in sociology and psychology to try to do without it[1]—there is a danger in a premature scrapping of the term. There are few enough words in the vocabulary of social science having wide generic implications. In some sense the very confusions about the word "alienation" represent an acute, albeit painful, testimonial to a conceptual complication that exists in consequence of the autonomous development of the social and behavioral sciences. The heavy freight placed on such words as "anomie," "aggression," "intuition," "instinct," and now "alienation" is a burden better met by clarifying the meaning of the term than by urging premature abandonment either on the grounds that any word admitting of multiple different definitions is meaningless, or because of the equally spurious aim of preserving formal symmetry.

First presented at the 42nd annual meeting of the American Orthopsychiatric Association in 1965. This study places the abundant alienation literature in a systematic framework by considering the tripartite context (psychological, sociological, and humanistic) of the term, as well as the way in which the word is transformed from its early nineteenth-century "objective" context into its twentieth-century "subjective" context. First published in *Philosophy and Phenomenological Research*, vol. 27, no. 2 (December, 1966); reprinted by permission.

1. For example, the following representative collections carry no information on alienation: Bernard Berelson and Gary A. Steiner, *Human Behavior: An Inventory of Scientific Findings* (New York: Harcourt, Brace & World, 1964); Solomon E. Asch, *Social Psychology* (Englewood Cliffs, N.J.: Prentice-Hall, 1952); and Robert K. Merton, Leonard Broom, Leonard S. Cottrell, Jr., *Sociology Today: Problems and Prospects* (New York: Basic Books, 1959).

The problem of the use of "alienation," like so many other theoretical issues, is a debt to the philosophical ambiguities of nineteenth-century German realism. Nascent within German philosophical sources were the current schisms and polarization of meanings in this word.

Hegel argued that the true meaning of alienation lay in the separation of the object of cognition from the man of consciousness, the philosopher. Hence, for Hegel the chief way of overcoming alienation is through philosophical understanding, an embrace of the rational world; as if to know the world is somehow to be at one with that world, to become identified with it. To be reasonable is for Hegel the same as being at peace. It was in this problem that the equation of reality with rationality was the resolution of the problem of philosophical alienation; just as the reduction of reason to reasonableness was the resolution of the problem of practical alienation.

In the philosophy of Ludwig Feuerbach, alienation comes to be seen as an anthropological problem. The word "anthropology" was being used as a surrogate for "psychology," since Feuerbach neither knew of nor really appreciated anthropology in any exact, empirical sense. Feuerbach considered the problem of alienation as a separation out, a parceling out, of human consciousness—one part of man is invested (properly) in the material world, and another to the world of God, the projective ideal world. In effect, the dualism in Feuerbach is almost Platonic. The material world's being dreary and dismal gives rise to a set of projections about a spiritual world of perfection. As long as these two worlds remain separated, there cannot be any resolution of the problem of alienation.

It is a disservice to consider Marx's notion of alienation within a strictly philosophical framework, since Marx insisted upon the necessity of a social scientific resolution of what had up to then been viewed as a metaphysical or humanist dilemma. It was Marx himself who made the clear and decisive break with the philosophical tradition of explaining alienation. No longer was alienation a property of man or of reason; it became a specific property of select classes of men in factory conditions who were, as a result of these conditions, deprived of its empty universal application, the labor context of alienation itself served as a scientific break with romanticism; a rupture consecrated in the bedrock of political revolution from below.

At its source the word "alienation" implies an intense separation—first, from objects in a world; second, from other people; third, from ideas about the world held by other people. It might be said that the synonym of alienation is "separation," while the precise antonym of the word is "integration." The main difficulty with the philosophical traditions is the assumption that those who are defined as alienated are somehow lacking and that they ought to be integrated. In both Hegel and Feuerbach, therapeutic values are assigned to alienation and to integration, to the distinct disadvantage of the former and to the advantage of the latter. That is how we come to the phrasing of the term "alienated from" as somehow opposite to "integrated with." This mystic faith in organic union invariably found its way into the work of Hegel and Feuerbach, the mystic organic union being for Hegel *man as idea*, and for Feuerbach *idea as man*. But to the same degree that alienation was seen as a negative concept, the philosophical approach was considered abstract and unreliable in terms of psychological and sociological facts.

The really important break, therefore, which began with Marx, is that in the modern usage of the concept of alienation, there is a distinctive concern for distinguishing therapy from description, and for separating recommendations from analysis. There is in the dialectical approach a common belief that alienation is no better and no worse than integration, and that either concept might serve positive social ends. Alienation is a driveshaft of revolution; and integration is a transitional equilibrium generating new forms of separation from the mainstream, *i.e.*, new forms of alienation.

II

Let us now examine three fundamental categories of the concept "alienation."

In the first place, let us take the psychological meanings of alienation. Perhaps the classic definition is that given by Fromm: "By alienation is meant a mode of experience in which the person experiences himself as alien. He has become, one might say, estranged from himself."[2] It is important to take note of the fact that Fromm severely modifies the Marxian concept. He gives a definition that converts a "mode of production" into a "mode of experience," while the Marxian proletarian laborer is neatly converted back into the Hegelian abstract person. It is evident in the work of Fromm that he is not concerned with just providing a psychological approach to alienation, but also with giving renewed vigor to the older German romantic categorizations.

Alienation is often used as a psychological surrogate in the literature. Instead of being employed as a phenomenon of separation, it is used as a phenomenon of negation, or even of "lessness"—a suffix prefaced by "power-lessness," "norm-lessness," or "meaning-lessness." In this kind of approach, alienation either becomes part of a major body of literature on anomie, or in turn swallows up anomie. The difficulty is that this definition of alienation as negation does not connect up various forms of negation. Further, alienation as anomie tends to describe the social system in terms of an assumed rationality: that which has the power, norms, and meanings, in contrast to the personality system or that which is not a condition of rationality.[3]

At its most elevated form, the psychological definition of alienation is linked to the notion of ideology. This in turn is fused with the notion of how intellectuals view their roles in a social world. "A great deal of contemporary thought finds a state of alienation precisely in those ideologies which profess to predict with high confidence the outcome of people's behavior. Intellectuals especially

2. Erich Fromm, *The Sane Society* (New York: Rinehart, 1955), pp. 120–121.
3. Melvin Seeman, "On the Meaning of Alienation," in *Sociological Theory*, 2nd ed., ed. by L. A. Coser and B. Rosenberg (New York: Macmillan Co., 1964), pp. 525–538.

find themselves alienated in a world of social determinism; they wish for a world in which the degree of social predictability would be low."[4] In Feuer's concept of alienation, the notion turns out to be much more positive in its potential effects than in almost any other theory. With Feuer it is almost as if one has to overcome integration, rather than alienation, to arrive at scientific truth. Integration is held to yield precisely the kind of normlessness which is characteristic of an identification with rootlessness and machinelike behavior in general. Feuer thus offers a prototype of what in the literary tradition of Zamyatin, Huxley, and Orwell is the alienated man as an anti-utopian—a social realist.

The main contribution of the psychological school of alienation has been to demonstrate the universality of the concept, its connection to the personality structure as well as the social structure, and therefore its existence in socialist societies no less than in capitalist societies.[5] The psychological school holds that the foundation, the reservoir of nonparticipation in the social system (or even refusal to participate in that system), may be constructive as well as destructive. In this sense alienation is more akin to deviance than it is to disorganization. It is not a synonym for neurosis or psychosis so much as it is a notion of marginality, which is consciously or unconsciously held. The problem of alienation stems more from a lack of accurate perception of the norms than an active defiance of these norms.

The sociological tradition is perhaps a consequence of this distinction between psychic disorganization and social disorganization. A whole new set of variables is called into force. In this Marx himself set the tone, since alienation was viewed as the particular response of the working man to the externality of the product he produced. It was, in effect, a class phenomenon.

What, then, constitutes the alienation of labor? First, the fact that labor is *external* to the worker, *i.e.*, it does not belong to his essential being; that in his work therefore, he does not affirm himself but denies himself, does not feel content but unhappy, does not develop freely his physical and mental energy but mortifies his body and ruins his mind. The worker therefore only feels himself outside his work, and in his work feels outside himself. He is at home when he is not working, and when he is working he is not at home. His labor is therefore not voluntary, but coerced; it is *forced labor*. It is therefore not the satisfaction of a need; it is merely a *means* to satisfy needs external to it. Its alien character emerges clearly in the fact that as soon as no physical or other compulsion exists, labor is shunned like the plague. External labor, labor in which man alienates himself, is a labor of self-sacrifice, of mortification. The external character of labor for the worker appears in the fact that it is not his own, but someone else's, that it does not belong to him, that in it he belongs, not to himself, but to another. Just as in religion the spontaneous activity of the human imagination, of the human brain and the human heart, operates independently of the individual—that is, operates on him as an alien, divine or diabolical activity—in

4. Lewis Feuer, "What is Alienation? The Career of a Concept," *Sociology on Trial*, ed. by M. Stein and A. Vidich (Englewood Cliffs, N.J.: Prentice-Hall, 1963), pp. 127–147.
5. Adam Schaff, *Philosophy of Man* (New York: Monthly Review Press, 1963).

the same way the worker's activity is not his spontaneous activity. It belongs to another. It is the loss of his self.[6]

Once Marx opened this Pandora's box of the social and cross-cultural locale of alienation, it was just a matter of time before others would see alienation of different social sectors from those Marx had dealt with. Thus, for example, in a modern view of bourgeois society, that held by C. Wright Mills, alienation comes to be understood as a lower middle class phenomenon, something that debases salesgirls, technicians, and even intellectuals in a similar way. In this Mills provided not only a bridge from one class to another, but even more importantly, a way of viewing alienation as a problem for all nonruling classes, not only the factory-anchored urban proletariat. "In the normal course of her work, because her personality becomes the instrument of an alien purpose, the salesgirl becomes self-alienated. Men are estranged from one another as each secretly tries to make an instrument of the other, and in time a full circle is made: One makes an instrument of himself and is estranged from it also."[7]

Most recently we have had the example of alienation as a specific artistic problem, as a problem connected to the marketing of ideas rather than the production of goods. In this sense alienation is seen to have different functional prerequisites. The new work by Moravia contains a clear differentiation of the alienation of the worker from the alienation of the artist. He offers a clearly defined expression of qualitatively different notions of alienation that are involved in different social sectors. In this approach there is an attempt to link alienation to specific types of work done, which leads to a fragmentation of the notion of alienation rather than fragmentation of the notion of stratification.

The standard sociological perspective is to see alienation as a phenomenon of a unitary type, with differences being attributed to the stratification system. In Moravia, quite to the contrary, we have the unique case of a stratification system giving rise to different forms of alienation. In this we have a more advanced sociological notion of alienation than any thus far given:

There is no relationship between the alienation of the worker and the alienation of the artist. The worker is alienated because, in the economy of the market, he is a piece of goods like any other and as such he is defrauded of his surplus value, or of what represents his value as a man, whereas the artist creates an object that has no market (or, if it has, it is not that of necessities that always have a market) and no real price in money or kind. The artist receives the price of his work of art in creating it. In other words, when he hands his book over to the publisher, his music to the conductor, or his painting to the art dealer, the artist has already been paid and whatever he receives after that is a bonus. Hence the

6. Karl Marx, *Economic and Philosophic Manuscripts of 1844* (London: Lawrence and Wishart, 1959), pp. 67–84.

7. C. Wright Mills, *White Collar* (New York: Oxford University Press, 1951; 1956–57, pp. 182–188.

alienation of the artist consists in the total or partial prevention of his expression, or of his true relationship with society.[8]

The third general variety of alienation theory is based on considering it as part of a general cultural milieu. Within this framework, we find ideology spoken of in national terms, that is, the American ideology, the Soviet ideology, etc.; whereas Marx, in dealing with the German ideology, dealt with that ideology as it was a reflection of the ruling class diffused throughout the general society of the times. The newer pluralistic approach emphasizes the mass culture. Boorstin offers a particularly interesting variety of this approach.

We expect anything and everything. We expect the contradicting and the impossible. We expect compact cars which are spacious; luxurious cars which are economical. We expect to be rich and charitable, powerful and merciful, active and reflective, kind and competitive. We expect to be inspired by mediocre appeals for "excellence," to be made literate by illiterate appeals for literacy. We expect to eat and stay thin, to be constantly on the move and ever more neighborly, to go to a "church of our choice" and yet feel its guiding power over us, to revere God and to be God. Never have people been more the masters of their environment. Yet never have a people felt more deceived and disappointed. For never has a people expected so much more than the world could offer.[9]

The culturalist approach is no less critical of alienation as a status than any of the other approaches. Even from the quotation just read, one can see their criticism is severe. What is new and particularly interesting is the assumption of the "national character" from which the concept of alienation flows. The mass cultural school at its peak, with men like Dwight Macdonald and David Riesman, represents an interesting fusion of the psychological and sociological approaches. Alienation comes to be seen as a discrepancy, a measurable discrepancy, between achievements and expectations. At the general sociocultural level it is a discrepancy between national demands or national purposes and individual demands for an extension of autonomy and pluralism.[10]

One final expression of this cultural style is the tradition of alienation as a religious phenomenon, specifically, alienation as characteristic of marginal religious groupings. This view of alienation, held by men like Karl Barth, Paul Tillich, and Martin Buber, has strong ties to Feuerbach. Commentary on the current status of Jews in America is illustrative. As Isaac Rosenfeld once said, "Jews are specialists in alienation." They are alienated from a Diaspora, alienated from a redemptive God, and alienated from nationalism as such.[11] Of

8. Alberto Moravia, *Man as an End* (New York: Farrar, Straus, and Giroux, 1965–66).

9. Daniel Boorstin, *The Image* (New York: Atheneum Publishers, 1961), pp. 3–6.

10. See in particular the recent collection of papers by David Riesman, *Abundance for What? And Other Essays* (Garden City, N.Y.: Doubleday and Co., 1964).

11. Irving Malin, *Jews and Americans* (Carbondale: Southern Illinois University Press, 1965). For an earlier consideration of Jewish alienation, see Simon Dubnow, *Nationalism and History* (Cleveland, New York: Meridian Books, 1961).

course, alienation as an authentic religious expression has become a major theme for all Western religions.

This view of alienation as marginal has a great deal in common with the psychological view, just as the mass cultural view has a great deal in common with the sociological view. One can begin to detect a synthesis taking place in present-day expectations of alienation: a systematic linkage of psychological states, sociological classes, and cultural forms.

The location of the problem has now decisively shifted. The problem is no longer a fusion of psychological or sociological cultural techniques. The study of alienation is now confronted with a distinction between two modalities of analyses, one formal and the other descriptive. The formal system tends to emphasize the root categories, such as those provided by Seeman in his work, or operationalized definitions capable of survey designs, such as those provided by Nettler.[12] Descriptive analysis tends to emphasize the weaknesses in the psychological approach by pointing out that the formal modes of analysis are invariably *ad hoc*. They provide little indication, however, of how the types of alienation or the models built are related to each other or why they should be restricted to three, four, or five in number. Descriptive approaches tend to see alienation in a problem-solving context. They have a big problem in settling upon the relation of alienation to deviance, marginality, creativity, etc. But they do have the value of being linked to empirical, rather than logical modalities.[13]

It might well be that this is simply a social scientific reflex of the ongoing debate concerning the analytical and synthetic modes of argument. Whatever the case may be, it is clear that the literature on alienation has tapped into something extremely meaningful in the emergence of modern social science. Once the various meanings and levels at which the term "alienation" is employed can be properly understood, then social scientists will be better able to employ alienation as a central variable in discussing other features of social structure and process. The task of philosophy in this area might be a clarifying one, to show how various usages of alienation are either synonymous, overlapping, or entirely different from one another. The philosopher might develop some kind of logical or periodic table of alienation. I am given to understand that this is what modern philosophy of science is all about.

12. Gwynn Nettler, "A Measure of Alienation," *American Sociological Review*, 22 (1957); and see his earlier paper, "A Test for the Sociology of Knowledge," *American Sociological Review*, 10 (1945).

13. Marvin B. Scott, "The Social Sources of Alienation," in *The New Sociology*, ed. by Irving L. Horowitz (New York and London: Oxford University Press, 1964), pp. 239–252.

8. *Social Deviance and Political Marginality: Toward a Redefinition of the Relation Between Sociology and Politics*

I. THE WELFARE MODEL OF SOCIAL PROBLEMS

The study of social deviance within American sociology has traditionally been based on a model that consigns delinquent behavior to the instruments of social welfare. This model has sought to liberalize the visible agencies of social control (the police, judiciary, and welfare agents) by converting them from punitive instruments into rehabilitative instruments. This underlying premise that punishment and rehabilitation are the only two possible responses to deviance yields the conventional tendency to evaluate deviant behavior in *therapeutic* rather than *political* terms.[1]

This paper represents an effort to restructure the fields of sociology and political science by presenting both the theoretical and empirical foci for considering deviance and marginality as gradually merging phenomena. It was written in collaboration with Martin Liebowitz, who is currently at work on a dissertation relating counter-guerrilla insurgency and local police activities. It was published in *Social Problems*, 5, no. 3 (Winter, 1967).

1. See, for example, Gwynn Nettler, "Ideology and Welfare Policy," *Social Problems*, 6, no. 3 (Winter, 1958–59): 203–212; also see his "A Measure of Alienation," *American Sociological Review*, 22, no. 2 (April, 1957).

The rehabilitation model seeks a more human redefinition of the moral code as its long-range goal. Its short-range goal is to indicate the superordinate role that agencies of social control adopt in ascribing subordinate status to deviants. Coser has recognized this role conflict in the welfare orientation to poverty when he indicated that "in the very process of being helped and assisted, the poor are assigned to a special career that impairs their identity and becomes a stigma which marks their intercourse with others."[2]

However serviceable this model has been in the past, and notwithstanding its use in resisting encroachments on the civil liberties of accused deviants, the social welfare model does not exhaust present options—either on logical or on pragmatic grounds. A relationship among equals is possible only in democratic politics, where conflicts are resolved by power rather than a priori considerations of ascribed status. Only in such politics can deviants attain the status of legitimate combatants in social conflict.

II. POLITICAL REQUISITES OF SOCIAL PROBLEMS

In the traditional welfare model, deviant behavior is defined as a social problem. This definition implies several important assumptions about the nature of deviance. First, it takes for granted that deviance is a problem about which something should be done. Second, it assumes that deviance is a *public* problem, which means that social agencies have the right to intervene. Finally, deviance is treated as a social problem in contradistinction to a political issue. Thus decisions concerning it are relegated to administrative policy rather than to the political arena. As a result, deviance is handled by experts instead of being debated by the very publics who are supposedly menaced.

These beliefs about the nature of deviance have scant empirical justification. They derive from no intrinsic characteristics of deviance. Rather, they are normative statements about how deviant behavior should be treated. Bernard has shown a singular appreciation of this. "Values are inherent in the very concept of social problems. The conditions that are viewed as social problems are evaluated by the decision-maker as bad, as requiring change or reform. Something must be done about them. The reason for coming to the conclusion may be humanitarian, utilitarian, or functional. In any case, a system of values is always implicit, and usually quite explicit."[3]

In this framework, identifying the values of the decision-makers is crucial. As Becker indicates, if we take the above seriously, the selection of decision-makers who define deviance as a social problem is a *political* process, not just a value problem:

The question of what the purpose or goal (function) of a group is, and, consequently, what things will help or hinder the achievement of that purpose, is very often a political

2. Lewis A. Coser, "The Sociology of Poverty," *Social Problems*, 13, no. 2 (Fall, 1965): 145.
3. Jessie Bernard, "Social Problems as Problems of Decision," *Social Problems*, 6, no. 3 (Winter, 1958–59): 212, 215.

question. Factions within the group disagree and maneuver to have their own definition of the group's function accepted. The function of the group or organization, then, is decided in political conflict, not given in the nature of the organization. If this is true, then it is likewise true that the questions of what rules are to be enforced, what behavior regarded as deviant and what people labeled as outsiders must also be regarded as political.[4]

The decision to treat deviance as a social problem is itself a political decision. It represents the political ability of one group of decision-makers to impose its value sentiments on decisions concerning deviance. The anomaly is that, although the political decision has been to treat deviance as a nonpolitical problem, deviance persists as a political problem. A comprehensive analysis of deviance must include political factors by determining which decision-makers define deviance as a social problem, and indicating why they consider deviance a problem. Lemert was almost alone among the sociologists of the past decade in contending that deviance does not pose an objectively serious problem:

In studying the problem-defining reactions of a community, it can be shown that public consciousness of "problems" and aggregate moral reactions frequently center around forms of behavior which on closer analysis often prove to be of minor importance in the social system. Conversely, community members not infrequently ignore behavior which is a major disruptive influence on their lives We are all to familiar with the way in which populations in various cities and states have been aroused to frenzied punitive action against sex offenders. Nevertheless, in these same areas the people as a whole often are indifferent toward crimes committed by businessmen or corporations—crimes which affect far more people and which may be far more serious over a period of time.[5]

III. A Conflict Model of Deviance

Deviance is a conflict between at least two parties: superordinates who make and enforce rules, and subordinates whose behavior violates those rules. Lemert noted the implications of this conflict for understanding the sources of deviance. "Their common concern is with social control and its consequences for deviance. This is a large turn away from older sociology which tended to rest heavily upon the idea that deviance leads to social control. I have come to believe that the reverse idea, *i.e.*, social control leads to deviance, is equally tenable and the potentially richer premise for studying deviance in modern society."[6]

The conflict model implies alternative formulations of deviance as a problem: the deviant behavior itself, and the actions of rule-makers to prevent such behavior. The political climate prescribes both the conflicts that will occur between deviants and nondeviants, and the rules by which such conflicts will be

4. Howard S. Becker, *The Outsiders* (New York: Free Press, 1963), p. 7.
5. Edwin M. Lemert, *Social Pathology* (New York: McGraw-Hill Book Co., 1951), p. 4.
6. Edwin M. Lemert, *Human Deviance, Social Problems, and Social Control* (Englewood Cliffs, N.J.: Prentice-Hall, 1967), p. v.

resolved. The struggle of groups for legitimation thus constitutes an integral part of deviant behavior.

Deviance has been studied by employing a consensus welfare model rather than a conflict model because, for the most part, decision-making concerning deviance has been one-sided. The superordinate parties who regulate deviance have developed measures of control, while the subordinate parties, the deviants themselves, have not entered the political arena. The conflict, though existent, has remained hidden. As Becker correctly notes, this leads to a nonpolitical treatment of deviance. Becker has duly noted:

It is a situation in which, while conflict and tension exist in the hierarchy, the conflict has not become openly political. The conflicting segments or ranks are not organized for conflict; no one attempts to alter the shape of the hierarchy. While subordinates may complain about the treatment they receive from those above them, they do not propose to move to a position of equality with them, or to reverse positions in the hierarchy. Thus, no one proposes that addicts should make and enforce laws for policemen, that patients should prescribe for doctors, or that adolescents should give orders to adults. We call this the *apolitical* case.[7]

As the politicalization of deviance develops, this apolitical case will become atypical—the hidden conflict will become visible, and deviants can be expected to demand changes in the configuration of the social hierarchy.

Although there has been scattered intellectual opposition to asylums in the past, patients have never been organized to eliminate or radically alter mental hospitals; or addicts to legalize drug use; or criminals to abolish prisons. Synanon, a center formed by addicts to treat drug addiction, is a striking exception to this pattern. Staffed completely by former addicts, it has no professional therapists. Thus, it represents an insistence that deviants themselves are best able to define their own problems and deal with them. Ironically, while Synanon challenges both the right and the competency of professional therapists to intervene in the lives of addicts, it has not discarded the value premises of an adjustment therapy. Nonetheless, as Yablonsky indicates, this marks a departure from the conventional welfare model. "Over the past fifty years, the treatment of social problems has been dropped into the professional lap and has been held onto tightly. The propaganda about the professional's exclusive right to treat social problems has reached its high mark. The professionals, the public, and even patients are firmly convinced that the only 'bona fide' treatments and 'cures' available come from 'legitimate professionals' with the right set of degrees."[8]

Even where deviant social movements have become powerful, they have avoided political participation as special interest groups. For instance, Synanon

7. Howard S. Becker, "Whose Side Are We On?," *Social Problems*, 14, no. 3 (Winter, 1967): 240–241.

8. Lewis Yablonsky, *The Tunnel Back: Synanon* (New York: Macmillan Co., 1965), p. 368.

has acted politically only when new zoning codes threatened its very existence. The politicalization of deviance is occurring, as groups like homosexuals and drug addicts pioneer the development of organizational responses to harassment. A broad base for the legitimation of deviant behavior will increasingly be made.

The political questions inherent in a conflict model of deviance focus on the use of social control in society. What behavior is forbidden? How is this behavior controlled? At issue is a conflict between individual freedom and social restraint, with social disorder (Anarchy) and authoritarian social control (Leviathan) as the polar expressions. The resolution of this conflict entails a political decision about how much social disorder will be tolerated at the expense of how much social control. This choice can not be confronted as long as deviance is relegated to the arena of administrative policy-making. For example, public schools are perceived as a repressive institution by many Negro youths, yet there is no political option of refusing to attend or radically altering them. This problem is now being raised by Black Power advocates who demand indigenous control over schools in Negro ghettoes despite the citywide taxation network.

IV. Political Marginality and Social Deviance: An Obsolete Distinction

Conventional wisdom about deviance is reinforced by the highly formalistic vision of politics held by many social workers and sociological theorists. This view confines politics to the formal juridical aspects of social life, such as the electoral process, and to the maintenance of a party apparatus through procedural norms. In this view, only behavior within the electoral process is defined as political in character, thus excluding acts of social deviance from the area of legitimacy.[9]

In its liberal form—the form most readily adopted by social pathologists—the majoritarian formulation of politics prevails. This is a framework limited to the political strategies available to majorities or to powerful minorities having access to elite groups.[10] The strategies available to disenfranchised minorities are largely ignored, and thus the politics of deviance also goes unexamined. The behavior of rule-makers and law enforcers is treated as a policy decision rather than as a political phenomenon, while a needlessly severe distinction is made between law and politics. Analyses of political reality at the level of electoral results help foster this limited conception of politics. Consequently, the shared inheritance of sociology has placed the study of deviant behavior at one end of the spectrum and the study of political behavior at the other.

9. See Angus Campbell et al., The American Voter (New York: John Wiley and Sons, 1960); V. O. Key, Public Opinion and American Democracy (New York: Alfred Knopf, 1961); Seymour Martin Lipset, Political Man (Garden City, N.Y.: Doubleday Book Co., 1960); Samuel Lubell, The Future of American Politics (New York: Harper & Bros., 1952).

10. C. Wright Mills, "The Professional Ideology of Social Pathologists," Power, Politics, and People, ed. by Irving Louis Horowitz (New York and London: Oxford University Press, 1963), pp. 525–552.

Conventional nonpolitical responses on the part of sociology were possible largely because the political world itself has encouraged this kind of crisp differentiation between personal deviance and public dissent. Political deviance is a concept rarely invoked by politicians because the notion of politics itself implies the right of dissension. Lemert points out that this has not always been true for radical political deviants.[11] There is a history of punitive response to political deviants in this country, involving repression of anarchists, communists, socialists, and labor organizers. This has spread at times to a persecution of liberal groups as well. What characterized the "McCarthy Era" was not the hunt for radicals, but rather a broadening of the definition of radicals to include all sorts of mild dissenters. Only on rare occasions has political deviance been defined as a major social problem requiring severe repression. Thus, with the possible exception of anarchists, communists, and socialists (and sometimes even including these groups in the political spectrum normally defined as legitimate), there is no way of dealing with political life as a deviant area. The nature of American political pluralism itself promotes dissent, at least in the ideal version of the American political system. The onus of responsibility in the castigation of a political victim is upon the victimizer. Rights and guarantees are often marshaled on behalf of a widening of the political dialogue. Indeed, the definition of American democracy has often been in terms of minority supports rather than majority victories.

The area of deviance is not covered by the same set of norms governing minority political life. The source of responsibility for deviant behavior, whether it be drug addiction, homosexuality, alcoholism, or prostitution, is not borne by the person making the charges but rather is absorbed by the victims of such charges. The widespread recognition of the juridical shakiness of the deviant's position serves to privatize the deviant and embolden those who press for the legal prosecution of deviance. While the right to dissent politically is guaranteed (within certain limits), the right to dissent socially is almost totally denied those without high social status.

One simple test might be the perceived reactions toward political radicalism in contrast to social deviance. If a person is accused of being an anarchist, there may actually occur a certain "halo effect." Perhaps a charge of naivete or ignorance will be made against the politically marginal man, but not a censorious response demanding nonpolitical behavior.

In the area of deviance, if there is a self-proclamation of drug addiction or alcoholism, the demand for therapeutic or punitive action follows very quickly. If one admits to being a drug addict, there is an attempt to remove the curse from everyday life by the incarceration of the "patient" into a total institution, so that at least the visibility of deviance is diminished.

The line between the social deviant and the political marginal is fading. It is rapidly becoming an obsolete distinction. As this happens, political dissent by

11. Lemert, *Social Pathology*, pp. 203–209.

deviant means will become subject to the types of repression that have been a traditional response to social deviance. This development compels social scientists to reconsider their definitions of the entire range of social phenomena—from deviance to politics. Wolfgang and Ferracuti have taken an important first step toward an interdisciplinary study of social violence.[12]

For the social sciences, this implies a new connection between social problems and political action. The old division between the two can no longer be sustained. In terms of theory, the new conditions throw into doubt the entire history of political science as an examination of the electoral situation, and of social problems research as a study of personal welfare. If politics is amplified to incorporate all forms of pressure, whether by deviants or orthodox pressure groups, to change the established social order, and if sociology is redefined to include pressure by deviants to redesign the social system so that they can be accepted by the general society on their own terms, then there is a common fusion, a common drive, and a common necessity between sociology and political science, not only on the level of empirical facts, but on the level of scientific interpretation.

Some sociologists have already adapted to this new situation. Cloward's work in organizing welfare recipients is a particularly striking effort, which is an outrageous idea to both the classical capitalist and socialist doctrines.[13] This marks the first time that a sociologist has been involved in organizing welfare recipients. This enlargement of roles demonstrates that changes are occurring in what constitutes political life and social work.

There are several other important directions that applied sociologists might follow: drug addicts might be organized to alter laws concerning drug use; students might be organized to change the character of schools; and mental patients might be organized to change the way they are treated. In each of these cases, change would be initiated from below by members of subordinate marginal groups. This would be in sharp contrast to the conventional elitist pattern of politics, where decisions are made from above by members of the prevailing majority. This is the primary distinction between the existing political party style and the political outsider style that is currently emerging.

V. THE POLITICIZED SOCIAL DEVIANT

A serious dilemma for many deviant and marginal groups alike is their failure to perceive any main-line organizations (either overtly political or social) as providing the sort of universal legitimation that governed an earlier, more tranquil period in American history. The entire array of formal and informal organizations seems arrayed against the kind of deviant particularisms expressed by hippies, Hell's Angels, or "acid heads." Thus, the subgroups, whether of

12. Marvin E. Wolfgang and Franco Ferracuti, *The Subculture of Violence* (London and New York: Tavistock Publications, 1967), pp. 1–14.

13. See Richard A. Cloward and Richard M. Elman, "Advocacy in the Ghetto," *Transaction*, 4, no. 2 (December, 1966): 27–35.

deviant lower class origins or marginal middle class origins, begin to align themselves with each other and against the mainstream of American life per se. A new set of cultural heroes, dance forms, and art forms coalesce to define not just a classical generational revolt for the rage to live, but a particularistic expression of immediate personal liberation as a prelude to distant public egalitarianism.

The key demonstration effect that such particularistic responses may prove extremely effective, even if they involve small numbers, is the rise of guerrilla insurgency as a military style in the underdeveloped areas. If "colored people" can conduct protracted struggles in Asia and in Africa, why can't the same sorts of struggles be conducted from the rooftops of Watts and Newark? Indeed, the expanding internationalization of the deviant and marginal groups can best be appreciated in new cultural heroes such as Franz Fanon, Malcolm X, and others connected with the demimonde of the Black Power movement. The seeds of this were long ago raised in the works of Padmore and DuBois, who urged precisely such ideological linkages with revolutionary forces elsewhere in the world—particularly in Pan-Africanism. What was absent before was the mechanism for success. In the guerrilla style, this mechanism, this critical missing ingredient, was finally supplied—and the linkage made complete.

The area of Negro struggles is a particularly fertile source for reevaluating the relationship between deviance and politics. Originally, there was a clear distinction between vandalism for personal gain and an act of organization for political gain. When the political life of Negroes was circumscribed by the NAACP, it was clear that political life entailed normative behavior within the formal civic culture. Similarly, it was clear that acts of personal deviance fell outside the realm of politics. Indeed, there was little contact between Negro deviants and participants in the civil rights protest.

The rise of civil disobedience as a mass strategy has blurred this distinction. Such disobedience entails personal deviance to attain political ends. Regardless of the political goals involved, it is a conscious violation of the law. The treatment of civil disobedience in the courts has therefore been marked by ambiguity. It is difficult to predict whether it will be treated as a political act of insurrection or a simple personal violation of the law. Many law enforcement officials see no distinction between civil disobedience and crime, and blame the ideology of law-breaking inherent in civil disobedience for rising crime rates and the occurrence of race riots.[14]

In turn, these officials may be responding to the large-scale denial by Negroes of the traditional role of the police as keepers of social order. This can perhaps best be gauged not only directly, in the expressed attitudes of political leaders from governors down to sherrifs, but indirectly as well, i.e., by the inability of local gendarmeries to cope with Negro mass rioting. The Watts riots of August,

14. In this connection, see Stanley Lieberson, "The Meaning of Race Riots," *Race*, VII, no. 4 (1966): 371–378.

1965, were, in this connection, prototypical of the current breakdown in traditional forms of police legitimacy. In that riot, which lasted four days, caused 34 deaths and 1,032 injuries, and ended in 4,000 arrests being made, the key fact was the role of the National Guard in quelling the riot. The Los Angeles police were thoroughly unable to cope with a situation once it achieved paramilitary proportions. This lesson has clearly not been lost on Negro ghetto communities elsewhere in the United States.

Confining ourselves to the cluster of race riots which took place in June and July of 1967, we can see how Watts heralded a new stage in the relationship between deviance and politics. In the main riot areas of Chicago, Detroit, Cleveland, Cincinnati, Buffalo, and Newark (we will disregard for present purposes the satellitic riots which took place in the smaller centers of Plainfield, Louisville, Hartford, Prattville, and Jackson) the following characteristics were prevalent in each community during the duration of the riot.

(a) Each city requested and received National Guardsmen to restore social order. Correspondingly, in each city, the police proved ineffectual in coping with the riots once the shield of legitimation was removed.

(b) In each city, there were deaths and serious injuries not only to the rioters but to the established police and invading guardsmen.

(c) In each city, the riots lasted more than one day, the duration being from two to seven days; which indicates the guerrilla-like nature of the struggle.

(d) In each case, the triggering mechanism for the riot was an altercation involving police officials (usually traffic patrolmen) and Negroes accused of reckless driving, driving without a license, or driving under the influence of alcohol.

(e) In each case, the major rioting took place during summer months, when the normal load of Negro male unemployed is swelled by students and teenage former students not yet relocated.

(f) In each city, property damage was extensive, with the sort of sniper tactics and "scorched earth" policies usually associated with so-called wars of national liberation.

(g) In each case, the major rioting seemed to lack official civil rights organization sponsorship; however, participation in the protests did take place on an individual basis.

Table 1 gives some indication of the character and extent to which the conflict model dominates current Negro deviance-marginality. The parallel with what Eckstein has termed "internal violence,"[15] and with what is more customarily referred to as guerrilla warfare,[16] is clear.

15. See Harry Eckstein, *Internal War* (New York: Free Press of Glencoe, 1964); and for a more specific account, Harold Black and Marvin J. Labes, "Guerrilla Warfare: An Analogy to Police-Criminal Interaction," *American Journal of Orthopsychiatry*, XXXVII, no. 4 (July, 1967): 666–670.

16. See Irving Louis Horowitz, "The Military Elite," in *Elites of Latin America*, ed. by Seymour Martin Lipset and Aldo Solari (New York and London: Oxford University Press, 1967).

Table I: Major Negro Riots in Urban Ghettos

Date	Place	Casualties			National Guard[a]	Riot Duration	PROPERTY DAMAGES (thousands of dollars)
		Killed	Injured	Arrested		Days	
8/65	Watts (Los Angeles)	35	1,000+	4,000+	14,000	5	50,000+
6/67	Buffalo	—	68	182	500	4	100+
6/67	Cincinnati	1	50	300	1,100	2	2,000
7/67	Cleveland	4	55	275	nd	5	4,000+
7/67	Chicago	2	100+	500+	4,200	4	nd
7/67	Newark	24	1,150	1,600+	3,375	6	15,000+
7/67	Detroit	36	1,500+	2,665+	13,000[b]	5	500,000+

[a]National Guard figures exclude city police.
[b]Includes 8,000 National Guard and 5,000 federal troops.

Source: Compiled from New York Times Index.

What this amounts to is a military rather than a civil definition of the situation in racial ghettos. The essential deterrent was the raw fire power of the combatants rather than the legitimated authority of the police uniform. Under such circumstances, the established welfare distinction between juvenile deliquency and guerrilla warfare mean very little.

The rapidly rising crime rates indicate a further ambiguity in the traditional formulation of social deviance. It is of decreasing sociological importance whether "crime" is perceived as an act of politics or of deviance. The consequences are the same in either case: cities are becoming increasingly unsafe for whites, and white-owned businesses are suffering mounting losses. Whether it is political insurgency or traditional crime, the consequences remain the same—a disruption in the legitimation system of American society.

VI. THE DEVIANT POLITICAL MARGINAL

At the opposite pole—minoritarian politics—a similar set of ambiguities plagues those in search of precise boundary lines. An example is the behavioral pattern of the left wing. Among the radical youth of the 1930's certain characteristics clearly emerged: a relatively straitlaced "puritan" ethos concerning sexual mores; a clear priority of politics over personal life—what might be called the ascetic purification of self; and a concern for a relatively well-defined ideology, combined with encouragement for all to participate in the life of the working classes. The radical Left of an earlier generation shared with the dominant cultural milieu a distinct, even an intense, disaffiliation from deviant patterns. Indeed, the Old Left pointed to social deviance as illustrative of the moral degeneration of bourgeois society. The need for social revolution came about precisely because the existing social order was considered incapable of controlling social deviance. Thus, the demands of the traditional Left with respect to social deviance were not very different from Establishment demands.

This contrasts markedly with the position of the New Left on conventional indicators of deviance. First, they exhibit substantial positive affect toward an extreme and libertarian ethos replacing puritanism. Second, there is an identification with deviant forms, stemming from a continued affiliation with the "beatnik" movement of the 1950's. There has been a considerable absorption of the Beat Generation of the 1950's into the Activist Generation of the 1960's. The ideology of the New Left, insofar as it has clear guidelines, is based on freedom of repression. It has both political and social components: freedom for the Negro from the effects of racial discrimination; freedom for the student from the constraints of university regulations; freedom for the young generation from the demands of their elders; and freedom of politically powerless groups from the growing authority of the centralized state. In this sense, Freud feeds the ideology of the New Left at least as much as Marx defined the ideology of the Old Left.

The traditional notion of a noble affiliation of radical youth with the working class has already dissolved in favor of a highly positive response to deviant and marginal groups in American society. There is a relative unconcern for the traditional class formations engaged in the struggle for upward mobility. If there is a hero, it is the alienated man who understands what is wrong and seeks escape. Often, escape takes the form of social deviance, which is considered no worse than the forms of behavior traditionally defined as normative. The traditional hero has been supplanted by the anti-hero, who wins and attains heroic proportions by not getting involved in the political process. This anti-hero is defined by what he is against as much as by what he is for; he is for a world of his own, free from outside constraints, in which he is free to experiment and experience.

What this means operationally is that the line between left-wing political behavior and personal deviance has been largely obliterated. Nowhere has this been more obvious than in the student protest movement, where it is impossible to separate the deviant student subculture from the substantive demands of the student revolt. Spence accurately describes the significance of this student movement at the University of California at Berkeley: "This was the first successful student strike at a major university in the United States. But more important, this was the first significant white-collar rebellion of our time. These sons and daughters of the middle class demonstrated and walked picket lines, not behind the moral banner of the oppressed Negro, but on the basis of their own grievances against a system that had deprived them of their rights of responsibility and self-expression."[17]

The student rebellion underlies a major thesis herein proposed, since it led not to organized political responses of a conventional variety, but rather to a cele-

17. Larry D. Spence, "Berkeley: What It Demonstrates," *Revolution At Berkeley*, ed. by Michael V. Miller and Susan Gilmore (New York: Dell Publishing Co., 1965), p. 217.

bration of deviance itself as the ultimate response to orthodox politics. Stopping "the operation of the machine," which for Mario Savio "becomes so odious, makes you so sick at heart that you can't take part; can't even tactically take part," led to only one conclusion: "the machine must be prevented from running at all."[18] It is interesting that victory was not defined as taking over the operations of the machine, not the classical capture of organized political power, but rather in nonparticipation and in nonacceptance. Savio himself, as if in conscious defiance of Michels' "iron law of oligarchies" governing the performance of organizations, simply refused to participate in any leadership functions in the Berkeley post-rebellion period. The definition of victory, then, is in the ability of marginal groups to disrupt the operations of political power either in its direct parliamentary form or in surrogate forms.

Among young members of the New Left, draft evasion has become an important form of deviance. The number of people who adopt the traditional political path by refusing to serve and going to jail as political prisoners is small compared with the number who adopt the deviant path, using mental illness, homosexuality, or drug addiction (whether these be real or feigned) to avoid serving. In effect, they are taking advantage of the prevailing established norms toward deviants. However, this path is made much more accessible with the merger of leftist politics and social deviance, since only politics can transform private desires into public principles.

An important social characteristic of the New Left is its self-definition as a "swinging" group, or conversely, not being "square." This new definition of leftism is also a central definition of the deviant subculture. So it is that Berkeley and Watts became the symbols of the twin arms of radical politics: the university campus and the Negro ghetto. Even in terms of social psychological definitions of friends and foes, the line between the political Left and social deviance is now largely transcended. Thus there is a deep distrust of formal politics and of the people who operate within the bureaucratic channels of the political apparatus. This definition of friends and foes is obvious at Berkeley, where many students feel that they cannot trust anyone over thirty.

The right-wing movement in America also illustrates this perspective. The Old Right was characterized by extreme antipathy for any kind of promiscuous or overtly immoral behavior. The American Right viewed with alarm attacks upon law-enforcement officials. The Old Right perceived itself conventionally as a paragon of law enforcement. This is the core around which the right wing has traditionally been established. But a phenomenon such as the Minutemen reveals a spin-off from law-abiding to direct action approaches to politics. The Minutemen, for example, are encouraged to acquire possession of fully automatic weapons, even though many such weapons are forbidden to individuals by law.

18. Jack Newfield, *A Prophetic Minority* (New York: New American Library, 1966), p. 27; on this general theme, see Irving Louis Horowitz, "Radicalism and Contemporary American Society," *Liberation*, 10, no. 3 (May, 1965): 15–18.

They are urged to join the National Rifle Association to become eligible for rifles and handguns at cost as well as free ammunition. The Minutemen *Handbook* contains lessons on such subjects as "Booby Traps," "Anti-Vehicular Mines," and "Incendiary Weapons Composition." The self-made saboteur is encouraged to improvise lethal weapons. Espionage and infiltration of established political groupings are also encouraged. A subunit called the Minutemen Intelligence Organization is in possession of a fairly sophisticated organization, not unlike those of paramilitary units.[19]

Breakaway segments of the New Right, like their opposite numbers in the New Left, are concerned with redefining the relationship of the person to the legal code in very loose terms. The appeals to youth are in terms of training in weaponry rather than in law. When confronted by the law, the Minutemen dissolved their public leadership and created a new underground leadership. This phenomenon could be an extreme situation in American life, precisely because so many armed forces veterans may be attracted to such a combination of politics and deviance. A situation is arising where the line between the deviant act of gun-toting in an undisciplined way for personal (or political) ends, and the use of "hardware" for the purpose of maintaining law and order, is largely dissolved. Political conflict may become marked by opposing marginal political groups confronting each other in armed conflict, with the legitimated state agencies of power the enemy of both.

VII. The Politics of Deviant Violence

Attention should now be drawn to the growing Latinization of Negro riots and student revolts in the present period. This was done in terms of rough macroscopic data. Here we wish to underscore this point by taking closer note of the workings of the new style of subculture in America. The largest Negro gang in Chicago, the Blackstone Rangers, numbering several thousand members, is a clear example of the breakdown in the distinction between crime and marginal politics, as well as the course which the politics of marginality is likely to follow. The Rangers act as an autonomous group, in conflict with both local residents and police. The strategies employed in this conflict indicate the style of the new politics. The gang entered into negotiations with the Chicago police, and reached a satisfactory (if temporary) settlement: they agreed to surrender their weapons and stop fighting other gangs if the police would drop certain charges against their leaders and disarm a rival gang. The negotiations thus served to "keep the peace," but only at the expense of enhancing the credibility of the gang networks.

Negotiation of this sort is a major strategy of international politics, although it has seldom been used to resolve conflicts involving marginal domestic groups. The negotiation process itself entails the recognition that marginal groups

19. See William W. Turner, "The Minutemen: The Spirit of '66," *Ramparts*, 5, no. 7 (January, 1967): 69–76.

represent legitimate political interests. So far, the art of negotiation has not been adequately developed for dealing with such situations, just as it has not been adequately developed for dealing with unconventional international conflicts.

The problem posed by marginal groups like the Rangers is not yet viewed as a political problem to be solved by political strategies. When police violated the negotiated settlement, the Blackstone Rangers planned to file suit in the federal courts to prohibit a pattern of harassment. It is novel for such deviant groups to engage in political conflict with legitimate agencies like the police, but it does indicate a step beyond the "good bad boy" approach of social welfare.

There is a growing impulse to develop political means of resolving conflicts that involve marginal groups, as an alternative to the military means that have thus far prevailed. The Woodlawn Organization, composed of local residents, received a federal grant of $927,341 to work with gangs like the Rangers and the Disciples. The Chicago police raided the first meeting between the gang leaders and leaders of The Woodlawn Organization, demonstrating a conflict between advocates of a political solution and proponents of what amounts to a military solution to the gang problem.[20] In the absence of acceptable political solutions, it is probable that increasing reliance upon domestic military solutions will be sought—just as the failure of political solutions internationally often leads to pressing for quick military solutions.

This trend toward marginal politics reflects a rejection of conventional political styles that have proven unsuited to the needs of marginal groups. In the past, the powerless had recourse to two choices for political action: legitimate means, to which they do not have sufficient access to be influential; or accessible but ineffective illegitimate means that bring little structural change. Marginal minorities are now searching for the development of political means that are both accessible and effective. It is probable that these new styles will be illegitimate rather than legitimate, and that the distinction between social deviance and political insurgency will be further reduced.

Race riots differ from both orthodox politics and personal delinquency. They offer some important insights into these new styles. Race riots have an ideological core, while many other forms of collective behavior do not. They are avowedly political, organized, and purposeful. Typically, deviant acts like theft, assault, and homicide have none of these attributes. For these reasons, race riots may be closer to organized unconventional warfare than they are to conventional crime. Once perceived in this way, they constitute a powerful if latent political weapon.

At present, in most American cities a relatively small police force can effectively control the populace. But this is true only as long as police are accorded legitimacy. When conflicts are defined totally in terms of power and force rather than authority and legitimacy, as during race riots, the police cannot effectively

20. Rowland Evans and Robert Novak, "The Negro Gangs," *Herald Tribune, International Edition,* July 5, 1967.

maintain control. For this reason, riots constitute a major departure from established patterns of interaction between police and deviants. Deviants are not organized to battle police, and they have no ideology that labels police as enemies to be attacked and destroyed. Police have legitimacy as long as deviants avoid rather than attack them. However, police traditionally mount an organized collective effort against deviants, who typically respond only as unorganized individuals. The existing conflict is a one-sided war. The emergence of a bilateral conflict situation promises to be a major development in the link between politics and deviance. Race riots are the first indication of this change.[21]

This conflict can take several alternative forms: on a *minimax* scale there could be de-escalation to the English system, in which both Negro militants (or deviants in general) and police would not carry arms; at the other end, there could be escalation to race riots, which are sporadic and constitute a relatively unorganized set of events. Beyond sporadic racial strife lies the possibility of sustained conventional war. This is most closely approximated in American history by the Indian Wars and the Civil War. Presently, unconventional warfare is coming into focus. The latter two possibilities indicate how social deviance could spill over into insurrectionary politics, given both the peculiar racial division that exists in American society and the consistent exclusion of marginal groups from political and social legitimacy.

This marginal style of politics is being adopted by groups of all "extreme" ideological persuasions. Marginals of both the Left and Right fear the growing power of the centralized government, which they feel will be used to repress them, and are opposed to the consolidation of power by the majority. This commonality is demonstrated by the high amount of social interaction that occurs, in places like Greenwich Village and Berkeley, between politically opposed deviant groups. Even such political opposites as the Hell's Angels and the opponents of the Vietnam war shared a common social network in California. Their political enmity was balanced by their similar enjoyment of deviant social patterns.[22]

The clearest example of this movement toward violence, and one easily overlooked, is the reappearance of assassination as a political style, coupled with the inability to know whether Left, Right, or Deviant is spearheading this style. It is almost impossible to say whether the assassination of John F. Kennedy, Malcolm X, or Martin Luther King, was a deviant act or a political act. No group took responsibility for the assassinations as overt political acts, and the assassins did not link the deaths to ideological demands. Without taking into account the breakdown in the distinction between politics and deviance, the meaningfulness of both sociology and political science is seriously compromised.

21. See Ed Cray, *The Big Blue Line: Police Power vs. Human Rights* (New York: Coward-McCann, 1967), p. 121.

22. See Hunter S. Thompson, *Hell's Angels: The Strange and Terrible Saga of the Outlaw Motorcycle Gangs* (New York: Random House, 1966), pp. 231–257.

VIII. Marginal Sectors and Deviant Values

Applied social science must take account of this new view of marginality in American life. If any group has emerged as the human carrier of the breakdown between political and private deviance, it has been the *Lumpenproletariat*, or the nonworking working class. This group has replaced the established working and middle classes as the deciding political force in America. Lang and Lang[23] point out in their discussion of collective dynamics that this is precisely the condition which breeds collective deviance. "Ordinarily the cleavages within a society are between clearly constituted social strata or between parties whose special interests seek recognition within a broader framework of order. When cleavages occur between constituted authority and those who do not accept it, or between those who feel unable to share in the established authority systems, we can refer to the condition as one of widespread and general alienation."

The army of marginally employed comprises a significant segment of *both* politically radical and socially deviant cultures. If in Western Europe the bureaucracy grew disproportionately to all other classes, the disproportionate rise of the marginally employed characterizes contemporary America. This group, rather than disappearing or, as Marx would have it, becoming a social scum to be wiped out by revolution, grows ever larger. At a practical level, there is now a new and powerful intermediary class that performs vital roles in the authoritarian political system, while at the same time it sets the style for a new libertarian morality.

The boundaries of American politics reflect the growing affluence that typifies the American social structure. However, a significant minority of disaffected marginals exists in the midst of this affluence. It is becoming increasingly clear that these marginals threaten to destroy the fruits of general affluence, and, indeed, to disrupt the entire situation. Race riots are a more serious indicator of the inability of the political system to maintain an equilibrium despite the general affluence.

The overlap of deviance and marginality is well captured in a current book on the Hell's Angels. The Hell's Angels—with the Swastika, German helmet, and Iron Cross as their main symbols—differ but slightly from the pseudo-Maoist organizations of the Left. Without wishing to equate Maoists with either Minutemen or Hell's Angels, it is clear that each of these groups is marginal and deviant with respect to established political norms. Further, it is even difficult to give conventional definitions to those holding a gun in one hand and a flower in the other.

The Angels have given up hope that the world is going to change for them. They assume, on good evidence, that the people who run the social machinery have little use for outlaw motorcyclists, and they are reconciled to being losers. But instead of losing quietly, one

23. Kurt Lang and Gladys Engel Lang, *Collective Dynamics* (New York: Thomas Y. Crowell Co., 1961), p. 18.

by one, they have banded together with a mindless kind of loyalty and moved outside the framework, for good or ill. They may not have the answer; but at least they are still on their feet. It is safe to say that no Hell's Angel has ever heard of Joe Hill or would know a Wobbly from a bushmaster, but there is something very similar about their attitudes. The Industrial Workers of the World had serious blueprints for society, while the Hell's Angels mean only to defy the social machinery. There is no talk among the Angels of building a better world, yet their reactions to the world they live in are rooted in the same kind of anarchic, para-legal sense of conviction that brought the armed wrath of the Establishment down on the Wobblies. There is the same kind of suicidal loyalty, the same kind of in-group rituals and nicknames, and above all, the same feeling of constant warfare with an unjust world.[24]

The policy response to this dilemma has been the Welfare State: an attempt to "cool out" the marginal underclass and minimize the potential danger it poses. It is an attempt to avoid the consequences of large-scale marginality without making any social structural changes. Schatzman and Strauss contend that this welfare style deals with the problem by avoiding its political implications:

America pours its wealth into vast numbers of opportunity programs to achieve its goals and names almost any conceivable group, event, or thing a social problem if it can be seen as threatening the achievement of these goals. Hence its concern for the culturally deprived, the under-achievers, the school dropouts, the job displaced, the aged, the ill, the retarded, and the mentally disturbed. This concern goes beyond that of the nineteenth-century humanitarians who involved themselves with the underprivileged out-groups on moral grounds. Now all these aggregates are seen as special groups whose conditions are intolerable to society, if not actually threatening, in light of today's social and economic requirements.[25]

This attempt to depoliticize a highly political problem has proved inadequate. The welfare solution has not erased the consequences of having a growing number of disaffected people in the midst of general affluence. Indeed, the very existence of affluence on so wide a scale creates demands that parallel those made by the "poor nations" on the "rich nations." Because of this, a political attempt to solve the problem is bound to emerge. If this attempt is not initiated from above within the legitimate political or electoral apparatus, it will be generated from below and probably take illegitimate paramilitary forms.

The implicit exchange system which formerly existed between the very poor and the very rich in American society was simple: "Don't bother us and we won't bother you." In exchange for the poor not disturbing the rich, the wealthy provided just enough money for the poor to live at Ricardian subsistence levels. This exchange has been the basis of American social work, and con-

24. Thompson, Hell's Angels, pp. 265-266.

25. Leonard Schatzman and Anselm Strauss, "A Sociology of Psychiatry," Social Problems, 14, no. 1 (Summer, 1966): 12.

tinues to define the boundaries of the welfare system. The rich have only vaguely appreciated the magnitude of the poor's potential power and their ability to disrupt the entire system. For their part, the poor only vaguely appreciate the power at the disposal of the rich, which accounts for the suicidal characteristics of many race riots.

This interchange system is now being threatened. The poor are gradually developing an appreciation of their own power, while at the same time they have a greater appreciation of the power held by the rich. For their part, the rich are becoming more aware of the power available to the poor, as seen in the generalized fear created by rising crime rates and race riots. In short, there is a greater polarization of conflict between the two classes.

The primary political problem of deviance can be framed as a Hobbesian dilemma. Hobbes sought the creation of the state as a solution to the problem of social disorder, in which individuals war with each other in pursuit of their individual interests. The dilemma is that the creation of the state creates a problem of social control. The solution to the problem of chaos or the *Anarch* is the *Leviathan*. But the *Leviathan* is the *totalitarian* state. Indeed, totalitarianism is the perfect solution to the problem of disorder. The dilemma for those who consider social problems obstacles to be overcome is that any true overcoming of social problems implies a perfect social system. And this entails several goals: first, the total institutionalization of all people; second, the thoroughgoing equilibrium between the parts of a system with respect to their functioning and the functioning of other sectors; and third, the elimination of social change as either a fact or value. Thus, the resolution of social problems from the point of view of the social system would signify the totalitarian resolution of social life.

The political problem posed by deviance is how to avoid social disorder while at the same time avoiding the problem of total social control. It is a dilemma precisely because of the impossibility of solving both problems simultaneously. Political decisions about deviance must reflect judgments about the relative dangers of these two problems, and must constitute a weighing process based on ethical no less than on empirical considerations.

Connections between deviance and politics take place most often when a society does not satisfactorily manage its affairs. For better or worse, a well-ordered society is one that can impose a distinction between responses to deviance and responses to marginality. Antecedents for the linkage of deviance and marginality exist in two "conflict societies." In the 1890's in Russia, the Narodnik movement was directly linked to the movement toward personal liberation. In Germany of the 1920's, the "underground" movement, aptly summed up by the Brecht theater, Nihilism, and amoralism, gave rise to both Nazi and Bolshevik political tendencies. The merger of the Beat Generation and the current Radical Student movements reveals this same pattern of connecting political revolution with demands for personal liberation.

These examples indicate how the fusion between deviant behavior and political processes is a prelude to radical change. If the fusion of politics and deviance is the herald of revolution, or at least indicates a high degree of disassociation and disorganization within the society, then radical changes in the structure of American social and political life are imminent.

What takes place in personal life has major political ramifications in contemporary society. Until now, American life has been resilient enough to forestall a crisis in treating marginality. This is a testimonial to the flexibility of the American system of political legitimation. But it might well be that the extent of deviance in the past was not sufficient to cause more than a ripple in the political system.[26] In the emerging system, with automation and cybernation creating greater dislocation and marginal employment, personal deviance may generate a distinct transformation in normal political functions; it marks the point at which the political system cannot cope with deviant expressions of discontent.

A political description of this condition begins with the inability of American society to resolve political problems that are important to *marginal* people. Almost one-third of the potential voting population does not vote and is therefore without even the most minimal political representation. The fact that these disenfranchised people have important problems in common that cannot be managed within existing arrangements creates a volatile situation.

Political styles evolve that are not presently labeled as political behavior, much as race riots are not now generally considered as political behavior. These new styles are characterized, first, by a rejection of the legitimacy of the existing political system (the challenge to the rules by which the game is now played); second, by a rejection of compromise as a political style; and third, by a willingness to oppose established authority with illicit power in order to change not merely the rules but the game itself. Ends will attain a primacy over means, whereas a concern with the legitimacy of means has traditionally characterized American politics. Direct expressions of power might assume a more important role than legitimate authority in resolving important conflicts.

Political legitimacy is itself subject to change in order to meet the demands of a society in which social deviants and political marginals have become more, rather than less, important in determining the structure of American society.

26. Rex Hopper, "Cybernation, Marginality, and Revolution," in *The New Sociology*, ed. by Irving Louis Horowitz (New York and London: Oxford University Press, 1964), pp. 313–330.

27. See E. E. Schattschneider, *The Semi-Sovereign People* (New York: Holt, Rinehart & Winston, 1960), pp. 97–114.

PART II. *The Academic Life of Sociology*

9. *On Learning and Teaching Sociology*

The sociology of education has had a long and modestly significant impact. Its tripartite focus on the school as (a) social institution, (b) cultural transmission belt, and (c) clearinghouse of ideas, attitudes, and ideologies has been particularly effective. As a matter of fact, there has, of late, been a considerable interest in the teaching of sociology and in the career opportunities for the student of sociology. But, thus far, there has been no corresponding concern in the learning of sociology, in the education of the users of sociologists.

When efforts are made in this direction, they are often severely circumscribed, including only the university upper-level student staking out a career line of sociology. I would like to address my remarks to the most cellular, yet perhaps most difficult to evaluate, issue—the learning of sociology at all educational levels. The basic strategic advantage of such an approach is that it enables the researcher to employ whatever "hard data" exists in this never-never land of the educational process, while the root intellectual advantage is that it takes seriously the existence of the many-sided publics for sociology.

Any definitive analysis of the learning and teaching of sociology is, by its complexities and infinite shadings, a collective enterprise. And faced with a

Prepared for a Conference on the Introduction of the Social Sciences into the Educational Curriculum, held at Cornell University in 1964. The purpose of this paper was to provide a preliminary design for a sociology program that would be attuned to the specific needs of students at different levels in the educational ladder. It also tried to explain some of the professional problems of sociologists in developing a clear educational standpoint. First published in a much abbreviated version in *Five Fields of Teacher Education*, edited by D. B. Gowin (Ithaca, N.Y.: Cornell University, 1965).

situation in which nothing exists for sociology comparable to the monumental *The Teaching of Anthropology*,[1] I was faced with the choice of either attempting to make a small point in a definitive way, or taking a risk and making big points in an impressionistic way. My impulse and my inclination both made me lean toward the latter choice, with what results the reader will decide.

Sociology in the United States is a cohesive multipartite body which has at its disposal a great accumulation of unique information. It also possesses some distinctive and disparate points of view. It is a fraternity with complex associations, which contains perhaps 7,500 "believers," in the sense that these are persons whose basic attitude towards life is dominated by the search for human meanings through sociological training and truths.[2] But in addition to this nucleus that derives its living from sociology either as school hands or field hands, there is a further stratification: along one axis are the strivers after immortality, the 350 or so bishops and archbishops who add to, subtract from, and are generally concerned with changing or, as is more often the case, interpreting the sacred scrolls. These are the theorists. The sociological College of Cardinals (the presidents of the American Sociological Association) is usually drawn from this pool of prophets. Along another axis are another 850 or so elite secularists, who seek their rewards on this earth, usually in the form of "hard cash."[3] The leadership of this secularist elite often has direct affiliation with, or access to, the great foundations—the sources of material rewards.

The feudal empire of sociology thus has two principal estates: the priests and the princes. The third estate of 7,000 nuclear members may be considered part of the officer corps of sociology—freemen who will rise in righteous wrath against enemies from the outside or transgressors from within, who provide

1. David C. Mandelbaum, Gabriel W. Lasker, and Ethel M. Albert, eds., *The Teaching of Anthropology* (Berkeley and Los Angeles: University of California Press, 1963).

2. For quantitative information on the number of degree holders in sociology, the places they occupy in the occupational order, and the institutions from which they received their training, see Abbott L. Ferris, "Sociological Manpower," *American Sociological Review*, 29, no. 1 (February, 1964): 103–114; and Elbridge Sibley, *The Education of Sociologists in the United States* (New York: Russell Sage Foundation, 1963), pp. 63–77. The first of the most significant of the findings was the continued hold the major educational centers had on the granting of higher degrees. Only five schools, for example, averaged five or more doctorates between the years 1950–1962. On the other hand, there is an encouraging tendency toward diversification, since at least thirty-five universities now have major graduate training leading to the doctorate in sociology. The second impressive fact is that students receiving baccalaureate degrees in sociology is twelve times higher than those receiving master's degrees; while in turn, there are three times as many receiving master's as receive doctorates. The fact is, therefore, that the design of even graduate education must become increasingly sensitive to the fact that the M.A. is rapidly becoming the terminal degree, and that training in sociology must begin to reflect this by a special emphasis on the needs of the M.A. student per se, and not just, as is now largely the case, view the M.A. as a "stepping stone" on the way toward receiving the Ph.D.

3. For pointing out to me this neat division between terrestrial rewards and the rewards of immortality, I am indebted to my colleague Alvin W. Gouldner.

professional counsel even though they may not always "know truth" at its most esoteric or creative levels. To this must be added the novices-in-residence, the large body of graduate "majors" in sociology, who, while intimately aware of the rights and obligations of lords, bishops, and guardians to their dominion, definitely feel that the actual "period of adjustment" from novice to the running of an independent parish or garrison is one of painful but necessary adjustment to a world defined by superordination and subordination. This period of adjustment depends on factors more subtle and complex than fulfillment of the formal requirements for an advanced degree. It is also expected that the novice learn the habits, manners, idiosyncracies, and expectations of the profession in general and the professors in particular. Indeed, a measure of student sophistication is how well he knows the men behind the sacred books, no less than their contents. In this process, the classroom, the corridor, and the bureau fuse—into the sociological Establishment as such.[4]

Interesting as this interior structure of sociology may be, and however fascinating the organization of the sociological profession, from an education point of view their numbers would doom the sociologists to insignificance. Nonetheless numbers do not uniquely determine importance. If they did, China would rule the earth, and economists would rule the social science roost. The actual publics of sociology are wide and varied. There are thousands of business and commercial firms who use, by either directly hiring sociologists or using sociological information, the findings of sociology. There are the allied professionals in the academic world, such as the political scientists of the avant-garde type and the behavioral psychologists, who are organically plugged into sociological activities. There are, in addition, architects who design urban renewal programs with sociological admonitions and cajolings in mind. There are political hopefuls who either throw their hat in the ring or throw the hats of others in the ring depending on the findings of the sociology of public opinion; there are television programs that are either maintained or discarded on the basis of mass communications research findings. There are social reformers who urge either mass contraceptive devices or mass fertility rites depending on what the demographers and developmental sociologists say. It is clear, then, that a public exists for sociological information. It is a commodity for sale no less than an established body of knowledge.[5]

The biggest audience of all is the student population. The introductory course in sociology—of either a semester or a year's duration—has become the basic commodity for sale. The packing of this product is usually in the form of the textbook, and the personality rendering the mysteries of the Book meaningful is the teacher of sociology. And behind both text and teacher stands the aforementioned princes and priests, the coercers and the anointers. Thus one can see

4. See Irving Louis Horowitz, "Establishment Sociology: The Value of Being Value-Free," *Inquiry: Journal of Interdisciplinary Research*, 6, no. 1 (Spring, 1963): 129–140.

5. See Hans L. Zetterberg, *Social Theory and Social Practice* (New York: Bedminster Press, 1962), esp. pp. 47–73.

that, although the teachers and researchers of sociology have received the attention, it is the learners of sociology who are the Great Underwriters of the social system called Sociology. While there is undoubtedly increasing interest among sociologists in the "methods of teaching," the great debates are still reserved for the content of sociology—for the character of the learning process and not for the nature of the teaching process. And this is as it should be. Otherwise, sociology would be bare bones and not the brawling, battling—but, above all, living—entity it is.

Just as the feudal world exhibited a struggle between the King's Two Bodies, so does the sociological world exhibit a conflict that ramifies and permeates the learning of sociology at every level. In its simplest form it is a struggle between those who see sociology as a discipline with the task of enlightening its publics, orienting its policy-makers, knocking over established pictures of the world, and in general infusing (or infecting) the learning of sociology with the critical humanistic spirit. On the other side stand the sociologists infused with a natural-science image of sociology, with an attitude of building upon established data rather than bowling over sociological deities, and with a stress on team effort, testable hypotheses, and quantitative analysis.[6] Elsewhere I have dealt with this in terms of the competing sociological ideologies of disciplinarianism and professionalism.[7] For our purposes it is sufficient to note that this division exists at every level of sociological performance and, no less, exists within any sociologist worth his salt.

We must be careful not to reify or polarize the interior problems of sociology in the Germanic way. The issue is one of tendencies in one direction or another, and not of flat choice of one style over and against another. Nonetheless, it must be frankly stated that the existence of these alternative modalities, while fertilizing and vivifying the domains of sociology, has placed the learner of sociology in a condition of cognitive dissonance—since in any one text, or by any one teacher, he may be taught that sociology is clarificatory and manipulative, is value-free yet permeated with value guides, is a discipline established by great men in the "classic" tradition, and a profession made by great schools and bureaus in the "modern" organizational tradition. The first major phenomenon which must be noted, then, is that to learn sociology, to learn it truly, is to understand the dialectic, the polarities, the controversies that define sociology at any given point.[8]

We can perceive the difference between the teaching and the learning of

6. Compare and contrast two recently prepared compendiums on the matter of sociology: Llewellyn Gross, ed., *Symposium on Sociological Theory* (Evanston, Ill.: Row, Peterson & Co., 1959); and Robert K. Merton, Leonard Broom, Leonard Cottrell, Jr., eds., *Sociology Today* (New York: Basic Books, 1959).

7. Irving L. Horowitz, "Disciplinarians and Professionals: Two Styles of Sociological Performance," *Philosophy of Science*, 31, no. 3 (July, 1964). See Ch. 14 of this book.

8. See Alvin W. Gouldner, "Anti-Minotaur: The Myth of a Value Free Sociology," *Social Problems*, 9, no. 3 (Winter, 1962): 199–213.

sociology. One can teach sociology as the story of some great books or some important figures, or one can teach sociology from a laboratory manual, mechanically modeled on a physics manual. In the former case, one can be infused with the heroes and legends of sociology, with the Platonic "noble lie," but never learn sociology. While in the latter case, one can come through a sociology class with the feeling that by hiding behind a lamp post (like the manual says) and observing the number of drivers who break the full stop sign (like the manual says), one can fully know the meaning of social deviance (like the manual says). But the ignoble truth is really in no way superior, and in many ways inferior, to the noble lie. I submit that in neither case does one learn what sociology is about. The assumption that sociology is an Imperium is itself thoroughly antisociological in its predilections and predispositions. Each false alternative is fraught with its paradox. If sociology is its collective heroes, why study the subject in a conceptually organized way? Why not simply read the writings of the greats? Obviously, to read the classics is not to confront the world directly, nor indeed to create new classics. There would be no need for learning sociology in an organized or systematic way. If sociology is a set of tautologies derived from manuals in guided observation, what is there left to teach? Simply turn over the podium to the laboratory assistant, and run through the formulas. The fetishism for "hard" data would result in absolute frustration. Jacques Barzun relates a story of the Ph.D. candidate who was being plagued at his oral examination by picayune criticism of his footnotes. He finally burst out with the following: "I did not discover America, I took it secondhand from Christopher Columbus."[9] Thus, in the very attempt to bypass the main fact that the learning of sociology is the master key to the whole business of knowing sociology, that it is the common link between the recruit to sociology and the emeritus professor of sociology, the floodgates to sociological self-annihilation are opened wide. For without the need to explain how and why people learn sociology, there is little need to teach sociology.

The irony of the present state of sociology is perhaps best revealed in a recent "reader" for the elementary course. In the first essay, on "the nature of sociology," the author offers a "political" typology of misanthropic social scientists—including "believers in absolute good," "reformer—evangelists," competitive power-type, traditionalists, humanists, rationalists.[10] We learn something about the antisociologist, but little about the sociologist or the nature of his belief system. But the very last essay in the same reader maintains that "To Be a Sociologist" is by no means incompatible with different life styles, political visions, and intellectual commitments. In answer to the question "What is a sociologist?" the author points out that it is a concern with human groups, "their

9. Jacques Barzun, *Teacher in America* (Garden City, N.Y.: Doubleday Anchor Books, 1959), p. 35.

10. Alfred deGrazia, "The Hatred of New Social Science," in *Perspectives on the Social Order: Readings in Sociology*, ed. by H. Laurence Ross (New York: McGraw-Hill Book Co., 1963), pp. 6–13.

statuses and roles, and the ways in which the patterns of interaction between or among them in any society or societies are transmitted, modified, or revolutionized."[11] This illustrates the fact that in science, and particularly in so sensitive a science as sociology, it is extremely dangerous to behave as a screamer—a *Gewaltmensch*—to rule out or to shout down the rest of the human race as "misosocioscientists." Sociologists have made serious blunders and mistakes— because of underenthusiasm and blandness no less than in consequence of passionate embraces of the prejudices of the moment.

The learning and teaching of sociology will be modified in many directions in years to come. Fashions and fads will change. Exact findings will replace old biases; new problems will compel intellectual realignments. New faces will create new hero images. New institutions will transform such images into schools. But just as long as the creative tension between teaching and learning sociology is maintained, just as long as the sociologist as scientist is not sundered from the sociologist as a human being by academic Gauleiters, the field of sociology can be counted upon to make itself steadily and increasingly felt within the interstices, no less than upon the total structure, that constitute formal education in America.

II

The originating basis and ultimate purpose of sociology, as of any other scientific discipline, is the formation of intelligent publics who are in a position to utilize that which they have learned and, as a matter of fact, who define the learning process precisely as the utilization and central sifting of information. The mind rejects the useless and resists absorption of the doubtful. Hence the purpose of learning sociology is the transformation of unformed and uninformed men into decision-making creative persons. In short, to transform a passive "mass" into an active "public."[12] Therefore, sociology, like any other science, serves as an antidote to emotive extremes of cynicism about the prospects of the social future and to equally unwarranted naive optimism, which is oftentimes the product of social environments that have rarely experienced defeat or suffering on a mass scale.

The dissemination of sociological finding has become a serious and full-scale matter in the United States. The fact that a huge audience exists for such books as William H. Whyte's *The Organization Man*; David Riesman's *The Lonely Crowd*; Michael Harrington's *The Other America*; C. Wright Mills' *The Power Elite*; and E. Franklin Frazier's *Black Bourgeoisie* (among others) is an indication that sociology has come of age as a public source of legitimacy. We determine biology's coming of age, not only with the findings of Charles Darwin, but with the ability of a wide audience to absorb the generalizations of T. H.

11. Janice Harris Hopper, "To Be a Sociologist," in *Perspectives on the Social Order*, pp. 452–465.

12. See C. Wright Mills, "Mass Society and Liberal Education," in *Power, Politics, and People*, ed. by Irving L. Horowitz (New York and London: Oxford University Press, 1963), pp. 353–373.

Huxley; and physics' coming of age not so much with the ability of Einstein to introduce a new concept of space, but rather with the capacity of Gamow and Giedeon to translate this fourth dimensionality into a style of art and architecture, and a style of life generally. What I am suggesting, therefore, is that every index points to sociology's having come of age, but that, unlike either biology or physics, the growing pains of sociology seem to remain in full force—in part, because the learning of sociology is arbitrarily delayed four years after the learning of physics and biology.

To a considerable extent, the retardation factor is a consequence of the lack of widespread understanding of sociology as a science on the part of educationists. And I am not here referring simply to the fact that books labeled "society and education" rarely make use of sociological findings, but to the broad-scale neglect of sociology by the policy-planners of secondary education. It remains a fact that, except in wildly experimental high schools, sociology is introduced into the curriculum only at the college level—despite the fact that high school students "talk sociology" in their everyday lives. Such phrases as "clique formations," "status groups," "role playing," and "influentials" are part of the common vernacular—but it remains an unstructured vocabularly because of the absence of the organized study of sociology in the American high school system.[13] Thus, in discussing the formal education of sociologists, it might be wise to begin with an "ideal type" model of how sociology can be made part of the growing-up educative process.[14]

It might well be asked: if the study of social problems is such a natural part of the growing-up process, and hence a natural part of any decent high school curriculum, why is there no concerted effort in this direction? Several answers suggest themselves: the general absence of a problem-solving orientation in the high school curriculum; the middle-class orientation of high-school planners who lack any profound orientation toward the special problems of the poor and the minorities; and the general issue of who is to define the main social problems —the city administrators of high schools? the principals of the school systems? the teachers of social sciences? the students? In short, a social problems approach organically introduces the issue of the teacher as social critic. Nonetheless, this problem is neither unique nor insurmountable, since the same line of objections can be raised about what should go into the teaching of American history or world literature in high schools. There is a much wider consensus on what the main social problems are than we are willing to admit in the midst of theoretical

13. See C. Wayne Gordon, *The Social System of the High School: A Study in the Sociology of Adolescence* (Glencoe, Ill.: Free Press, 1957).

14. For two excellent case studies of the discrepancies in high school programs between self and society, ascribed and achieved status, work and leisure values, etc.—all fundamental problems for the high school community, no less than for sociology—see Dorothy Lee, "Discrepancies in the Teaching of American Culture," in *Education and Culture*, ed. by George D. Spindler (New York: Holt, Rinehart & Winston, 1963), pp. 173–191; and Jules Henry, *Culture Against Man* (New York: Random House, 1963), esp. pp. 147–282.

disputation[15]—poverty in an age of affluence, many poor nations dominated by a select few rich nations, inequality in a tradition of equality, elite policy-making in a structure of democratic norms. Seen in this light, the objections to the teaching of social problems in high schools often come down to inhibitions about social problems as such, as well as a fear that this or that pressure group would find classroom discussion of a social problem objectionable. The fact of the matter is that such an argument rests on conjurers' tricks. The long-standing myth that Roman Catholics would find the teaching of human hygiene objectionable was dispelled only when such courses were introduced into the curriculum—as part of physical education. I venture to say that a similar outcome awaits the introduction of a social problems curriculum in the American high school system.

A one- or two-year program could be designed around the master social problems of the modern period. Now that technology has come to displace theology as an ideological style, no less than as a functional fact, social problems can be considered a part of what is within the dominion of young people to correct. The social problems approach is rich with possibilities; a model type of curriculum might contain the following:

1. The problems occasioned by the changes in social ties and obligations, which have been dichotomized alternately as traditionalist-rationalistic, particularistic-universalistic, rural-urban, etc.

Example: How do the transitions in life-styles affect family obligations, community links, national loyalties?

2. The problems that arise in a society defined by achievement instead of ascription, education rather than birth, occupation rather than inherited rank.

Example: What does this do to the youngsters with parents who have "arrived?" What is the relation between socially defined achievement and personally defined satisfaction?

3. The problem of the transition of American society from an agricultural society to an industrial society.

Example: What is the effect of mass production techniques on cultural tastes, choice of mates, style of living?

4. The problem of racial and religious minorities in adjusting and being adjusted to.

Example: Who defines color and religion? Why, if men are biologically equally endowed, are some socially deprived? What can be done to insure greater opportunities for mobility?

5. The problems of mass culture. How tastes are formed; individuality in mass society; the psychological effects on patterns of living of such technological innovations as television, radio, films, phonographs, etc.

15. See on this, Leonard Reissman, "Social Structure and Social Problems: Issues and Perspectives," paper delivered at a plenary session of the Society for the Study of Social Problems, Los Angeles, August, 1963 (mimeograph).

Example: What are cultural "standards"? How is the "generational problem" or the "class problem" reflected in sharp cleavages of tastes?

6. The problem of institutional bureaucratization and the professionalization of work; what happens to classic distinctions of economic class, classic ties to the work environment, etc.?

Example: How does automation affect the behavior of employees toward employers?

7. The problem of social organization: the place of a nation in a world of competing nationalisms, disorganization at various levels—delinquency, homicide, and warfare.

Example: How does the fear of war transmit itself into early marriages, sexual experimentations, marital instability, etc.?

8. The problems involved in marriage and child rearing: the nature of romantic love, its sociohistoric origins; class differentials in married life; the special problems of the student-father and the student-mother; planned parenthood schemes; religious and ethnic factors in marriage and divorce.

Example: Given the increasing propensity of people to become engaged and to marry at young ages, either in high school or just after graduation, what are the social problems which arise from the need to make a living and the short-run absence of monetary gains in continuing education? What are some solutions postulated?

The fact that so much of this is fairly obvious to professionals should not obscure the point that for a high school student, a study of contemporary life through the prism of social problems gives him a sense of how society changes, how it hangs together, and how changes in one part may effect changes in other parts of society; who is in charge of changing and maintaining a society, etc. It has the additional value of making the study of such disciplines as history and economics, which are now a disconnected part of the "social studies" curriculum, more meaningful—a part of the general shared learning process for which all citizens are responsible.

To carry out such a program means the abandonment of many features that have become standard operating high school procedure, such as mindless "crash programs" in area studies, communism, democracy, etc. It may also entail the abandonment of history courses as such; that is to say, their absorption into a social problems focus. The historical backgrounds to social problems would be made an intimate part of the sociological workload. Undoubtedly this program would meet with stony silence from those engaged in preparing history courses, but such fears are groundless. To speak of history as such is meaningless—there is the history of things, of people, of institutions, of ideas—and the history of society. Such a program would therefore not displace history so much as vitalize what is now a program in chronological recitation and sterile repetitions of ethnocentric verities.

Sociologists have the organizational chore of giving high status value to the teaching of sociology in high schools. At least at first, this would mean the activation of some of the very best sociologists in such programs. School administrators would have to take a less jaundiced view of their teachers taking an interest in research and writing activities even at the expense of immediate student needs. Boards of education would have to offer sociology instructors salaries that are competitive (and then some), much the way they are now compelled to recruit language teachers. Parent-teacher associations must encourage academic experimentation and potentially volatile ideas. This is a tall order, requiring the sort of meshing of organizational gears that is thus far notable for its absence.

As long as the present methodological muddle remains, the title "social studies" remains a truer description of the situation than the words "social science." On the other hand, the introduction of sociology as the study of social problems would necessitate a recognition of the social *sciences* as something much more intimately connected with the learning process in general, and with the needs of a technological society in particular. At present, there is a dichotomy between the learning about society that every high school student must engage in (if for no other reason than to survive the social structure of the high school community) and the teaching about society as a set of objective recorded facts.

III

In moving from the high schools to a discussion of sociology in colleges, we move from the realm of conjecture and projection to something more substantial. Indeed, few of the sociologists who are now preeminent did not have their initial ordeal by intellectual fire in the undergraduate centers of America.[16] Europe may have had its great sociologists and its great *universities*, but sociology in Europe remained (and continues to remain in nations as advanced as Italy and France) a marginal form of employment. In great measure this is because they have lacked what the United States has provided in abundance—the great *colleges*. Not that the American colleges opened their doors and their hearts to sociology without considerable procrastination and trepidation. Considerations of religious affiliation and sometimes sheer political and ideological backwardness oftentimes impeded the professional and administrative acceptance of sociology as a legitimate scientific discipline worthy of consideration in the college core curriculum. Nonetheless, in comparison with the hardships that European sociologists endured during the formative period of sociology, the American college provided sociologists with the necessary relief from economic pressures that allowed them to prepare the ground for its empirical researches.[17]

The American college is, in the main, defined and circumscribed by the

16. See Research Division, National Education Association, *Teacher Supply and Demand in Universities, Colleges, and Junior Colleges, 1959–60 and 1960–61* (Washington, D.C.: National Educational Association of the United States, May, 1961), pp. 41–56.

17. See Howard Becker and Harry Elmer Barnes, *Social Thought from Lore to Science: Sociological Trends Throughout the World* (Washington, D.C.: Harren Press, 1952), vol. II.

phrase "liberal arts." It has as its fundamental purpose the enlightenment of the whole person, and seeks to provide intellectual and ethical preparation for worldly enterprise. This factor, more than any other, has continued to define the limits as well as the contents of the learning and teaching of sociology at the college level. Graduate schools increasingly have become professionalized and specialized. They have come to view the content of sociology in terms of strict models of verification rather than as general education. Perhaps this is as it should be. But there has to be some place where the content of the field at any given time is integrated as fully as it can be in order to be displayed as attractively and as usefully as possible. At the liberal arts college the contents and perspective of sociology should be, and often are, made relevant to the cultural sensitivities and historical background which the student is acquiring.

Sociologists are quite conscious of their tasks as innovators, if for no other reason than that the long uphill battle for acceptance and legitimation has compelled innovation. But the "low status" of the sociology of education, combined with the widespread growth of "bureaucratic" sociology after World War II, threatens to blunt sensitivity to the needs of the liberal arts college in relation to sociology. The impact of sociology will be prevented from full realization if new lines of advance are not carved out with respect to the American colleges. There are only 20 major graduate centers of sociology in the United States, but there are 2,000 colleges where sociology courses are taught.

Sociologists have to think through how sociology ought to look in the undergraduate colleges: the kinds of texts and course materials actually employed in the teaching process, possibilities for small-scale research, the kinds of personnel recommended by university chairmen for college-level positions. This must be done not simply because of a desire to influence what comes to be known as sociology over the next several decades, but because by directly influencing the shape of undergraduate teaching, sociologists can, within a relatively brief period, improve the quality of students who continue their studies at graduate centers—not to mention raising the level of receptivity and appreciation for sociological performance among the community and business leaders.

At the liberal arts colleges, sociologists are in the fortunate position of being able to exploit a rising general interest in innovation. Most college sociology staffs are still small, and hence new appointments can be made in line with new ideas on curriculum. Innovation is easier to accomplish at the college level than at postgraduate centers, where a considerable amount of formalization has set in. There is also a decent balance between departmental autonomy and the college administration at the better colleges; particularly as the "cash value" of sociological research begins to filter through administrative domes. At the liberal arts college, there is additional "natural" advantage that is all too rarely appreciated: allied social sciences feel kinship ties with sociology, rather than the animus often characteristic at graduate centers. Finally, it must be recorded that the students at the liberal arts colleges are as good as, if not better than, the undergraduate students found in attendance at the major university centers. A basic appeal of the liberal arts college is necessarily a high threshold of innovation and experimentation. This gives the sociologist much greater latitude with his students than he might be in a position to exercise at a university center which is self-conscious of its functional roles and ideological position in the sociological firmaments.

The most single important question that can be asked about any educational endeavor is that suggested by James: What kind of a man do you expect to turn out?[18] The liberal arts college differs from other educational efforts in that it is designed to do something to and for the "whole man" and not merely to his capacity to play a more or less specific occupational role. The ideal has been stated in many ways: the fully rounded man, the man capable of continuous rejuvenation through learning, the person capable of self-cultivation, the alert citizen, etc. The matter can be ideally stated as follows: the colleges are charged with turning out a person and not a product—someone who in his every activity employs the basic habits of intellectual workmanship. This means that the "good" college graduate comes to experience things and people not as a passive receiver, but as someone capable of linking experience with a conscious tradition of ideas and ideals. When this "ideal" undergraduate comes upon a problem in his vocational performance or in his personal affairs, he knows how to operationalize it as an answerable issue; he also knows where to go for help and information. The liberal arts graduate is entitled to receive cultural and historical background to evaluate what is taking place. More important, he needs the knowledge to keep finding out what is going on—to pursue a problem to its resolution. The liberal arts college at its best provides an individual with a perspective and a life-technique of reflection.

The liberal arts college stands in contrast to the vocational institute which is concerned exclusively with the capacity of the student to fulfill, with the necessary skill, a given type of occupational role. In ideal at least, the professional school is an attempted synthesis of the two at a more advanced level of training.

The sociology taught at the liberal arts colleges must serve the ends of pre-professional training, no less than of liberal arts programming, if for no other reason than the growing percentage of college students who go on to post-graduate work in the social sciences. What is the role of sociology in this pre-professional training? It scarcely suffices to recite slogans of how important it is for students to be alerted to the social world they live in and made aware of the available traditions within it that seem appropriate.

Sociology at the liberal arts institution should focus upon an understanding of the organizations and work habitat in which professionals work, and upon the social and psychological implications of the role they are called upon to play. Sociologists should provide students with the consciousness of both their special tradition and the moral obligations they will be called upon to exercise. This should be done not so much to orient students in their future professional

---

18. William James, "Democracy and the College-Bred," in *The Intellectuals: A Controversial Portrait*, ed. by George B. de Huszar (Glencoe, Ill.: Free Press, 1960), pp. 285–289.

capacities as to show them what is entailed in the practice of professions in modern society. Pedagogically, the task is to seize upon a students' pecuniary interest in the professions and provide him with a full-scale view of the sociology of the professional persons and their institutions. This is a somewhat different meaning than that conventionally attached to the concept of "preprofessional" training. And given the fact that the liberal arts department of sociology has a manifest or latent proselytizing function—that is, to make converts to the faith out of intellectual heathens—one of the most useful and least applied approaches would be to provide an adequate curriculum focused on the meaning of the professions.

One major source for cross-fertilization of social ideas and for recruitment of students as "majors" in sociology is the "common course" or the "core course" in social science. In such courses, the student often becomes acquainted with the historic institutions and ideas of Western civilization, and further becomes aware of persistent contemporary problems, primarily the economic and political issues of our time. Too frequently, sociology offerings are arranged without serious scrutiny and close reference to htis basic set of courses. The education of the budding sociologist might be accelerated by viewing these core programs in social science and Western civilization as a testing ground for sociological perspectives in relation to other social science perspectives.

There are major areas left untouched by this core programming. Within the aims of the liberal arts college, these might be fulfilled by sociology; or if they are already filled in part, they should be elaborated, and can be so elaborated, by an adequately integrated sociology curriculum. These untouched or partially examined areas are of such a character as to permit the connections of sociology to social life to be made much plainer. They are also areas which not only make sense in their own terms, within the general aims of college life, but which are very much open as links to other social sciences in the total college offering. Sociology courses ought to be integrative in their effect with respect to the functioning of the college as such.

Let me briefly indicate what some of these themes and areas might involve:

The Professions

As has been pointed out, a liberal arts college offers an integrative and terminal formal education, but along with this function it is increasingly a center of preprofessional training. It would therefore be the better part of wisdom to seize upon this interest and generalize the student's understanding of what it involves sociologically. Instructors should attempt to provide students with the tools, conceptions, and perspectives with which to work out an orientation and understanding of modern society from the standpoint of the professional role he is going to play in that society. The student should receive a rounded and full description of the social conditions of the major professions, and he should get an imaginative view of other institutions from a standpoint from which he is likely to encounter them in the course of a professional career.

Comparative Social Structures

College survey courses are too often wholly concerned with *Western* civilization.

They pay little or no attention to Latin American, African, or Eastern cultures. They should concern themselves explicitly with those areas affording a sharp comparison with our own cultural tradition. A first step in this direction would be a sociology offering of one full year, in the junior year, of comparative developmental institutions. This kind of a basic course might or might not be worked out in collaboration with other departments, notably economics, political science, history, anthropology, or even modern foreign languages. At the larger colleges, the process of social development might be elaborated by detailed courses in given nations. Such questions cannot be gone into in detail because they depend upon such intangibles as staff interest and collaborative modalities of work. A starter, however, is to inaugurate one such basic course in the area of social development.

Cultural and Psychological Implications of Modern Society

A great portion of the best current work in sociological research and theory is in the area of social psychology. Through this literature, the student can best work out a model of personality and social structure. This area of sociology has the added feature of being immensely attractive, for it leads directly into student reflection and self-reflection—something not to be frowned upon so much as channelized. Apart from a basic course in social psychology, there ought to be specialties in the mass media and aspects of popular culture. The aim of the study of mass media and aspects of popular culture in the liberal arts college is quite different from its aim in a research center. In the liberal arts curriculum it must raise, as an explicit problem, the question of values. The sociology department ought to turn out a man who, after taking such a specialty, can never see a motion picture without enjoying it—not merely at a consumer level, but as an observer of the structure and technique of the cultural commodity and its meaning for his enjoyment. What is the good of exposing a student to "literature" for years and then turning him loose in a world of "mass culture," if he has not considered fully and in detail the scale of sociological differences between the two? By raising such questions and making very clear the differences in the functions of the two in self-development, sensitivities, and enjoyment, standards of taste and habits of self-cultivation can be inculcated.

American Society

Many texts in sociology take data exclusively from the United States, mixed with a few random illustrations from preliterate societies. This is mistaken and pedagogically inept. If sociology is going to deal so extensively with American materials, it should raise the major questions squarely: What is the social character of this society? What kind of class and status structure underwrites this society? How does it work out for the predominant types of people enacting it? The sociology of American society could take the fragmentary fields of the family, the city, and the community, with the rest of the "group" courses that now are standard offerings, and knit them together into a full-length statement of the American social structure. The offering of courses in the American family, urban communities, etc., are useless unless they tally up to a general perspective.

And the average American college is in such a marginal financial state that it would be foolish to teach such specialties before basic sociological courses are well developed and properly staffed.

One must be wary to develop these areas in more detail or to elaborate their implications for the liberal arts college offerings as a whole. Course programming can only be done in connection with a specific staff in mind, and with forethought to the stated objectives of a college. Nonetheless, one must avoid being evasive or coy. Hence, the following course design should be taken as my own views on the matter of junior and senior level courses, not as a *diktat* or mandatory operational procedure.

An adequate upper-level liberal arts curriculum in sociology might be divided into three divisions.

I. Courses of a general nature, which deepen knowledge of man and society. These are especially recommended to students who are minoring in sociology and therefore have only limited time or interest. (1) Social-historical Change (with special attention to theories of history: de Tocqueville, St. Simon, Toynbee, Spengler, Marx, Weber, etc.). (2) Comparative Sociology (world demographic information, revolutionary movements, industrialization and urbanization, etc.).

II. Courses specialized according to subject area. Each of these is to be handled with attention to the range of comparative and historical institutions. Any one of these "areas," of course, might be split into more than one course. The idea is that it is better to present a wide range of courses rather than a heavy dosage in any single field—as might be expected or even desirable at the graduate level. (1) War and Military Institutions, (2) Sociology of Religious Institutions, (3) The Kinship Order, (4) Sociology of Political Life, (5) The Social Contexts of Economic Institutions, (6) Educational Institutions, (7) Mass Communications and the Public, (8) The Sociology of Cultural Life and Its Products (including popular and fine arts).

III. Seminars requiring independent research. These would be arranged according to the interests of the staff and the talents of the student. The main problem is to have independent research carefully (and this means modestly) structured to produce meaningful results. Research should open up the thrill of discovery, and not simply be an extended or amorphous "paper."

Of the courses which are usually offered, but which I personally find to be rarely appropriate for undergraduates, I would mention Methodology, History of Sociology, and General Sociological Theory. These properly belong in first-year graduate programming. Such courses might be made available to seniors going on to graduate school. But this is the minimum problem, and not, as it is so often pictured, the big problem.

What makes the entire programming "go" or not is the sociologist with a total commitment: who knows how to learn, no less than to teach; who develops a style of work that is sensitive to the sociology of college administration no less than to the administration of sociologists The college teacher cannot forget that he is engaged in a competition for the minds of men and women who *count*. He has no "captives," only interested and interesting people. Insularity from practical problems, arrogance in the conduct of his classes, mechanical work patterns—all count very heavily against the college teacher. Therefore, a "bad" teacher who is perhaps a "good" sociologist can be a serious misanthrope at this kind of work. And it would be well for sociologists to increase their concern with general educational problems, lest they attribute a lack of studied interest in sociology to the difficulties of the field rather than to the clumsiness of the personal performance.

But the deeper we move into such problems as staffing and orientation, the more we must examine the graduate school programs of sociology.

IV

Everyone seems to agree that graduate training in sociology means professional training. The problem inheres in the word "professional." Is professional training defined by the details, or is it defined by the proportions, the form, the style, and the quality beyond the accumulation of information? Does "professional" imply a level of knowledge or a level of technical competence? Does "professional" imply the ability to teach the subject matter of sociology, or to engage in independent sociological investigations? Plainly, these are not mutually exclusive conditions. The ideal would be to achieve a fusion of the polar elements. But invariably, there will be a "tilt" in the "mix," which is to say that no fusion will ever be quite a harmonious synthesis of opposing elements. A graduate department will lean in one direction or the other. Graduate students must thus learn not only the subject matter of the discipline, but also just what the "tilt" is in the sociological mix. And given the propensity for intolerance that any proud group of sociologists must necessarily possess, it would be injudicious of a graduate student to dismiss out of hand such psychological factors in the composition of the sociological higher learning.

Instead of offering a plea for tolerance and mutual understanding, which often is rhetoric untranslated into departmental practice, it might be wiser to first isolate those factors common to entering graduate students which make (and sometimes break) graduate departments of sociology. Among some of the central problems that have arisen in graduate education are those which are a consequence of growth as such. If we take as axiomatic the rapid expansion of sociology, it is almost inevitable that we would face the rapid multiplication of problems.

At the level of graduate student activities we might mention the following factors: (1) The graduate student of sociology is but rarely a passionate devotee of knowledge. More often than not he has a general but unstructured interest in sociology which becomes crystallized only to the degree that he becomes plugged into a monetary system of rewards; that is, insofar as he is part of the "granting" mechanism through which his department becomes a large-scale operation. If we can speak of "hard money" and "soft money" aspects of graduate sociology departments, we can also speak of "hard" students and "soft" students—those who would be quickly pared away if appropriate funds were not available (or if a "spillover" from such funds did not exist). This is a dangerous line of criticism insofar as the graduate student is in fact being acculturated to the process of professionalization. What probably needs more sober investigation is this process of professionalization, of living the life of facts without passionate dedication instead of learning the facts of life. The by-product of this monetary system of rewards is that research in sociology has a higher status than teaching—an honor system which is in part a consequence of there usually being more funds available in research than in teaching; and also a status derived from the feeling that engaging in research is more specifically sociological than teaching introductory courses.

Because of the unique bipolar structure of funding in graduate sociological education, we find the graduate student tailoring his points of view or trimming his intellectual sails to meet those of his senior professors. This is not done with guile, but simply in consequence of a belief (often false) that employer-employee relationships are the university rule, while professor-student relationships are the exception. This has a manifest dysfunction of subordinating independence of thought and independent research projects in favor of going where the money is, and in mimetically reproducing the research activity of the senior professor.

One astute analyst noted the following properties of the incoming graduate student: (a) a deeply imbedded system of middle-class values; (b) a concept of equality and democracy which tends to be highly ethnocentric; (c) an atomistic view of the world as carved into discrete parts; (d) a psychological view of the learning process, *i.e.*, self-understanding rather than systematic thinking; (e) little training in research procedures and even less capacity to engage in systematic criticism.[19] Before we engage in the great game of allocating blame, it should be appreciated that this set of guideposts is common to society and to college society as well. We have spent such a great amount of educational effort in outfitting the college student for social life that his tendency is to "work the system," to forget that the process of learning is considerably different from the process of making a living. The fact that many features of graduate training, especially in sociology, approximate a "profane" bureaucratic business and not a "sacred" institute of higher learning only reinforces the degenerative features in the ideology of the graduate student.

The worst consequence of this is that in the very process of "cooling the mark out" the graduate student who learns to manipulate the situation at the same time slowly loses a sense of purpose in going to graduate school. The high rate of attrition in most graduate departments of sociology bears little resemblance to the quality of the student. The drop-outs stand as a constant reminder not only of student dilemmas, but more profoundly of the dilemmas of their professors and administrators.[20]

19. See Solon T. Kimball, "Teaching Anthropology in Professional Education," in Mandelbaum, Lasker, and Albert, *The Teaching of Anthropology*, p. 496.

20. See Theodore Solotaroff, "The Graduate Student: A Profile," *Commentary*, 32 (1961): 482–490.

One major administrative step to correct the imbalance between learning and research would be efforts to increase "hard money" in relation to "soft money." While this is now common practice in establishing professorial "lines," the same cannot be said of the young researcher or graduate assistant. There must be a university-wide demand that agency funding be in some part "nondirective." This would enable a university and its department of sociology to increase the amounts of monies available for unattached scholarship and the amounts put aside for teaching assistantships. This would have the further effect of upgrading teaching assistantships financially and ideologically—to place teaching sociology on a par with research activities for the graduate student. While no university can any longer reach maximum efficiency and strength without the resources of the big government agencies and private foundations, it is just as true that no university *qua* university can survive as an independent (and sometimes even inefficient) organization that is thoroughly dependent on the circumscribed needs and requirements of such big public and private foundations.[21] The student could then be exhorted to consider that to be a sociologist means considerably more than meeting formal requirements or gaining an appreciation of methodological devices. One could then emphasize immediate occupational roles no less than promissory-note long-range professional goals.

As for the professorial side of this same coin, perhaps the most serious problem is the inadvertent, but no less exacting, exploitation of student labor; first, in the form of wage differentials for teaching and research; second, in the form of unrecognized assistance on research projects; and third, in the narrowing down of the purposes of advanced sociological training to meet the needs of projects funded for special functions having little interest to the graduate student. The amount of time taken away from studies itself constitutes a potential blow to student degree ambitions and career aspirations. It serves to stretch out graduate training beyond the required number of years; and hence often has an infantilizing effect on graduate students who complete their training period, and an embittering effect on many of those who do not.

This ambiguous situation generates undefined and unstructured rules of progression, since the length of time in training becomes a function of the type of work performed rather than of actual learning requirements. Admittedly, this is a harsh view to take of graduate sociology training. There can be no doubt that the research experiences achieved, the teaching activities engaged in, the financial security offered, etc., are themselves highly educational and instructive in the performance of professional obligations. But this does not signify nor excuse the widespread use of graduate students for reasons quite extrinsic to the educational process. At the least, the present "soft money" situation of graduate programs introduces considerations of judgment that fall outside any legitimate overview

21. For an important memorandum on the relationships between academic departments and federal agencies, see Carnegie Foundation for the Advancement of Teaching, "Twenty-six Campuses and the Federal Government," *The Educational Record*, 44, no. 2 (April, 1963): 95–136.

of a graduate student's capabilities and desires. It creates an unwarranted toleration of the "organization student" and, no less, an unjust harshness toward the "marginal student."

In this network of circumstances, demands for orthodoxy become an implicit part of professorial performance. Since academic orthodoxy is itself often a functional imposition of the research project, it is not viewed as being dictatorial in character. Often the project director is unaware that he is imposing a demand for othodoxy. From the point of view of a project director (who is usually a professor as well) student criticism becomes deviant with respect to the task assigned to him. Thus, instead of a dialectical relationship of ideas, there is a mechanical relationship between people of superordination and subordination in the one area where this is intolerable, the realm of ideas.

It must be mentioned that there is a very dangerous tendency to confuse two distinct and discrete factors in graduate sociology training: professional job placement and the conferring of degrees. Which is to say that sometimes an M.A. or a Ph.D. will be granted not on the basis of the observable merits of the graduate student, but rather in terms of his amenabilities and his attractiveness as a person. The role of style in sociological job-placement often rests on socialization processes which favor conformist students. Since the senior professional staff derives its status at least in part from *where* it sends its graduate trainees, nothing becomes more symbolic of failure in the eyes of a professional staff than granting a higher degree to an unsociable person, to a maverick, or to any deviant from sociological norms. A chain of conformism is established which itself represents a serious violation of the canons of sound sociological work.

One way in which many of these problems can be overcome would be to make graduate training more standardized, to make the "rites of passage" more easily identifiable on the part of the graduate student. The graduate student in sociology needs to know, like his colleagues who enter medicine or law, that the period of his professional training will take a definite number of years and require a definite level of competence, no more and no less. As matters now stand, in the absence of standardization a professional capriciousness takes command, which can only lead to the depletion of the ranks of sociologists and certainly to the depletion of those kinds of students who find it difficult to "cool the mark," "dig the professor," or "work the system."

In addition to the standardization procedure, there has to be a much greater awareness on the part of the administrators and faculty of the differences between candidates for the master's and doctorate degrees.[22] They have to begin to be treated as two kinds of professional training rather than as steps with

22. Apparently the graduate students, at least in one major university, have an awareness of the differences. In a study of student characteristics based on degrees sought, approximately 65 per cent are in search of a M.S., 25 per cent desire to gain a Ph.D., while 10 per cent are aiming at special certificates. See Solon T. Kimball, "Teaching Anthropology in Professional Education," in Mandelbaum, Lasker, and Albert, *The Teaching of Anthropology*, p. 495.

one leading to the other. We must begin to think of the master's as terminal with respect to all sociological occupational roles. Since 40 per cent of the sociologists are now in a nonteaching category, we must begin to ask ourselves the question: "What kind of research student do we want, and what kind of training does he get?" Without laboring the point, one should expect that the master's candidate would, in the main, be plugged into social problems at a more action-oriented level. He should be equipped in terms of specific jobs, such as those available in industrial organization, penology, and gerontology.

The Ph.D. candidate should be viewed in terms of his teaching, not as a minor responsibility, but as a major aspect of his future work orientation. Teaching assistantships should go primarily to those graduate students concerned with teaching as a career, just as the research assistantships should be extended to those who have scholarly efforts as their goal. This is not to deny that the curriculum required for the master's or the doctorate must necessarily remain fluid and flexible. It must respect and be a response to particular vocational interests no less than to specific professional capabilities.[23] A resolution of the M.A. muddle by making it an "occupational" degree, while reserving the Ph.D. as a "professional" degree, by no means represents a perfect solution. Continuities between the master's and the doctorate should be available, as the new Yale educational degrees aim for. Nonetheless, by differentiating the two types of training involved, sociology has much to gain (as the librarians and social workers have found) through satisfactory distinctions between the M.A. and Ph.D. degrees.

Given the widespread difficulties in recapturing the traditional status of teaching sociology, following its displacement by government and business-sponsored research activities, there are two alternatives to the present situation: a completely vocational graduate training orientation; or something far less drastic (but much more satisfactory), the transformation of the research project into a major educational experience. If necessary, a research project could carry

23. One basic factor often overlooked, which could be instrumental in the design of an M.A. sequence that is significantly different from the Ph.D. program, is that many of the masters in sociology go into federal, state, and welfare employment programs. Hence, the M.A. orientation might take as a point of departure the emphasis on the practical aspects of sociology; e.g., urbanism, mental health, criminology, demography, marriage and the family, mass communications; while the Ph.D. could be geared toward the inclusion of this "field approach" to a larger, and perhaps less instrumental, "theory approach." Thus the Ph.D. could lay emphasis on social stratification, political sociology, social structure and social change, the sociology of knowledge, etc. What needs pointing out is that within the shortest possible time, the graduate student along with the graduate faculty (or subcommittee thereof) should determine whether a candidate is equipped for a master's program *or* a doctorate program. They ought not, in short, be viewed simply as "blocks" or "obstacles" to be removed step by step. For quantitative information on nonteaching employment opportunities in sociology, see Nahum Z. Medalia and Ward S. Mason, "Position and Prospects of Sociologists in Federal Employment," *American Sociological Review*, 28, no. 2 (April, 1963): 280–287; and also, "The Non-University Social Scientist: Where He Works and What He Earns," *The American Behavioral Scientist*, 7, no. 6 (February, 1964): 15.

a course description and course credits. It could become a credit-granting system for research assistants. The basic weakness in completely converting research graduate training into vocational training is (a) it would be discontinuous with respect to liberal arts training; (b) it would lead to the further dehumanization of research procedures; and (c) it would create new forms of rifts and jealousies between "researchers" and "teachers." The King's Two Bodies would be sundered, with unintended (and undesirable) consequences sure to follow.

A great deal can be said for using research projects as fundamental laboratories of sociological inquiry. There is already a belief in the need for an infusion of empirical findings into classroom programs; the reverse is no less required—the infusion of classroom values into research activities. Thus far this has been a one-way bridge: while classrooms are in fact increasingly being used for the general presentation of research findings, the research agencies continue to deal with fundamental educational needs in contemptuous terms—as an obstacle to the completion of the research. An advantage of building a two-way bridge would be an increment in the democratization of the learning process in graduate schools. Since research activities are inherently more informal, person-to-person affairs, the structuring of these activities in a classroom atmosphere would also, one can hope, carry over these democratizing properties that go under the name of scientific method. It would impart the status of teaching to the researcher and greatly improve the graduate assistant's opportunity for maintaining or creating a meaningful exchange of views. Such experiments are now being undertaken at the major universities, and their results should prove most interesting for the future reform of graduate education in sociology. In sum, the notion of research "training" and classroom "educating" is a hoary inheritance that sociology would do well to shed at the earliest possible moment, lest the functional differentiation between the two harden into ideological postures with a net balance of destructive consequences for both.

A critical reason for insuring a proper "mix" between classroom and research functions, and, at the larger graduate centers, between departments and bureaus, is the intrinsic weaknesses of "contract sociology"—of sociological activities geared to the needs of a highly selective (and by inference a nonrepresentative) clientele. Lazarsfeld has put the matter forcefully:

There are a number of important problems which are not being studied at all because there just doesn't exist an interested client. Some of the more obvious social evils like juvenile delinquency do find their tie-up with organized research, but how about studying the conditions under which a desirable political candidate wins out over a well-heeled political hack? Who makes studies as to how true participation among workers in factory management could be organized, overcoming resistance of management as well as apathy among workers? What is really known about the victory of manifestly corrupt union leaders in union elections or about the informal relations between businessmen and members of Congress? It has repeatedly been pointed out that applied social research in this country is especially handicapped by our general laissez-faire philosophy. If we had more social planning there would be more opportunity to study its effectiveness and shortcomings.[24]

The maintenance of a strong departmental orientation can insure that the "mix" does not dissolve, for within the classroom interplay between professor and students, "inner-directed" issues can be thrashed out. With the "free" funds that a department has at its disposal, a redress of balance between research and teaching can be achieved. If no such funds exist, then every effort should be made to impress upon donors, clients, foundations (and no less the professorial applicants) the need to structure into grants an "unattached" portion that can be used in any way the department or the university sees fit.

The most serious problem at this end is not the foundations or even the clients, but senior faculty who are "go-getters" with the ability to "squeeze water from a stone." They are like the wealthy taxpayer who decries his tax rate on the grounds that if the poor would work hard, there would be no need for the kind of support presently required. Thus, while sociologists must learn to live with administrative activities, like physicists, they must also instruct their donors and their clients of the *general educational* obligations incurred in granting funds. Hopefully, as the novelty of departmental affluence wears thin, and as *nouveau riche* sociologists become transformed into a sub-branch of the *anciens riches*, a certain "aristocratic" bearing can be made manifest. Instead of personal "empire building," a genuine feeling of departmental solidarity will serve to preserve the autonomy between sociological theory and social research that now threatens to get lost in the financial shuffle.[25]

For a variety of reasons, administrative, organizational, and intellectual, no significant "blueprint" of an ideal graduate program in sociology can be provided. In the first place, classroom activity declines in significance the closer one gets to the dissertation stage in graduate education. Second, a good set of courses depends on the type of personnel available. It is thus not so much the course content but the professorial content that becomes increasingly significant. Third, individual differentiation among senior student ranks becomes pronounced, especially beyond the first year of graduate study. And fourth, the character and structure of the university has a profound effect upon the content of sociological graduate work. If the university has a good medical school, then the possibilities for joint studies are magnified. Similarly, interdepartmental research with law school activities can only take place if such a school exists and is interested in a reciprocal and interdisciplinary efforts. In short, extradepartmental, intradepartmental and interdepartmental orientations are largely defined by the university setting as a whole.

24. Paul F. Lazarsfeld, with the collaboration of Sydney S. Spivack, "Observations on the Organization of Empirical Research in the United States," *Bureau of Applied Social Research* (Reprint No. 351) (New York: Columbia University, December, 1961).

25. See on this, Wilson Record, "Some Reflections on Bureaucratic Trends in Sociological Research," *American Sociological Review*, 25, no. 3 (June, 1960): 411-414.

Rather than belabor organizational and administrative problems, it is necessary to note that however "plugged in" the student is to the double hierarchy of department and bureau, there are certain obligations that the student has toward the faculty and, in turn, obligations that a faculty has toward its students. These might be placed under the general heading: the making of a professional socio-logist. Whatever the heading chosen, the foci are similar: there is a need to develop a mastery of methods, contents, and orientations. The trouble would seem to be not in the failure of sociologists to recognize this division of labor; but rather in their overzealous identification of scientific method with atomic, discrete, "middle-range" research. The character of qualifying examinations, specialized subjects, dissertation topics, all strongly reinforce an atomistic, mechanical vision of sociology.[26]

By common consensus, the most difficult aspect of advanced sociological training seems to be "methods." In part, this is a consequence of the difficulties American students have with quantification procedures, model construction, and multivalued logics. Insofar as this is the case, the problem cannot be con-sidered sociological except in the abstract sense that every human problem is somehow social. But Elbridge Sibley has pointed out some special aspects of the problem of sociological methodology:

The courses in methods required in the first year [of graduate work] are often frustrating to both students and teachers. Comparatively few students find abstract study of tech-niques intrinsically interesting; those who come with the strongest interests in substantive problems are impatient to get down to the business of finding common-sense answers. The instrumental importance of formal methods can be preached, but the preaching falls on deaf ears if it is not paralleled by involvement of the students in research that seems to them significant.[27]

Several major ways are available to minimize the shock of methodology. In the first place, it can be taught in an open-ended way which reveals interesting aspects of methods by pointing out its problematic elements. Different ways of structuring a questionnaire, alternative questionnaire systems as such, probabil-istic and rigorous forms of statistics, the situational resolution of what constitutes an adequate sample, conflicting methodological viewpoints on the nature of theory construction, the role of qualitative analysis in a quantitative study. A second, concomitant way could include acquaintance with the rationale of inquiry. This would include an appreciation of the difference between a fact, an hypothesis, and a problem as such. It could focus on the "uncommon sense" of science and on the philosophy of the social sciences in general.

A vital factor in training sociologists is to connect statistics with substantive

26. See Irving L. Horowitz, *The New Sociology* (New York: Oxford University Press, 1964), pp. 3-48.
27. Elbridge Sibley, *The Education of Sociologists in the United States* (New York: Russell Sage Foundation, 1963), pp. 118-119.

problems at the earliest possible stage in methodology. The use of quantitative information in deciding between alternative and contrasting policy decisions might be one way this could be done. Another might be to "reduce" problems of anomie and alienation to codifiable and operational terms. Yet another might be to place methodology within a framework of political and social decisions that are within the purview of the graduate student. The entire field of war and peace research might be used as a sociological source book—equivalent to the attraction youngsters find in baseball statistics: probabilities of damage, given a certain level of weaponry; simulation techniques providing for anticipatory responses to crisis situations; strategic decision-making based on simple two-person nonzero sum games; dyadic and triadic models of inter-nation conflict.

Whatever the social problem treated, the mathematical materials could be viewed as instrumental, as a means toward getting substantive results. The focus on empirical issues would also enable the student to distinguish between the necessary and the unnecessary aspects of methodology with respect to a particular social problem. Examples of the use of statistics and methods should not become specious, or too distant from the human materials of sociology. There must always be a reality dimension to statistics: first, as a reinforcement of the utility of methodology; and second, to avoid the common feeling that methods in sociology are a necessary exercise in ritual without real applicability. For if such a view comes to be rooted, the consequences might be a disenchantment not simply with methodology, but with sociology as such. And there are enough antisociologists in the country without adding new recruits to their numbers by foolish and mechanical views of statistics as a trial by fire.

The second point concerns the broad contents of graduate training. Here the problem is not one of multiplying course work so much as it is to develop some kind of programming that would take aim at the present-day situation in society. From my own point of view, the extraordinary fact of twentieth-century living is the constant drive towards a technological foundation to society. The processes of industrialization and socialization should therefore become the core of graduate sociological training in complex organizations, the modern bureaucracy, the process of urbanization, changes in the professions, the rise of a scientific intelligentsia, and the growth of a mass cultural apparatus. But these processes have also been accompanied by the rise of new social movements on a class scale, on a national scale, and on a racial scale. Indeed, from an historical point of view, it might well be that the age of nationalism which reached its high point in the eighteenth century came to an end with the class revolutions of 1848; and the class revolutions in turn gave way to revolutions on a continent-wide scale after World War II. The breakdown of social orders, the redistribution of political power, indeed, the cross-over from an economic to a political basis of power—all of these have to find their way into the curriculum.

The present tendency to develop courses on political sociology, on the sociology of knowledge, on social movements, etc., does not hold out the promise of a big-range sociology—of a picture of the situation as it now stands. This is not to say that precise empirical work is not required. It is to say that precise empirical work requires a magnified framework for its elaboration and its inclusion into the general system of knowledge. Thus what is required, in terms of content, is some historical perspective; in particular there has to be a concerted effort to develop a knowledge of the nineteenth century, at least as a background for the rise of industrialism, socialist revolutions, colonialism and anticolonialism, etc. This does not mean a multiplication of courses in history as such. It does mean that the graduate student of sociology must come to consider his area as part of the human sciences, and hence, his technical responsibility as extending beyond departmental corridors.

The vast social changes which have taken place in the twentieth century are reflected in feelings, attitudes, emotions, and values, in what might be called *la sensibilité* or *l'esprit* of a society. Most of the social movements that have arisen in the twentieth century have been efforts to demythologize life and to define freedom in rationalistic terms. This has profoundly affected the nature of modern values. If the nineteenth century searched out religious equivalents to hostility and world conflict, the twentieth century can be measured by the degree to which it seeks out scientific equivalents to the tendency toward conflict. It is not only that religion has been displaced, but that the nature of the religious commitment has increasingly become ethical rather than supernatural. Thus it is that the sociology of religion as a course is intimately bound up with the sociology of mass movements on one side and the sociology of mass communications on the other. And if at the lower levels of the learning process there must be a concerted effort at making the parts specific and clear, at the highest levels there is an obligation for providing some kind of social synthesis. If the task of education is the creation of the whole man, then whatever the level of study, there has to be a whole curriculum. This point might be summed up as the study of modern consciousness as it relates to the study of modern institutions. At the present time, courses in social institutions and courses in social consciousness are much too far apart to provide for a maximum "enrichment" program at the graduate level.

From what has been said about the methods and contents of sociology it is clear that the orientation I am calling for is one in which sociology is not considered only as subject matter, but as a distinctive framework for studying society. Such an orientation allows a graduate student to develop a consciousness of his own role in the teaching of others. Such an orientation would emphasize themes of socialization, group and group pressures, status feelings, motivations, and social constraints in the light of a body of knowledge already accumulated. The graduate student must begin to share the same problems and the same agonies as his professors, in the sense that he ought to become aware of how he as an individual and as a mature member of a professional community forms and receives his values, and how others who differ from him form theirs. He should be able to apply his perspective creatively and at the same time embody the research of other fields. The sociology student who reaches full maturation is in some sense weaned away from sociology as a special field. He learns to look upon his field as not just a beatific thing in itself, but as a style of life, a style of observation, and a style of evaluating everything from literature and law to medicine and government. To become a fully matured sociologist thus means to become sophisticated about the world, for only such a person can assist others, whether in research projects or in teaching roles, to become sophisticated themselves.

Sociology at the graduate level is increasingly involved with cross-disciplinary programs—such as area studies, comparative developmental structures, world conflict and conflict resolution. It is not the job of a graduate department of sociology to abandon its main principles for the sake of "crash programs." It is the job of sociology to make available its data-gathering, model-building, and interpretive techniques for investigations into heretofore neglected nooks and crannies of society. Sociology must surrender falsely modest claims of being strictly "middle range," and, as A. Whitney Griswold puts it, "revise the intellectual map of the world to make it coincide with the physical map."[28]

Given the limited resources of any single university, much less any one graduate faculty of sociology, the distribution of labor must be rationalized, across departmental lines and even university lines if need be. Communication between sociology and allied social sciences must be drastically improved. The present tendency toward departmental insularity is fostered by ecological separation, differential budget allocations between academic departments, bureaucratic styles of work, and contempt for "other" social science approaches. The latent fear that cross-fertilization implies a reduction in the professional status of sociology needs to be seriously challenged and overcome, if the graduate training of students is to be successful in developing fully rounded scholars and policy-planners. While many such programs are formally advocated, they fail to get off the proverbial pot, since teaching and research assistantships, and departmental written and oral examinations, are still designed in old-fashioned ways. Thus the graduate student hazards into marginal fields or allied departments, often at his own risk—and alas, often at the displeasure of the professors who recite the rhetoric of cross-disciplinary research, but who design rules and regulations that thwart such practices. In brief, reform must begin with the reformers. The elegance of a position is less significant than encouraging the graduate student to "cut loose" from the department and its leading figures and explore the "world" of the university as such.

The development of cross-disciplinary programming could have a large-scale feedback in terms of sociological production. For example, a sound course in the foundations of law, might provide the sort of knowledge of the differences between Roman law and common law that could then be applied to advanced research on the operations of bureaucratic organization. It could furthermore

28. A. Whitney Griswold, *The University* (An Interview) (Santa Barbara, Calif.: The Fund for the Republic, 1961), pp. 20–21.

help explain why Max Weber developed a theory of authority, while Roberto Michels developed a theory of European legal superstructure. The study of the contemporary novel could likewise be instrumental in all sorts of strictly sociological undertakings: the continuing ethnic and religious divisions between Americans; the character of mass communications and mass culture; the changing beliefs concerning marriage and the family; the intimate description of anomie and alienation.

The ideal of the "rounded man" need not necessarily be subverted by professional and technical education, if only we avoid the confusion between sociological specialization and sociological trivialization. The precedent for this is clear: sociologists often seek advanced training in mathematics and statistics because such training is best in departments of mathematics and statistics. The need is only to extend this attitude to include science and the humanities as part of the purview of sociology. No department is so flexible that it can encompass all possible varieties of useful professional training—and none is so large as to contain all varieties of cross-disciplinary interests. Thus, the liberal spirit is not something confined to the liberal arts college, but a useful style at all advanced levels of research and theory.

V

In summation, the issues can be put in the following way: The teaching of sociology at the high school level suffers from an acute condition of status deprivation for the instructor, and the learning of sociology suffers simply by its absence. At the college level there is a general state of confusion between a liberal arts orientation and a preprofessional outlook. And at the graduate level, there is an excessive degree of rigidification of departmental orientation in place of cross-disciplinary orientation. The most unfortunate aspect of the situation is that it does not admit of easy or piecemeal solution. A basic reason for the role confusion at the college level has to do with the absence of sociological consciousness at the high school level; thus there are as many orientations to the teaching of sociology in a college as there are institutions themselves. The graduate school has responded to this eclecticism by adopting the attitude of "flushing out" the student during his first year of graduate work, attempting in this way to take responsibility for the entire training process of the student.

The person learning sociology is in a double bind: whether or not he has had a satisfactory undergraduate education, he is placed at the same level as the student having an unsatisfactory education. Paradoxically, he is compelled to make advanced decisions about the content and the character of sociology and his work orientation in the field, something he is not readily able to do.

To resolve these problems there must be an "across the board" approach. The outline given here of a social problems approach at the high school level, a humanistic liberal arts approach at the college level, and a preprofessional approach at the graduate level can only work insofar as each part of this total educational system is operative. Since the character of American education beyond the elementary school level is definitely tripartite in character, there has to be some way to provide elasticity and continuity in the learning process of any given discipline, within an essentially inelastic and discrete educational apparatus.

The widespread development of two-year colleges might change the situation drastically. However, as of now, the infusion of a broad social science course in the curriculum has only served to take up the slack in the high school teaching of the social sciences. It has not added anything dramatically new in the orientation that we have herein given. The problem with the two-year college curriculum is not only that it merely takes up the high school lag, but that it also heaps up confusion by giving a survey course in the social sciences which is neither fish nor fowl. It is, however, conceivable that the area of penetration and experimentation will be made at this junior college level, since of all phases in American education, it is the least structured and the most subject to experimentation. Therefore, it is possible, if experimental pipelines are to be fitted, that this might be the appropriate place.

There are texts designed for junior college use that offer some promise of an introduction to social problems at one level and an introduction to theoretical issues at another. Perhaps one reason why a breakthrough can be made at the junior college level is that the two-year program offered is often viewed as terminal by most people who attend. Hence the design of sociological work is not burdened by supposed obligations the junior college ostensibly has to the higher learning.

What is needed is the kind of programming that provides terminal training and is at the same time continuous with the next higher level of work. For this reason, educationists cannot themselves resolve the problem of the learning of sociology, since by nature a solution must be based on the intrinsic contents of a sociological education and not on the functional requirements of educational plants. Just how this fusion between educationists and sociologists can be made is difficult to assay. One prima facie solution is to urge every educationist to become a sociologist, and there are ample grounds for assuming that this is not an altogether negative solution. In fact, there is an increasing tendency of educationists to draw upon sociological materials, and some graduate educational centers have developed powerful institutes of sociology in their own right. Similarly, it might be urged that the sociologist should become an educationist. This is sometimes countered by the plea that the sociologist is an educationist, that is to say, he has to function in terms of general problems of the teaching and learning process as a whole. But this is simply a ploy. The fact remains that numbers of sociologists are becoming concerned with formal problems of educational systems and not just with classroom pedagogy. To conclude this point, the future for increased rapport between sociologists and educationists is most promising. Whether this promise will be realized or not depends on factors that are largely outside the control of departments of sociology and schools of education, but are in the realm of the social system as such.

The sociological community is undergoing one of its periodic big-scale transformations. Old localisms are yielding to new cosmopolitan features—witness the growth of cross-disciplinary research in developing areas. It is, to be sure, simpler to locate what is passing away than what is coming into existence. The present seems to be witnessing a rising clash between two views of sociology; the natural science approach and the social science approach—behaviorism on one side and humanism on the other. But interestingly, and what is qualitatively new about this period, at the same time this is taking place, there is an increasing consensus as to what the chief features of a sound learning process in sociology are. And if the professional debates between methodologists and theorists become sharper, the spirit of both camps is that the student should at least be familiar with both sides, so that his choice is based on real decision rather than artificial stereotyping.[29]

The learning and teaching of sociology may be as paradoxical as ever. But at the very least it is clear that the paradoxes can act as a stimulant to creativity, not necessarily as a bind to sociological development. It is a sign of maturation that sociologists no longer confuse uniformity of opinion with knowledge of the truth. There is a declining dogmatism which can be observed throughout the length and breadth of the profession. Cooperation is not only possible, but existent, between sociologists having conflicting valuational bases. Science has always been compelled to live in suspension of absolute judgment, and it is therefore little wonder that now that sociology has come through its first hundred years—battle-scarred from intra-mural strife, and a trifle shell-shocked from the blasts of antisociologists—there is a considerable degree of pride (among men in all "camps") in the achievements registered.

This is not a sign that fundamental criticism has ground to a halt. It does signify that criticisms can now be made more responsibly than in the past. No longer is it true that criticism from within (or from without) is necessarily viewed as a threat to the discipline as such. Only now can criticisms be made in the knowledge that sociology is not "on trial." Sociology has a language and realistic, if flexible, boundaries. Sociology has an audience of over a milllion users, and untold millions of listeners. Sociology has an organizational basis, even if bitter debates between the organizational parts continue unabated. Sociology has a firm anchor in the colleges and universities of America. Sociology has penetrated the East-West barrier by means of international conferences. This does not mean that sociology must continue to flower. A science has staying power only to the extent that it helps in the betterment of the human condition. When a science is sundered from its uses, when it seeks justification and rationalization as a "thing in itself," unhinged and unrelated to human needs, it must surrender its place as a science and become part of the world of esoterica. It must be judged on aesthetic grounds, rather than scientific ones.

29. See Robert K. Merton, "Social Conflict over Styles of Sociological Work," Reprint No. 286 (New York: Columbia University, Bureau of Applied Social Research). Reprinted from *Transactions of the Fourth World Congress of Sociology*, 1959.

The increased uses of sociology in policy formation, in privately inspired research, in the general problems of education, is no cause for undue pride on the part of sociologists, or undue alarm on the part of the citizenry. The coming of age of sociology means only that sociology must become increasingly conscious of its social role, its place in social affairs, its educational functions. It demands the opening up of new centers of graduate training, new efforts at remodeling sociology in colleges, intensification of efforts to infuse sociology into the high school curriculum. It requires new periodicals for the dissemination of socio-logical findings to the general public, and improvements in the quality of old ones. It means making sociology a way of life for increasing elements of society. Above all, sociology as a science means that although all may not know its methods, all may enjoy its benefits.

10. *Establishment Sociology:*
The Value of Being Value-Free

THIS IS AN EXCURSION into the sociology of American sociology. It is an attempt to present a typology of the relationship between sociological empiricism as an ideology, and the preeminence and power of empiricist sociologists. Toward this end, such concrete factors as recruitment practices, educational orientations, status strivings of the social scientists, forms of financial subsidization, and the professionalization of the field are taken into account. The article concludes by noting the limited field of investigations open to sociological empiricism, and its general impoverishment as the leading *ideology* of the science of sociology.

The rhetoric of explaining the rise of empiricism in American sociology customarily hinges on references concerning the pitfalls of doing sociology in any other way. Thus, its practitioners will speak of empiricism as a reaction to an exaggerated historicism. Some may offer an explanation based on the growing secularization of the social sciences in general. Others offer the grim view that sociological empiricism coincides with the *Zeitgeist*, with the general analyticity of the age. Finally, there are those who see in this view the best method for obtaining factual results independent of ideological or valuational claims or considerations.

This paper examines the notion of an Establishment in sociology and specifies five variables that would seem to demonstrate the existence of such a phenomenon. It is the organizational counterpart of the paper on "Social Science Objectivity and Value Neutrality." It was first published in *Inquiry: Journal of Interdisciplinary Research*, 6, no. 1 (Spring, 1963).

In these brief remarks it is not my intention to challenge or confront any of these hypotheses directly. What I have in mind is an outflanking maneuver. I should like to restrict myself to the question "how" rather than "why." That is, I shall examine the second-line issue of how, for the past quarter of a century, sociological empiricism has retained its preeminence in the face of challenges from all quarters—including antisociologists no less than those working within the field of sociology who have not found the conversion from empirical sociology to sociological empiricism either simple or necessary.

It is my contention that, in answering the question "how," we are also offering a causal expanation, albeit a partial one, for the present preeminence of one style of sociological research. And beyond this, we are perhaps offering an inventory of the practical barriers that will have to be overcome if there is to be a further release of what Mills aptly termed the sociological imagination.

I say practical barriers. By this I do not wish to minimize theoretical objections, only to indicate that such abstract objections seem directly connected to a complex of concrete factors.

I. RECRUITMENT POLICIES AND PRACTICES

It is clear from an investigation of professional social science jour nals'annual listings of higher degrees awarded and in progress that while there is a sharp numerical rise over the years, there is no corresponding growth in the number of institutions granting higher degrees. By far the highest proportion of degrees granted in social science, and in science generally, is made by a highly selective and restrictive group of universities. This observation is confirmed in studies made by Wilson, Barber, and Berelson.[1] Thus the power and prestige of these selective universities and, more specifically, the departments in which this power is directly lodged, show a growth pattern far in excess of the increase in higher education as such. "Team work," the drive for consensus, the pressure to state findings in quantitative terms only, are reinforced by the financial and occupational need for the graduate student to get his degrees. This power of the large department is not diminished after graduation. The communications network is kept open in terms of grants and awards, university press publications, journal articles, efforts of promotion and relocation—all of which in some measure require the sanction of the major institutions and their various departments. Barr offers this interesting account in "fictional" form. "The fact that his desk (that is, the head of the economics department's) was a clearing house for teaching posts with swank research organizations and private business corporations gave him absolute control of his graduate students. They knew they would be taken care of if they won his favor. They knew likewise that if they failed to win it they would not even get a degree, no matter how strong a dis-

1. Cf. Logan Wilson, *The Academic Man* (New York: Oxford University Press, 1942), p. 33; Bernard Barber, *Science and the Social Order* (Glencoe, Ill.: Free Press, 1952), pp. 142–143; and Bernard Berelson, *Graduate Education in the United States*, p. 226.

sertation they wrote."[2] With such a situation, the younger men are under obvious restraint not to do violence to the group norms that prevail. The most serious criticism of value premises is thus confined to the upper echelons of the discipline, or to those scholars working in different areas of social science.

What Mills has called the "feudal structure" of graduate education in itself encourages empiricism—first as a degree-getting posture and later on as a theoretical position. Solotaroff describes this process as a general one. It does not have to be emphasized that this process holds even more firmly in sociology, where empiricism is king. The graduate student

learns to go along with the acceptable style of scholarly thinking, in which "originality" means mainly finding a problem, or segment of one, that is still to be explored, "pertinence" means mainly the amount of fresh factual documentation that can be accumulated, and "soundness" means mainly working within the existing body of "scholarly opinion." Moreover, he begins to find satisfaction in the close, skeptical examination of evidence, in the thoroughness of research, in accumulating a great deal of knowledge about a particular question. He develops a respect for factuality and for careful arguments that remain within clearly defined terms.[3]

In brief, the process of recruitment emphasizes the mechanical values of working in areas where information is already available and, by the same token, discourages research into problems where evidence is lacking, where information is tentative—that is, the kind of intellectual situation that would entail potential resistance to entrenched attitudes, thereby making for considerable difficulties in getting on with the practical needs of graduation, promotion, and eventual placement. The total institution pattern is simulated, with emphasis on "working the system" replacing the older canons of systems of intellectual work. Empiricism is thus not simply a sociological methodology, but a social ideology.

II. EDUCATIONAL ORIENTATIONS

Closely allied to recruitment practices is an orientation in which there is an excessive concentration, particularly in sociology, on experimental efforts as something apart from theory construction. Specialized techniques of questionnaire design, codification, and compartmentalizing allow for the interviewing process to become the end of research rather than an instrumentality. The spate of literature on survey design and sampling techniques leads to a strict methodological view of the purposes of sociology. That this is not confined to any one branch of social science is confirmed by a UNESCO survey of political science. The editor of this survey indicates that "a good deal of political research carried on in universities today is aloof from the real problems of political life. Too often

2. Stringfellow Barr, *Purely Academic* (New York: Simon & Schuster, 1958), pp. 51–52.
3. Theodore Solotaroff, "The Graduate Student: A Profile," *Commentary*, 32, no. 6 (1961): 482–490. For an earlier estimate, see C. Wright Mills, *White Collar: The American Middle Classes* (New York: Oxford University Press, 1951), pp. 129–136.

research seems to be conducted for the sake of research. The topics chosen have no apparent significance, and the investigation does not throw light on any contemporary problem of importance. There is no driving force behind such research, no vital motives inspiring the work, no useful potentialities in the conclusions which emerge."[4] There seem here to be two intertwined problems: establishing criteria of significance and, equally important, an unwillingness to break through the data barrier. There are obviously a multitude of reasons for this, but I believe that Lerner and Hilgard have caught the essence of the problem when they note that

the prestige of the natural scientist is high in American culture, where the developed industrial civilization and high standard of living are commonly attributed to scientific advances. This fact may lie behind the self-conscious wish of social scientists to become scientists like other natural scientists (chemists, physicists, biologists). Hence, those in the social disciplines turn to the natural sciences for their models of system-building. They wish to attain the generally accepted criteria of good science: objective and reproducible observations; precise and valid instruments for refining observations; hypotheses that help to initiate inquiry and to direct research; general theories; and laws that satisfy the esthetic demand for an articulated and harmonious system.[5]

III. Status Strivings of Social Scientists

Policies and orientations in social science are clearly related to the reconstruction of the image of sociology held in the past. While Lerner and Hilgard have indicated some of the major reasons for the attempt at mimetic reproduction of natural science methods, there remains the matter of the lingering identification of sociology with social reform (if not worse). The peer group in sociology has thus felt a special obligation to cleanse the word of its inherited "socialist" connotations. And this could be done either through the substitution of methodology for actual useful results or by direct appeals to members of the profession to rethink any lingering moral residues or biases—especially any bias against the business and industrial world. The manipulative values of sociology, which for a while were viewed as a necessary, if discomforting, by-product of research, have now become something of a matter of principle. In his "Reflections on Business," Lazarsfeld bemoans the lack of interest, if not the historic antipathy, of the professional social scientist for the business calling. Drawing attention to the mutuality of interests between sociologists and businessmen, Lazarsfeld points out that it is the businessmen who have done most of the work. This he shows through a content analysis comparing the *Harvard Business Review* and the *American Journal of Sociology*.[6] There can be little question that a parallel analysis

4. William A. Robson, *The University Teaching of Social Sciences: Political Science* (Paris: UNESCO, 1954), p. 116.

5. Ernest P. Hilgard and Daniel Lerner, "The Person: Subject and Object of Science and Policy," *The Policy Sciences: Recent Developments in Scope And Method*, ed. by D. Lerner and H. D. Lasswell (Stanford: Stanford University Press, 1951), p. 38.

6. Paul F. Lazarsfeld, "Reflections on Business," *American Journal of Sociology*, LXV, no. 1 (Julo, 1959): 1–26.

of the contents of the *American Journal of Sociology* for the following decade, beginning with 1960, will show an appropriate response to Lazarsfeld's plea for tolerance, understanding and fair play. As social research itself begins to take place in an atmosphere resembling that of a highly rationalized business organization, the status possessed by the latter is presumably going to rub off on the former. Whether this is so remains to be seen.

It might be argued that a commitment to a businesslike way of doing sociology is not necessarily a commitment to business values as such. Nonetheless, if the researches of Elton Mayo and Chester Barnard betoken anything at all, it is that "industrial" sociology does indeed start with assumptions of the parity of labor and management, the need to further class consensus, and the worth of maximum output at minimum costs. When we add these to the empiricist redefinition of authority as legitimate power, the results are disastrous for any serious "reflections on business." Lazarsfeld's recent calls for the sociologist to assume his proper administrative functions amounts to absorption of business values, not reflections on such values by an autonomous social science.

IV. SUBSIDIZATION OF THE FIELD

With the growing emphasis on sociology as a heuristic device has come a concomitant notion of "applied" sociology as something that can be of service to the customers who purchase the commodity. In this way the subsidization of sociology has increasingly come to be underwritten by corporate elites. The extraordinary expansion of business interest in sociological research is underscored by the Institute for Social Research at the University of Michigan. "The staff of the Institute for Social Research has grown from the original group of 12 persons who established the Institute in 1946 to over 350 individuals in 1961." In a list of sponsors of this Institute, which is typical of similar Institutes elsewhere, we are presented with a veritable "Who's Who" of the business world. Especially well represented are chemicals, oils and refining, communications, public utilities, banking and investment, philanthropic foundations, food and drug manufacturers, auto, steel, aircraft, and insurance corporations, and last, but by no means least either in number or significance, leading federal agencies.[7] Interestingly enough, the list does not contain a single labor union nor, with the exception of the Boy Scouts of America, any noncorporate agencies or societies.

What this makes quite plain is that (a) the selective subsidization of sociology has developed at an extremely rapid rate; (b) although the research findings are open to all in theory, they are open only to corporate wealth in fact; and finally (c) the center of gravity in sociology has shifted away from "pure" or academic research to "applied" or institutional research. To term this development the "secularization" of the field is simply to provide a misanthropic label for the simple fact that the tenacious clinging to the "value-free" doctrine and to the

7. *Institute for Social Research, 1946–1961* (Ann Arbor: University of Michigan, 1962), pp. 35–37.

"functional" method is a consequence of the sales values of a nihilistic posture in actual research undertakings.

The hovering of the corporate image over the activities of sociology has caused a considerable shift in the subject matter treated by the discipline. Such areas as sociological theory, the history of sociology, the sociology of religion, have been outflanked in the course of the development of sociology as a heuristic discipline. "Who pays how much for what"—and not any imagined "revulsion" with the traditional content of sociology—best explains the dominant *motif* in American sociology. And what pays are survey design, communication and influence analyses, studies of leadership and organizational behavior, etc. The *slogan* is "separate facts from values"; the *substance*, however, is "suppress values at the expense of facts." For it is no more the case that studies in the social structure of interpersonal relations in an automobile factory. But it has been precisely this assumption of certain aspects of social life as being "sacred" and others "profane" that has driven a wedge into the sociological establishment, between the academic departments and the corporate-sponsored institutes.

V. Professionalization of the Field

The process of professionalization, which involves a gamut of subprocesses—from being *au courant* with the vernacular of the moment to an appreciation of the number of variables the latest IBM calculator can deal with in a single computation—serves the classic purpose of distinguishing peer-group members from outsiders. Fossils and deviants of older generations, or those who have come through the educative process with a concern for value questions intact, must still face the prospects of the highly organized professional societies. An English sociologist has pointed out the situation with respect of professionalization: "A professional association seeks privileges at the expense of the common good. It attaches more importance to respect for seniority, conformity to professional rules of conduct, and the growth of tradition than it does to individual freedom and inventiveness. Its members are conditioned to interpret their duties more in terms of professional skills than in terms of the needs of clients."[8] Clearly, the basis of professionalization has increasingly come to rest on a notion of consensus that often carries over into conformism. The social scientist is asked to comport himself as a physicist or physician, yet, unlike the former, he dare not establish a *Bulletin of Atomic Scientists* lest the charge of meddling in political affairs come back to haunt him; and, unlike the latter, he is not authorized to make prescriptions (only descriptions and perhaps recommendations) lest the charge of moral concern be raised.

An examination of the concept of sociological neutrality might begin by devising a quantitative test for distinguishing the extent to which it is based on indifference to policy problems, on the desire to achieve a higher scientific rank-

8. Peter Townsend, "A Society for People," *Conviction*, ed. by N. MacKenzie (London: MacGibbon & Kee, 1958), p. 105.

ing in the eyes of policy-makers, or simply on the belief that non-neutrality might result in a loss of position and professional ranking. Such a study might be extended to include information on whether ethical and political neutrality is simply a manifested pose, disguising a latent antipathy or sympathy for certain movements and ideals. For this purpose, a typology of social science attitudes toward specific social classes, occupational groupings, and ethnic affiliations might be a worthwhile starting point. The work of Lazarsfeld and Thielens on *The Academic Mind*[9] and that of Caplow and McGee on *The Academic Marketplace*[10] provide useful anchor points.

In lieu of substantial findings, we must carefully examine the current cautious criticisms of ethical neutralism and functional necessity from the *avant-garde* themselves. To the extent that the policy-making sector of sociologists becomes discontented with the quality of work being produced, we will get increasingly sharp appraisals of the situation. Indications from a number of sociological centers is thus a clear-cut index of things to come. The increased demands for relevance, openness, and imagination from scholars such as Homans, Moore, Williams, and Bierstedt can not be ignored.

This might appear to contradict the "material bases" for the rise of sociological empiricism in the first place. Yet I think not. For in addition to those who adopted empiricism for "practical" reasons, there are many—and by no means the least able—whose empiricism reflected a direct concern with oracular and ideological distortions of fact in the name of value. The inherited European currents reflected a lack of patience with scientific controls. We might just mention their impressionist approach to evidence, intense individualistic appraisals, attempts at exclusively long-range predictions (decline-and-fall type of problems), absence of specific surveys to settle specific issues localized in space and time, the failure to establish any organized pressure toward data realiability, etc.[11] But with the solution, at least partially, of these methodological considerations, attempts at a more coherent picture of the function of value premises in social science can be made. It would do violence to the facts to consider the present situation without due regard to this admittedly nascent current in American sociology.

The forging of a valuable sociology depends in part on the creation of a social science of values. Here we come to the greatest impediment to an advance in sociological research—the empiricist refusal to view the social sciences as essentially a human enterprise, bound at one end by the biological-psychological

9. Paul Lazarsfeld and Wagner Thielens, *The Academic Mind* (Glencoe, Ill.: Free Press, 1958).

10. Theodore Caplow and Reece J. McGee, *The Academic Marketplace* (New York: Basic Books, 1958).

11. Cf. Robert K. Merton, "The Sociology of Knowledge and Mass Communications," *Social Theory and Social Structure*, rev. ed. (Glencoe, Ill.: Free Press, 1957), pp. 439–455; see also Kurt H. Wolff, "The Sociology of Knowledge and Sociological Theory," *Symposium on Sociological Theory*, ed. by L. Gross (Evanston: Row, Peterson Co., 1959), pp. 567–592.

constitution of men, and at the other by the historical career of mankind. Red-field, in a most important statement, has summed up the reasons for considering anthropology a human science. His observations, which I shall paraphrase, seem to me to hold true for other social sciences (particularly sociology) as well.[12] (1) However clever the design of an experiment, there is a clear difference between humanity and nonhumanity, between history at the upper level and physics at the lower level. (2) To reduce culture to physics is to decompose humanity into parts, and thus into something other than the study of man or society. (3) The dominance in the social sciences of natural science models and methods is not matched by any corresponding success in executing studies based on these models and methods. (4) The basis of any one social science is the study of some portion of humanity. It thus shares a common frame of reference with, first, the other social sciences; second, the humanities; and third, philosophy. (5) The development of an explicit concern with values—the values of those doing the investigating no less than of those who are under investigation—makes quite out of the question even the striving for, much less the realization of, a pure "natural science" of man devoid of value functions and value orientation.

Given this tabular outline of the shortcomings in sociological empiricism, its violation of observed human relations and hence of an empirical approach as such, it is time for the practitioners in the field to move beyond the institutiona-lized molds of *wertfrei* empiricism as a sociological ideology. If sociology is to avoid becoming a "dismal science," if it hopes to free itself for some of the larger tasks characteristic of the classic tradition in social science, then it will have to move beyond an image of the field based on commodities for sale, and a corres-ponding self-image based on an overly generous estimate of the need for academic salesmen.

For when we really come down to brass tacks, sociological empiricism has specific policy-making ramifications. We live in a social science era (in the United States) in which huge funds are put at the disposal of the researcher—without any appreciable net benefits for society. In Europe, operating with much smaller financial resources, but with a much wider sociological horizon, the sociologist has had much greater success in affecting national and regional policies. Why should this be so? One answer herein offered is that empiricism as a sociological ideology leads to gamesmanship and pseudointellectual one-upmanship. But this has a boomerang effect. Society has learned not to take the sociological empiricist any more seriously than he takes himself. This is the dreary and dismal result of a sociological method *claiming* to have effected the "secularization" of sociology, but only *producing* yet another form of the ideo-logical distortion of social realities.

12. Robert Redfield, "Relations of Anthropology to the Social Sciences and to the Humanities," *Anthropology Today: An Encyclopedic Inventory*, ed. by A. L. Kroeber (Chicago: University of Chicago Press, 1953), pp. 728–738.

11. *Sociology for Sale*

THE BREAK-UP of a scientific system proceeds in two ways: first superior results from a competing system and method create dramatic rifts; second, discontent and disaffiliation develop from within. *Social Theory and Social Practice* by Hans Zetterberg offers a remarkable example of the escond type of disintegrative process. Mr. Zetterberg is a sociologist long associated with the methodological empiricist wing of sociology. His work is an expression of discontent with the results obtained by empiricism, and, even more, a disaffiliation from the concepts which dominate sociological research agencies. Thus, if by virtue of Zetterberg's "insider" position alone, one must treat his work seriously.

What exactly is Zetterberg's uneasiness with the course of sociological professionalization in America? His answer is framed in terms of five shortcomings of social practitioners and three fallacies in their theoretical armor. To paraphrase these basic flaws: (1) The theory of group work is normative; it serves to give a social or moral legitimization of professional practice, not a scientific legitimization. (2) The practitioners' use of case study method is capricious and lacks the reliability associated with science. (3) What passes for accumulated knowledge is often accumulated ignorance and malpractice organizationally enshrined. (4) A collection of descriptive facts and trends does not result in specific advice on what action to take. (5) Often advice is given without either conducting original research or drawing upon available scientific laws.

This was first prepared as a review essay of the work of Hans Zetterberg in his effort to create a more therapeutic and practical orientation to sociology. His work was singled out as one of the major attempts to break out of the impasse in which the functionalist orientation placed sociology as it entered the present decade, but one which seemed to raise as many problems as it resolved. First published in *Studies on the Left*, 3, no. 4 (Winter, 1963).

As for the "fallacies," they are the beliefs, first, that social science practice is the same as popularizing its content; second, that the content of knowledge to be applied must match the content of the problem faced by the practitioner; and finally, that the number of social problems is nearly infinite, and by implication, unmanageable.

At the outset, it should be noted that criticisms such as these, while quite severe, have been made before and often—by sociologists not enamored with the "purity" of empiricism and, even more sharply, by philosophers of science hardly taken with sociology at all. But what is important is that such a powerful broadside is for the first time launched from within the Establishment. Zetterberg reflects the anguish of a man who *experiences* disintegration, rather than one who *understands* it through ratiocination. That is why his critical remarks have a fresh and authentic ring to them, despite the fact that the content of his remarks is by now well understood among many professional and practicing sociologists.

Zetterberg is reacting to "grand theory" the way William James reacted to "dialectical idealism" at the turn of the century. Sociology must be practical. It must understand the difference between tough-minded scholarship and tender-hearted sentiment. It must offer useful consultations to useful businessmen. It must make recommendations to policy-makers and it must provide a service to industry worth the cost. The notion of impersonal and abstract research must give way to, or at least share the wealth with, the "scholarly confrontation"— which of course is personal and highly concrete. However distasteful the word must sound to the author of *Social Theory and Social Practice*, he presents us with a manifesto, a prophecy of the shape of sociology tomorrow and a warning of what can happen if the prophecy is ignored.

We come now to the heart of the matter: How well does Zetterberg's manifesto succeed? Is he offering a revolutionary boost to sociological theory and practice, or a nostalgic glance back to a time when social science was keenly related to worldly affairs? Is this really a worthwhile track to ride along or a smashing dead-end?

Perhaps the strangest aspect of Zetterberg's volume, given his justified reputation as a methodologist, are the logical problems posed by his work. The error of looking at the social world in terms of mechanical polarities, or as it is sometimes called by philosophers of science, the problem of reification, is everywhere present. Human action is divided into "executive" and "emotive" types. People are divided into "tough-minded" and "tenderhearted," "pioneers and protectors," etc. Pattern variables are set up in terms of "contingent" and "impersonal" forces. And then there are a number of triadic relations: "realms, values and stratifications"; "description, evaluation and prescription," etc. Now while this approach serves to formulate typologies for the way men behave or the way institutions function, it involves a prima facie reductionism, since the die is cast strictly in terms of black and white, positive and negative variables. The advantages of this sort of reductionism are that social laws can be framed with relative ease. But there is an overriding disadvantage. The laws so framed tend to be highly general phase statements with a very low level and narrow range of predictability.

What Zetterberg leaves us with, then, are not really laws so much as experienced invariant occurrences or simple logical tautologies. Illustrative of the first kind is the following: "The more a person deviates from a prescription given by his associates, the more unfavorable evaluations the latter tend to give him." One might just as well say that "The more a dog disobeys his master's order, the more unfavorable evaluations the latter tends to give him." But this neither *explains* the mechanisms of disobedience and the *reasons* for negative feelings, nor forms the basis of *predictions* since Zetterberg's "law" is only a tendency. And counterfactual conditions can be shown to exist in which *deviation* from norms brings rewards and favorable evaluations no less than its opposite. Or take the kind of "law statement" which says that: "The greater variety of offerings in a market call, the greater the response." This is a simplistic truism. It is like saying that more people go to Macy's than to the local dress shop because a department store has a greater variety of goods. But this "law," while implying an invariant relationship between numbers of people and numbers of offerings, does not account for a host of intervening factors. A law of diminishing returns may be operative if there are already a large number of department stores in one neighborhood. A specialty store might take more money with a smaller financial investment in such a situation. The costs of providing a saturation range of goods might diminish and not increase profits, etc.

Yet a third kind of "law" that Zetterberg adduces is that: "The more visible control of an institutional value a person has, the more favorable evaluations he receives from his associates." This is plainly debatable. Such psychological phenomena as resentment, envy, jealousy, are simply not accounted for. No one has ever proven a direct relationship between power and favorable evaluations. Empirically, the opposite is more nearly everywhere the case. If not, rulers would have no need to insist on social changes. In this context Zetterberg's law generalizes the reaction of small numbers of people whose activity is related in simple organization. There can be little relevance for problems connected to complex organization. The possessor of "visible control" impresses immediate associates or only those in a position to strive for or be affected by it. It cannot extend itself to the larger social realm where the "invisible hand" governs.

In general, it must be said that Zetterberg's "laws" suffer from four principle defects: (a) they are framed to exclude changes in the relationship between variables; (b) they are often simple phase rules and not applicable to a wide range of social phenomena; (c) they tend to assume that since the form of law-statements must be logicial, the *content* of law-statements is nothing but the formal mode as such; (d) above all, the laws offered have no ability either to explain past behavior or to calculate future responses. The reification of social events is thus a handicap and not an advantage to investigation. Zetterberg's "laws" are too easy: they are not wrested from social forces in painstaking effort, but flow with suspicious ease and simplicity from faith in a bivariant logic.

A large-scale problem which Mr. Zetterberg seems not to understand, or at least not be willing to confront at this point, is that the contextual situations of the sociological consultant and the psychiatric consultant are not quite of the same order of magnitude. In a patient-analyst relationship it is clear that the relation is one in which the paying customer (patient) is in a subordinate position, while the paid consultant (analyst) is in a superordinate position. Now in a policy-maker (patient)–sociologist (analyst) relation, it is not clear that the former needs clarification. He may simply require rationalization of his behavior or need guidance in manipulation of the actions of others. Thus the paying customer (policy-maker) in this case is in a *superordinate* position, while the paid consultant (sociologist) is in a *subordinate* position. This role reversal is of decisive importance for those who might like to draw the fee as well as the analogy of the psychiatric consultant. The structure of the particular relations is so different that one must assume not the likelihood of the sociologist performing critical consultation services, but rather the improbability of this happening. The organizational advisee seeks to arrange and order his hired human machinery for ends of perpetuation, efficiency, competition, and advancement of special interest, whether or not for socially useful purposes and without their knowing consent— leading only to reinforcement of function already established. The inadequate neurotic acquires greater powers of self-direction for purposes of altering his relation to the social milieu. The former seeks to engineer unknowing consent. The latter acquires the powers of knowing, voluntary assent. The sociologist-consultant *reinforces* an ongoing process. The psychiatrist-consultant (discounting instances of incompetence) restores balance and the power of change to his needy patient.

One cannot help marveling at the ingenuous and naive aspects of Mr. Zetterberg's thought. He discovers the "motivational basis for class struggles" in the "lower class" taking over the "methods of measuring worth that prevail in the higher strata." Clearly, the "motivation" of poor nations desirous of becoming rich nations is the models provided by the latter. But just as clearly, class struggle has an apocalyptic dimension. The root of class struggle is not the desire to adopt upper class values, but often the wish to negate them and replace them with an utterly different set of values. Underlying Zetterberg's sociology is a simplistic hedonism, in which "motivation" is equated with the desire to have what others already possess. Religious history no less than political history teaches that motivations may be altruistic no less than egoistic, messianic no less than opportunistic.

Because of this hedonistic psychology, Zetterberg can never really derive a set of workable social laws, since he flatly denies that things social really change: "... history shows no exception to the rule that class struggles succeed only in modifying existing stratification or in replacing one form of division by another. In no society, ever, has stratification been abolished or equal control of institutional values achieved by all." Here Zetterberg simply misses the point—and the point is that what counts in sociology is the *direction* of events, the tendencies toward *mobility* and away from fixity. The replacement of social divisions may entail, and in the revolutionary process usually does entail, not simply a re-division of power but very often an enlargement and expansion of the policy-making and policy-involved sector of society. It is presumptuous nonsense to declare that all history is simply a change in who rules, without acknowledging the fact that history also records the expansions and retrenchments of *how many* rule. Naturally, if one liquidates social *change* from social structure, the formulation of "laws" is a simple undertaking. But such a negation has only the merit of simplicity, not of truth. Why is it more "lawful" to say with Zetterberg that the history of class society is a history of the redivision of labor than to say with Marx that the history of class society is a history of the progressive emancipation of humanity? This subject is not a matter of law but a matter of empirical studies. And despite Zetterberg's constant warning to be "concrete" and to avoid the "abstract," his work has precious little concreteness. His exploration of social theories is an exhortation on behalf of antitheory. The actual content of social history is nowhere to be found. Motivations are transplanted from history to hedonism; thus enshrining the metaphysical pathos of "inevitable" differences between types of men.

With all of these criticisms made, one can yet in a sense be grateful to Zetter-berg for his provocative reappraisal, not only of the relation of recommenda-tions to research, but for a general estimate of the stakes of sociology in the modern world. Unfortunately, there is an overriding difficulty; namely, that Zetterberg has been carrying around the baggage of empiricism for so long that, even though he has opened it to find that it was stuffed with Confederate paper rather than solid gold nuggets, he has really lost sight of the gold nuggets as well. Everything comes as a surprise and a discovery to Zetterberg. It is as if he has imbibed rather than digested the classical tradition in sociological theory. If an inadvertent by-product of Zetterberg's work is a greater attention to sociological tradition, the fact that it is inadvertent is disconcerting in itself. It would probably surprise Zetterberg to know that a deceased colleague of his, C. Wright Mills, said as far back as the mid-1940's: "It is one thing to talk about general problems on a national level, and quite another to tell an individual what to do. Most 'experts' dodge that question. I do not want to."

If I understand Zetterberg correctly, he does not want to "dodge" this ques-tion either. But what distinguishes empiricism from a sociology of real content, from a big-range sociology, is that he *does* want to dodge the question of *res-ponsibility* for the decisions taken at the sociologist's recommendation. What would the colleagues of a surgeon say if the surgeon undertook to make a prog-nosis or a diagnosis of an illness and then washed his hands of the case—as if the diagnostic process were completely cut off from the operative process. To kill a company by improper diagnosis is logically no different than killing a person by improper medical diagnosis. In either case it is patently absurd to limit the "scholarly confrontation" to analysis in isolation from the results obtained. If Zetterberg really wishes to adopt a hard-nosed pragmatic line, he must see the means-ends continuum as extending to the sociological diagnostician; and that would mean sharing in the agony as well as in the ecstasy. Pious words to the effect that the sociologist makes "consultation," while decision-makers must still suffer "agony and anguish," can only deepen the rift between society and sociology. It increases the suspicion that the sociologist is not so much performing a role as society's doctor as the role of the quack selling spiked rum as mother's milk and then running to the next town before the truth gets out.

Given a more rationally coordinated social order, Zetterberg's kind of approach would prove most helpful and salutory. But in an irrational social order (and with twenty million American souls under some form of psychiatric treatment, who can deny the presence of irrationality?) the rationalization of the crackpot does not lead to more reason in relations between men, but only to more dangerous varieties of social madness. One's respect for Zetterberg's impulse to practical theory must be seriously tempered by the fear that his approach would smooth the ruffled feelings of the businessman or museum curator, but do little to really connect up the words "theory" and "practice" in a socially, as well as sociologically, meaningful fashion.

It was inevitable, once empiricism in sociology made it canon law to view sociology as an academic commodity rather than an intellectual pursuit, that someone would come along and "package" the commodity in a fancy package and hang a "for sale" sign on it. With all the ingenuity of a top-flight sales executive, Hans Zetterberg has written a book free of jargon, free of complications, but above all, free of anything even remotely embarrassing to the potential buyer of the "specialized services" of the sociologist. Here we inhabit the happy world of "consultants" and "clients," where "tough-minded" professors give advice to "tenderhearted" curators. Why, there are untold numbers of human resources the narrow psychoanalyst never dreamed of. Leave the neurotics to the psychoanalyst; Zetterberg's sociologist will claim the even bigger market of the normals. The game goes to the quick. And nobody dealing with sociology in the past decade is quicker than our author! Who, after all, but an empiricist in sociology would have the nerve to display the wares of nothingness and think it only fair to get something in return?

This is not to say that Zetterberg's sociology for sale has not met with stiff opposition. The men in the academy are not unaware that it is one thing to busy oneself with patchy little research projects that don't really harm anyone (they don't really help anyone either, of course), but quite another thing for an enthusiast to get so caught up in the commodity values of empiricism as to go out into the world and tell people he's got a salable package. What makes this enthusiasm awkward and dangerous is that people will pay for "right" recommendations, but they will howl like made at "wrong" or unsuccessful recommendations. The physician who makes a wrong diagnosis has the advantage of polishing off the patient. The sociologist who makes a wrong recommendation has only a lifelong, embittered opponent. Perhaps this is why Zetterberg's researches have not had the kind of enthusiastic support from like-minded colleagues that he might expect as his due.

Zetterberg points out that the sociologist in relation to a businessman may function as an "anxiety-reducing ritual." He then offers as an analogous situation the wedding ceremony. "The minister asks if the man wants this woman for better or worse. The man's answer to this anxiety-provoking question has already been decided. However, it is not a useless ritual. After the ritual the man and the woman do the same things they did before, but they feel more comfortable about it." There is no use embarrassing our Victorian sociologist about what the sly "it" is. However, it must be pointed out that the analogy is utterly fallacious. The "anxiety-ridden" couple may end up in a divorce suit, but they hardly blame the minister for the shortcomings of their marriage! And of course, the very purpose of "hiring" a sociologist to sanctify a decision is the very reverse. For as Zetterberg himself notes on the next page, "the research or consultation ritual establishes a scapegoat should the decision prove to be disastrous." Too many such disastrous decisions, and the sociologist-turned-cynical-money-grubber-turned-guilt-alleviator may arrive at the beginning of the end of Establishment sociology. Little wonder that Zetterberg's own professional family in the Bureau of Applied Social Research at Columbia University "did not want to house consultations based on these premises." Businessmen are not stupid feudal emperors. If they do not *see* the fine garments, they will loudly shout that the sociological kings go naked. And this just won't do. The "market" and the "consultation room" are not fit places for naked kings. The files of the Bureau must remain locked—the enthusiasm of enthusiasts notwithstanding!

12. *Anthropology for Sociologists: Cross-Disciplinary Research as Scientific Humanism*

ONE OF THE MAJOR ironies of the present period in the social sciences is that the sociologist, that professional charged with "the study of society," is probably further removed from the sources and object of his study than any comparable group of scholars. Marshall B. Clinard put the matter directly when he said that "the sociologist has probably had less first-hand experience with the actual data of his science than any other social scientist." Not really knowing about human beings, social institutions, and communities at firsthand he obviously feels ill-equipped to devise action programs that may have considerable immediate consequences."[1] Whatever the deformities and deficiencies exhibited by anthropologists, the discipline as a whole has the merit of encouraging and establishing contact with the peoples and cultures its practi-

This paper is a review of recent literature from allied fields of anthropology and ethics that appeared to have a great potential bearing for the reorientation of sociological research. It attempted to place interdisciplinary research in a modest context of cross-fertilization of ideas, rather than the systemic interpenetration of theories promoted by functionalism. First published in *Social Problems*, 11, no. 2 (Autumn, 1963); and *Trans-Action*, 4, no. 4 (March, 1967).

1. Marshall B. Clinard, "The Sociologist and Social Change in Underdeveloped Countries," *Social Problems*, 10 (Winter, 1963): 207–219.

tioners seek to understand. The anthropologist, in comparison with the socio-logist, tends to be empirical rather than empiricist, concerned rather than detached, and full-blooded in his reportage rather than vaguely rationalistic. The anthropologist tends to point out things that need doing, while the socio-logist too often ends with a plea for more research or more data. And if I may be permitted a personal observation, the anthropologist seems to *enjoy* his work, whereas the sociologist often acts as if he is *enduring* his work.

But there is another side to the matter, one not so pleasant to anthropological sensitivities. In comparison with sociology, anthropology is still in a stage of methodological underdevelopment. The "science of culture" makes only the vaguest distinction between objective facts and subjective opinions, and rarely does the anthropologist take the trouble to distinguish between what is and what informants say something is. But perhaps the greatest difficulty for the anthro-pologist is getting over an ingrained professional provincialism. He too often worries about and busies himself with the archaic and not the actual. It is not pottery-making but policy-making that is foremost in the minds of Africans and Brazilians. It is not cultural continuity (or social structure) but cultural discon-tinuity (or collective dynamics) that needs more attention. The reverence for continuous cultural elements too frequently disguises an unconcern with social change and, sometimes worse, a fear that attention to the tradition of the new would upset the professional anthropologist's applecart.

But any discipline operating at its maximum capacity transcends the pettiness and parochialism that infiltrate the rank and file. And anthropology performing at its maximum efficiency is a thing of brilliance and illumination that sociologists can ill afford to ignore. Sociologists have done more talking about interdisci-plinary research, but it has been the anthropologists who have taken the lead in concrete measures. Since sociologists must also meet the challenges of a new social science age of interrelation and cross-cultural exchange, the books under consideration here must be considered as more than a plea to read on a wider front. It is simple common sense to examine what has been done by our sister science on a wide variety of fronts before venturing forth ourselves. At the least such a procedure guarantees that we will avoid a senseless repetition, and at the most it may provide sociologists with the necessary initial thrust to get into interdisciplinary orbit.

Of course, talk about interdisciplinary research is commonplace. It forms the essential rhetoric of the grand theorists and the empiricists alike. Unfortunately, too many sociologists have conceived of interdisciplinary research in terms of superordination and subordination. Thus, for the Parsonian School, nearly everything under the sun is conceived of as a "subsystem" of society. Economy is "part of" the social system. Politics is "part of" the social system. Culture is "part of" the social system. We ought not confuse sociological imperialism, however benevolent, with interdisciplinary work. And as a matter of deeper significance, the phrase *interdisciplinary studies* ought not to be viewed oppor-tunistically, as enabling an arbitrary linkage to a "good image" field such as medicine or physics. In this connection, the sharp words of Ernest Becker are most instructive. Arguing the case for a transcultural psychiatry, he points out that the arbitrary linkage of psychiatry to medical physiology has had destructive consequences.

In the first place, psychiatrists have a prestige contingent on their medical *bona fides* that they do not deserve; only a small portion of behavioral malfunction can be traced to underlying physiology. In the second place, a medical education does not provide a broad view of human malfunctions which have nothing to do with physiology. This is a vicious circle of a kind, and we should not wonder that psychiatrists are claiming larger and larger sums of federal-grant money for research into the physio-chemical bases of behavior malfunction.[2]

In short, interdisciplinary effort is neither image-making nor a simple mechanical (and verbal) relation of distant fields. Such false alternatives can only result in poor social science; *e.g.*, the use of psychoanalytic categories of the normal and the pathological in testing the behavior of other cultures.

Arbitrary graftings may result in monstrosities. That is why interdisciplinary *research* needs a general *theory* of human behavior as a base. This must be a theory from which all social scientists and humanists (the latter are usually the rub, for who wants to connect up with the inhabitants of the academic poorhouse!) can derive benefits. The work of the late Robert Redfield was consistently outstanding in this sphere, not only because he insisted upon a connection between anthropology and the humanities but, more profoundly, because he forged the tools of a humanized anthropology. A review of the titles of Redfield's major papers itself offers a clue to how interdisciplinary work can be done: "Social Science among the Humanities," "Social Science as an Art," "Social Science as Morality," "The Peasant's View of the Good Life," "Art and Icon."[3] If Redfield were a young instructor today he would probably be called aside by his department chairman and gently informed that he was "spreading himself too thin" and that he "ought to get himself a technical specialty before it is too late."

Perhaps Redfield's most illustrious paper on the subject of interdisciplinary effort first appeared in a 1953 compendium on *Anthropology Today* and is reprinted in the first volume of his collected papers. It is titled "Relation of Anthropology to the Social Sciences and the Humanities"—and the contents match the title. The point of Redfield's policy paper is not the convenience of social science linkage, but its necessity for social scientific survival. In advising men of action, in participating in social change, in performing as agents of change, the anthropologist must face the problem of the "good" and the "beautiful" as part of his work. In treating the human person as a modifier and a creator of his culture, the social

---

2. Ernest Becker, *The Birth and Death of Meaning: A Perspective in Psychiatry and Anthropology* (New York: Free Press of Glencoe, 1962).

3. Robert Redfield, *Human Nature and the Study of Society: The Papers of Robert Redfield*, ed. by Margaret Park Redfield (Chicago: University of Chicago Press, 1962).

scientist necessarily moves over into the study of the humanities, the study of the producers and the creative products of man.

Redfield's theoretical explorations have already borne fruit in the recent work of Oscar Lewis on a "transitional" Mexican family.[4] In such an undertaking the writer must fuse the art of biography, the insight of history, and the facts of society. The extension of anthropology to include civilized peoples as well as preliterates places the researcher in the historical stream as such. As long as the anthropologist dealt with preliterate peoples, a case could be made out for the "history-less" nature of anthropology. But this condition no longer obtains. To deal seriously with "developing" societies and "transitional" cultures entails an explicit commitment to the historical muse. Similarly, the intimate study of group life entails no less a commitment to biography. There is no doubt that, viewed in cross-disciplinary terms, the demands on the social scientist, no less than the problem areas as such, mount considerably. But this is a comparatively small price to pay for the boundless enrichment of the study of man in society. Just imagine the kinds of problems that could be treated if there were a true social science cross-fertilization: Does reference group theory exist in a comparatively static society? Does the preliterate operate with our sense of time and space? Does the fact that all past societies exhibit a religious factor signify that all future societies must also contain such a factor? Do Indians have the same notion of overpopulation as Western sociologists? One can multiply these kinds of *important* questions indefinitely. The point is that the present sterilities in research reflect the impotence of a bloodless methodology, and not the disappearance of what Robert Park called the "Big News."

There is a regrettable condition, in the academic and social science worlds, of terrible anxiety and self-consciousness when confronting materials that defy disciplinary definitions. This is a large reason why Lewis' work on La Vida[5] is severely underestimated by academic journals, and left to reviewers in the popular media to celebrate. It is difficult to be convinced that Lewis himself is entirely immune to the crisis created in his now work. He is so intent on seeing his effort as cultural anthropology that he has appended a 55-page introduction to prove his contention.

From my own point of view, the sterling qualities of La Vida are apparent in the utter unconcern of this panoply of a Puerto Rican family with problems of academic discipline, or who gets what for being an anthropologist, sociologist, or economist. The unity of human experience is herein fully captured. Lewis exhibits a remarkable intellectual integrity by not allowing his own prejudices to intrude upon the people of San Juan and New York whom he examines. In this volume the "subjects" have as much to teach the reader (skilled or general)

4. Oscar Lewis, *The Children of Sánchez: Autobiography of a Mexican Family* (New York: Random House, 1961).

5. Oscar Lewis, *La Vida: A Puerto Rican Family in the Culture of Poverty* (New York: Random House, 1966).

as they in turn must learn if an escape from a barbarous poverty is to be achieved. More bluntly: Fernanda, Soledad, Felicita, Simplicio, Cruz, and the assorted cast of characters linked to the Rios family may, as Lewis says, have to fight clear of the culture of poverty even before they are liberated from its economic restrictions.

Here, I should like to deal extensively with Lewis' introduction. In the public-relations acclaims for *La Vida*, what has seemingly been left out of account is discussion of the author's methodology and theory. The obvious novelistic and revelatory aspects have been discussed as if this were a cheap piece of porno-graphy, or as if anthropology were a surrogate of voyeurism. The lasting merit of *La Vida* is that its parade of witnesses confronts the methodology and goals of social science theory with a series of practical dilemmas to which we must all address ourselves, or risk seeing one or another of the social sciences become a twentieth-century phrenology.

The *culture of poverty* (or subculture of poverty) concept which Lewis once more employs, far from being the strongest part of his introduction, is the weakest. It must be plainly said that the *culture of poverty* notion is methodologi-cally unsound and at times flatly contradictory. We are told that "the culture of poverty transcends regional, rural-urban, and national differences and shows remarkable similarities in family structure." But earlier in the introduction Lewis states the opposite: that in his studies comparing the Sánchez and Ríos families "a number of differences emerge, differences which are undoubtedly related to the different histories of Mexico and Puerto Rico." Also contradictory is the psychological characterization. We are told of the Puerto Rican family's "fortitude, vitality, resilience, and ability to cope with problems which would paralyze many middle-class individuals." But apparently, it has not done any better for lower-class individuals, since we are told of the Ríos family's "uncon-trolled rage, aggression, violence, and even bloodshed . . . their extreme impul-sivity affects the whole tenor of their lives."

The author tells us that "the culture of poverty is both an adaptation and a reaction of the poor to their marginal position in a class-stratified, highly indi-viduated, capitalistic society." Yet, in the most thoroughly capitalistic nation in the world, the United States, the author must admit that a "relatively small number of people in the United States have a culture of poverty." The more extensive Lewis' attempt at definition, the less satisfactory it becomes. The culture of poverty is equated at one time or another with the urban poor, the *lumpenproletariat*, and finally those who simply believe in the "reality of the moment . . . enjoyment of the sensual, the indulgence of impulse, etc." Simply put, Lewis' attempt to escape the twin evils of brutality and sentimentality is methodologically uncertain. One escape route might be an inversion of termin-ology. Not the culture of poverty, but the poverty of culture is what the Sánchez and Ríos families have in common. Hence, what should be considered as a goal is not abolishing "basic characteristics of culture of poverty" but, more impor-tant, a search for the abolition of poverty itself. After all, Erasmo's critique of

Puerto Rican modernization—"roads and more roads and the poor live as they always did"—is that this is "the kind of thing that is killing the working class." His advocacy of statehood for Puerto Rico (like Simplicio's belief in closer ties with the United States) is precisely in terms of ending poverty—and the devil take the culture of poverty!

Happily, the introduction contains a great deal more than a discussion of the culture of poverty. The description of methods used in *La Vida*, as well as the remarkable execution of those methods, constitutes a major contribution to ethnography. Not since Paul Radin, Robert Lowie, and Robert Redfield have I seen a more useful "how to" about anthropology. The seven points deserve outlinging:

(1) The use of the day as an investigatory device, since the day orders family life, yet is brief enough to permit intensive direct observation.

(2) The structuring of the previous day's interviewing, so as to examine observations for perspective and typicality.

(3) The development of rapport between investigator and investigated *before* attempting to record an actual day with a family.

(4) The use of the tape-recorded interview as the best instrument for capturing the slang, nuances, hesitations, as well as substance, of the conversations.

(5) The use of a complete family profile and genealogy, however painstaking and time-consuming, so that the remarks of one person can be systematically linked.

(6) A detached analysis of the material possessions of the people involved, so that the real wealth and real values of a people can be appreciated.

(7) An inventory of all household items and methods of purchase (cash, installment plan) for the same reason.

It is good to have this from Lewis. He is clearly a methodological innovator. The systematic working out of these seven parts in the actual interviews is impressive. The reason Lewis' work has so few imitators has nothing to do with its "simplistic" character; on the contrary, it has to do with its foundation of sophisticated and painstaking research.

An additional insight into the methodology guiding *La Vida* is Lewis' sure-handed "plugging in" of his suburb of San Juan to existing data. The choice of *La Esmeralda* was dictated by its being one of the four sample slums in greater San Juan studied in special census surveys. This appreciation of the total picture, linked as it is to Lewis' study of seven generations of the Ríos family, not only strengthens the empirical basis of Lewis' researches, but enables him to avoid the vacuous generalizations that frequently characterize "functional-structural" analyses of Puerto Rico.

The editorial judgment and skills exercised by Lewis are remarkable for their sensitivity to the nuances of language. Although the book is written in English, one can "hear" the Puerto Rican origin of many terms. Lewis does this through a clever sampling of Spanish terms and Puerto Rican localisms. He translates phrases rather than words, so that the rhythmic values of the language are retained. These same skills were present in *Five Families*, *The Children of Sánchez*, and *Pedro Martínez*, but whether it is because of the heightened pitch of life of the Ríos family, or simply Lewis' stylistic maturation, the recording of language is better in *La Vida* than in the previous books.

The living core of Lewis' methodological contribution is his belief in the "possibility that studies of the lower class may also reveal something that is distinctive of a people as a whole." This conscious rejection of elite definitions of a culture is in marked and refreshing contrast to the dominant tendency of the social sciences to equate the holders of culture with the holders of power. Lewis' admirable humanism lies precisely in his capacity to distinguish power from culture, and education from wisdom. Unfortunately, his drive to provide *unique* properties to the culture of poverty at times blunts the thrust of any effort to achieve a *general* theory of culture.

One of the major advantages of Lewis' technique is that it permits theory-construction of a sort implied by the narrative rather than stated in the introduction. I should like to draw attention to several aspects of the Ríos family either not dealt with by Lewis, or treated in a peripheral manner.

The Ríos family, like the Sánchez family, displays the earmarks of a transitional culture rather than a poverty culture. The high degree of physical *motility* and low degree of social *mobility* make this clear. What is particularly acute is the extent to which Puerto Ricans tend to have ecological latitude without much significant upward movement in a status hierarchy. They exhibit a low environmental responsibility and a high familial responsibility. In the act of high motility, family life is central as a thread providing cultural continuity.

This point might be carried a step further. Each member of the Ríos family constantly returns to the family unit for solace—as to an ancestral womb. The role of the male tends to be highly practical (wage earner, mover, repairman, etc.), while the female role is linked to the more intimate considerations of love, affection, and family stability. A repeated phenomenon is the return of the errant husband to the family matriarch. The Puerto Rican family minimizes frustration and resolves dilemmas privately, not so much in the larger world of labor, business, or community organization. At the first sign of frustration the family serves to alleviate pressures—especially in the case of mothers and sons. Lower-class Puerto Ricans seem tough in comparison with their Mexican counterparts (especially in the relations among the female members of the family), but they too are linked to the Latin ethos of compassion for the male victims of the socioeconomic world. And this extension of compassion comes across as a sign of female superordination.

The intimacy of family existence tends to weaken the organizational basis of Puerto Rican political life, or at least lower-class participation in political affairs. Demands that in advanced industrial cultures are placed upon the economy and the polity are left in family hands. This absence of functional specialization is indicative not so much of cultural style as it is of relative ignorance or mistrust of welfare services. Only Cruz among the Ríos clan seems seriously aware of the social resolution of her dilemmas, and this is only because of her relative dis-enchantment and isolation from the family as she grows to maturity. Paradoxi-cally, her personal *anomie* seems to foster certain forms of social interaction, while the family integration of the other Ríos tends to foster social *alienation*.

The Ríos family exhibits an all-pervasive monetary determinism. This is clearly revealed in the absence of any real knowledge of the economic founda-tions of power, and the absence of any real measures of wealth and poverty. The impression is given that the Puerto Rican conception of wealth is a patheti-cally low sum not far above the poverty lines established by social scientists. These are a Ricardian people, living in terms of marginal economic subsistence; not a Keynesian people, living in terms of credit extensions and measuring wealth through expenditures and investments. The general attitude toward the United States is that "everything's worse up here except the money." The world of secondary services and the obviously greater opportunities are less impressive to Puerto Ricans than to those foreign peoples in a relatively more advanced stage of the modernization process.

One must finally draw the conclusion that the attractions of the traditional island culture make adjustments to the mainland United States culture extremely difficult. One piece of evidence that there may be a distinctive Puerto Rican culture (whether or not it be termed a culture of poverty) is the number of those returning to the island. The flow of reverse migration is as extensive as immi-gration to the mainland. The Ríos family seem to move about without any great concern for differences between San Juan and New York ghetto living. One piece of indirect evidence of this insularity is the attitude of Puerto Ricans toward other minorities, especially Negroes, but sometimes Jews and Italians. There appears to be a uniform hostility toward Negroes as a people. And while Puerto Ricans also seem aware of the need to grant the Negro formal equality, their perception of Negro life is at the least as stereotyped and as suspicious as that of any white racist. It may be that just as the family is the safety-valve insuring against failure in the economic world, Puerto Rico is a gigantic mother insuring against the failure to become integrated into the modernizing sectors of United States society. One goes back to the mother; or, lacking that, one goes back to the land of birth and life.

These qualities seem to be as characteristic of the Ríos family, and as typical of Puerto Rican lower-class culture, as factors explicitly suggested by Oscar Lewis. They do not necessarily contradict Lewis' thesis. Yet there is a good deal more that can and ought to be said about Puerto Rican family life than the introduc-tion allows. Of course, it is significant to draw attention to the sturdy Puerto Rican habit of showing moral concern without issuing moral condemnations of others, and certainly it is important to draw attention to the naturalness with which matters of sex and family life are handled. But these are not exhaustive, and they perhaps are traits which intellectuals find more admirable than anyone else in United States society. It is characteristic of a modern culture (not a traditional culture) to make such fine distinctions between moral behavior and moral judgment. And if it is important not to become brutalized in our attitudes toward Puerto Ricans, it is no less important to avoid romanticism.

The doubts and differences concerning Lewis' work will certainly not be resolved by a single review. It is enough to say that not only has Oscar Lewis given us a work of great imagination, but has made the most profound use of personal biography. Lewis' combination of the findings of psychiatry and sociology, linked as these are to an ethnographic form, represents a significant step toward the reintegration of the social sciences. And his exposition of the Ríos family is a crushing blow to those who have fatuously declaimed the joys of Puerto Rican poverty. And if Lewis' volume assists in redefining social science, perhaps it may also have the far greater effect of showing the way toward a redefinition of society.

How fascinating it is to read how a brilliant anthropologist (and magnificent person) like Ruth Benedict approaches sociological problems with fresh insight. It has become so fashionable to criticize Benedict's "cultural relativism" that we sometimes tend to slight her concrete work. It is no exaggeration to note that Benedict said more on the subject of race prejudice in three pages than most sociologists have squeezed out in 300 pages. In this connection, it should also be noted that Redfield's essay, "The Cultural Role of the Cities," is the basic essay on comparative urban sociology, yet I have not seen it mentioned in a single text on urbanization! Pitifully few sociologists have dared say the obvious with anywhere near the clarity of Miss Benedict: "Race prejudice is deeply entrenched in American routine life and probably, measured by any objective standard, only South Africa goes further in segregation, discrimination, and humiliation."[6]

Our sociologists too often assume that the present condition is a permanent condition. This is one reason why the field of race relations has fallen into a kind of torpor. So barren has the "area" become, in fact, that it is being rapidly subsumed into the "high status" field of "small-group research"—at a time in American history when the racial problem has reached a peak of critical importance. Why is it that the most significant *sociological* statements on the racial question come from James Baldwin writing in *The New Yorker* and from Norman Podhoretz writing in *Commentary*? Is it not possible that the humanities may teach sociologists, no less than the other way around? Similarly, on questions of conflict and conflict resolution the sociologist needs to know the comparative data that the anthropologist makes available for public distribution. How can such notions as the biological and instinctual "impulses" toward war be put to deserved rest without reference to evidence derived from the preliterate societies?

Benedict's theory of "lethal" and "non-lethal" types of conflict squares very well with present researches into "safety-valve" equivalences for the prevention

6. Ruth Benedict, *An Anthropologist at Work: Writings of Ruth Benedict*, ed. by Margaret Mead (Boston: Houghton Mifflin Co., 1959).

of total conflict through programmed and controlled conflict. But perhaps what we need above all is the sagacity of a Benedict: "We wage the lethal variety of the genus War and the poisonousness of it comes not from what man is but from what society is." What a herculean challenge! If the problem is social and not rooted in man's "nature," how can sociologists continue to shirk their responsibilities for the study of conflict?

Each of the books under consideration introduces, either through design or by inference, a strong sense of humanist concern. It would take a lengthy search to find any series of books by sociologists that reveal the same set of concerns. Perhaps the chief reason lies in the fact that anthropologists show an intimate concern for problems of mind, while the behavioral-actionist emphasis in sociology tends to make its view of man "mind-less." Only that which is translatable into forms of action tends to be included in the sociological purview. Is this realistic? Can it actually be the case that sociologists believe that all acts exhaust the contents of the mind? The world of artifacts and symbols, myths, ideologies, and slogans has been relegated to a subordinate position in a desperate and futile effort to rid society of culture. The sociologist has become so alienated from cultural life as such that the assumption that he can in turn study the cultural forms of social life as a subsystem becomes transformed from an assumption into a presumption.

The work of Abraham Edel and May Edel is a happy family fusion of cross-disciplinary interests.[7] Abraham Edel is a philosopher, his wife a skilled anthropologist. The pivotal value of this book is its synthesis of materials on ethical beliefs in preliterate cultures. There is so much prattle in sociological quarters concerning the "separation" of facts and values that one might imagine that there is a papal ban on the empirical study of values as such. Utilizing the work of Benedict, Redfield, and Kluckhohn in anthropology, and the naturalist tradition in American philosophy, the authors have fashioned a first-class volume. The Edels work at many levels: they offer an accounting of ethical systems, wide and narrow, primitive and civilized; they present an inventory of what different cultures conceive of as the valuable, the good, and the useful; and above all, they offer a typology for the scientific study of ethical systems. The important social science element in their work is a transcultural analysis of different ethical systems and how they relate to an overall valuational base; *i.e.*, how a moral premise serves basic needs and meets fundamental aspirations.

The Edels ask of a moral system no less and no more than we ask of a scientific system: that it satisfy needs and fulfill aspirations. This does not mean that science and ethics are identical in orientation or in methodology. Science reflects the human need to solve the immediate and the commonplace, while ethics reflects the needs of men for transcendence, for adventure, emergence, and creativity. The Edels insist that a scientific study of ethics would resist a foreclosure on

7. Abraham Edel and May Edel, *Anthropology and Ethics* (Springfield, Ill.: Charles C Thomas, 1959).

further evaluations. The transcultural approach of the Edels dovetails with the similar demands of Becker that a continuing look at such psychiatric phenomena as schizophrenia and depression in the light of changing circumstances and a wider social science perspective would also have profoundly practical benefits in the fashioning of a useful ethic for modern man—a humanistic credo without the necessity of oracular misrepresentations. Supplementing the theory of a "common humanity and diverse cultures," the Edels and Becker seem to be insisting on the need for a "common ethos and diverse moralities."

The monograph written by Becker goes further along an interdisciplinary path than most books attempting to correlate anthropological and psychiatric information. Becker's book is unique in its steadfast refusal to take either the going shibboleths of Freudianism as Divine Law, or legalistic definitions of mental illness as sociologically meaningful. The work of Becker, along with that of Szasz in psychiatry[8] and Goffman in sociology,[9] is leading the way toward a truly synthetic social psychological account of mental strain in the industrial world and physical stress in the "total institutional" set-up of insane asylums and prisons. The attempt to transfer psychiatric analysis from instinctual grounds to a cognitive base can have the most revolutionary effects on future discussions of mental health and mental deterioration. Becker's use of the naturalistic tradition in American philosophy is as worthwhile and meaningful as the Edels' use of the same tradition to revise our stereotypes about moral beliefs. These books leave no doubt that interdisciplinary research has a radicalizing agent as an intrinsic component. Everything from academic departmentalization to hospital bureaucratization will be subject to scrutiny and change. Those who doubt this need only to reflect on how capricious and tenuous departmental separation and professional bureaucratization are to understand that the future organization of social science will scarcely resemble its present forms.

Extensive commentary on the papers contained in the Benedict and Redfield volumes is not possible here. Nonetheless, it is instructive to compare the types of editorializing done in each. The Redfield volume, edited by Margaret Park Redfield, is beautifully realized. Mrs. Redfield supplies brief sketches to most of the essays, while Raymond Firth's introductory note is both to the point and in excellent taste. Ruth Benedict was not quite so fortunate. Her papers, subtitled *Writings of Ruth Benedict*, are edited by Margaret Mead. Unfortunately, one gets the distinct impression that Mead is running in competition with her deceased colleague. Each section is prefaced by an essay by Mead, oftentimes far more indicative of the editor's biases than of Benedict's position. The editorializing is a trifle too cloying and pretentious for the occasion and seems singularly inappropriate to the nature of the book. Mead's remarks sound like a prepared brief urging Benedict's canonization but offer little illumination of her as an anthropologist.

8. T. S. Szasz, "Politics and Mental Health," *American Journal of Psychiatry*, CXV (1958), esp. pp. 507–509.

9. Erving Goffman, *Asylums: Essays on the Social Situations of Mental Patients and Other Inmates* (Chicago: Aldine Publishing Company, 1961).

In conclusion, the plea of the previous generation of anthropologists for inter-disciplinary effort has been turned into the practice of the present generation. And with this have come new strategies for the social sciences as a whole. The uses of this kind of "anthropological" research for sociologists are such that, with even a modicum of redirected energies, it is possible to forecast a large-scale improvement in the quality of the sociology of the sixties.

13. *Max Weber and*
the Spirit of American Sociology

IF THERE IS ONE figure in the sociological firmament who needs no special *Festschrift* one hundred years after his birth, it is Max Weber. Why? Simply because we celebrate him every working day in every scholarly way. Indeed, Weber has become the Benedict Spinoza of sociology. Just as all major wings of modern philosophy find something in Spinoza to take seriously— pragmatists praise his liberalism, historicists adhere to his concept of freedom through necessity, Thomists praise his God-intoxicated universe, while Marxists are equally fervent in honoring his materialist ontology—so too has this univer- salizing trend unfolded in relation to Weber. It is almost as if Weber does not just provide a *theory* of status legitimation, but in his person brings a special form of legitimation to the sociologist. Parsonians can identify with Weber's notions of bureaucracy and social stratification; Mertonians can identify with Weber's concepts of career patterns of scientists and theologians and their stimulus to social change; and Millsians can identify with Weber's concepts of authority and dysfunctionality of raw power no less than the belief that at its source every social problem is a moral paradox.

First presented at the annual meetings of the Midwest Sociological Society, in its special program honoring Max Weber, in April, 1963. The study deals with the specific impact Weber has had on the three major wings of American sociology, as they are represented in the work of Parsons, Merton, and Mills. It is seen that Weber functions as a legitimation device, no less than a source of social concepts; and that in fact it is this former aspect of legitimation that may be paramount. First published in *Sociological Quarterly*, 5, no. 4 (Autumn, 1964).

The irony of the situation is that the "Midwest tradition" in sociology, that tendency sometimes covered by the rubric "Chicago school" and points west, should be celebrating Weber's centennial. For if there is one tendency in contemporary American sociology that owes relatively little to Weber and, indeed, offers slender obeisance to him, it is the Midwestern style of work—the style identified with Mead, Dewey, Veblen, Cooley, and Park, among others.[1] So I take this gathering of mainstream American sociologists, insofar as it represents a common core of ideas, to be unusual not in its celebration of Weber, but in being the one group that can still afford to maintain an aura, if not the substance, of intellectual detachment and dispassion in the face of the lionization and canonization process Weber is undergoing elsewhere in the United States.

Since this is a discussion, not on Max Weber per se, but on how his work is perceived as it is channelized into the mainstream of American sociology, we necessarily have something less than a balanced view of Weber. The reader will hopefully not rest content with my interpretations of Weber but will turn to Weber himself. This made clear, let us simply point out that the degree to which the "Chicago style" in sociology has ignored Weber is sufficient to call forth some explanation. While the Weber celebration was going on from coast to coast, it seemed to leave the midsections of America unimpressed.

Howard S. Becker's recent studies on deviance have not a single mention of Weber;[2] Erving Goffman's pioneering work in social psychology and his similarly unusual work on behavior in bureaucratic institutions are also without noticeable indebtedness to Weber's sociology.[3] Even where one would expect some real intellectual grappling with Weber's problems, e.g., in social stratification, we find W. Lloyd Warner making only the most casual references to Weber.[4] He speaks of the "obsessive" concern which Marxians have for the problem of power and rank, and mentions Weber as less dogmatic about the problem but no less obsessive. In a single reference to charisma, Warner sees this concept as "little more than one form of personal *mana*." Taking these as typical, several hypotheses suggests themselves—and the proportion of the "mix" depends upon the wing of Midwestern sociology under consideration.

First, Weber has little to say of the demi-monde, of the underworld in which

1. One of the very few efforts dealing with the pragmatic aspects of the Chicago style of work in the dissertation written by C. Wright Mills before he became a Millsian. See *Sociology and Pragmatism: A Study in the American Higher Learning*, ed. by Irving Louis Horowitz (New York: Oxford University Press, 1964).

2. Howard S. Becker, *Outsiders: Studies in the Sociology of Deviance* (New York: Free Press of Glencoe, 1963).

3. Erving Goffman, *The Presentation of Self in Everyday Life* (Garden City, N.Y.: Doubleday & Co., 1959); *Asylums: Essays on the Social Situations of Mental Patients and Other Inmates* (Chicago: Aldine Publishing Company, 1961). It is not that Goffman finds nothing useful in European intellectual life. Quite the reverse. He is no less fond of citing the work of Sartre and de Beauvoir than he is that of Kenneth Burke.

4. W. Lloyd Warner, *Social Class in America* (Chicago: Science Research Associates, Inc., 1949; reprinted, New York: Harper & Row, 1960), especially p. 272.

life is not "rationalized and bureaucratically structured" but basically unstructured, deviant, and marginal. Even the notion of charisma is directly related by him to political authority. This reflects Weber's general neglect of the dysfunctional and personal elements in his system of social stratification; a theme which has been developed by many of Weber's American commentators and needs no elaboration here.

Second, Weber is a European sociologist par excellence. He sees things in grand world historic terms. Thus, even when he comes to the United States and sees "the Greek shining the Yankee's shoes for five cents, the German acting as his waiter, the Irishman managing his politics, and the Italian digging his dirty ditches," his real interests are not focused on the persons performing such roles but on the "Yankee" for whom the work was being performed.[5] True enough, this is circumscribed by his general belief in the waste created by capitalism. But unlike the muckraking tradition which wafted out of the stink of the Chicago stockyards, unlike the studies of ethnic minorities, racial groups, psychologically dislocated and sociologically deformed types, Weber uttered no cry for social change, for just laws, or for extending human rights. Like the Marxist "other," he saw only the "hopelessness of social legislation in a system of state particularism." Thus, his very totalism clashed with the reform instincts of Chicago-style sociology.

Third, there is the point almost accidentally hit upon by Warner. Weber was concerned with power and authority, how they became legitimized, how status depends on authority. The world of the Chicago school, even of its conservative echelons, never could accept such a formulation, which seemingly denigrated status in deference to power and economy. Indeed, it is little wonder that while Weber himself viewed his work as on a scale with that of Marx, the provincial sociology of the Midwest saw him as one more footnote to the power and authority school that could claim such an unlikely blend as Plato, Machiavelli, Marx, and Rousseau. From the American perspective, Warner may be right. It may indeed be the case that what Weber conceived of as "world historic" is simply the decayed reflection of crumbling European intellectual edifices musing over their own past while taking a breather from war.

A fourth reason may be adduced here. Weber was "discovered" by a special kind of American: the worldly eastern sociologist trained in Europe, or at least learned in the languages and customs of central and northern Europe. Thus learning about Weber was sifted through a filter called *The Structure of Social Action*.[6] And the mood of the Chicago school in the 1930's was analytic rather

5. Cf. *From Max Weber: Essays in Sociology*, ed. and trans. with an Introduction by H. H. Gerth and C. Wright Mills (New York: Oxford University Press, 1946), p. 15.

6. It is not that the work of Weber went unnoticed or was unknown prior to the efforts of Parsons. But Parsons "internalized" or "operationalized" Weber. The working sociologist learned from Parsons how to use (Duncan might say abuse) Weber's work. See *The Structure of Social Action: A Study in Social Theory with Special Reference to a Group of Recent European Writers* (New York: McGraw-Hill Book Co., 1937).

than synthetic, symbolic rather than historic. How was the Chicago school to know of Weber's interests in such things as the ecology of the city, property rights, and the personal situation, plebeians and patricians, when the filtering process tended to minimize Weber's *Wirtschaft und Gesellschaft* precisely at those admittedly rare points where he ceased being systematic and grand, world historic and theoretic?[7]

This is said to make clear that the American response to Weber is considerably differentiated. The East Coast developed styles of sociological research that became increasingly gentlemanly and remote in form and bureaucratic in substance. It was obviously easier to place Weber in this kind of professional context. The West Coast rekindled an interest in Weber by shifting the emphasis to Weber as the political sociologist par excellence. There was also a clear shift in how the West Coast operated with the data—even though many of these men were East Coast products. There was an increasing emphasis on qualitative over quantitative findings. Nonetheless, the basic valuational posture remained unchanged. Coastal sociology retained an insistence on detachment over involvement, pure research over applied research. In such matters the Wild West was a product of the Columbia-Harvard-Yale styles of work. It was common to the Weberians that when they looked at the relationship of rich and poor, elites and masses, their personal *sympathies* may have been with the poor and the masses, but their professional *interests* were clearly focused upon the rich and the elites.

The role of Parsons in the dissemination of the spirit of Max Weber can scarcely be overestimated. It is not simply that the design of *The Structure of Social Action* gives the critical anchor to Weber's writings. As translator of *The Protestant Ethic and the Spirit of Capitalism* and later, with Henderson, of *The Theory of Social and Economic Organization*, Parsons set the tone for what was considered the essential Weber for a long while. Indeed, as Duncan has made clear, the very idiosyncracies of the Parsonian language find their ways into the corpus of those works of Weber he translated. If in the 1930's Parsons' definition of *Weberstudien* was rooted in the essay on the relationship of Protestantism to Capitalism, by the 1950's—and with a heavy dose of translations available—the shift of emphasis was made from Weber as illustrative of a "voluntaristic theory of action" to Weber as "illustrative of universalism and functional specificity." It is also Weber the analyst of the "Western world" and of the "Anglo-Saxon" world to whom Parsons responds. He sees or creates, as the case may be, Weber in his own image, as someone who understood both "the uniqueness of our social system" and no less "its precarious state of instability."[8]

7. In this respect, Don Martindale's work rounds out our vision of Weber considerably. See the translation he and Gertrud Neuwirth made of *The City* (Glencoe, Ill.: Free Press, 1958), and, in particular, his "Prefatory Remarks: The Theory of the City." See also Don Martindale, *The Nature and Types of Sociological Theory* (Boston: Houghton Mifflin, 1960), pp. 377–399. For a sound and impartial appraisal of the "Chicago school," see John Madge, *The Origins of Scientific Sociology* (New York: Free Press of Glencoe, 1962), pp. 88–125.

8. Talcott Parsons, Introduction to Max Weber, *The Theory of Social and Economic Organization*, trans. by A. M. Henderson and Talcott Parsons, ed. with an Introduction by Talcott Parsons (New York: Oxford University Press, 1947), pp. 82, 84.

That science can feed the needs of totalitarianism and of modern bureaucratic structure tended to be minimized by Parsons. This is really a consequence, hypothetically at least, of the Weberian tendency to overlook and minimize the dysfunctionality of bureaucracy as such. I say "tendency" because fascism did temporarily shake Parsons' insular belief in conservative solutions and led him to emphasize, between 1945 and 1949, the *checks upon* authority rather than the *rationality of* such authority.

It is not only what Weber stood for specifically that attracted Parsons, but rather the sense that Weber, unlike Durkheim, Marshall, Pareto, or even Freud, made possible the consideration of the social system as a *general theory*. Weber allowed for the evolution of a kind of sociological "imperialism" in which everything from family and personality to politics and economics could be viewed as a subsystem of sociology.[9] For example, in introducing his first volume of selected papers, Parsons notes the existence of two big problems for social science: the development of a unified language, which is converted into a need for a conceptual scheme as such, and a theory of the relation of the institutional structures to human behavior. On the latter score, Parsons identifies his view of function with that of Weber, since only when human motivation is linked to the operations of a social system are generalizations about people "sociologically relevant."[10]

On both counts, as a conceptual scheme and as a general theory, Weber offered Parsons a way of transforming sociology from a parochial discipline, confined to local, small, and middle-sized issues, to a discipline of universal, large-scale issues in which total systems proceed always and everywhere in the direction of increased rationality.[11]

To be a Parsonian became for a long time the only way a person in American sociology could tolerably deal with big issues without being condemned as a Marxist. And this very insight undoubtedly accounts in part for Parsons' profound animus for Marxism and socialism. His cold, analytic stance with respect to any sociology that came within sniffing distance of a positive appraisal of "dialectics" or any other aspect of Marxology differs markedly from his Olympian disregard for critics in general.[12]

Robert K. Merton, insofar as he represented a response to Weber, was interested not in systematizing but in secularizing him. Weber became one of

9. Irving Louis Horowitz, "Introduction to the New Sociology," in *The New Sociology* (New York: Oxford University Press, 1964), pp. 14–15.

10. Talcott Parsons, *Essays in Sociological Theory, Pure and Applied* (Glencoe, Ill.: Free Press, 1949), p. x.

11. On this point see Robin M. Williams, Jr., "The Sociological Theory of Talcott Parsons," in *The Social Theories of Talcott Parsons*, ed. by Max Black (Englewood Cliffs, N.J.: Prentice-Hall, 1961), pp. 88–89.

12. See Parsons' rare polemical reaction to Llewellyn Z. Gross's "Preface to a Metaphysical Framework for Sociology," *American Journal of Sociology*, 67 (September, 1961): 125–136. Parson's comment was carried in the same issue on pp. 136–140.

the classic figures to whom the good sociologist turns for inspiration and for new ideas about old themes. The great theme of bureaucratization in modern society, for example, was not an illustration of universalist-instrumentalist action, but rather a challenge for further social research. It provided an opportunity to "build a Solomon's House for sociologists"—which opportunity, indeed, they have not missed. Bureaucracy enabled Merton to treat critically what Weber had failed to deal with substantively: the dysfunctions of certain bureaucratic structures, the ineffective consequences of overconformity and maximum rule-boundedness, and, above all, the possibility that Weber's pessimism, if not uncalled for, may have been slightly premature—since as a matter of fact, "bureaucracy is a secondary group structure" oriented toward depersonalized achievement of "certain activities" only when primary group relations fail to solve problems and "run counter to these formalized norms."[13] Indeed, the trend toward increasing bureaucratization raises for Merton a set of interesting problems, which he outlines, and to which many of his students turned in subsequent years.

Likewise, Merton's use of Weber's sociology of religion is radically different from that of Parsons. Instead of offering a propaedeutic review of Weber's position, Merton tried his hand at a slightly adjacent, related, and markedly distinct problem: the differential tendency for German Protestants to pursue scientific career patterns. It is not that the results are particularly astonishing, nor are they intended to be. In a bibliographical postscript Merton says that the results arrived at, at the empirical level, are "conceived as an effort to follow" and extend the "mandate . . . which Weber had opened up."[14] And as if to underscore his nonpolemical attitude toward the work of Weber, we find that an extremely important paper by Merton, employing roughly the same analysis with respect to Protestantism and the rise of scientific societies in England, is published in *Science and Society*, which at that time (the late 1930's) was an avowedly Marxian periodical. In other words, the problem of capitalism and its relation to the Protestant Reformation, and how capitalism ramifies outward, is seen by Merton as a scientific problem bequeathed to modern sociology by Marx and Weber, stripped of its inherited ideological squabbling over whether economy or religion is the originating causal base of social development. But the scientific problem in turn is seen as a social problem, a problem in democracy.[15]

Merton undoubtedly responded to Weber as the sort of scholar who, above all, represented cosmopolitanism and not some form of localism. Merton is no "easterner," but rather a sociologist in touch with the world of learning. Indeed, just how important this is to Merton is reflected by his criticism of provincialism,

13. Robert K. Merton, "Bureaucratic Structure and Personality," in *Social Theory and Social Structure*, rev. and enlarged ed. (Glencoe, Ill.: Free Press, 1957), pp. 204–205.

14. "Puritanism, Pietism, and Science," *ibid.*, p. 595.

15. "Science and Democratic Social Structure," *ibid.*, pp. 550–561.

which he rejects twice in the same sentence of his Acknowledgments to his omnibus collection, *Social Theory and Social Structure*. Sorokin is acknowledged as having helped him "escape from the provincialism of thinking that effective studies of society were confined within American borders and from slum-encouraged provincialism of thinking that the primary subject-matter of sociology was centered in such peripheral problems of social life as divorce and juvenile delinquency." But since Sorokin has already gone off to "become absorbed in the study of historical movements on the grand scale," the search in Europe focused very heavily upon Marx, Durkheim, Weber, and, in terms of interest, the problems selected for study by Weber—bureaucracy and the social structure, and the role of religion in social change—were uppermost for Merton over a long span of years. Even in such recent papers of Merton as "Social Conflict over Styles of Sociological Work," the impact of Weber upon Merton's liberal-heterodox view of the field is noticeable. In it, he argues for a Weberian middle position, against the *wertfrei* and *partinost* alike, and for Weber's concept of a sociology that is *Wertbeziehung*—value-relevant. And to the charge that this is a fuzzy concept, Merton answered much the way Weber did: that its very ambiguities allow for open debate and differing evaluations.[16]

Thus we might conclude that if for Parsons, Weber was the conservative, almost Prussian, sociologist par excellence, a serious student of bureaucracy, elites, and charismatic authority, for Merton he is the liberal European (rather than German) sociologist par excellence, a man who upheld the dignity of learning over and against the indignities of nationalism. The interesting thing is that Weber is such a magnificent ambiguity that he can easily uphold both interpretations—as well as a third, to which we now turn.

To be described as influenced by a figure is not necessarily a form of flattery. And perhaps the best case in point is the influence of Weber on Mills. As he was for Parsons and for Merton, so too Weber was for Mills a part of the classic tradition in sociology. But unlike Parsons and Merton, Mills' consciousness of Weber stemmed from German emigré sources. Mills learned about Weber from a German sociologist—from Hans Gerth. But with his Midwest intellectual roots, Mills found his interest in Weber tempered by a range of considerations raised by other classic figures, such as Veblen in economics, Mead in social psychology, and Dewey in philosophy. Thus from the outset, Mills was uncomfortable in the role of interpreting Weber. What he did, in effect, was to pragmatize Weber. This is most obvious in the introduction that he and Gerth wrote for the Max Weber translations. He sees Weber, like Dewey and James, as "one of the last of the political professors who made detached contributions to science, and, as the intellectual vanguard of the middle classes, were also leading figures."[17]

16. Robert K. Merton, "Social Conflict over Styles of Sociological Work," *Transactions of the Fourth World Congress of Sociology*, vol. 3 (1959), Reprint No. 286, Bureau of Social Research Publications, pp. 34–35.

17. Gerth and Mills, *From Max Weber*, p. 25.

Thus Weber is the educator and exemplar of intellectual courage. It was not refined pedagogic aspects of education but the moral infusion that found such response in Mills.

It is interesting to note that aside from the introductory essay to *From Max Weber*, Mills wrote very little about Weber that did not carry an at least implicit critical tone. In part this derived from his early work with Gerth. Nonetheless, it is a tendency which Mills seemed to push even farther and harder than his mentor, if we are to judge the respective paths which they took. For it was, after all, Gerth who was responsible for the monumental translation projects of Weber's religion-sociology, and it was Mills who placed decreasing emphasis on the Weber legacy as such. Mills saw early that Weber was indeed something less than the radical savior of sociology. He understood that this kind of identification of charisma with irrationality was linked with totalitarianism, which, if Weber did not approve of, at least he had no defense against. Similarly, Weber's notion that bureaucracy would remain fairly stable throughout revolutionary shifts in power was a generalization that did not obtain for twentieth-century bureaucracy.[18] Indeed, it astonished Mills, even toward the close of his career, that this highly questionable formulation of the bureaucratic continuity should remain unchecked and uncritized for so long.[19]

One item from Weber that Mills picked up, which he saw as potentially revolutionary in its consequences, was the difference between Marx and Weber on the social organization of modern capitalism. The idea of Marx that capitalism represents an anarchy of production is subject to a jeering criticism by Mills, who saw this as one of Marx's basic generic errors; and with Weber, Mills understood that what makes capitalism so viable or at least durable is that Western capitalism is rational and planned in the extreme.[20] He also learned from Weber that what makes the development of a true revolutionary experience so difficult in modern capitalist society is that rationality has shifted from the individual and is now lodged in the total institution; because of this, the increased education of modern man has no revolutionary consequences, but only goes to feed the needs of the giant institution for happy and well-educated robots. Another place where Mills linked up with Weber, and in truth the only other place he could, given his radical posture, was in Weber's critique of the behavior of the intellectual; the sacrifice of the intellect that was involved in the outfitting of the scientific soul with antiquarian ideologies. Weber's notion of value-relevance was translated by Merton as the need for heterodoxy, but by Mills as the need for commitment lest the sociologist become one of those easily manipulated plebeians unable to perform an authoritative national role.

This point cuts deep. Along with Weber, Mills saw the need to connect intel-

18. C. Wright Mills with Hans Gerth, "A Marx for the Managers," in *Power, Politics, and People: The Collected Essays of C. Wright Mills*, ed. by Irving L. Horowitz (New York and London: Oxford University Press, 1963), pp. 54, 68–69.

19. "Two Styles of Social Science Research," *ibid.*, pp. 557–558.

20. "The Nazi Behemoth," *ibid.*, p. 171.

lect with power and not to shy away from the challenging dangers of possible corruption; and the need to face squarely the choice between what should rule— intellect or passion. He was contemptuous of fears as to whether intellect can be saved by avoiding problems of power and authority. At the very root, one would have to say that this is what Mills learned from Weber. Methodologically, he learned from Weber to deal with society not simply as total social structures (as Parsons had done), but a step beyond that, as total social structures in a comparative context, so that systematic sociology becomes somehow transformed into historical sociology without losing touch with empirical reality.[21]

Mills created such an aura of individuality, even down to idiosyncratic behavior, that we can easily overlook or minimize the extent to which he offered a solid bridge between European and American traditions in sociology. What made Mills unique was that theoretically he closed the gap between the materialist and the positivist traditions in philosophy, the abstract and the pragmatic traditions in educational theory, the historical subject and the empirical methods in sociology proper. In American sociology he was one of the few men who could study Puerto Rican migration patterns, Detroit labor intellectuals, and high-class New York prostitution in an intimate "Chicago style," with the methodological tools fashioned at the Bureau of Social Research and also with the systematic theoretical orientation fashioned by classicists such as Weber, Pareto, and Durkheim. And perhaps because of his very electicism, Mills could speak as the *American* sociologist par excellence, and yet be viewed throughout the world as the American *sociologist* par excellence.

We have seen that Weber was instrumental in opening up a vast network of problems handled quite differently by Parsons, Merton, and Mills. Weber became in American sociological history the form of legitimation or the conservatism of a Parsons, but no less for the liberalism of a Merton and the radicalism of a Mills. And it is the irony of the "immortal" that though he bends every effort to summarize and synthesize problems, his very act of synthesis, his very engagement in a dialogue with past intellectual gods, only opens up once again the perennial problems that sociology has in common with the humanities. It is precisely those problems that make all talk of sociology as a pure natural science profoundly suspect. And surely, if there is one lesson that Weber teaches all his disciples and all of his critics, it is simply that sociology is a human science and not merely a social science.

21. C. Wright Mills, *The Sociological Imagination* (New York: Oxford University Press, 1959); see, in particular, his critique of Parsons, pp. 25–49.

14. *Mainliners and Marginals: The Human Shape of Sociological Theory*

"*A SCIENCE WHICH* hesitates to forget its founders is lost." With these proud words culled from the philosopher A. N. Whitehead, the sociologist Robert K. Merton introduces his justifiably famous collection of papers on *Social Theory and Social Structure*.[1] One is tempted to make a quick retort to this sentiment by recalling the words of Sören Kierkegaard, to the effect that the man who would forget the past "has condemned himself and deserves nothing better than what is sure to befall him, namely, to perish."[2] Both positions have avid, not to mention livid, followers in the sociological ranks. And in the hands of its supreme practitioners, there is, and has been for many years, a forceful effort to

This paper is a typological integration of the various personnel found practicing sociology. It is also an effort to integrate the ideas of E. C. Hughes in *Men at Work* and C. Wright Mills in the *Sociological Imagination* with respect to the operations of professionalism as an ideology and as an organizational style. It was published first in the *Philosophy of Science*, 31, no. 3 (July, 1964); and in an expanded version in *Sociological Theory: Questions and Problems*, edited by Llewellyn Gross (New York: Harper and Row, 1967).

1. Alfred North Whitehead, *On Understanding Education*. Quoted by Robert K. Merton in the Preface to *Social Theory and Social Structure* (New York: Free Press, 1957).

2. Sören Kierkegaard, *Repetition: An Essay in Experimental Psychology* (Princeton, N.J.: Princeton University Press, 1946), p. 5.

get beyond the apparent contradictions involved in these two philosophic stand-points and, at the risk of a nasty word, try to *synthesize* them.[3]

If we drive the contradictions between Whitehead and Kierkegaard far enough, or examine the differences between modern sociological titans such as Samuel Stouffer and C. Wright Mills, what remain are the basic questions and root metaphors of contemporary sociological theory: Should sociology concern itself with its own history as part of theory, or should sociology, like medicine, view its history as part of a humanistic hubris which is better flushed out and forgotten? To what extent can self-awareness be considered part of scientific understanding? And to what degree is self-consciousness a literary intrusion upon the vigorous and rigorous character of all true science? From these questions we can clearly perceive the importance which the choice of sociological stylings has for the character of sociological theory.

To sharply demarcate boundaries between men who fundamentally share the same universe of scientific discourse may be viewed as a cursed scholastic inheri-tance—a navel-picking exercise out of proportion to the actual worth of the differences that obtain. While there can be no quarrel with those who would caution against drawing the internal differences of sociology too exactly and too tightly, it is surely no answer to grab hold of the opposite intellectual pole and refuse to make any distinctions in the name of an engineered consensus. The care-fully drawn ambiguities with which the word sociology is modified—"field," "craft," "profession," "occupation," "convention," etc.—indicate just how sensi-tive the man of sociological learning can be to his hard-won efforts. Let us therefore try to overcome the false option between exclusive self-reflection and its infantile rejection of its own history. This we will do by treating problems of sociological theory as basically being responses to the emergence of the field of sociology as an organizational framework and, more decisively, as a human enterprise.[4]

3. We may take the current raft of books on the subject of sociological self-analysis as being precisely concerned with this task of synthesis. See in particular the following: Arthur J. Vidich, Joseph Bensman, and Maurice R. Stein, eds., *Reflections on Community Studies* (New York: Wiley, 1964); Phillip E. Hammond, ed., *Sociologists at Work: Essays on the Craft of Social Research* (New York: Basic Books, 1964); and Gideon Sjoberg, ed., *Politics, Ethics, and Social Research* (Cambridge, Mass.: Schenkman Publishing Co., forthcoming).

4. While the treatment of sociological theory from the viewpoint of the organization of sociologists is not a commonplace, certain forceful antecedents to such a perspective should not go unnoticed. For good examples, see the following: Pitirim Sorokin, "Some Contrasts of Contemporary European and American Sociology," *Social Forces*, 8, no. 1 (September, 1929): 57–62; Robert K. Merton, "The Role of the Intellectual in Public Bureaucracy," *Social Forces*, 27, no. 4 (May, 1945): 405–415; Talcott Parsons, "The Professions and the Social Structure," *Social Forces*, 17, no. 4 (May, 1939): 457–467; C. Wright Mills, "Two Styles of Research in Current Social Studies," *Philosophy of Science*, 20, no. 4 (October, 1953): 266–275; and most recently but on a more general level, Walter Hirsch, "Knowledge, Power, and Social Change: The Role of American Scientists," *Explorations in Social Change*, ed. by G. K. Zollschan and W. Hirsch (Boston: Houghton Mifflin Co., 1964); Everett C. Hughes, "Professional And Career Problems of Sociology," *Men and Their Work* (Glencoe, Ill.: Free Press, 1958), pp. 157–168.

I

What we must concern ourselves with is the evolution of a language that will permit a description of the organization and the ideology of sociology within a single framework. To do this means, first of all, to describe four types and two pairs of sociological styles. Those who conceive of it as an occupation constitute the particular pairing we will call *mainliners*—those who are in the center of sociological activities and disputes. The second coupling of sociologists is less easily defined. At their extremes they are the unsociologist, the individual who is trained in the discipline, but whose fundamental allegiance is to the institution for which he works; and the antisociologist, who, while likewise trained in sociology, has a fundamentally different allegiance, to the intellectual horizons which inform all the social sciences. This pairing can be called, with some qualms, to be sure, the *marginals*.[5]

To those who feel that science is some sort of monolithic enterprise performed by marching soldiers given their orders by an elite corps of knowers, these pairings will appear to slash at the very flesh of sociology. But for those less given to a romantic view of science as the virgin birth of knowledge, the pairings will be perfectly understandable. Thus far, the most incisive contribution to this concept is Merton's evidence that norm inconsistency is characteristic of all social systems, and certainly characteristic of science in the form of the growth of "contradictory pairs of norms."[6] For the purpose of this study we will explore each pairing separately, and then see how they connect with each other in the actual conduct of sociological theory.

Toward the close of the fading fifties, in 1958 to be precise, an organizational confrontation took place. The formal issue before its membership was this: Should the American Sociological Society (ASS) be rechristened the American Sociological Association (ASA)? The results of the vote conclusively demonstrated that for a majority of the participants it was preferable to be known as a group of ASA's rather than a collection of ASS's. But, frivolity aside, the debate on nomenclature introduced matters of deep substance, which have increasingly come to disturb the sociological community. It became evident that underlying the manifest problem of bureaucratic nomenclature is the more serious choice of scientific images and ethical guidelines. The big question continued to be unresolved: Should the practitioner of sociology be considered primarily as a member of a scientific profession or is he to be viewed as associated with a scientific discipline? It does little good to say that "profession" and "occupation"

5. This formulation owes a profound intellectual debt to the paper by Alvin W. Gouldner, "Cosmopolitans and Locals: Toward an Analysis of Latent Social Roles," *Administrative Science Quarterly*, 2 (December, 1957, and March, 1958): 281–306, 444–480. This debt is herewith acknowledged.

6. See Robert K. Merton, "The Ambivalence of Scientists," *Bulletin of John Hopkins Hospital*, no. 112 (February, 1963): 79–97. And for a creative application of this concept, see Marvin B. Sussman, "The Social Problems of the Sociologist," *Social Problems*, 11, no. 3 (Winter, 1964): 215–225.

are not incompatible. This mediating formula leaves open exactly the issue that must be settled: whether "profession" is a more meaningful sociological designation than "occupation"; or, indeed, whether these concepts are at all scientifically relevant or simply represent strategies for upward mobility.

Actually, what has taken place in sociology represents in a most acute form the basic rift *within* empirical modalities, between pragmatism and positivism. It is not an argument *between* the empirical and the nonempirical, for that discussion has been resolved, with rare exceptions, in favor of empirical techniques and definitions. We might say that the pragmatic currents supply the intellectual cement for occupationalism; while the positivistic currents supply the same sort of support for professionalism—with the "machine runs" and the "machine room" providing the web of data justifying a heuristic approach to sociology.

But even within such a common modality, profound differences obtain. The professional is concerned with developing a picture of the world, a model of the universe, which to all intents and purposes jumps up at him from the data. A good example of this is the account by James A. Davis of his work "Great Books and Small Groups." His concluding remarks reveal an almost mystic reverence for the self-revealing properties of data. "Those few moments when a new set of tables comes up from the machine room and questions begin to be answered; when relationships actually hold under controls; when the pile of tables on the desk suddenly meshes to yield a coherent chapter; when in a flash you see a neat test for an interpretation; when you realize you have found out something about something important that nobody ever knew before—these are the moments that justify research."[7] The occupationalist, for his part, has a more affective approach toward the object of his study, and his disposition is toward developing theories of behavior, which are more likely to be imposed upon the data than to jump up from them. In describing Riesman's attitude toward a project on sociability, a project that could just as well have been conducted in the circumstances of Davis' Great Books groups, we find out that "his own forte lay in the more anthropological methods of observation and description. His approach to the study of parties was to ask what a whole party was like: what were its major, often concurrent themes; what were its blockages, frustrations, liquidities, accomplishments?"[8] This is not simply a distinction between statistical and ethnographic information, but between differing notions of what constitutes the proper relationship between investigator and informant.

Pragmatism supplied the intellectual ammunition for two wings of the famed "Chicago School"—the educationists as well as the sociologists. Men like Mead, Dewey, Morris, and Veblen insisted upon an orientation in the social and behavioral sciences towards values of ameliorating and understanding the plight

7. James A. Davis, "Great Books and Small Groups: An Informal History of a National Survey," in Hammond, *Sociologists at Work*, pp. 233–234.
8. David Riesman and Jeanne Watson, "The Sociability Project: A Chronical of Frustration and Achievement," in Hammond, *Sociologists at Work*, esp. pp. 278–279.

of the poor. It was this picture of the world that played a large part in the drive behind the sociological wing. While it is true that the Chicago type of sociologist makes a posture out of appearing "hard," "tough," and "unsentimental," this is partially due to the easy sentimentalism that has been popularly associated with those kinds of human materials with which he works. The pragmatism of men like Louis Wirth, Robert E. Park, Walter Reckless, and Everett C. Hughes rests on the fact that they wrote not only about urbanization, but about how crime can be minimized or channelized; not only about Negro-White relations, but on how such relationships can be humanized. Their commitment then, sociologically, was strongly influenced by their belief in reform. The occupationalist emphasizes the connections of the social problem to the social program, and in so doing defines the core tasks of sociology in a unique way.

The idea of sociology as an occupation squares well with the "good craftsman" view of the field. Style, literary "punch," and publicity are genuine values for the pragmatic mind, as they are for the occupationalist. Both want to provide not just "hard data," but much more than that—sociological awareness of social marginality. Only a sophistication about the world could save the sociologist from falling into the square mold. And such sophistication is integrally linked to sociology as doing, as exposure. Active knowing, implying action programs, made for a pragmatic fusion of theory and practice in the best populist manner. Living was its own reward; action generated its own further consequences. Sociology thus acquired an open-ended property in the occupationalists' hands. It meant informed policy, easy movement between the scholar and the policy-maker. It meant making the sociologist aware of himself as a social actor in the very act of making sociology. The Chicago School product attempted to develop a "package" that contained not only hard data but also ethnographic observation and value orientations.[9] And in its most recent and most sophisticated form, it is an approach that readily grants, and indeed insists upon, the positive value of facing up to the "irreconcilable conflict between the interests of science and the interests of those studies."[10]

Within empirical sociology a new strategy of research has evolved. The positivistic wing, with its emphasis on observation independent of action, nomological laws apart from real laws, logical stipulations apart from ontological status, and above all, criteria of verification apart from standards of valuation, has come along to challenge older holistic conceptions of the field. It is clear that for this positivist tendency, the control of variance is far more important than an impressionist understanding of social problems. The dilemma is then that the control of variance rules out examination of a whole range of variables that might impede or impinge upon the experimental situation. It might well be that

9. See Irving Louis Horowitz, "Max Weber and the Spirit of American Sociology," in *The Sociological Quarterly*, 5, no. 4 (Autumn, 1964). See Ch. 13 of this book.

10. See Howard S. Becker, "Problems in the Publication of Field Studies," in Vidich, Bensman, and Stein, *Reflections on Community Studies*, pp. 276–277.

the tendency of this group to lean toward social psychology is not so much a reflection of intellectual preferences as of methodological pressures for exactitude.

To speak of the professionalist as a positivist should not conjure up memories of August Comte and the "engineering of the soul" attributed to social science. For the Columbia School would be most vociferous in its denial of offering recipes for social change. It deals in "implications for action" rather than actual policy recommendations. By positivism is meant the development of a total portrait of man derived from the combination of discrete questionnaires, surveys, and other "atomic" facts. Professionalism is a sociological ideology emanating from the sharp distinction between facts and values. It considers sociology as a positive science in the special sense that the ends for which it is used are independent of the findings as such; and it views professional expertise as something apart from intellectual luster. If the pragmatic Chicago School was defined by the particular problems that sociology should at least confront, the Columbia School is no less clearly defined by the emphasis on the universal and scientistic values of sociology. Indeed, it views with contempt "social dilettantism" and is hostile to any notion of sociology that would deprive it of its "systematic," "serious," or "austere" characteristics.[11]

On a different plane, professionalization, by virtue of its grim fight for status, ironically permits a kind of irresponsibility with respect to the future of the social world. The professional can, by virtue of his professionalism, exempt himself as a scientist from responsibility for the ends to which his scientific findings are put. It is not that the positivists are politically more conservative than the pragmatists. Perhaps the very reverse is the case. The positivists were in all likelihood more radical in their political beliefs, more dedicated to the idea of socialist change, more convinced of the corruptness of the bourgeois social order than were the pragmatists—who at the most were (and remain) "worldly" men in a limited demi-monde setting. Therefore, the main difference is not in the beliefs held, but in what is expected in the way of sociological reinforcement of such beliefs.

The positivist methodologically oriented sociologist has a compartmentalized view in which the quality, the formal elegance of the sociology performed, counts for more than the quantity or the purposes for which sociology is employed. The European positivist tradition gave a special warrant for a sociology that could be considered scientific without at the same time outraging the sensibilities of other scientists. The pragmatists, for their part, developed a series of intellectual networks—groups of people responsive to larger pressures— and in turn they sought to act as a pressure group on the larger society.[12] The

---

11. See the most interesting "Acknowledgment" to Paul F. Lazarsfeld in Merton, *Social Theory and Social Structure.*

12. C. Wright Mills, *Sociology and Pragmatism: A Study in the American Higher Learning,* ed. by Irving Louis Horowitz (New York: Paine-Whitman Publishers, 1964), pp. 35–83.

positivists, on the other hand, developed a series of "circles"—and like a circle, the people included were responsive only to one another's pressures, acting as insulating material against the general pressures of society. The extreme intellectualism of the professional ideology is thus, in an American context, either akin to, or a direct response to, the kinds of positivism brought to America from Vienna, Berlin, and Warsaw.[13] The actionism of the occupational ideology tends to be more of a response to immediate situations and to "nativistic" tendencies in social thought. The positivist wing in sociology desires logical coherence, firm rules, and the kinds of inner-directed rituals geared to satisfy collegial standards. The pragmatist wing in sociology desires connection, guidelines to action, and the kinds of outer-directed experiences geared to satisfy recipients of service and information.

This point may be summed up by noting that the sociologist who emphasizes professionalism tends to have as his main reference group other working sociologists; while the sociologist emphasizing an occupational orientation has as his main reference group a directly concerned public, whether real or imaginary. The positivist wants *to know* as an end; the pragmatist wants *to act* as his end. This distinction is shown clearly in the attitudes expressed in writings emanating from traditional centers of graduate education, as in such works as *Sociology Today* and *Sociologists at Work*; as compared with work being done at the newer centers of graduate training, and evident in such works as *The New Sociology* and *Reflections on Community Studies*.

In the 1940's, at a time when sociology had to choose between humanist and scientist affiliations, positivism offered an incredible opportunity to justify the latter. The positivists provided the fundamental critique: humanism provided a series of emotions; science provided facts. Humanism was dialectical; science was cumulative. Humanism was brilliant but got nowhere; science was prosaic but got somewhere. It was easier to sell government agencies, private business, and foundation funds information that was cumulative and went somewhere than emotions that were woven into a fine mosaic but not into a salable package. The rhetoric of "hard" science eased the path toward El Dorado. The gold rush was on. Professionalism served to keep the grubby amateurs and dilettantes out of the picture. The occupationalists, with their touching faith in the practicality of sociological activities, could not offer a systematic critique to this process of the bureaucratization of sociology. The spillover in accoutrements and advantages from the professionalization process was large enough for the entire field to prosper. And no ideal argument can overcome material affluence. For every sociologist prepared to put his discipline "on trial," there were a hundred others prepared to put the sociologist-turned-apostate on trial. Robert Lynd's *Knowledge for What?* remained an isolated outburst—tolerated because his earlier

13. See Ernest Nagel, "Impressions and Appraisals of Analytic Philosophy in Europe," in *Logic Without Metaphysics and Other Studies in the Philosophy of Science* (Glencoe, Ill.: Free Press, 1956), pp. 191–246.

Middletown studies helped to professionalize the field of sociology, but thunderously ignored by the new breed of sociological positivists who had been taught that Lynds' sort of old-fashioned queries could be easily and profitably ignored.

The good sociological Schweiks of the 1950's assumed their professionalist poses with a disconcerting naturalness. The sociological institute or bureau became a way of life, on a par with the college or university. Sociology was more than a discipline; it offered work, jobs, careers. An uncomfortable argument by analogy arose that somehow established an equation between non-academic work routines and scientific substantiation.[14] But the routinization of sociological work entailed something more profound; namely, the assumption that any second- or third-rate person, particularly if his young mind was uncluttered by knowledge or cultivated opinion, could be transformed into a first-rate methodologist. This fact was to provide a demonstration effect that sociology had little to do with humanistic learning.[15] Actually, a reverse Pygmalion effect took over. The bright-eyed student, direct from the undergraduate schools and a world of sociological classics, found himself confronted with a concerted effort to disabuse him of "inherited" styles of thought. Indeed, the basic measure of his "successful adjustment" to graduate school was exactly his capacity to be liquidated as a "theorist" and resurrected as a "methodologist."

II

The present period in sociology reveals a rising tide of discontent and self-criticism that may well foreshadow the *Götterdämmerung* of professionalization as such. After a full generation of domination and control, after establishing a sociological rhetoric that has been parlayed into a universe of "soft money," the professionals find that training and precision can be purchased at the price of objectivity itself. Such phenomena as the Cold War come to be viewed as "stable states," so that one comes to analyze "alternative future states of affairs of the Cold War," rather than the sort of "intervention research" needed to show how to finally end the Cold War.[16]

14. The first person to note the illicit character of this equation between career patterns and science was John Dewey, in "Liberating the Social Scientist: A Plea to Unshackle the Study of Man," *Commentary*, 4, no. 4 (October, 1947): 378–385. But at that time, few sociologists were ready to pay attention to such "logic chopping"; particularly not in the vast laboratory at Columbia University.

15. The most forceful advocate of this position was Samuel Stouffer. See his paper on "Some Observations on Study Design," *American Journal of Sociology*, 55, no. 3 (November, 1950): 355–361. Ironically enough, Stouffer's work on *The American Soldier* and on *Loyalty and Disloyalty in Post-War America* obviously could not be done except by a man who retained a criterion of brilliance and not simply competence.

16. See Paul F. Lazarsfeld, with the collaboration of Sydney S. Spivak, "Observations on the Organization of the Empirical Social Research in the United States," Information Bulletin of the *International Social Science Council*, no. 29 (December, 1961): 26. (Reprinted by Bureau of Applied Social Research, Reprint No. 351.)

While this does not exhaust the problems of bureaucratic research technique, it is indicative of the new role that sociological theory must play in the future development of the field. For example: What is the relation between government agencies' expectations and the design of sociological research projects? How does the canon of secrecy affect the character of sociological findings? When should an individual cooperate or not cooperate with federal decision-making units? Where should the intellectual lines be drawn?[17]

The rush is now on to prove that everyone can really do the important things as well as the trivial; big-range sociology no less than two-person group analysis. It is at this point that self-reflection must be converted into substantial theoretical gains and not simply applaud "big-range" efforts because of their bigness. What needs to be established in sociology is some recognition that the grounds of the field still rest on people no less than powers, masses no less than elites, spontaneity no less than equilibrium, revolution no less than reaction, conflict no less than consensus. And for this a dialectical sociology must be brought into force; whatever may be the number of people or the size of the organization being studied. Whether it be called thinking in pairs, thinking triadically, concretely, or what you will—the full scientific weight of sociology will not be realized unless the present "two sides" to every story become transformed and elevated into one whole with many sides.[18]

Sometimes the occupational orientation is thought to be earlier in time than the professional orientation; namely, occupationalism is a less sophisticated, more primitive version of the same thing—the drive toward the specialization and bureaucratization of learning. While it is true that in certain fields, such as sociology, the occupational orientation, as symbolized by the Chicago School, gained preeminence earlier than the professional orientation, as symbolized by the Harvard and Columbia styles of work, this is by no means a general rule. In such spheres as engineering, for example, occupational orientations are relatively recent, and have come into being as responses to the dysfunctional aspects of professionalization.

We might say that occupationalism is itself something of a professional ideology, since it rests not simply on a critique of professionalization but, more profoundly, on a defense of the "field" against amateurs and dilettantes. A recent instance of this irony is Martin Rein's blistering "insider" critique of professionalism among the social service and social workers. He points out several major shortcomings in professionalization that hold not only for social work but for social science in general:

17. See Gilbert Shapiro, "Social Science Research and the American University," *The American Behavioral Scientist*, VIII, no. 2 (October, 1964): 29–35.

18. See Reinhard Bendix and Bennett Berger, "Images of Society and Problems of Concept Formation in Sociology," in *Symposium on Sociological Theory*, ed. by Llewellyn Gross (New York: Harper & Row, 1959), pp. 92–118; and also Llewellyn Gross, "Preface to a Metatheoretical Framework for Sociology," *American Journal of Sociology*, LXVII, no. 2 (September, 1961): 125–136.

When a group of persons who perform a service band together to control the body of persons who may legitimately perform that service, certain inevitable consequences follow: a striving to raise their own prestige and rewards; a tendency to overdefine the skills needed to do the work; a limit on those who may do it, and to whom it may be done; and an increasing concern with "professional standards," personal satisfaction, and income. The danger is that the interests of the recipients can easily become subverted to serve the interests of the dispensers.[19]

The core of the occupationalist's ideology is in the last analysis determined by his belief in the primacy of the interests of the "recipients" over those of the "dispensers." The occupationalist sees his role as determined, in the long haul, by the needs of the recipients. Hence, his view of the field must be by definition more flexible and fluid than that of the professionalist—whose prime concern is building up organizational security against the vagaries of the future. Indeed, the occupationalist views the drive to build up security as in fact a move toward bureaucratization—a direction that is at the same time a violation of the scientific ethos.[20]

III

Thus far, we have presented illustrative material to support the thesis that the mainliners within sociology have been divided between two styles of empirical work. Only when we turn to an examination of marginality do we encounter nonempirical or even antiempirical tendencies. Clearly, what is being said here in the rough requires careful documentation and clarification. But such tests are eminently possible. Career lines can be traced. Publishing habits can be examined. Mobility among sociologists can be charted.[21]

What I herein want to content myself with is a formalization of the inner sociological disputes as they now exist. Whether this will yield some "higher synthesis" is problematic. Nonetheless, the forthright presentation of the dilemma as it works its course in a scientific field provides powerful case material for the view that while theoretical issues may be sidetracked, they can scarcely be permanently outflanked. Theoretical principles are embedded in the core of research strategies. This may prove small comfort for those who take sociological theory to be a device for ordering the world, but for those who take a more modest view of it, a formal inventory of available postures and policies may be of some utility.

19. Martin Rein, "The Social Service Crisis," *Trans-Action*, 1, no. 4 (May, 1964): 3-6. Similar statements by sociologists and political scientists have also been recorded. See Peter Townsend, "A Society for People," *Conviction*, ed. by Norman MacKenzie (London: MacGibbon E. Kee, 1958); and William A. Robson, *The University Teaching of Social Sciences: Political Science* (Paris: UNESCO, 1954).

20. See Alfred McClung Lee, "Annual Report for 1963–1964 of the SSSP Representative to the ASA Council," *Social Problems*, 12, no. 3 (Winter, 1965): 356–360.

21. See Elbridge Sibley, *The Education of Sociologists in the United States* (New York: Russell Sage Foundation, 1963).

Any effort at a systematic account of a field, particularly when framed in terms of polar opposites, is justifiably open to the charge of oversimplification. Yet the need to formulate the lines of division between sociologists, no less than those between sociological styles, is pressing enough to chance erring on the side of simplicity. Further empirical probing, research techniques to test propositions, and simply reflection on the issues raised may all serve as essential correctives. For our purpose, it will be sufficient to make plain just what undergirds present sociological cleavages.

Several precautionary measures are in order prior to a review of the forces upholding the integrity of the profession on one side and defending the honor of the occupation on the other.

The first precaution is to bear in mind that by a "professional" we do not imply a bigoted upholder of any one concept of sociology, nor by an "occupationalist" do we imply an intellectualist posture in general. The professional may be of any political persuasion and have any number of interests. He may be connected with nonacademic agencies, but he is largely affiliated with colleges and universities. His commitment to the idea of professionalism, however, forms an ideological set of beliefs which may be said to produce a sociological ideology, but which nonetheless has a line of development independent of other ideological strains in the field of sociological theory. The occupationalist, for his part, is also obliged to justify himself in terms of the field, and, unlike a free-lance intellectual, he cannot make "ideas" as such his frame of reference. The terms "profession" and "occupation" are not directly transferable to denote narrow specialist and broad intellectual. However, there does seem to be some rationale for believing that the professionals see themselves in a physicalist image, while the occupationalists are more likely to seek an image based on political and even literary sophistication.

The second precaution is to avoid assumptions about the professional and the disciplinarian either preceding or following each other in time. The question of chronological evolution is a difficult one, and worth pursuing, but not subject to a simple answer. The serious rifts between members of the Royal Society about this question make clear that even in former centuries, divisions existed between professionals and occupationalists (sometimes called *dilettantes*) within a professional organization.[22] Similarly, even within a dedicated occupational and intellectualist chore such as the *Encyclopédie*, men like D'Alembert upheld the notion of professional standards. In effect, (a) when dilettantism is replaced by some sort of formal organization of a field, (b) when it becomes sanctified as a science, and (c) when findings become serviceable to purchasers, at that point "hard-line" divisions between professionals and occupationalists tend to emerge. The growth of a science is not a straight-line phenomenon, but one that pro-

22. See M. Ornstein, *The Role of Scientific Societies in the Seventeenth Century*, rev. 2nd ed. (Chicago: University of Chicago Press, 1938); and Richard S. Westfall, *Science and Religion in Seventeenth Century England* (New Haven: Yale University Press, 1958).

ceeds "dialectically"—through a conflict of different tendencies and orientations. Science itself can be viewed as a struggle for a style of work—with the victors crowned as the epitomizers of truth by the ever-present epigone.

The third precaution is to avoid any assumptions that popularization is a unique property of occupational or professional types. The mainline members of a scientific community embrace both those who believe in sociology as an 8-hour a day profession and those who believe in it as a 24-hour occupation. They are united by a roughly common educational background (although emphasis on different "minor" subjects may provide a revealing distinction) and by a set of personal relations and associations in common. From this the marginalist is often excluded. This is not to deny the role of popularization; the work of social science journalists like Dan Wakefield, Michael Harrington, Thomas Morgan, and Vance Packard represents a significant dent in the public consciousness of the role of sociology in public affairs. Yet, this role is performed from the outside. One need simply compare the above-named "outsiders" with such occupationalists as C. Wright Mills, David Riesman, and Erving Goffman; or with such professionals as Talcott Parsons, Robert K. Merton, or Kingsley Davis to see how thoroughly marginal the popularizers remain.[23]

The fourth precaution is to guard against ignoring the powerful kinship ties between sociologists. They have a shared emphasis on standards of quality and on the need for formal educational requirements, as well as a common attitude concerning the worth of sociology as such. In a real sense, both professionals and occupationalists are "professional" in their fundamental connections with a university, and both are "occupational" in that the criteria for such appointments and promotion often depend upon originality, brilliance, and intellectual productivity.[24] Thus, the differences described take place within the same "interior." This stands in marked contrast to conflicts between the various social sciences, which appear to stimulate "worldly" conflicts, that is, competition for public approval and policy domination. Intradepartmental struggles also differ from interdepartmental struggles in that the conflict between professional and occupational positions are ultimately supplementary rather than antagonistic to one another. Each must check its activities against the other so that a mutual dialogue continues openly, which can give vitality to the field of sociology.

Several additional points must be stressed. Both professional and occupational types represent fully elaborated tendencies *within* the main line of sociological activity. They are "ideal types," which, however logically consistent, do not

23. One test for the extent to which "mainliners" and "marginals" are subject to differential treatment is the reviews of their work in the sociological journals—the respect accorded the most extreme "insider" of the sociological community in contrast to the rejection accorded the latter.

24. Despite the monstrous abuses of universalistic criteria, "professional judgment" is based on performance and is as equitable as conflicts of viewpoint permit. See Theodore Caplow and Reece J. McGee, *The Academic Marketplace* (New York: Basic Books, 1958), pp. 87–93.

imply their extreme crystallization in any one person or among any one group of practitioners.

Nor should it be imagined that this model can be mechanically assigned to any particular research method or general philosophic orientation. Functionalism, for example, may be used in both professional and occupational styles. Naturally enough, the emphasis will be different. The same holds true for believers in the "natural history" theory. In some sense the differences between these two groups seem to be directly connected to the social-academic position and to the goal orientations of the sociologist. They are related to the attitudes of the individual sociologists about the utility of varying methodologies only indirectly and in a mysterious "long run." The work of a sociologist can center on the "small group" and still fall within an occupationalist orientation. If this were not the case, the problem of "styles" in sociology would be considerably simplified. "Mind" would no longer stand as a specific factor to be examined on its own terms, since "behavior" could be directly inferred from "interests."

This brings us to a major question mark: What exactly is the relationship between style of work and quality of results? After all, both professional and occupational types have as their ultimate court of appeal the utility and longevity of their work. And both mainliner sectors have come to appreciate the weaknesses in past sociological theory. But for the professional such weaknesses were a function of the relative scarcity of time and funds to think about theory. The retort of the occupationalists is that since there is, at least in the present, sufficient time and funds, why is there no corresponding improvement in sociological theory? Perhaps sound theoretical development is a consequence of the seriousness with which problems are thought about, rather than simply a function of available material resources at the disposal of the scholar.[25]

To complicate the problem, there is the stark and ever-present fact that there may be first-rate professionals and second-rate occupationals (and vice versa). We then have to explain whether or not there is a relationship between styles of work and qualities of results. But this deserves the full attention of a separate study. It is sufficient to say that there is a prima facie value in making this distinction between believers in an occupational orientation and believers in a professional orientation with such clarity as the field of sociology permits. But it is no less important to indicate that this prima facie value may be far more limited than is here stated. It might turn out that challenges from outside forces—political critiques, other social science encroachments, widespread withdrawals of foundation support, etc.—may turn out to be more cohesive elements in sociology than any legislated consensus or "gentleman's agreement" to withhold criticism.

25. On this whole set of issues, the reader might compare and contrast Paul F. Lazarsfeld, "Reflections on Business," *American Journal of Sociology*, LXV, no. 1 (July, 1959): 1–31; with Dennis H. Wrong, "The Oversocialized Conception of Man in Modern Sociology," *American Sociological Review*, 26, no. 12 (April, 1961): 183–193.

PROFESSIONALISM

1. Sociology is defined by the people who have been educated in the field and who go on to work and earn their living in the same field. A heavy premium is placed on the "boundedness" of sociology. This usually comes attached to a highly socialized attitude, or set of attitudes; *e.g.*, problems of priorities in research discoveries resolved in bureaucratic terms.

2. The professional tends toward an estoteric attitude toward his activities. He believes in the need for a special language (jargon). He places a high premium on professional associations, and upon special status awards and rewards. He further tends to insist upon an early choice in specialization. In short, the professional operates within a theory of *exclusivity*.

3. Professionalism tends to accept the effective working of institutions as a norm not to be impeded and, indeed, to be aided. It is an assumption of the right of public institutions to define the character of their actions and the consequences of such acts. (The defense of social myths.)

4. There is a strong emphasis on the "team," on not breaking the "consensus," and on the testability of the propositions used in research reports. A premium is placed on reliability and on measurability. (The classical image of perfection.)

OCCUPATIONALISM

1. Sociology is defined more in terms of the contents of the field and much less by its practitioners. The occupational type has a greater interest in intellectual activities taking place in adjacent or even distant disciplines. This usually comes with a linkage to an "individualistic" attitude toward such matters as primacy in discovery; *e.g.*, problems resolved in terms of personal identity.

2. The occupationalist has an esoteric attitude toward his activities. He believes the common language is good. He places a high premium on associations outside of the profession-reward system based on some sort of public acclaim or policy utilization of efforts. Membership in professional organizations is often considered as peripheral. In short, the occupationalist operates within a theory of *inclusivity*.

3. Occupational orientations tend to an irreverence for authority and established institutions. It is a tendency not to treat public institutions as sacred, or to accept their self-definitions of the social situation. (The populist frame of mind.)

4. There is a strong emphasis on individual uniqueness which in turn is accompanied by varying intensities of disaffection and disaffiliation. A premium is placed on "quality of mind" and not on doing the quality or kind of work which may not be subject to standard forms of measurement. (The romantic image of innovation.)

5. The assumption made about sociological information is that it is derived basically from informants. The field is held to be a series of generalizations derivable from a public. Emphasis on questionnaire design and model building. There is a further assumption that methodology and training techniques can compensate for original differences in levels of ability between sociologists. Professionalism implies standards of competence.

6. On the grounds of either belief or utility, the professional holds that there is a clear and distinct separation between factual commitment and valuational consequences. Thus, part of a definition of the field includes the proposition that research findings are neutral with respect to those who may use such findings. They are neutral in themselves, values being added by those who apply the findings.

7. For the professional the question is: For whom is sociology useful? The answer is usually made in terms of whoever can utilize the information. (The marketplace conception of knowledge.) For the professional, utility is heightened insofar as technique and efficiency have reduced the area of intellectual conflict and increased the capacity to anticipate conflict. Method is held to lead to intellectual resolution of doubt.

8. The "image" or chain of associations instilled is that of other

5. The assumption made about sociological information is that it is derived basically from the investigator. The field is held to be essentially a dialogue between the present generation of disciplinarians and the inheritance of the field. There is a further belief that, while methodology can produce a minimal level of competence, it cannot and it does not eliminate different levels of insight and talent. Occupationalism thus implies standards of excellence.

6. The occupationalist feels entitled to examine questions of value, *i.e.*, ethical questions, insofar as they are intrinsically entailed in sociology. Sociology is defined in its interplay of fact and value, and of description and prescription. Thus, the findings of sociology are held to imply values which have proper and improper application. Those who apply the findings also draw their value implications.

7. For the occupational the question is: What are the values of sociology? The answer is usually made in terms of integrity of the field, *i.e.*, rejecting sociology as marketable service in favour of sociology as knowledge. (Humanistic conception.) For the occupationalist the intellectual "dialogue" is valued above the canon of efficiency; these being mere evasions from position-taking in the area of conflict. Technique and efficiency are not seen as assurance that the resolution of debate is either possible or desirable.

8. The "image" or chain of associations instilled is that of other

professions, usually of a high prestige standing. In the case of sociology: physics, mathematics, and sometimes engineering. Images are often linked to those areas which have achieved a high grade of systematization and qualification, and no less a clear and distinct separation of theory-building from historical antecedents.

fields, usually of high prestige but low systematization. In the case of sociology: history, biography, and sometimes fiction. Images are often linked to those areas which have a high degree of interest relevance and which resist systematization. There is an emphasis on auto-consciousness, on an awareness of the historical continuities of social problems and social forces.

9. Professional emphasis is on the institutes that act as clearing agents for the dissemination of sociological information. The sociologist has some rationalized authority, with a high degree of work routinization. He considers the field as a job rather than a calling.

9. Occupationalists, because of their departmental emphasis, rely heavily on the sociologist as teacher and writer. There is a disinterest in, or a disavowal of, agencies that impersonally disseminate information. He views the field as a calling rather than as a job. The sociologist is a charismatic figure who defies routinization.

10. The professional often operates within a framework that assumes the existence of a clear understanding of the rules of research, rites of passage, and stability of the social order. He is more concerned with problems of mobilization. That is to say, his concern is the maintenance of set standards that have been agreed upon by the elite within the profession. This leads to a general downgrading of novelty and individuality.

10. The occupational often operates within a framework that assumes a high degree of social conflict and a low degree of social cohesion. He tends to transfer from this image of reality an image of the field which is also basically unstructured. There is a pragmatic view of roles, and a looser view of academic roles. Under such conditions, novelty, generalization, and new modalities of relations to the general public are countenanced if not encouraged.

11. Professionalism involves an emphasis on technique, on the formal elegance of a presentation, and on approval from peer groups. The professional thinks in partialities, in terms of adjusting, correcting, and ameliorating. (The reformist imagination.)

11. Occupationalism involves an emphasis on criticism, on the deftness of presentation, and on approval from an amorphous but relatively large-sized public. The disciplinarian thinks in totalities, in terms of overhauling and transforming. (The revolutionary imagination.)

IV

The concept of marginality has many meanings and avenues of expression. One can infer from it a person living in limbo, between intellectual worlds as it were. It might be used to signify a self-conscious alienation, a feeling of the positive values being outside the mainstream. It may also be employed as a concept going against the mainstream, so that marginality becomes a function of a belief system rather than of the social system.[26]

This last strikes closest to my use of the notion of marginality. The antisociologist employs marginality, whereas the unsociologist simply lives out this process in his institutional environment. In a sense, marginality is a response to traditionalism, the critique of present trends in terms of past achievements, and therefore will always be required. However, as it is herein used, marginality is a response to mainliner behavior, a belief that in some sense, nuclear membership in an organization or a profession is destructive of some major value which is in itself more social than sociological. For the antisociologist the power necessary to maintain onself in a central organizational position violates the scientific and/or ethical need for the maintenance of principles and scruples.

However that elusive word "knowledge" is evaluated, there is a sense in which the assertion of marginality is a demand for the sociologist to concern himself with action programs, with intervention in social affairs, and with value considerations. The marginal man is concerned with immortality—conceived by the unsociologist as a remembrance for services rendered to the alma mater, and by the antisociologist as the supreme critic combing poetry and science into a universal synthesis. Hence, to deal with marginality is to deal with powerful and contradictory forces motivating men toward extremes of self-sacrifice and self-centeredness.

In discussing the marginal sectors within sociology, it should be emphasized that the antisociologist has certain functional similarities to the unsociologist. Both have standards of professional judgment that are determined not so much by sociological performance as by patterns extrinsic to such performance. The antisociologist for his part penetrates the field with a series of aesthetic judgments and often adopts a critique of sociology from the point of view of consciously applied literary techniques.[27] The unsociologist for his part has an entirely different starting point. He reflects a collegiate set of values, the point of view of practical judgment. His framework and frame of reference are not sociology,

26. The notion of marginality is sometimes used to express the relationship of the "immigrant scholar" to his new environment. I shall not be dealing with this kind of marginality. Nonetheless, several interesting observations of marginality in general were made in this special immigrant connection. See Franz Adler, "The Marginal Man on the Faculty," and John Kosa, "The Immigrant Scholar in America," both in *Arena*, no. 17 (January, 1964): 33–34, 7–32.

27. For a fine essay developing this, see Maurice R. Stein, "The Poetic Metaphors of Sociology," in *Sociology on Trial*, ed. by Maurice Stein and Arthur Vidich (Englewood Cliffs, N.J.: Prentice-Hall, 1963), pp. 173–181.

but what is good or what is perceived to be good for the university or the college with which he is affiliated. The irony is that the profoundly alienated sociologist shares with the thoroughly integrated unsociologist a virtual abandonment of sociology as a system of strategy for engaging in social research.

Keeping in mind both the dissimilarities in starting points, and the similarities in terminal points, let us work up a diagrammatic profile of the relationship which obtains between the antisociologist and the unsociologist.

ANTISOCIOLOGIST

1a. The antisociologist owes a functional allegiance to a source of authority, or to a set of ideas that is outside the control system of sociology. This may at times carry over into a critique of academic life as such, but it does not have to. It may be restricted to a critique of sociology as such, using criteria of judgment generally found in either mathematics or the humanities.[28]

2a. The antisociologist, by virtue of his ideological orientation, does a considerable amount of writing. He generally adopts a polemical style in his work. He sees these writings as transcendental, in contrast to most sociological writings, which he sees as transient in value and temporary in significance. As a writer, he "converses" with the classical figures—both dead and alive.

3a. Antisociologists tend to be drawn from the pool of cosmopolitans. They have view sociology as placing arbitrary limits to debate and discussion. In this way,

UNSOCIOLOGIST

1b. The unsociologist's primary allegiance is not so much to "main line" attitudes or to alternative forces which are contesting for preeminence in sociology, as it is a profound sense of obligation and loyalty to the institutional agency (usually a college or university) that employs him. The unsociologist has a perception of himself as a defender of an educational institution even at the risk of negating sociology as such.

2b. The unsociologist tends to do very little writing beyond the requirements for graduate training. Writing is not a value for the unsociologist, since the terms of promotion and advancement depend upon institutional loyalty and perhaps on teaching ability. When the unsociologist does write, he tends to do so more as an educationist than as a social scientist.

3b. Unsociologists tend to be local. They are concerned with a small range of problems, generally those kinds of problems which deeply affect the administrative apparatus of

28. One finds among the antisociologists such diverse types as the methodological model builder who uses formal logical criteria rather than empirical criteria for the judgment of sociological work; or, at the other end of the spectrum, the antisociologist who employs literary or metaphysical judgments. The singular unifying trend is that the judgment about sociology is generally made from the point of view of another discipline.

sociology comes to be considered an essentially parochial activity, having dubious scientific merits.

4a. Antisociologists tend to be messianic. They see themselves as men with a mission. They make an effort to proselytize; but the proselytization process is not so much of the heathen as it is of the orthodox and the entrenched. They apply the pressures of the cultivated to the organization men of the field.

5a. The antisociologist is usually located at major universities and in large departments of sociology. In this role he functions as a critical pivot, addressing himself to the larger dilemmas of the profession. He is also able to connect up with the main intellectual currents of either the university or the community.

6a. The antisociologist starts with a critical ideological posture, generally well thought out and not infrequently involving radical political premises. As a matter of fact, oftentimes the antisociologist can be found arguing not so much against sociology as for politics.

7a. The antisociologist adopts an alienated view of the world. In the very act of identifying with marginal groups of society, he often considers himself as part of the breakdown in sociological solidarity. He tends to picture his own role as being

college life, and in consequence their attitudes towards sociology are conventional and nonemotive. They see it in terms which are value-neutral.

4b. Unsociologists do little to win adherents. Instead, they function in such a way as to lessen the desires or the drive to engage in fundamental sociological effort. They are organization men. Their power within the profession largely derives from administrative sensitivities. They are more interested in administration than in intellect.

5b. The unsociologist is usually located at small colleges where his administrative prowess is appreciated and needed; and also where the demands for his continued professional achievement are at a minimum. The unsociologist may be "cultivated" in a general sense, but, unlike the antisociologist, he has no need of performing critical catharsis.

6b. The unsociologist generally adopts a consensualist posture, one based on organizational agreements and oriented towards getting the job done, whatever the task may be. He tends to be, therefore, politically indifferent and mildly conservative in his "outlook."

7b. The unsociologist takes a gentleman's view of the field. He tends to be pleased with sociological activities insofar as they create a "halo effect"—an image which is respectable and can create an additional "line" to the school he is alienated with respect to the work processes of sociology as such.

at. He is sometimes enmeshed with the creation of sociological rituals—which are neither offensive nor innovative.

8a. It can be surmised that the antisociologist has his personal background in a big city, prefers urban life, and works on a set of problems that derive in part from the big issues in world affairs. He tends to view sociology as good when it addresses itself to total issues in a total way and bad when it ignores such issues, or delves into them from a "social problems" or partial way.

8b. The unsociologist tends to be from a small town and rural background. He therefore is interested in the utilization of sociology only as it addresses itself to small or middle-range problems; problems that are susceptible to immediate control and that can be resolved without raising theoretical issues having much of a "cutting edge."

9a. The antisociologist has a well worked-out philosophical system, or is at least pro-philosophy. He may draw upon a network of doctrines such as dialectical materialism, neo-thomism, existentialism, intuitionism, etc. He sees empiricism as a philosophically crude system which "mystifies" the terms of ordinary language by leaving them in a "repressive" universe of discourse.

9b. The unsociologist tends to be an antiphilosopher. His theoretical premises rarely move beyond the doctrine of common sense. He is willing to forgo philosophic implications of scholarship if this impedes bureaucratic development. He is a "pragmatist" only in the sense of being discontent with "European ideologies" or systems of thought, which impede direct access to the materials of course work in sociology.

V

With this set of characterizations now completed, we might summarize the relationship between our broad sociological types by means of a chart. This chart, hopefully, illustrates what I take to be the core relationships that are found between the four types of sociologists herein dealt with. It can be seen that from the viewpoint of the ethos (the vertical line), professionals and unsociologists tend to "line up" together, as do occupationals and antisociologists on the other side of the diagram. This factor of "ethos," "ideology," "world outlook"—or what you will—has been the victim of neglect in these pages for two reasons. First is my belief that immediate "organizational" relations shape the ideology, and not the other way about. Second is the admittedly personal reason of wanting to draw the lines between sociological types in such a way as perhaps to ease tensions between competing styles by showing how such styles are keyed to organizational developments of science in general, and to the social sciences in particular.

Rather than suggest an outcome to this analysis that would be a beatific vision of the sociological horizons deprived of the creative tensions which make sociology one of the more dynamic social sciences, I propose a reading of those elements in the occupational-professional orientation, and in the antisociological-unsociological orientation, that can serve to increase the value of the research done and the theories devised.[29]

A Double Interchange System for the Study of Sociological Types

Organization

Mainliners

	Professionalism		Occupationalism	
Ethos				*Ethos*
	Unsociologists		Antisociologists	

Marginals

Organization

Although professionalism provides an organizational basis for sociology, it also contains dysfunctional elements—degenerative devices for enforcing early career decisions, ensuring consensual indoctrination, and crystallizing conventions into dogma. Professionalism does indeed provide mechanisms for the increase of public awareness and acceptance of sociology; but it too often does so at a cost of hindering scientific openness and experimental innovation among sociologists. Its demands for universalism, for competence at the expense of excellence, too often spill over into an attack on heterodoxy—the very charge that the sociological tradition has consistently addressed to the European ideologies from which it broke away.[30]

29. The reader should be apprised of the fact that this study represents one chunk of an ongoing effort of mine to develop a sociology of sociology. For other related aspects of this effort, I should like to draw attention to other chapters in the book, especially Chs. 1, 3, 10, 12, and 13.

30. For critique of professionalism along these lines, see Ralf Dahrendorf, "Out of Utopia: Toward a Reorientation of Sociological Analysis," *American Journal of Sociology*, 64, no. 2 (September, 1958): 115–127; Robert W. Habenstein, "Critique of 'Profession' as a Sociological Category," *Sociological Quarterly*, 4, no. 4 (Autumn, 1963): 291–300; E. C. Hughes, "Professional and Career Problems of Sociology," *Men and Their Work* (Glencoe, Ill.: Free Press, 1958), pp. 157–168; and most recently, David J. Gray, "Sociology as a Science: A Dysfunctional Element," *American Journal of Economics and Sociology*, 21, no. 4 (October, 1962): 337–346.

The person who views sociology as an occupation has the distinctive advantage of being central to the development of the field without losing sight of the connections between sociology and allied disciplines. He has a vested interest in the idea content rather than the bureaucratic norms of a field. Of all the strategies the sociologist is eligible to adopt, occupationalism offers maximum intellectual flexibility. He can function both "inside" and "outside" professional confines with equal ease. He can maintain a critical posture without reducing his position to sheer negative demands for the self-liquidation of the field. And finally, the occupationalist can appreciate the fact that the word "society" is larger and more embracing than the word "sociology."

This statement of optimal outcomes, however, leaves much to be desired. The occupationalist too often suffers from a ready default of sociological effort. His cultural concerns are at times misanthropic, since they entail an unwillingness to state clearly the basis of judgment and the grounds of action. The occupational orientation has grown content with being part of a sprawling discipline, a sort of "loyal opposition" too ready to condemn and too slow to correct. Occupationalists have too frequently mistaken their intellectual orientation for a need to avoid organizational involvement and participation—as if the critique of professionalism necessarily carries with it a mandate to frown upon organizational solidarity.[31] This in turn stems from a long tradition in which ideas and power were considered as not just different, but antagonistic.

The antisociologists in the sociological ambience provide a necessary reminder that a totalist critique of the field is a necessary stimulant to serious work. It is a constant reminder that sociology is a human science, and as such is intimately connected to human foibles. The antisociologist at his best is the outsider within. He reminds us how many of our grants are due to the conservatizing needs of a welfare establishment; how many of our positions on standards and measures are really postures taken defiantly in the absence of firm standards; how much of our insistence upon the appropriate rites of passage rests on primitive puberty rites—oftentimes designed to weed out the different rather than the deviant.[32]

31. The literature that is either critical or positively disposed towards an occupational orientation remains surprisingly slim. This in part may be a reflection of its "emergent" status. And it may also be, as I have elsewhere indicated, a consequence of an absence of a self-conscious, well-articulated strategy on the part of the professionals. The best single exposition which seeks to defend an occupational orientation, in the "classical tradition," is C. Wright Mills' *The Sociological Imagination* (New York: Oxford University Press, 1959); and along roughly similar lines, see Irving L. Horowitz, *The New Sociology* (New York: Oxford University Press, 1964). While no single sustained attack on occupationalism has yet been made, one may take as typical the olympian statement in *Sociology Today: Problems and Prospects*, ed. by Robert K. Merton, Leonard Broom, Leonard S. Cottrell, Jr. (New York: Basic Books, 1959).

32. See, for example, Herbert Marcuse, *One-Dimensional Man: Studies in the Ideology of Advanced Industrial Society* (Boston: Beacon Press, 1964); and from a different perspective, Daniel J. Boorstin, *The Image, or What Happened to the American Dream* (New York: Atheneum, 1962).

But this does not preserve the antisociologist from overreacting to an admittedly difficult cultural environment. How much weight can someone pull if he disbelieves in either a professional or an occupational view of sociology? Isn't antisociologism a reactionary view of social change disguised as super-revolutionism? Isn't it a contempt for social problems and social adjustment in much the same way as old-fashioned nineteenth-century revolutionism, which was dismayed with every attempt at reform lest it weaken the revolutionary "impulses" of the people? The antisociologist may drift into the higher irresponsibility. He takes seriously only his criticism of the field; and not the need to do something about the society he studies. The antisociologist is metaphysically proper and right, since in fact every attempt at social amelioration must fall short of the mark. But in the concrete, profane sense, an antisociologist is always wrong, since his totalist critique never gets us nearer the utopia he so clearly craves. He can only "possess" the future in poetic imagery; unfortunately he can never work for a realization of that future with a perhaps prosaic imagery that gets us one step nearer to a meaningful future.[33] The drive to possess the future *en bloc* usually comes out fitted with garments inherited from the past. What is celebrated is not so much that which is to come, but an idyllic past that has already been. That is why the reactionary-revolutionary pendulum has more than surface attitudes in common.

The unsociologist is the most difficult to categorize of our four types. He is least likely to articulate his position in an intellectually convincing way. Yet, there is much to be said for the unsociologist, who at least takes his duties as a teacher and a member of the faculty seriously. He can, under optimal circumstances, provide the kind of elementary grounding in sociology from which careers are launched. He can prove to be innovative with respect to academic needs. He can employ his sociological skills to constructive ends in the university-college establishments. He can provide the link between the personalized student and an impersonal college administration.

However personally attractive the marginal type may be, he is involved in an objective default. In his accommodation for functional tasks, in his gentlemanly search for local power independent of sociological tasks, or in his assiduous avoidance of power as such, he represents the kiss of death—the man who can do more to destroy student interest in *sociology* than to stimulate such interest. His passions are for administration and college gentility. His discomfort with intellectual brilliance, with sociological effort, makes him intolerant of those dedicated to sociology. Thus, throughout the small colleges of America are to be found elder statesmen who feel more threatened by sociological talents than inspired by them. Like his antisociologist compatriot, he reveals the repressed

33. Sociological "antisociology" has a long and honorable tradition within the field (which is perhaps the most difficult phenomenon of all which the antisociologist has to account for). The best recent symposium on this position is *Sociology on Trial*, ed. by Maurice Stein and Arthur Vidich (Englewood Cliffs, N.J.: Prentice-Hall, 1963).

fear of the demands that sociology as a science makes on the time, the energy, and the talents of the sociologist.

There is no single answer to the problems herein posed. Obviously each of the four sociological types in our profile-in-diagram has points of utility as well as inutility. Insofar as the social position and perspective of the sociologist determine the quality of the work done, it remains an empirical task to figure out which of the four types does indeed lead to greater sociological creativity. But we should not overlook the fact that there is an autonomous element involved in sociological creation and that we are just as likely to get brilliant work from an unexpected marginal source as from an expected mainliner context. There is a functional autonomy between individual creativity and organizational connections. Were this not the case, the size of the university and the quality of creation would be perfectly correlated. If it were indeed possible to establish a definite correlation between professionalism and maximum creativity, the dispute would be settled then and there. It is precisely because this cannot be done that it becomes useful to develop profiles of various sociological types and to insist upon refinements and changes in various forms of sociological norms.

For example, at the most elemental level, the unsociologist, the one who is willing to subordinate his entire interest to the teaching apparatus, is most unlikely to be in a functional position to make any sort of theoretical breakthrough. On the other hand, it might with equal assurance be said that a professionally oriented sociologist may be inhibited from making any breakthrough at the level of educational methods, if for no other reason than a fear of alienating any possible lines of "worldly" organizational support. At the extremes, the problem is capable of a general formalization. But it is unlikely that the sociological dilemmas will be broken out of, independent of a general resolution of academic and university affairs.

Without wishing to minimize the contributions of the "marginal," it must be said in all frankness that the main struggle for the emergence of a new sociology can be engaged in only by those willing and capable of entering the arena; that is, by the "mainliners." In this competition between sociological styles, the unsociologists and the antisociologists confine themselves to the role of spectator, so that, at least in the present period, the struggle over the kind of theories and methods sociology should have is directly proportional to the institutional questions—what kind of agency should the sociologist have, and what kind of man should the sociologist be? Indeed, in the very process of fashioning institutions appropriate to the solution of these concrete questions, we will travel some distance on the road to answering ethical questions. But to lose sight of the fact that institutions are responses to moral demands is to build castles in the air that cannot be defended intellectually or inhabited practically.

Perhaps the most damaging aspect of marginality is that it encourages premature expressions of cynicism and resignation about the organization of sociology and the strategies of its practitioners. However, at the present period in American sociology, the responsibility for fostering this premature futilitarian attitude also belongs to the professionals. It is the organizational kingpins who, after all, have insinuated the ideology of homogeneity, and not their critics. They have urged the sorts of monolithic organizational identities that make a hetero- dox sociology difficult to bring about. Thus the problems created by professional- ism require the most immediate concern.

The idea that once a science becomes "professionalized" it is "lost" in terms of any radical transformations is simply an erroneous and dangerous myth. Just as we have found that bureaucracy has many "irrational" and dysfunctional features, so too professionalism has been found, by many of the sciences, to be likewise dysfunctional, and in much the same way as any complex organization is something more and something less than rational.[34] (1) Professionalism leads to great stress because of its overstructuring of the field of sociology—its ritualistic demands for codification gradually slip over into demands for con- sensus and finally cohesion, having little to do with scientific standards. (2) Pro- fessionalization tends to reduce experimentation to a minimum, by setting arbitrary definitions of sociological activities, and by circumscribing the kinds of positions found acceptable. (3) Professionalization sets up a bureaucratic chain of command and, for that very reason, endures the same complex of pains that all other bureaucratic structures undergo. (4) Professionalization is an ideological posture which, insofar as it removes the sociologists from the social problems he writes of, tends to weaken his stature in the research efforts to the degree that he becomes professionalized.

These conditions have evolved more fully in other sciences, particularly those not engaged in the process of image-building. Hence, the revolt against profes- sionalism as an ideology of science (or at least against its obvious dysfunctional elements) is at a more advanced stage in physics and engineering than in sociology or social work. We may take the following sharply critical statement on the reduction of knowledge to information as characteristic of the present vigorous assertion of the antibureaucratic concept of scientific man as expressed among contemporary natural scientists:

The huge "think factories" of our times are the equivalent of the Lancashire cotton mills of the industrial revolution. The scientists are many, and they are very busy producing staggering quantities of "knowledge." Their product, however, is increasingly taking on the character of a mere commodity; and their work takes on the alienated character of assembly line production, with no rhyme or reason or discernible relation to a meaningful whole. To call this mushrooming mass-production of information a flowering of science makes only a little more sense than to call the booming output of television commercials a flowering of poetry and dramatic art. Without integrative understanding, without theory, science is not really possible. All the electronic computers in the world, both those present and those to be built, storing and analyzing all the myriad pieces of detailed infor- mation, produced by countless technical workers, do not constitute science, because they

34. See, for example, Herman D. Stein, "Administrative Implications of Bureaucratic Theory," *Social Work*, 6, no. 3 (July, 1961): 14–21.

cannot provide effective knowledge and understanding *for us*, the human beings. They cannot make a meaningful, humanly livable world *for us*.[35]

The enormous increase in experimental programs, in cross-disciplinary research, in demands for humanistic preprofessional training in such areas as medicine and engineering by leading graduate schools, is a strong indicator that a narrowly conceived professionalism can no longer hold the day in the court of ideas. The emergence of different styles and strategies in sociology can only augur well for the future development of what is, after all, a public body of information produced by scientific men and not a mystic sect interested in sealing off knowledge from action.

35. Paul R. Zilsel, "The Mass Production of Knowledge," *Bulletin of the Atomic Scientists*, XX, no. 4 (April, 1964): 29; see also C. Wright Mills, "The Bureaucratic Ethos," in *The Sociological Imagination*, pp. 100–118.

15. *From Social Psychology to Social Performance: The Generational Gap in Sociology*

CHANGES IN SOCIAL science are now taking place with such dramatic speed that those actually engaged in such transformations may themselves be too busy to provide evaluations of their nature. In the much maligned field of social psychology, those who no more than a decade ago would have given their intellectual lives to the laboratory as a goal in itself are now engaged in all forms of social activity—from using the laboratory as a miniature kindergarten for underpriviledged children to using it as a simulated training center for interplanetary travel.

And while changes in experimental social psychology have not entailed any weakening of methodological rigor, the sense of infatuation that dominated the field in the 1950's has given way to a sober realization that tools and goals ought not to be idly confounded.

While these shifts are in the main a consequence of concrete social demands—

This paper is a composite of two extended review essays showing how the critical frame of reference to social psychology has been converted into a constructive, neo-positivist, framework. Social psychology has increasingly become a central focus in sociology, but how it moves from structural analysis to action therapy has been little examined. These studies first appeared in *Frontier*, 16, no. 5 (March, 1965), and *The Behavioral Science Book Service* (October, 1965).

demands to "do something" about the crises in race relations, group relations, and nation relations—they are also a consequence of the relative sterility of much work done in the past. If one takes even a casual evaluation of the main contending schools of thought in social psychology in the 1950's, it becomes plain, at least in retrospect (where even the most obtuse problems become plain), that the battle of intellectual styles would have to yield something more useful for the world if it was to sustain itself.

What I would like to do here is take two books—the Gerth and Mills *Character and Social Structure*, and the Gouldner and Miller *Applied Sociology*—as indicative of the larger trends each represented for the 1950's and 1960's respectively. For while the two volumes do have a rough continuum in ideological sentiment, their sharp divergence in scientific statement throws the two decades into bold relief—at least insofar as the stated purposes of a social psychology can be used as a bench mark in the general rerouting of sociology that has taken place in recent years.

I

During the early summer of 1960, Mills was working on everything from the "classic tradition" theme, which was to introduce the *Images of Man* reader, to some initial thoughts on Castro's revolutionary system in Cuba. On one occasion we had for a free-floating conversation, talk drifted to *Character and Social Structure*. In discussing the work now, and recalling comments made at that time, the matter of priorities, of whether Gerth or Mills was chiefly the architect of the book, will be discarded as irrelevant. At the time of its appearance in 1953, the book had striking and positive attractions for me: a strong dose of Marxism, some conventional progressive ideas about the death of liberalism and the insipidities of conservatism, plenty of good philosophical *Weltschmerz*, indeed some of the best social theorizing produced in the dismal decade. All of which goes to prove that a reader finds what he wants in a book, especially one as rich in eclecticism as this.

Mills indicated that this was the book he was least satisfied with, the one least likely to succeed, and the book most in need of drastic revision. With characteristic flamboyance, he dismissed the work as intellectual "crap," and blamed his excessive reliance on Max Weber as the cause. I have never spoken with Professor Gerth on this matter, and presumably he had his own set of responses to the book. Indeed, *Character and Social Structure* is a big book. It has many pages, many themes, many ideas, and—the kicker—many points of view.

Eclecticism is often resented because of its complexities rather than its errors. This takes place when Gerth and Mills tell us that "we have no objection, if the reader prefers, to use the names George H. Mead and Max Weber, although of course they differ from Freud and Marx in many important ways." In this way the "classic tradition" was employed to cover a multitude of sins; as if these four names could be plugged into each other without causing the most violent types of short circuits. But the authors had little choice. They were confronted by a mélange of ill-shapen theories of social psychology, and they confronted each other as alien traditions of American pragmatism and European sociologism confront each other. One can go through the book and pick out those passages and paragraphs that are characteristic of either Gerth *or* Mills. What is profoundly more difficult is to isolate the characteristically Gerth *and* Mills portions.

The learned Gerth could speak of everything from *Klatsch* to Kant in discussing symbol spheres. He spoke of social control and command in big international terms—of comparative social structures—Prussian Junkers, Japanese Samurai, and British Gentlemen. Collective behavior, the sociological term meaning uncontrolled or unstructured action, was seen by Gerth in terms of mobs of storm troopers hunting Jews in boulevard cafes, or Klansmen beating up Negroes in race riots. The garrulous and Americanized Mills discussed symbol spheres in such terms as Mead raised, in terms of the motivational functions of language. He spoke of social control and command in terms of the administrative policies of the New Deal and the organization of a labor bureaucracy in the American Federation of Labor. Collective behavior did not mean much to Mills. Storm troopers and hunger riots were outside his empirical purview. And that which Mills did not experience he rarely appreciated. In addition to this honest-to-god pragmatism of Mills, there was his emphasis on structure, his fixation with it, so that spontaneous events hardly dented his sociological imagination, as they had Gerth's.

With all of that, there are powerful unifying themes and faiths in *Character and Social Structure*. Gerth and Mills shared a strong propensity to think in terms of conflict models, rather than any consensual scheme. As such, problems of social psychology are happily liberated from the ugly cliches of deviance and disorganization—catchall words that have little to do with science and a lot to do with the sociologists' distasteful acceptance of police definitions of reality. They are also both committed to worldliness, even if that term is differentially understood. Gerth was cosmopolitan about the world. Mills at that point in his career had not gotten beyond the American shores. But neither of them could be chased into hapless slogans about the "corruptions of power" or the "struggle between democracy and totalitarianism" or "the human impulse to . . ." or such similar tripe. There are breathtaking passages about historical epochs, about Caesarism and Sultanism, about monarchism and Bonapartism, that are more than simple echoes of the Weberian past. They are downright reminders to the future generation of sociologists as to just what we stand to lose in the way of historical insight with the liquidation of big-range sociology. For example, I have seen dozens of essays and studies on Soviet society written by sociologists— not any collection of which can compare or compete with the plain history of an E. H. Carr on an Isaac Deutscher. Thus, despite an incredible eclecticism, the unspent force of a comparative and historical social psychology was able to carry the freight of methodological shortcomings.

How does this relic of the hapless fifties shape up against the other productions of that decade, and against the new breed of social psychologists? There seem to be four distinctive trends competing for audience attention in the swing-ing sixties.

The most important group are the experimentalists. This legion of researchers may be found under any technical rubric ranging from the behavioral to the zoological. The key methodological concept is the laboratory. This wing has a hard-nosed belief that replication and control of the experimental situation, fol-lowed by a statement of the findings in mathematical or statistical language, is the only real social psychology. Taking B. F. Skinner as typical, the root meta-phor is that man is an animal; and hence, the conditions for studying animals in laboratory conditions can be simulated in the study of the human animal. In this world of "stimulus-response" and "fields of action," the language of ideology and theology is banished. The peculiar thing, however, is that this experimental social psychology should pursue its own special aims with a zeal and militance not unbecoming to the political dogmatism these gentlemen so roundly con-demn. The mortifying aspect of these very modern researchers is their lack of self-consciousness, an inability to detect their own professional marginality. They possess an intellectual narrowness which threatens to engulf them, and convert these "hard scientists" into soft sentimentalists—into crib manufacturers for the rearing of bigger and better children.

The form of experimentalism that dominated the 1950's was small-group research conducted in "natural settings," in which select variables could be controlled. For men like Theodore Newcomb, observations must be so codified as to yield "orderliness in things" out of "raw behavioral components." By "orderliness" the small groupers mean systems of interaction in which "the stronger a given A-to-B positive attraction, the lesser the perceived discrepancy on A's part between his own and B's attitudes toward X." Equilibrium and strain, consensus and cooperation, individual and collective systems, are all paraded forth as we find out the attraction of Bennington College sorority students or University of Michigan dormitory graduates toward each other. The study of social psychology becomes an analysis of attitude variance—attitudes toward making friends, living together, and sexing together. The outside world shrivels up into the life-styles of hothouse students. Lest anyone be deceived into thinking that the findings can be generalized, we are continually warned, in the name of science, that findings may be of local value only. The result is often a sterilized, hygienic social psychology with little practiced "pay-off." Students "mount tirades" but we never know why. Colleagues are liked and disliked without objective causes. The world of Newcomb's small group is one where a "triple confrontation" (objects, others, and ego) takes place, and we must some-how solve the problem of adaptation. Just what happens if we don't, or worse, don't want to, we are never told. Presumably, violators of the consensus system must be properly dealt with, so that the sociologist may proceed with his search for orderliness and tranquility in the human world.

At the other end of the spectrum were the ethnographers who turned their gaze on the sociopsychological. The leader of this wing, Erving Goffman, occupies a place across the intellectual hall from B. F. Skinner. The books of Goffman, like those of B. F. Skinner, have served to revolutionize the way in which we talk of human interactions: "presentation of self," "cooling the mark out," "total institutions." What Goffman did was build a brilliant, ethnographic system out of the atomic units of personality structure. The jazzed-up language provides the reader with the feeling that these social psychologists really swing. Yet strangely, the experimenters and the ethnographers share a common unconcern for structure. The flux of events, whether under laboratory or field conditions is unconnected to cognitive definitions. It is an operationalized world, in which the definitions of things—living, dying, singing, or swinging—are embedded in the symbols and rituals with which these things are done. The Goffman school is the ultimate in nominalistic orientation. No reality stands behind the event to certify its reality. The world is a performance. People are the performers, and the social psychologist becomes the literary theater critic turned loose on an unsuspecting universe of role-playing, manipulating and/or manipulated actors.

Another type of social psychology attempted to combine, in effect, the previous two (wherever there is a new style, old synthesizers are sure to follow). The game theorist accepts all the role theory and rule-making of the Goffman wing, while insisting that its logic and its methods are not unlike those employed by experimentalists working either in "natural" or "laboratory" settings. They inhabit a world of bargains and bargainers; of players who have the goods, and of those who bluff. Every event is made into a psychological sweat—in which parliamentarians and presidents are pictured as playing the game of life with the whole universe, while the little people of the world are seen as playing exactly the same game at lesser levels and with smaller tasks. The social psychologists who have gone into military strategy are large—in numbers if not in quality. I have yet to learn of one new civilian militarist casualty in Vietnam—the gap between policy-making and physical execution is approximately 10,000 miles— the same distance that this group is from effecting the grand synthesis of everything from children playing Monopoly to their daddies playing Big Business. The social psychological gamesters are distinguished from the experimenters and the ethnographers in that they deal with possibilities but not with people.

There is another style of work in social psychology which had a marked success toward the close of the 1950's. It is the thundering totalism of the alienation school—particularly the work of Herbert Marcuse and Erich Fromm. Marcuse, a severe critic of Fromm, nonetheless shares with him—and with many others from an older generation of European gentlemen—a nostalgic yearning after the lost paradise of the Viennese or Berliner twenties—a snobbish democracy of the educated that never really was. One can never be sure as to when this school is resting on autobiographical honesty—on a system of self-revelations, which, like many good revelations from Aesop to La Rochefoucauld, tell important truths and make some genuine observations about the world. More often than not, this is not a school of sociologists so much as they are avid and *good* newspaper readers—able to detect world historic trends and frame them in humanistic terms. The radicalism of this school is, however, slightly soiled by the fact that they have created a world of political devils without political angels. Indeed, it is the latest and the greatest form of *anti-politique*, *i.e.*, "pure negativity." "Man" is alienated, never select portions of the population. "Industrialization" is the culprit, never any specific process in production. "Urbanization" is horrible, cities stink as such, never the poor section of the city. "Nationalism" is horrible, never any one nationalism more so than another. The noisiness of this kind of writing does a great deal to cast doubt on the seriousness of macroscopic approaches. It represents, in fact, a step away from the sobriety and seriousness that characterized such great social psychologists as Hull and Koffka, no less than Mead and Freud. If Skinner made the initial incision, and divorced morals from science in an entirely irrevocable way, Marcuse performed the miracle of divorcing science from moral writing—in an irresponsible way—so that one is left either to share the morality of the thundering totalists, or be cast into the valley of the shadow of death. Each claiming substance casts away the other as shadow.

The ultimate question about *Character and Social Structure* is why, since it is such an invigorating text, has it fallen into such disuse? The answers are complex in the extreme. In the first place, Gerth and Mills employed Freudianism in a more than fashionable sense. It was woven into the fabric of their work as no other American sociologists had dared to use it. However powerful Freudian thought was in a clinical, patient-analyst setting, it never gained respectability in departments of either psychology or sociology. And without such academic respectability, a book that used Freud in such an extravagant way was doomed to academic oblivion. In the second place, the very employment of Freud by Gerth and Mills pointed up the painful, nontherapeutic way in which they used Freud. In England, in such places as the Tavistock Institute, Freud was used in factory studies, in experimental situations of all sorts. The social psychologists were thus exposed to Freud in a public, practical setting—which retained a firm grip on the therapeutic, pragmatic side of psychoanalysis and its offshoots. In the United States, the strictly Germanic impulses prevailed. Even a pragmatist like Mead was an impractical man, caught in the vise of abstract metaphysics. The Freudians became critics instead of constructors. And to this very degree to which criticism replaced construction, ideology replaced therapy. In the United States, Freudianism was cleaved: the "analysts" simply ignored the critical cutting edge of their master; while the "academics" simply ignored the therapeutic setting of Freudian analysis. And while there are momentary flashes in *Character and Social Structure* that show some understanding of this issue, the problem could not be tackled straightaway—by two authors who already were poles apart methodologically, and moving further away from one another with the passage of time. Thus it is that the career of an intellectually exciting book had such an abrupt termination point.

With such a cacophony of sound and fury, the republication of *Character and Social Structure* must be viewed as a welcome event—if only for the opportunity it provides for looking at the progeny with greater scrutiny than is usually the case. I must say that for me, this is the best book on the subject written during the dismal decade. Indeed, the clumsy confusion between social roles and institutional roles, the traditionalist, almost Parsonian, relegation of social change as a footnote to the "model of social structure," which anchors the book to the least viable part of Weber's *Wirtschaft und Gesellschaft,* clearly "date" the book. But my, oh my—what a pair of minds can accomplish even within such a theoretically loose framework! When Gerth and Mills speak of hypocrisy and posing as "the stylization of self-presentations," they clearly anticipate the theoretical innovations of Goffman. When they speak of the status sphere in terms of "the claimant's side and the bestower's side," they go far into subsuming game analogies under their wing. And while they are too enmeshed in the Freudian and Meadian approaches to symbols, language, gesture, and motivation to make any experimentalist happy, it cannot be said that they are ignorant of the findings made by physiological psychology. And at the macroscopic level of political sociology, Gerth and Mills are eminently sounder on questions of economic development, dictatorship, psychology, or bureaucracy than are the thundering totalists. They see the double process of convergence and competition between East and West as a long-standing one. And if their statements on "sea power" and "land power" are obsolete in a thermonuclear epoch, their underlying appreciation of the differences between socialism and capitalism, democracy and totalitarianism, is far more welcome than the denunciations of the modern world that have come to define the limits of radical ideology in the American universities. *Character and Social Structure* is thus more than a book: it is a statement of dissatisfaction with the decade, but also a demand for attention to those structural variables that the psychologizing of sociology dismissed with impunity.

II

The war of words between sociological styles is different in content, but hardly less sharp in polemical form than the ideological battles waged between Hamiltonians and Jeffersonians, or Trotskyites and Stalinists. Pure sociologists view applied sociologists as interlopers, surrogates for social workers. Charges abound: applied types have an investment in social ailments to the point of inventing ills when none obtain. They are considered parasitical in theory and opportunistic in practice. Applied sociologists accuse "grand theorists" of forgetting the human content and context of social science. It is said that if confronted by a man in the act of suicide, the theorist is more concerned with discovering if it is a case of anomic, altruistic, fatalistic, or egotistic suicide than with pulling the "subject" off the bridge. Examining closely, however, I cannot but feel that the gap between the two groups is largely contrived. The war of words deserves a better underpinning in reality than it has received up to now. But the call to reason is perhaps the least appreciated of all by those who need social science the most. This is why *Applied Sociology: Opportunities and Problems* has practical importance apart from its general merits.

Let us take up the results that this book shows arising from sociological field work. The first immediate finding is the *interference effect*. This is a sociological counterpart of the Heisenberg effect in physics, in which the role of the experimenter in the natural setting is itself a consideration in defining a problem. While it took a decade to confirm this after Elton Mayo's factory researches, the interference effect is continually being reconfirmed in new situations. Second, there is the *marginal effect*. The social scientist operating in a practical situation is in some ways necessarily marginal with respect to the people he is dealing with. If he is studying local elites, he is outside the power structure and at best makes salutary recommendations. If he examines delinquency, he risks violating the law by participating in the gang culture. Therefore, in the attempt to remain legal, he is marginal. Third, we may speak of the *reinforcement effect*. For example, in a delinquency subculture, the experimenter may tend to spend much time with the leadership, who may in fact be the most extreme and "anti-social" in the group. Fourth, we may speak of the *involvement effect*. This generally takes place among industrial sociologists or sociologists in a bureaucratic setting, who are in a position to alter the decision-making process and hence tend to spill over from noting options and their consequences to becoming involved with the decision the corporation takes. A fifth item is the *God-like effect*. This is usually found among sociologists working in underdeveloped areas, where the tendency is to view the social scientist as a magician, a seer, and a prophet. This is particularly so when recommendations result in better crops, higher cash payments, a shorter work week, or better living conditions. God help this God-like sociologist if the intended results do not come about! Finally, there is the *investigator-client effect*. In any practical setting it is difficult for the social scientist who is being paid directly by a client to know what the *best* decision is, not merely the *range* of decisions possible. The advice given may be tailored to expected norms. This sometimes occurs among industrial sociologists, who, in their desire to settle labor-management tensions, raise issues of a peripheral nature that conform to a management viewpoint. Here, then, is a whole set of problems raised in the papers of Rodman, Kolodny, Gardner, Jordan, and Miller, among others, which once would simply not have been perceived honestly by the sociological brotherhood.

The contributors to *Applied Sociology* illumine a set of applied results arising out of established theory. A knowledge of David Riesman's concept of veto groups can be employed to arrive at the desegregation of a southern town. Localism, or Toennies' concept of *Gemeinschaft*, may explain an essential link between the individual and the amorphous cosmopolitan center, and thus contribute to the solution of racial tensions in the South. In criminology, the definition of criminal behavior may be considered a complex pattern of decision-making involving discretionary choices by those who administer the law. In the area of community leadership, Merton's notion of influentials may help to describe the actual relationship of power by indicating levels of influence as a function of monetary position in the community. One study shows that the dominants among the leadership elements are business people, while the subdominants are professional people. The key to the distinction between high status groups remains economic wealth. It may also be the case, as is pointed out in another study, that alienation is not the same as marginality; that mediators in small-town life may be so involved in the routine of daily leadership that they become alienated from the larger chores of community life. This lends substance to current sociological views on alienation. Finally, Leon Festinger's theory of compliant behavior can be used to show that the law can act as an educational force in changing people's behavior. Therefore, the passage of civil rights acts is not merely justified in terms of moral necessity but may in fact change the sentiments of those who might otherwise be noncompliers. In sum, sociological theory indicates that while you may not be able to teach racial equality, you can engender respect for the law that aims at racial equality. The papers by Breed, Robbins, Newman, Pittman, Lowry, Greer, and Evan offer this kind of work.

Then there is a special set of papers in which established sociological theory challenges established social welfare notions. One study points out that the continued conceptualization of the aged as a minority group, whatever its political interests, is not justified regarding the aged as a social force. Since the aged lack group identity, they do not perceive of themselves as a social movement, and therefore it may be more dangerous than helpful for sociologists in an action framework to conceive of them in this way. In another paper, it is pointed out that the family casework approach often assumes that solutions to family problems automatically improve parent-child relationships, when, as a matter of fact, in the so-called normal family, strife between generations may be most manifest. Thus, in these two papers by Streib and Sherwood, you have an interesting indication of the role of theory in contradicting applied research and in this way promoting the search for new applied results which challenge old theory.

This brings us to another departure from the expected. Jury behavior, far from being "angry," tends to be extremely judicious. People who in normal circumstances are given to exaggerated responses behave with extreme caution in courtroom situations. Here in the essays by Moore, Feldman, and Simon we have another set of pioneering studies where new applied research negates established theory.

Applied Sociology is a volume not easily ensnared by a paradigm. The final portion of the book points up the continuing dialogue, even the continuing agony that sociologists feel about the relationship of social theory and social action. The papers in this section seem to represent not so much a consensus as a range of alternative possibilities for viewing the famed "value problem." One end of the continuum is represented by Ralph Ross. He sees science as a value in itself. As a matter of fact, he declares that the core value which the scientist bears is that of science per se, namely, truth-seeking. Somewhat less extreme is the position taken by Robert Bierstedt, who sees the dualism between scientific and public service as everlasting, and as equivalent to the distinction between sociology and action as such. But he also goes on to note the need of the sociologist to be responsive to both his public and his scientific role, even though the twain shall never meet. Occupying the middle ground, Mabel Elliot argues that the solution of this science-action dualism lies in greater cohesion and coming together of sociologists and psychologists. Once they close the gap organizationally, certain problems will fade away. For Llewellyn Gross the gap is already closed, since the question consists of how to look at the problem in terms of facts and values rather than resolving the relationship. He notes that a dualism between the two cannot be maintained since the conditions and consequences for both factual and value statements are similar in many respects; hence the facts and values used for identifying and resolving social problems may be scientifically defined and prescribed. Alfred McClung Lee takes this line of reasoning to its ultimate by noting that the defenders of the dualism between science and action really have a psychological investment in science as something clean and action as something dirty. He urges those who want respectability to seek a comfortable cult instead of converting social science into a ritual-ridden secular faith. "Scientific innovation of a fundamental sort has never been legitimate even though it may be later legitimated. It is always unorthodox, agitational, and irreverent."

The final paper in the work, by co-editor S. M. Miller, is a companion piece to Gouldner's opening paper. Gouldner indicates the challenges and responsibilities in developing an applied social science, in achieving the kind of social science in which the rift between policy-maker and social scientist can be mended, much as the clinical treatment of patients resolves the "natural" illness of the patient in the "unnatural" setting of the hospital. Miller, for his part, points out the dangers involved in an applied sociology. He notes how easily the applied sociologist can serve rather than harness power and how readily he can drift into working within the discursive terms set by the interests of his organization. This pioneering effort to introduce the problems of applied social science to a general lay public is subject to many of the strains which may afflict the intended clientele. But unlike that clientele, and as an instruction for it, the book, its contributors, and its editors have a shared appreciation of self-awareness and of current limits as well as a creative potential in designing a future. This is what makes *Applied Sociology* significant reading for those interested in changing, no less than living in, the world.

Certain major tendencies appear clear and irrevocable. First, there has been a turn-around process from small-scale studies involving limited sized groups to large-scale studies involving expanding units of investigation. The very computer technology that was earlier used to prove the need for careful, if limited, studies, has become sophisticated enough to call into being the demand for a general scale enlargement in social psychology. Second, there is a constant demand to move the field from criticism to construction. The shift from analyticity (whether of a Millsian or Goffmanesque variety) to application (whether of a conservative penological variety or a radical educational variety) proceeds, after all, on the assumption that sociology is a commodity that has achieved enough sanction to warrant a marketing orientation.

Any prognostication should consider the anomaly of the present situation: both those emphasizing methodological precision and those arguing for greater relevance are probably going to get their wishes fulfilled—or perhaps over-fulfilled. The possibilities of social control are such that methodologists are going to be spending a great deal of time worrying over the policy implications of this situation. On the other hand, the general consensus established in the sixties on the need for relevance is going to produce a greater concern for the question of "relevance for who?" Now that the Lynd question—knowledge for what?—has been generally answered in terms of making social life better; the next question that needs attending to is "relevance for who?" And until an answer roughly equivalent to *everyman* can be ensured, we can expect the mission of social psychology to remain plagued by doubt and bathed in ambiguity.

The doubt and ambiguity are multiplied by the fact that nearly all current appraisals in applied sociology take application as a cause rather than as a fact. In this sense, theoretical advances have been few and far between. It made good sense for Emory Bogardus, Robert E. Park, and Stuart Chapin to structure their worlds in terms of a confrontation between generalists and applied researchers. In the early 1920's, in the halcyon days of *The Journal of Applied Sociology*, the applied researcher insisted that "the times are calling loudly for the social puritan." But the situation is considerably altered now. Sociological issues can no longer be formulated in the painfully naive terms that guided Comtian puritans like George Elliott Howard. Increasingly, the challenge to applied sociology comes from its "allies" the policy-makers, and not from its "enemies" the grand theorists. The old struggles, after all, permitted a certain moral smugness—the self-righteousness of the engaged versus the poor devils inhabiting the ivory towers of the academy.

However, after fifty years of applied research, the problem of justification has become much stickier. The claims for doing "important" and "meaningful" work come not so much from the sociological Left as from the political Right. And until this challenge is met in a forthright manner, suspicions concerning applied research will persist. As a start, the political character of much applied research must be appreciated, for only then can its overt political uses be challenged. There should be a clear recognition that application is not the alpha and omega of sociological theory, but only that application and intervention research confirm that sociological theory does indeed exist. If general theorists have been disdainful of applied research, the applicationists have been no less contemptuous of general theory. Yet, the need to allow sociology to pursue non-significant (in the manifest sense) activities is essential for the wider recognition that sociology has had, and must continue to have, an autonomous development. Every science has an inner life, an internal history. Without this, the very independent nature of the scientific enterprise itself is menaced. The task of applied research is to utilize fundamental theory in the solution of new and difficult problems. This should not spill over into any fatuous claims that theoretical work is unimportant or superfluous. The task of applied sociology is to make self-evident the options available and to administer guidelines for acting on such options. It is not the job of applicationists to pull every chestnut out of every policy agency fire. Only when the distinction between social practice and self-promotion is made clear will the promissory notes offered in applied sociology be redeemed.

PART III. *The Political Life of Sociology*

16. *Functionalist Sociology and Political Ideologies*

THE UNSETTLED QUESTION of the place of political belief and bias in sociological analysis has been a major source of irritation since Marx in the *German Ideology* implanted the problem of ideological variables, and Spencer in *The Study of Sociology* attempted a first full-scale resolution. Indeed, from the time of Spencer until the present, the claim has been made that functionalism has settled the issue of the relationship between sociology and the "class bias."[1] The purpose of this chapter is to explore the statement that sociology, to the extent that it employs functionalist canons, is liberated from the long-standing charge that political commitments and prescriptions underlie both the conscious theory and the unconscious tendencies of sociological investigation.

This charge (made both by those who are sympathetic and those who are hostile to sociology) has been met in contrasting ways. First, there has been the

This paper examines the claims of functionalism to be a theory and method of sociology that is free from extraneous, political criteria. It is found that the claims are largely unsupported and, more, unsupportable. The ideological premises and commitments of functionalism are considered against a background of growing demands for greater specificity and application in sociology.
This study was first published in *The Journal of Politics*, 25, no. 3 (May, 1963).

1. Cf. Herbert Spencer, *The Study of Sociology* (New York: D. Appleton and Co., 1873), pp. 65–74. For a modern variation on this theme see Karl Mannheim, *Ideology and Utopia* (New York: Harcourt, Brace & Co., 1936), pp. 97–136.

admission that sociology does have to do with political beliefs at some level, whether in originating questions, in styles of research, or in the aims of inquiry; but that this does not impugn the integrity of sociology any more than Keynes' commitment to the welfare state nullifies the importance of his studies in fiscal policy and monetary circulation, or any more than Einstein's concern for world federalism invalidates the theory of relativity. A second way of meeting the challenge has been to deny the premise, by an insistence that sociology is, as a matter of fact, free of value considerations of a political nature. This second approach, usually adopted by the school of structural-functional sociologists, further goes on to state that to the extent that a strict separation of facts and values is maintained, sociology is scientific; while insofar as it is not maintained, sociology is tainted and unscientific.[2]

Structural-functionalism has, with but rare exceptions, assumed the burden of the second way of meeting the charge that sociology is conditioned by political presuppositions. It is my intention to explore how and in what sense the denial of the connection of sociology to political beliefs achieves the intended goal of purifying sociological research. Simply asserting a link between sociology and politics no more destroys sociological objectivity than does the denial guarantee objectivity. As Schumpeter has shown,[3] ideologies—those unconscious agencies of interest rationalization and justification—at certain times may serve as a stimulant to the kind of continuing self-evaluation that nourishes the scientific community.

In his recent paper on functionalism as a sociological method, Kingsley Davis sums up the dilemmas of functionalism in decisive fashion. He introduces five major allegations against its continued use: (a) Professional consensus on even a minimal definition of structural functional analysis does not exist. (b) Most work done under the functional label is equivalent to sociological analysis as such; and when divergencies do occur, functionalism shows itself to be social philosophy rather than a unique methodological tool. (c) To debate sociological questions under the guise of evaluating functionalism exhibits teleological qualifications which are not open to scientific evaluation. (e) Terms such as "function," "dysfunction," and "eufunction" are semantic artificialities that hinder rather than promote sociological research.[4]

I shall not counter this broadside set of criticisms. To be sure. Davis has independently arrived at a negative view of functionalism earlier made by the

2. Cf. Bennett M. Berger, "Sociology and the Intellectuals: An Analysis of a stereotype," in *Sociology, The Progress of a Decade*, ed. by S. M. Lipset and Neil Smelser (Englewood Cliffs, N.J.: Prentice-Hall, 1961), pp. 37–46. See also Seymour M. Lipset and Neil Smelser, "Change and Controversy in Recent American Sociology," *The British Journal of Sociology*, 12 (1961): 41–51.

3. Joseph Schumpeter, "Science and Ideology," in *Essays of Joseph Schumpeter*, ed. by R. V. Clemence (Reading, Mass.: Addison-Wesley Publishing Co., 1951).

4. Kingsley Davis, "The Myth of Functional Analysis as a Special Method in Sociology and Anthropology," *American Sociological Review*, 24 (1959): 757–773.

philosophers of science, in particular Braithwaite,[5] Nagel,[6] and Hempel.[7] What I wish to do here is further develop these aforementioned analyses of functionalism in terms of its effects upon the relationship of sociology to political beliefs.

Specifically, the main contentions which I wish to make and support are as follows: (a) Functionalism, to the extent to which it distinguishes itself from sociology as such, intrinsically entails political commitment although it does not logically imply any single type of political belief system. (b) Functionalism offers no safeguards for the exclusion of political value judgments either in the formation of hypotheses or in the results obtained. (c) Where value considerations do not obtain in any form, the term "functionalism" is being employed tautologically, and not as a special research method. (d) Those who have maintained a functionalist orientation generally confuse a historical strategem with a logical inference. If these four points are correct, then it follows that functionalism, by presenting sociology with the misanthropic enterprise of liquidating political considerations, has blunted the more viable and practically realizable task of studying the place of political beliefs in and for sociological theory and social research.[8]

The classic formulation of the idea that functionalism involves no basic political or ideological commitment is that offered by Merton:

The fact that functional analysis can be seen by some as inherently conservative and by others as inherently radical suggests that it may be inherently neither one nor the other. It suggests that functional analysis may involve no intrinsic ideological commitment, although, like other forms of sociological analysis, it can be infused with any one of a wide range of ideological values.[9]

This suggests that considerations of political ideology are extrinsic to functionalism. It should first be noted that political beliefs and ideological values are not the same. They are as distinct from each other as unconsciously held interest positions are from consciously adopted value preferences. Thus, even if we grant the claim that functionalism is intrinsically free of ideological elements, it

5. Richard Bevan Briathwaite, *Scientific Explanation: A Study of the Function of Theory, Probability and Law in Science* (Cambridge: Cambridge University Press, 1953), 319–340.

6. Ernest Nagel, "A Formalization of Functionalism," in *Logic Without Metaphysics, and Other Studies in the Philosophy of Science* (Glencoe, Ill.: Free Press, 1957), pp. 247–283.

7. Carl G. Hempel, "The Logic of Functional Analysis," in *Symposium on Sociological Theory*, ed. by Llewellyn Gross (Evanston, Ill.: Row, Peterson & Co., 1959), pp. 271–307.

8. For a recent effort to develop a sociological appreciation of values in and for the social scientist, see Abraham Edel, *Ethical Judgment: The Use of Science in Ethics* (Glencoe, Ill.: Free Press, 1955) and *Science and the Structure of Ethics* (Chicago: University of Chicago Press, 1961).

9. Robert K. Merton, "Manifest and Latent Functions: Toward the Codification of Functional Analysis in Sociology," in *Social Theory and Social Structure* (Glencoe, Ill.: Free Press, 1957), p. 39.

remains a distinct task to examine the extent to which pragmatic criteria of workability entail a series of value perspectives opening wide the floodgates of political commitment.

Even such a formulation grants too much. It is by no means self-evident that the liberation of functionalism from pragmatic assumptions of utility would solve the problem. Insistence on maintaining the strict dichotomy of fact and value, far from offering a satisfactory solution, has only made the functionalist less attentive to political considerations in general, and to the political perspective inherent in specific sociological work in particular. Emphasis on the words "inherent" and "intrinsic" tends to obfuscate the facts of observation. Functionalists do indeed adopt political frameworks of a more or less explicit nature. Any inventory of sociology textbooks would make that clear. The question of whether these commitments are intrinsic or not is thus quite apart from the observed situation. To assert a gulf between political commitment and ideological values is only to make the functionalist attachment to a set of political beliefs more palatable. As a matter of fact, it does not overcome the paradox of asserting on one hand the need for a politically neutral sociology, and on the other, the fact of politically conditioned findings. However tenuous the evidence might be for functionalism as a special methodological adjunct of social research, there is even less evidence that can be adduced for it as an ideologically liberated approach.[10]

In this connection it is intriguing to note that Merton himself has exhibited the greatest sort of anxiety over the "neutral" claims of functionalism. He sharply condemns those who would solve problems "by the abdication of moral responsibility" as in fact being "no solution at all." The posture of value neutrality "overlooks the crux of the problem: the initial formulation of the scientific investigation has been conditioned by the implied value of the scientist."[11] Merton's use of the "narcotizing dysfunction" concept is indeed a direct attempt to shake up the self-satisfied claims of classic functionalism. For it is clear that Merton's urgings not to "mistake *knowing* about problems of the day for *doing* something about them" is a use of dysfunction, not in terms of the social order as such, but in terms of a *democratic* social order.[12] Given such impressive qualms, it is difficult to fathom the dogmatic insistence on the political neutrality of functionalism as such.

The idea that functionalism, at least in its Parsonian form as a theory of pattern-maintenance, is not *intrinsically ideological* tends to avoid an encounter with the primary issue, which is that functionalism is *intrinsically political*.

10. Cf. Irving Louis Horowitz, "Laws and Levels in the Sociology of Knowledge," in *Philosophy, Science, and the Sociology of Knowledge* (Springfield, Ill.: Charles C Thomas/ American Lecture Series, 1961), p. 116.

11. Robert K. Merton, *Mass Persuasion* (New York: Harper & Bros., 1947), pp. 187–188.

12. Robert K. Merton and Paul Lazarsfeld, "Mass Communication, Popular Taste and Organized Social Action," in *Mass Culture: The Popular Arts in America*, ed. by Bernard Rosenberg and David Manning White (Glencoe, Ill.: Free Press, 1957), p. 464.

Whereas the emphasis thus far has been on the terms "intrinsic" or "extrinsic," the more realistic emphasis might better be placed on the terms "political" or "politically neutral." The substance of the matter is not whether functionalism evolves out of any single ideological context, but rather in what forms it serves as a meta-sociology channelizing research along lines that are deemed compatible with any given political structure. Functionalist advocates speak of need satisfaction as something radically apart from want satisfaction. But in the process of social interaction, needs, wants, and desires are frequently defined by the same content.

In a recent paper, Brotz has given substance to the problem of functional reduction by taking note of the fact that the level of human association shows differential elements not to be found in the physiological or biological sciences.

In contrast to the world of human affairs, the heart does not have to plead to be allowed to perform its function, does not have to make a case that it is more important to health and life than other "dispensable" organs, does not have to defend itself by political *action* in the literal meaning of this term. The mechanisms of defense are such only metaphorically. The heart is not a political agent and as such makes no political claims. This is the obverse of the fact that the organs of the body are not ranged in political parties or interest groups with conflicting standards of health. They do their work, without raising the question of relative rights, or the organism as a whole perishes; and if it does they don't even care.[13]

This indicates that even if the language of physiological functions is legitimate within the biological sciences, itself a dubious assertion, this would still not constitute proof for either the sociological relevance or political neutrality of functionalism. The evidence would indicate that functionalism is not only infused with political values, but also intrinsically committed to position-taking and policy-making. What is open to question is the type of commitment, subject to the political and intellectual moorings of the individual investigator; but not the fact of commitment as such.

One of the difficulties with many criticisms of functionalism is that they have insisted that functionalism leads to only one possible style of polity.[14] If this were in fact the case, the myth of functionalism would have been dispelled with the first shafts. The very absence of consensus as to the political implications entailed by functional analysis leads one to assume that the nature of those political commitments is variable, subject to the particular moorings of the investigator. This however does not signify the neutrality of the given *ism* known as functionalism.

13. Howard Brotz, "Functionalism and Conflict Analysis," in *Conference on Conflict, Consensus and Cooperation*, ed. by Irving L. Horowitz (Geneva, N.Y.: Hobart and William Smith Colleges, 1962).

14. Cf. W. L. Kolb, "Values, Positivism, and the Functional Theory of Religion," *Social Forces*, 31 (1953): 305–311; and from another perspective, Ralf Dahrendorf, "Out of Utopia: Toward a Reorientation of Sociological Analysis," *American Journal of Sociology*, 64 (1958): 115–127.

In his famed work on *The Acquisitive Society*, Tawney has a chapter entitled "The Functional Society." In his view, if we accept the principle of functional requirement, we are led to ask what the purpose is of ground rents, royalties, interest on investments, profits, etc. Clearly, to pose the problem in this teleological form is to go far in supplying an answer. In Tawney's opinion, capitalist economic relations are organized for the maintenance of *rights* rather than for the performance of socially worthy *duties*. Hence this economic order is nonfunctional. Tawney goes on to present a straight functionalist accounting for the "polite ushering out of the State."

The course of wisdom in the affairs of industry is, after all, what it is in any other department of organized life. It is to consider the end for which economic activity is carried on and then to adopt economic organization to it. It is to pay for service and for service only, and when capital is hired to make sure that it is hired at the cheapest possible price.[15]

What this involves for Tawney is the liquidation of all nonfunctional aggregates, such as private property holdings beyond their actual use; profits extracted from industry which serve the cause of conspicuous consumption; and, in general, ownership divorced from production. In short, to achieve a functional society would involve the mass of mankind in a gigantic social upheaval. Tawney's attitude toward functionalism is equivalent to his attitude toward the need for socialism. But whatever socialism is or is not, the desire for a radical overhauling of society is based on a set of political beliefs concerning the worth of an egalitarian economy. It is not in itself neutral in virtue of its being "a functional society."

In an equally familiar work, Alexis Carrel deals with the "Adaptive Functions" not simply, or even primarily, to show how the chemistry of the human body works, but to evolve a system of "practical significance of adaptive functions," or, as it is put later in the book, "the remaking of man." Involved in this refurbishing process is a theory of the bodily adaptation to the external environment, such as mechanisms of compensation which bring a steady balance into play between biological and mental processes. "These movements of the functional systems express the apprehension by man of the outer reality. They act as a buffer for the material and psychological shocks which he unceasingly receives. They not only permit him to endure, but they also are the agents of his formation and of his progress."[16]

But Carrel wishes to carry his brand of adaptive functionalism far beyond the claims of homeostasis. The truly functional view involves a consideration of "natural health," a knowledge of the "inner mechanisms" responsible for some men being naturally weak and others naturally strong. The entire view of

15. R. H. Tawney, "The Functional Society," in *The Acquisitive Society* (London: G. Bell & Sons Ltd., 1921), pp. 96–104.

16. Alexis Carrel, "Adaptive Functions," in *Man the Unknown* (New York: Harper & Bros., 1935), pp. 233–234.

functionalism is thus something which ultimately is said to entail the eugenic purification of the human race. All sorts of overtones emerge in this equation of the "functional" with the "healthy": conceptions of the *Übermensch*, biological elites, and the cleansing force of genocide all find a home in this functional view of society. The functionalism of Carrel does not prevent him from advocating an overhauling of civilization no less drastic than that implied by Tawney, although radically different in practical implications, to be sure.

We now have to reestablish, in the fullness of his personality, the human being weakened and standardized by modern life. Sexes have again to be clearly defined. Each individual should be either male or female, and never manifest the sexual tendencies, mental characteristics, and ambitions of the opposite sex. Instead of resembling a machine produced in series, man should, on the contrary, emphasize his uniqueness. In order to reconstruct personality, we must break the frame of the school, factory, and office, and reject the very principles of technological civilization.[17]

We do not have to carry further Carrel's design for a fascist community of fate to see that functionalism in this case does absolutely nothing to prevent the manipulation of "scientific" information to specific political ends. Indeed, functionalism has meaning for Carrel precisely because it affords a scientific convention by means of which questions of politics can be discussed. Contrary to the claims of its adherents, functionalism has by no means represented in sociology what relativism meant in the development of physics. A clearer parallel can be drawn between functionalism and the general tendency of modern sociology to place a premium on any heuristic device which holds out the promise of being politically noncommital. But this only establishes functionalism as a specie of *anti-politique*. It does not guarantee its status as either a method or a system of sociology.

While Merton is discomforted by the "motley company" claiming the functionalist mantle, he nonetheless draws astonishingly positive conclusions about the worth of functional theory for sociology. The very existence of a "motley crew" suggests again that "agreement on the functional outlook need not imply identity of political or social philosophy."[18] True enough, but since it *does* as a matter of fact imply *some type* of political commitment, where does that leave the widely repeated claim for the *neutrality* of functionalism? I submit that it entirely nullifies the claim.

It will be objected that the uses of functionalism to support either socialist or fascist claims are few in number and represent only eccentric uses of the doctrine. While this is quite so, the alternative uses of functionalism, while not as politically uncongenial, are nonetheless political in nature. The employment of functionalism by liberal and conservative ideologies constitutes a proof of the intrinsically political nature of the functionalist canons no less than its uses by

17. *Ibid.*, pp. 314–315.
18. Merton, *Social Theory and Social Structure*, p. 47f.

extreme political doctrines. Indeed, in sociology and anthropology, the ideology of functionalism is in large measure connected with the fusion in the late nineteenth century of the liberal tradition in politics and the secularist tradition in scientific affairs.

We might select as antipodal poles of functionalist accounts, which yet reveal a shared regard to accept liberalism and scientism as the epitome of sound sociology, the work of Durkheim and Malinowski. It will be seen that however "hostile" the Durkheim circle and the followers of Malinowski are to each other, they have a basic ideological frame that derives from a common attitude toward the liberalist implications and meaning of functionalism.

In Durkheim's case, the notion of function as general social needs has its roots in the concept of social solidarity. But the conservative implications of this doctrine seen by later critics were not drawn by Durkheim himself.[19] He saw social solidarity as developing in time. The function of social solidarity is to guarantee human fraternity, technological and scientific growth, and economic progress. Beyond that, Durkheim plainly looked forward to a universal commonwealth "where war will no longer be the law of international relations, where relations between societies will be pacifically regulated, as those between individuals already are, where all men will collaborate in the same work, and live the same life."[20] Similar sentiments are expressed by Durkheim in nearly all of his major works. The functional society is one in which there is a progressive liberation of the individual from the tyrannies of custom and habit. This is a liberation which, given the social nature of man, must take place through the agencies of society, that is, through organic solidarity and collective thought. To be sure, Durkheim is to sociology what John Dewey is to modern philosophy, the prophet of liberalism through social involvement. "The kingdom of ends and impersonal truths can realize itself only by the cooperation of particular wills."[21] As a perceptive commentator recently put matters, Durkheim "was far from being a radical pessimist in respect to human nature or the condition of society. All his strictures against egotism, his phrases about the necessity of discipline, reveal the bourgeois citizen, the *Dreyfusard*, not the conservative authoritarian."[22]

In Malinowski's case it is even clearer that functionalism operated to enforce the liberal canons of an England caught in the counterclaims of imperialism, nationalism and world war. The functionalism of Malinowski bears a strong

19. Cf. Lewis A. Coser, "Durkheim's Conservatism and Its Implications for his Sociological Theory," in *Emile Durkheim, 1858–1917*, ed. by Kurt H. Wolff (Columbus: Ohio State University Press, 1960), pp. 211–232.

20. Emile Durkheim, *The Division of Labor in Society*, trans. by George Simpson (New York: Macmillan Co., 1933), p. 405.

21. Emile Durkheim, *The Elementary Forms of the Religious Life*, trans. by Joseph W. Swain (New York: Collier Books, 1961), p. 494.

22. Melvin Richter, "Durkheim's Politics and Political Theory," in *Emile Durkheim, 1858–1917*, ed. by Kurt H. Wolff (Columbus: Ohio State University Press, 1960), p. 202.

resemblance to the kinds of doctrine advocated in an earlier generation by John Stuart Mill and Lionel Hobhouse. Malinowski never failed to use his anthropological and ethnological findings to twit the English bourgeois, as if in this way a restoration of the liberal consciousness could be effected. Even Malinowski's emphasis on individual psychological criteria, rather than upon social solidarity, seems best explicable in terms of his deep and abiding faith in the sort of liberal canons of utility commonly associated with the British philosophic tradition. Certainly, there is no more a "functionalist imperative" for Malinowski's individualism than there is for Durkheim's socialism.[23]

Malinowski established the "overall functionality" of primitive cultures on grounds quite like those employed by Mill to justify the claims of the minority conscience. In all of his work, Malinowski urges upon us a view of primitive man that takes into account the symbolic regulation of conflict through law and custom rather than through force and coercion. Further, he sees in all primitive groups an established system of mutual obligations involving the recognition that social consensus is integrated with self-interest in a form approximately like Adam Smith's self-regulating laissez-faire economy. Other major functional attributes in all going societies are an established system of rewards and punishments judiciously meted out and, above all, a belief that in a functional society every man must count as one and equal, irrespective of racial inheritance, level of economic growth, or types of local mores, customs or habits.[24]

A deeper reading of Malinowski's more general writings only reinforces the impression that his functional imperatives are but liberal political imperatives, dressed up so as to be palatable to a scientific audience. His summary of functionalism contains statements urging an appreciation of the ongoing nature of culture, the dangers of ethnocentricism for both the man of civilization and the man of science, an urging of an evolutionary, progressive view of man (the essence of which is the progressive adaptation of institutions to their functions), a judgment of the worth of social institutions based on what they do for any specific community and on the numbers of people they do things for.[25] In brief, liberalism is built into the very method of social science which Malinowski was urging upon his colleagues.

The attempt to see Malinowski's use of functionalism as a pathological deviation from a truly scientific functionalism quite misses the point.[26] And the

23. Cf. Irving L. Horowitz, "Crime, Custom and Culture: Remarks on the Functionalist Theory of Malinowski," *International Journal of Comparative Sociology*, 3 (1962): 229–245.

24. Cf. Bronislaw Malinowski, *Crime and Custom in Savage Society* (London: Routledge & Kegan Paul Ltd., 1926), pp. 20–21; and also *Magic, Science and Religion and Other Essays* (Glencoe, Ill.: Free Press, 1948), pp. 50–71.

25. Bronislaw Malinowski, "Functionalism in Anthropology," reprinted in *Sociological Theory: A Book of Readings*, ed. by Lewis A. Coser and Bernard Rosenberg (New York: Macmillan Co., 1957), pp. 519–540.

26. A. R. Radcliffe-Brown, "Functionalism: A Protest," *American Anthropologist*, 51 (1949): 318–320.

point is simply that all forms of functionalism thus far devised contain political imperatives. Malinowski's form of functionalism has received the widest sort of publicity not because it is either superior or inferior to other varieties, but rather because of Malinowski's remarkable capacity to sum up the ambitions of the social science researcher to fuse, once and for all, the faith in science *and* liberalism.

The important aspect remains the constancy of political presuppositions in functionalist appraisals. It remains an essential task to uncover and stipulate the prescriptive elements in sociological research as such, and not to seek a way out of the *problem* of the cognitive status of sociological knowledge by the use of a rubric: by pious declarations of the neutrality of a method which in the main represented the extension of liberal politics to the social sciences. Either sociology recognizes the claims (legitimate and illegitimate) of political prescription upon its efforts, or it runs the steady risk of being victimized by an inherited equation of *scientific* social analysis with *functionalist* analysis.

Perhaps the strongest demonstration that functionalist analysis, insofar as it signifies methodological properties other than those usually associated with scientific procedures, has firm political commitments is the earlier work of Kingsley Davis himself. We may here content ourselves with two representative chapters from *Human Society*. His analysis of the "Functional Theory of Religion" which is contrasted with "Outmoded Theories of Religion" bears out the apprehensions expressed in Davis' more recent position paper on functionalism. He moves from the necessity of social solidarity for the maintenance of society to the conclusion that only religion seems capable of fulfilling this functional requirement. "Among the societal requirements, the necessity of ideological and sentimental cohesion, or solidarity is outstanding. . . . One of the functions of religion is to justify, rationalize, and support the sentiments that give cohesion to the society."[27]

Now it might be said that Davis is merely pointing out what religion does without prescribing as to its worth, that is, without making any value judgments. However, in his elaboration upon this functional role of religion, it seems that "religion makes a unique and indispensable contribution to social integration."[28] Nowhere in the text does Davis test this proposition of the *unique* functionality of religion, or suggest criteria of measurement, or stipulate conditions for its proof or disproof. Davis does not, as a matter of fact, show that a society cannot live without religion and yet maintain itself intact. Nor does he show that there are any properties that can be designated as uniquely religious. Each of his criteria, from the supposition of supernaturalism, common sentiments, furnishing of sacred objects, to the ultimate source of rewards and punishments, can be readily fulfilled by secular institutions; and indeed are increasingly being so fulfilled by non-church institutions. The industrialization process has often exhibited

27. Kingsley Davis, *Human Society* (New York: Macmillan Co., 1949), p. 519.
28. *Ibid.*, p. 519.

a parallel process of secularization of formerly sacred instituions. To call this "functional compensation" or "dysfunctional" is simply a clumsy admission that a religion is not necessarily functional in the sense of social utility.

Furthermore, it is dubious whether religions the world over entail the sort of commitments to supernaturalism and utilitarianism that Davis says make a religion functional to begin with. One would have to place a highly restrictive geographical boundary on the meaning of religion to make any sense out of any ethnocentric theory of religion. Thus, rather than show religion to be either indispensable or unique, Davis has only shown that, given the extreme application of functional canons to problems of social solidarity, certain conservative inferences can be axiomatically implied.

Directly conservative political judgments are involved in Davis' functionalist vision of social stratification. Indeed, not since William Sumner's equation of liberty, inequality, and the survival of the fittest, has a sociologist spoken so decisively in favor of the functional *necessity* of inequality.[29] Sumner's justification of conservatism was made in the name of evolutionism. His position is meritorious in that there is no pretense as to the political neutrality of this brand of sociology. Davis' functionalist account of stratification systems is said to be apart from any such extraneous judgments. Yet it is difficult to fathom how Davis can offer an explanation of social stratification in terms of the "functional necessity of stratification," and then recoil in amazement that this is, to be sure, a cornerstone of conservative theories of natural law, and not a scientific explanation. Davis' functional necessity turns out to be a defense of the universal necessity of social inequality.

If the rights and prerequisites of different positions in a society must be unequal, then the society must be stratified, because that is precisely what stratification means. Social inequality is thus an unconsciously evolved device by which societies insure that the most important positions are conscientiously filled by the most qualified persons. Hence every society, no matter how simple or complex, must differentiate persons in terms of both prestige and esteem and must therefore possess a certain amount of institutionalized inequality.[30]

If Davis desires to speak in defense of Platonic political verities he certainly has the right (and even necessity) to do so. However, what is not his prerogative is to assert that there is a scientific and sociological mandate for this way of speaking. For it is no more clear that functionalism supplies a mandate to Davis' competitive society than that it does so for Tawney's cooperative society. The function of social stratification as defined by Davis cannot be empirically studied

29. William Graham Sumner, "The Challenge of Facts," in *Essays of William Graham Sumner*, ed. by A. G. Keller and M. R. Davie (New Haven: Yale University Press, 1934), vol. 2, p. 95.

30. Davis, *Human Society*, pp. 367–368; also see Kingsley Davis and Wilbert E. Moore, "Some Principles of Stratification," *American Sociological Review*, 10 (1945): 242–249.

unless what is understood by "inequality," "stratification," "unconscious devices," "qualified persons," etc., is made explicit. If no restrictions are placed on these terms, the question of whether a system of social stratification is a "must" is not a factual one to be decided by empirical examination, but a logical question to be decided by fiat. This is so because Davis' idea that every society necessarily possesses patterns of invariant social relations is taken to be an axiom of the system to be explained. Davis' "functional imperatives" are, like Malinowski's "indispensable ingredients," based upon teleolgical considerations rather than upon causal explanations. As Nagel recently indicated, such imagined functional requirements rest on a non sequitur, on "a transfer without warrant of the admitted indispensability of *tradition*, to a particular means or instrument that happens to be employed in certain societies for sustaining tradition."[31] In Davis' case, this amounts to a *support* of inequality in the name of functional explanation.

As a matter of fact, and as if to prove the ancient adage that two can play the same game, Tumin has offered a powerful catalogue of "negative functionality" of stratification systems of the sort advanced by Davis. While the word "function" is retained and repeatedly used, Tumin quite properly offers his counter-hypotheses as subject to further empirical study. In Tumin's view, stratification (a) limits the discovery or use of the full talent of a society; (b) sets arbitrary limits upon the expansion of the productive forces of society; (c) provides the elite with the political power necessary to secure its dominance; (d) distributes favorable self-images unequally throughout a population; (e) encourages hostility, suspicion, and mistrust among the various sectors of society; (f) distributes the sense of prestige and status unequally; and (g) distributes loyalty unequally in the population, *i.e.*, distributes motivation unequally by making some apathetic and others energetic about their life chances.[32]

The crux of the matter is not simply that functionalism does nothing to prevent the penetration of the sharpest sort of political opposition within its domain, but that this is so for reasons beyond the control of the functionalist method. Sharp differences arise because social systems are in continual interaction with political systems. It is only natural, therefore, to expect sociology to be deeply concerned with questions of political policy—either in a manifest form or in a latent form. What has thrown too many sociologists off stride is the equation of neutrality with objectivity.

Functionalism presents itself in the linguistic garb of such neutrality, holding out the hope for some sort of methodological superimperative which could once and for all demarcate factual and valuative questions. What has in fact occurred is the multiplication of terminology, obfuscating rather than explaining basic

31. Ernest Nagel, "Explanation and Understanding," in *The Structure of Science: Problems in the Logic of Scientific Explanation* (New York: Harcourt, Brace & World, 1961), pp. 520–535.

32. Melvin W. Tumin, "Some Principles of Stratification: A Critical Analysis," *American Sociological Review*, 18 (1953): 387–393.

political loyalties and ambitions. Can it seriously be doubted that Tumin's loyalties are first to a social radicalism and second to assumed functional imperatives, to the degree that they support this radicalism? Can it be seriously doubted that Davis' loyalties are first to a social conservatism, with the functional imperatives as such useful to the extent that they provide support for this conservatism? The contrary uses of functionalism are logical contradictions, and hence no proof of the value of functionalism; unless, that is, one is willing to brave the logical paradox of assigning scientific importance to tautological statements.

The assumption of political neutrality has too often resulted in an unreflecting insipidity. The further assumption of a *wertfrei* methodology called functionalism has not had the intended consequences; namely, the reduction (if not the elimination) of political judgments in sociological analysis. The plain fact is that functionalism has neither altered nor modified the basic political commitments of sociologists *qua* sociologists. If from this fact it be deduced that functionalism is *eo ipso* free of political implications, then it still must be explained why certain sociologists employ functionalism for very definite political ends. Until better explanation is provided, we must conclude that functionalism is a strategy (and at times even a posture) that enables the sociologist to make political statements without the necessity of defending these statements in the court of public opinion.

Instead of following through on Weber's clear mandate to distinguish between taking a practical political stand on one side, and examining political structures sociologically on the other, the functionalist device has increasingly tended to muddy the waters by equating political noncommitment with scientific wisdom. In this connection, Weber's precise formulation should be recalled. "To take a practical stand is one thing, and to analyze political structures and party positions is another. When speaking in a political meeting about democracy, one does not hide one's personal standpoint; indeed, to come out clearly and to take a stand is one's damned duty."[33]

How many sociologists have performed their "damned duty" in this way? Indeed, the myth of functionalism has promoted a concept of the social researcher as a purveyor of puerile information for sale to the highest bidder, while the purveyor himself is said to be protected from the marketplace by his magisterial methodology. In place of "Here I stand; I can do no other," the functionalist seems to have adopted as his pivotal slogan, "The world is stupid and base, not I." Expertise has been improperly preempted as a private possession of the functionalist, a possession which conveniently does away with the need for *either* analysis of *or* commitment to any political position. The *anti-politique* of most varieties of functionalism has not led to better sociology, but to puerile sociology. This is not a question of equating the secular with the puerile, for puerility can take many forms, scientific as well as theological. To convert a vice into a virtue by an intellectual sleight of hand, by assuming that sociology

33. "Politics as a Vocation," *ibid.*, p. 127.

has "fully matured" because it is now as dismal a science as economic theory is reputed to be, is to shortchange the adventure of science no less than to muddle the tasks of present-day sociology—which I take to include an examination of the conditions under which a society does not work as well as the conditions under which it does. Further, it perilously ignores Weber's dictum that "no science is absolutely free from presuppositions, and no science can prove its fundamental value to the man who rejects these presuppositions."[34]

The very completeness with which an historical strategy has been accepted as a methodological first principle serves to show how thoroughly functionalism and liberalist politics have been intermeshed in the first half of this century. This does not, however, constitute a scientific proof for the language of functionalism. From a scientific viewpoint the question is not whether functionalism is intrinsically any one kind of political ideology, but to what extent it can be distinguished from political ideology as such. A rich tapestry of practical and ultimate political considerations is connected with the generic concept of function. Moreover, since the line between sociology and politics is hardly an impassable barrier, the central issue is not how "liberated" functionalism is from political concerns, but rather the exact line of intersection between functionalism as a political ideology in its own right, and functionalism as a rationalization and justification for more conventional divisions in the political spectrum.

Far from bringing about so euphoric a status as an "end to ideology" in sociology, or a "secularization" of the discipline, or any other gratuitous forms of self-praise, functionalism has only shifted the locus of the ideological dialogue. So clearly is this the case that rather pronounced political differences have come to the foreground in recent discussions of functional sociology. In so far as functionalism is a political *ism*, it suffers the factional fate of other systems of social analysis which preceded it, such as evolutionism, marxism, organicism, and historicism. To consider ideology as "an irretrievably fallen word," when it continues to inform the writings of even those who speak of its "exhaustion," only serves to show how pernicious the mechanisms of psychic and social self-deception are.[35]

From an analytical as well as an historical point of view, functionalism has not prevented sociologists from splitting up into competing political camps, not even those who claim functional doctrine as a protective covering. In large measure this has been due to functionalism's inability to settle the question of the relationship of political beliefs to sociological inquiry—the main question it set for itself since the writings of Spencer. Even if we grant the ability of functionalism to establish its neutrality *vis à vis* radicalism and conservatism, it must still come to terms with a world that is neither black nor white, but a thousand

---

34. "Science as a Vocation," *ibid.*, p. 153.

35. Cf. Daniel Bell, *The End of Ideology: On the Exhaustion of Political Ideas in the Fifties* (New York: Collier Books, 1961), pp. 400–401; and also Seymour M. Lipset, *Political Man: The Social Bases of Politics* (New York: Doubleday & Co., 1960), pp. 403–417.

shades of gray. Only by assuming a bipolarized world of political positions, and by making a hidden assumption that liberalism is not a political ideology, has functionalism been able to present itself as a bearer of neutral scientific truths. What happens if such a bipolarization is not assumed is the decomposition of the functionalist canons into some special code by means of which the world of political reality can be safely ignored.

17. *International Social Science Research: The Case for a National Social Science Foundation*

FOR PRESENT PURPOSES, I will eschew the relatively familiar ground of relations between social science and public policy—either at the level of what these relations now are, or what, ideally speaking, they ought to be. Rather, I should like to concentrate on organizational matters: specifically, the connection of how both policy-oriented research and basic social science requirements could be helped by new agencies and improved financial arrangements. Such arrangements should be made in order to assure a healthier benefit to the research dollar and, equally important, a greater return for the social sciences than what now obtains.

First presented as a statement before the United States Senate Committee on Government Operations, Subcommittee on Government Research, Washington, D.C., in July, 1966. The statement attempts to provide a basis for support of a National Social Science Foundation, particularly in terms of how such an agency might be able to underwrite, politically and financially, international social science research that is not beholden in any way to various policy agencies. In the preparation of this study, I had the collaboration and cooperation of Herbert Blumer of the University of California. First published in *Federal Support of International Social Science and Behavioral Research* (Washington, D.C.: U.S. Government Printing Office, 1967).

I. Imbalances between Basic and Policy Research

In a recent statement before the House of Representatives, Congressman Dante B. Fascell of Florida has pointed out that the bulk of research relevant to the achievement of U.S. national objectives is being conducted by agencies that do not now have direct responsibility for the execution of our foreign policy. This points up several issues: the need for greater agency coordination, the need to clarify how research is to be conducted and under what auspices, and ultimately, what can be or should be subject to congressional scrutiny and support.

Congress has to concern itself with what may be an already dangerous imbalance between heavy policy-oriented research and too little basic research. The legislative branch must take into account the fact that, even in advance of its creation, some tend to view National Social Science Foundation as a means to strengthen the hands of those who look upon the various social sciences simply as national security resources, while others see in such an agency a nonpolicy-oriented foundation. I think that Congress should safeguard itself against the possibility that the creation of still another agency might give rise to the sort of unholy alliances that at times are established between virtually autonomous federal agencies and entrepreneurial empires scattered throughout the world of social science.

There is a consensus forming on the part of Congress, in our opinion, to enact legislation that would create a National Social Science Foundation (NSSF). This would parallel present efforts of the National Science Foundation (NSF) in the physical and biological sciences.

Whatever the pragmatic sources behind such measures (such as recent policy debacles in the field of foreign area research), it is clear that such legislation would be a welcome event. Unquestionably it will elicit the support of most social scientists and, we believe, the interested public as a whole.

The encouragement of basic research in the social sciences is vital to the maintenance of American society in a healthy condition. The insistence upon the independence of such an agency through its constitution as a neutral, nonpolicy institution is also a worthy objective. The various mechanisms for making the organization of an NSSF fully responsive to the widest needs of the social science community cannot fail to elicit public approbation. The implementation of such an organization is certainly facilitated by the years of experience gained by the NSF. Doubtless, there would be great value to interchange of ideas on organizational matters between the NSF and the proposed NSSF.

I don't think it is too early to raise questions and search for answers to problems that confront the initiation of such an NSSF. In the briefest possible way, we should like to examine at least a few of these. For the most part, these observations and queries are intended to be supportive of an NSSF. We pose issues as sharply as possible only to safeguard the integrity of the proposed legislation by highlighting the difficulties that must be coped with in the very near future.

The nature of the social and behavioral sciences, no less than the historical circumstances of their emergence, makes the sort of consensus about methodology and goals that exists in the natural sciences highly unlikely in the behavioral sciences, at least at this time.

Whether or not one chooses to describe the social sciences as continuous and contiguous with the natural sciences, or as involving a sharp break with the "nonhuman" sciences, is not here in contention. While it would not be the function of an NSSF to answer such conjectural matters, neither would it be prudent to place too much faith on any one approach now fashionable. It would be appropriate for such an organization to support studies that would precisely assist in the settlement of these long-standing debates as to the proper nature and proper subject matter of the scientific study.

II. The Problem of Research into Controversial Areas

Turning to another matter, the conduct of basic social science research deeply and directly affects policy issues and political sentiments. What is required is an appreciation that intellectual and ideological sensitivities that cannot be ignored are involved. To convert the meaning of pure social science into an operational code book for noncontroversial social science would be self-defeating and even, in my opinion, suicidal.

There are already social science organizations supporting nonsensitive research—such as the Twentieth Century Fund, the Bolligen Foundation, and many others. What should be encouraged by congressional legislation is precisely research into dangerous areas. The oversimplified identification of social science with natural science techniques may lead away from this search for truth. Granting agencies should not assume that a noncontroversial style is equivalent to a maximum yield in substantive scientific findings.

We have a tradition, which is inherited from the feudal world, of *noblesse oblige* and of being very kind to one another since we live in a world where words are equivalent to fists among our lower class members, so that we tend to be overly sensitive, we tend to be overly solicitous, and as a result, we oftentimes tend not to be as sharp with one another as we ought to be.

The formation of an NSSF would involve a higher concentration of organizational energies, intellectual talent, and financial sources than has hitherto ever been the case in the social sciences. It is therefore extremely important that the pluralistic basis of social science research facilities be strictly maintained. Care should be taken to prevent the multiple forms of social science research from being smothered or obscured by the development of a monolithic agency committed to a single, limited orientation.

III. The Government Uses of Basic Research

We should encourage Congress to stimulate among the various policy and non-policy-making agencies alike a desire to use basic social science research findings and originate social science projects within legislative and executive agencies. The creation of an NSSF should be an occasion for vitalizing the research services of existing organizations, and not for demoralizing them. From the poverty program to the Pan-American Union, efforts to generate independent social science research must be redoubled.

It would be easier to stimulate basic social science research through an independent institution such as an NSSF than to simply allocate more funds for policy agencies, since in fact existing agencies are concerned, most of the time, with fostering special ends of their own rather than the autonomous goals of the social sciences. Furthermore, there would be a strong foreign resistance to work commissioned through an NSSF that had a direct policy commitment. Since it would be the only social science voice in government, the findings generated by a policy-oriented NSSF would more nearly represent an official "line" than anything now done by social scientists working under federal grants or contracts. To avoid this possibility the independent character of any NSSF must be guaranteed as far as possible by legislative safeguards.

The founding of such an organization should not be allowed to become a centralized research center which encourages consensualist responses and conforming research designs. Such bureaucratic tendencies are not calculated to improve the breed of the social sciences. In any pluralistic democratic society a certain strain between science and policy is not only inevitable, but valuable.

This strain may provide a sounding board of hard truths against which policy-making must echo its sentiments. American society would be far weaker if its policy outcomes were exclusively guided by, let's say, public opinion polls, than by the gamut of social scientific data now in use. To convert the proposed National Social Science Foundation into a policy adjunct is to run a grave risk of a loss of independence. The potential loss of intellectual nerve can easily be translated into action when other avenues of government financing of social research projects become narrowed. The creation of a new agency of social research should therefore be used to inform existing agencies of the need for basic social science findings in the conduct of their own work. Not to do so may create competitive attitudes between present *policy research* agencies such as RAND Corporation or the Institute of Defense Analysis, and *basic research* agencies such as the Ford Foundation or the Russell Sage Foundation.

One basic guarantee for the widest and deepest dispersion of NSSF goals would be to provide funds for university training programs. A model for this already exists in the National Institutes for Mental Health training grant system. What is required is the disbursement of funds to graduate students and junior faculty members for the acceleration of their advanced training. These should be in a form that is not necessarily tied to policy contracts. Support for training programs would have two additional merits: it would stimulate cross-disciplinary programs in new fields of endeavor, and it would lodge increased educational responsibility where it belongs, within the departments of social science.

IV. Guidelines for Conducting Policy Research

The creation of an NSSF does not of itself alleviate the burdensome tasks of coming to terms with policy-oriented research. Clearly, the main catalyst to the formulation of an NSSF is not the problems involved in pure research, but those connected with policy research thus far. Thus, while our remarks thus far are intended to be supportive of the creation of an NSSF—along the lines proposed in the House vote—we should like to devote the remainder of this chapter to the relationship between behavioral science and federal policy, and possible activities of Congress in this very vital field.

The first point in this connection we should raise with policy issues is the need to make policy-oriented research subject to the free enterprise system. By this we simply mean that every piece of research requested, involving nonclassified contract work, ought to be subject to open and intense bidding. If the government seeks the creation of a new weapons system or, for that matter, a new Senate building, it would indicate the specifications, the length of time available, the design of the environmental conditions, etc., and make its requirements known to the relevant professional publics. There is no reason why the same set of guidelines should not obtain in the creation of research projects involving social scientists.

The payoff for such a shift from a system of purchasing research privately, based on feudal premises of *noblesse oblige*, to public sector purchases based on capitalist laissez-faire premises, are numerous. (a) It would enable the government to draw upon the expertise available on any given subject, irrespective of the arbitrary boundary lines social scientists draw between themselves. (b) It would enable the government to select from many contract bids, and perhaps divide the contract among competing bidders to see if scholars using different methodologies and having access to different resources do, in fact, turn out the same kinds of answers. (c) It would assure the social scientist bidding on any contract of direct access to the design that wins a contract. In this way, whether or not he succeeds in obtaining a contract, his next submission of a bid might be improved upon. (d) It would make the social scientist increasingly aware of the need to deliver on his grant, since it would anchor his bid to specific goal requirements. (e) Finally, the law should be written to prevent any excessive commitments on the part of individual social scientists. An individual could scarcely fulfill more than a handful of contractual obligations. The system of subcontracting research, or farming out contract work to graduate students in exchange for degrees, should be strictly supervised and done with circumspection.

Several agencies have already accepted the advantages of public disclosure of their research undertakings—the U.S. Arms Control and Disarmament Agency, for example, publishes a list of its research activities in the Commerce Business Daily. What is now required is simply to advertise the requirements needed, not just the designs that are accepted.

Where open and public bidding for contract work is not feasible—as for example, in studies deemed to be of a sensitive or confidential nature, or studies involving the type of expertise that only one or two organizations or one or two universities in the United States can possibly fulfill—then a portion of the funds earmarked for the project itself should be allocated for calling in expert opinion from other sources as to how, given specific funds and resources, he or they would go about designing such a project. There is altogether too much energy directed to responding to problems raised by prearranged designs, where social scientists' investments are, in effect, in the designs they construct, rather than in what they are really looking at.

Now, once the investment in any one design is minimized, the elbow room for innovation—after a study gets underway no less than beforehand—might be maximized. This can best be accomplished by a set of alternative models that can be chosen, revised, or even discarded. This is the best guarantee I know of for involving expert opinion even if the final research bureau chosen for the work is somehow determined by objective limiting factors.

V. Decentralizing of Policy Research

Organizationally, it is important to provide an ecological setting for policy research that would be conducive to prudential judgment. Toward that goal, we would urge policy agencies to center as much research as possible in university or university-affiliated groups. This would serve to facilitate a number of worthy objectives:

First, drawing upon the best available talent with a minimal amount of re-location on the part of the social scientists involved. (The first big problem is recruitment. That problem is somehow magnified by having to have the experts you want relocate for a year or two, and thus perhaps losing a good deal of the tried personnel that we want to do important research. Very often we have to design lists of five, six, or seven names, and we don't get the first five or six people we want because of reasons of family and personality, rather than because of a substantive disagreement with doing policy research.)

Second, linking policy research to basic types of analysis, insofar as this is possible. For example, if there are going to be studies on the relationship between the Watts riot in Los Angeles and how to allocate federal poverty funds, they ought to be linked in terms of social science communities with some basic analysis of, for example, the nature of the American ghetto system, the nature of the Negro in American life, the kind of identification he has, and the peculiar qualities that may inhere to southern California politics; as well as all kinds of general basic issues that do not get resolved if we are to think of policy as being in one room and basic research in another room. There ought to be an anteroom where they meet once in a while.

Third, by acting on the first and second propositions, we would make the institutionalization of yet new satellite subgroups and subagencies in Washington unnecessary. And I think that is all for the good.

Clearly, policy recentralization will not always be either advisable or possible.

But in such instances, the policy agencies ought to offer the widest academic supports for the policy enterprises. In this matter, as in many others, I think the economists offer a sound model worthy of emulation. The National Bureau of Economic Research, composed of eminent economists, is also involved in the selection of the Council of Economic Advisers. The close-working relations that exist between the executive branch of government and the economists is indicative of the fact that there need be no hard line drawn between policy research and basic research. Indeed, the operation of the Brookings Institute in Washington is indicative of just such freewheeling linkages. In addition, economists have been in the business of foreign research a long time without any of the negative repercussions that sociologists and psychologists have received; perhaps one of the prime studies initially ought to be how the economists work, since apparently they work well.

In brief, what is required is decentralization of policy-rooted research when possible, or, when this is not possible, the infusion of basic scholarly considerations and personnel into such efforts.

VI. Secrecy, Science, and Policy

The various agencies of government tend to be the keepers of secrecy. Our Congress is uniquely qualified to be the keeper of science. We will not go into any prolonged examination of the latent and manifest contradictions between scientific inquiry and secret and selective uses of data. But it is apparent that Congress must avoid secrecy as a norm of scientific behavior on at least two fundamental grounds: (a) It is extremely uneconomical, since it gives rise to multiple projects done in isolation from each other, and without any appreciable benefits to federal policy-making personnel as a whole. (b) Secrecy in research is calculated to frustrate policy by creating extreme (and dysfunctional) competition between agencies and, no less, by creating in the minds of the researchers standards of work having more to do with being an "inside dopester" than in terms of being an "objective scientist."

Obviously Congress, either as a whole or in its committee system, cannot supervise the gamut of projects offered and accepted by policy-related agencies. But short of this, Congress can enact legislation that would limit the uses of secrecy and maximize the open exercise of science. It can designate the creation of a committee on scientific operations for the purpose of mapping out a policy statement to be used by government agencies in the conduct of their research programs.

The spelling out of the philosophy of research could make important contributions to the conduct of inquiry. It could make clear that the purpose of contract research is valid knowledge, not reinforcement or rationalization of the agencies' needs. The integrity of applied social research is particularly acute, since it directly affects foreign policy considerations and sensitive domestic programs such as the war on poverty.

Perhaps the creation of an ad hoc watchdog committee would be in order.

This committee would make sure that congressional appropriations for research purposes were not irresponsibly handled: that each grant be open unless otherwise stated; that each contract be fulfilled, insofar as possible, by the contracting parties; and that each subcontract arrangement be reported for congressional action insofar as this is feasible. All sums used for social science research ought to be so designated in the budget, and not be placed in miscellaneous or secret categories. The long and short of this point is that the burden ought to be upon those who assert the need for secrecy in research, and not on those who insist on open research.

VII. Contracts, Grants, and Unguided Inquiry

The blurred distinction between contracts and grants ought to be cleared up. Grants represent research in which the originating impulse comes from the individual scholar, whereas contract work is initiated through the efforts of the federal sponsoring agency. Both kinds of research are bona fide; the difficulty until now has been that nearly all contract work has been of a policy-making nature, while perhaps an equally large number of grants are for pure research. Policy agencies exhibit a strong bias in favor of contract work.

The creation of an NSSF will provide a major channel for the initiation of grants. The question is, who will then fulfill the policy-making contract? The answers are, however, not as insurmountable as critics of grants may note.

First, a number of scholars prefer the excitement of policy-oriented research. Second, some scholars prefer the material conditions of such contract work: concern with manipulating social or political events, the belief in contributing to world history, the immediacy of results. And finally, contract work could bid competitively for scarce talent, and in this way create a better economic climate for the social scientists.

One additional point in this connection, which mutually affects contracts and grants, is the need for a financial pool arrangement. On every grant proffered or contract fulfilled, there should be a set portion—as a start we would suggest 10 per cent of the funds—set aside for free research unconnected with the grant or contract and irrespective of whether the research is basic or applied.

The disbursement of such funds should be without regard to either the disburser or the recipient of the grant or contract. For this reason, the supervision of such a "kitty" should be in the hands of the institution with which the scholar is connected. In those cases when the scholar is unconnected to any agency or institution of learning, special arrangements can be made. If so much attention by administrators can be given to "overhead" costs, surely some can be paid to intellectual overhead.

VIII. Legislative Uses of Social Scientists

Congress ought to set the pace for relationships between social science and public policy by making much more extensive use of social science findings. The precedent for this already exists in the use of applied political scientists in the foreign affairs field, and of anthropologists and sociologists in the field of race relations. Perhaps far more innovative than even an NSSF would be a motion for increasing the staff factor for each senator and each member of the House by hiring a full-time social scientist assistant.

I venture to say that such a congressional resolution would elicit a tremendous positive reaction from the social scientific community. It would further serve to make congressional decision-making more aware of the complex demands of various pressuring agencies, and more competitive with technical personnel now involved with the executive branches of government.

A parallel innovative device would be the encouragement of new forms for the organization of the social sciences, which would be independent of both university and federal sponsorship, and yet avoid the negative consequences found so often in presently constituted unresponsive and irresponsible private agencies. It is our feeling that the strengthening, rather than the elimination, of private research agencies should be encouraged by any NSSF legislation.

We will need enormous change in the character no less than the number of personnel recruited from the social sciences because of the way in which government agencies have reorganized themselves. Traditionally, the agencies viewed their needs in terms of dollars necessary for personnel in each division. Today, these agencies compute financial needs on the basis of operational designs. The new planned program-budgeting (PPB) requires the kind of input-output analysis that economists, rather than political scientists, are best acquainted with.

The need for social science personnel as a consequence of organizational transformations within the legislative branch of government requires a wider recognition of the merits of social scientists than has thus far materialized. It also creates a decision-making problem: who is to decide whether research is to be "farmed out" to universities, or produced on an "in-house" basis?

Involved in the present situation is the world of contracts that link the academic social scientists to political policy roles; and the world of operations research, which links the social scientist with policy-making roles in a much more systematic, and perhaps more dangerous, way.

The role of Congress is to assist in mediating between basic scientific research and policy requirements. There are few satisfactory answers at present. Perhaps the most important condition of all would be to maintain the dynamics of the tension, of the differences.

Congress should see to it that the rewards of direct government employment do not become a tyranny of intellectual voyeurs over all other social scientists; at the same time, it must not expect the leading social scientists to work full time on government work without much higher salaries than have thus far been forthcoming, and, equally important, without providing for intellectual outlets such as much easier access to publication and promotion.

Many social scientists connected with government work also want to be related to academic work. This is evidenced by the high amount of part-time teaching they do. The sensitivities of social scientists on this score ought to be fully recognized by the hiring policy of basic research organizations. An academic man, even when he comes to Washington, does not want to leave his profession. There is not enough recognition of this. This is perhaps a central reason why there is a great deal more mobility away from rather than toward Washington on the part of the important segments of the social science community.

The greatest wisdom that can be offered is that no total solution to the relationship between social science and public policy can be made until applied research becomes a viable alternative for social scientists, and until pure research gains the full respect of all government officials. But in the absence of such an ideal-typical resolution, perhaps we ought to accept the fact of role strain between science and policy-makers, and attempt to frame a grid of organizational relationships that simply makes this strain bear greater fruit than it has in the past.

I have spoken about a National Social Science Foundation, in support of such an independent agency, and have indicated what might be done by an agency of that kind. But I have left out an answer to the choice between two alternatives: a National Social Science Foundation or a beefed-up Social Science Division of the National Science Foundation.

Let me first give the range of reactions and alternatives spoken of among social scientists.

The first reaction was that the NSF provides well at the present time for certain kinds of social science research, and also provides a backlog of legitimate basic social science inquiry.

To bifurcate the present organizational situation would perhaps lessen the operational capability of the NSF. Instead of two strong organizations, we would have two weak organizations. In brief, what now exists is one relatively strong organization; and it should be enlarged upon, but not divided.

The people who made this point raised the additional consideration that the NSF has a legacy and a history backing it which is noble and untainted. It is felt by some that anything that would weaken such a structure might not be healthy. Thus some believe we might better have an NSSF Division of the NSF.

Now I will add that that is a minority point of view among the men I have spoken to (although not necessarily a minority view of all professionals). It is not my point of view. I should like to address myself to this issue.

Organizationally, in terms of academic life, there is a strong division between the natural sciences and the social sciences. From my point of view, I cannot rightly answer whether that is going to shrink or grow with time. But at present, organizationally, within the life of academic affairs, there is a firm division along those lines. Those divisions were necessary in order for the social sciences to grow, to come to fruition. Even those social scientists who are keen on the natural sciences, on the methodology of natural sciences, have recognized this fact. Therefore, we have a near unanimous consensus on the merits of the division of social sciences from natural sciences.

Thus, whether or not there is a methodological reason for wanting to see the social sciences divided from the natural sciences, there seem to be very powerful organizational reasons. Further, inspecting the operations of the NSF, you will find that there is a strong propensity of the NSF to support that kind of research which can be considered hardened or firmed up; having to do with methodological commonalities with the natural sciences. There is a propensity to favor experimental designs in social psychology rather than historical researches or, for that matter, sociology proper. There is also a heavier emphasis on social psychology than on macro-sociology or the sociology of international behavior.

It is possible that this objection can be removed by making the NSF directorship more aware of the feelings of social scientists on this issue, but I rather doubt whether this is as easy to do as setting up either an independent agency or, for that matter, an independent branch of the NSF.

The difficulty with the latter scheme—with making the NSSF a branch of the NSF—would be that social scientists, even though they may not be entitled to see themselves on a par intellectually with the physical scientists, do consider themselves on a par psychologically, ethically, and in every other way. Social scientists would feel like stepchildren to a parent organization. I doubt whether they would be content with that kind of rearrangement on a long-range basis.

The social scientists are now in the process of flexing their muscles. They are growing very rapidly. I think the formation of an NSSF in fact would help that process and would accelerate that growth.

I would add one other point in this connection. I think the NSF itself might prefer an NSSF rather than see its own operations changed in a substantial degree. It is my impression that the scholars in NSF feel keenly their own limitations scientifically. They too have scientific prides and scientific prejudices. Hence they might just as soon have an NSSF as an expanded operational role in the area of the behavioral sciences.

This conjecture depends so much on the personnel within the organization. But if you move in the direction of expanding the NSF, it will merely constitute a postponement of the inevitable. That is one reason for now initiating an independent NSSF.

There is a spillover from science to policy that can be controlled, but not cancelled. Perhaps one can even say that the natural scientists, by the nature of their advanced role, are more implicated in policy matters than they even desire to be. The NSSF would be able to point out the policy implications of natural scientists and their work. In this way, an NSSF could become an asset to the natural scientists in their activities.

Right now there seems to be no way of getting research on policy issues within the NSF on these kinds of matters. If you wanted to fund a large research project on the role of Robert J. Oppenheimer and Edward Teller and their respective decisions or attitudes toward the manufacture of hydrogen weapons, who would do that work or who would sponsor that work within the present allocative systems?

This is not simply a matter of ideology. Organizationally, no agency is now prepared to handle the above kind of "sensitive" theme. Again this is conjectural.

Conceivably an NSF could support policy studies. But it would be far easier for an NSSF to do it. Thus even the NSF would welcome such a new and independent organization come into being.

One can easily envision an agency such as the NSSF becoming a form for legitimizing research activities of all sorts that are now being done in a haphazard way. In fact, I am not sure but that some congressional sentiment on the other side of the Hill leans in this monolithic direction. In their vision, an NSSF could not only be concerned with policy, but would in effect be an umbrella for various policy-making agencies.

It might be good to have some kind of supervisory procedure guiding independent entrepreneurial groups. But I am not sure that it would entail anything more than throwing out the baby with the bath water. There have been deep problems involved in previous research projects, but I do no think that the resolution of such problems is enforced security or the utilization of an organization such as the proposed NSSF for such purposes. Indeed I think that police functions would be illicit. Yet, unless there is a conscious, legislative mandate for a nonpolicy base to an NSSF agency, its chores could easily deteriorate into simple-minded data collection rather than the stimulation of fresh research tasks.

18. *Social Science and Public Policy: An Examination of the Political Foundations of Modern Research*

ECONOMICS, SOCIOLOGY, psychology, and the other social sciences have in recent times begun to play a new and problematic role with respect to national and international policy. The problem of social policy has become acute precisely to the extent to which social science has become exact. Legitimation of policy recommendations from social scientists has emerged in this period and not in previous periods because of a demonstrable feasibility of putting social science and social theory into a framework of political action. Demand for operations research analysts, tactical data systems, war-gaming, and simulation experts now rivals the search for basic engineering personnel. There is a paucity of exact information on how this transvaluation took place, due in part to the novelty of the situation and in part to the novelty of self-examination in the social sciences. What is at stake as a result of this newly acquired influence

First presented at the sixth meeting of the International Sociological Association at Evian, France, September, 1966. This study explains the special circumstances surrounding the growth of social science in different sociopolitical contexts. It is chiefly concerned with strains between social science and political requirements in the United States, with particular emphasis on the ways in which financial and institutional arrangements effect the norms of social science. First published in the *International Studies Quarterly*, II, no. 1 (March, 1967); reprinted by permission.

is not the feasibility of social science, but the credibility of social scientists.

Any discussions of villains and values, which inevitably is what the study of social science and public policy boils down to, involves two distinct areas. One is the empirics of present relationships between social science and public policy, its formation and its execution. The other is the question of what the relationship between social science and public policy should be. In connection with both *what is* and *what should be* there are two variables. The first is the utilization of social science in the formation of public policy; the second involves the *relation* between social scientists and policy-makers. The fact that an ever increasing number of individuals can with some legitimacy claim both scientific and policy-making status tends to blur the lines between these issues.

I. THREE STYLES OF POLITICAL EXHORTATION

The first problem we come upon concerns the factual issues in the character of the relationship between the social scientists and the policy-makers; that is, how this relationship differs in various social structures. What is the relationship of sociologists to society in a totalitarian state? Or in a welfare state? Or in a laissez-faire state or system? What are the stresses and strains upon the social scientists and policy-makers in each type of national system?

Most social science disciplines require open-ended conditions for their functioning. Invariably and almost necessarily, established dogmas about society must be challenged. In this sense, sociology has been as much a problem for the socialist ideology as astronomy was for a seventeenth-century Catholicism. For example, do women go to church more often than men in the Soviet Union? From the point of view of Marxism, this is a ridiculous question. Men and women are equal by definition. Only historical antecedents are considered in accounting for differentiation by sex in response to religious practices in a socialist nation. Therefore, the sexual variable itself tends to be suppressed as a legitimate area of inquiry for Soviet researchers, despite the noticeable difference in church attendance between male and female, not only in the Soviet Union but in many other countries displaying similar political structures and levels of industrialization.

This discrepancy between fact and theory leads to the conclusion that in a pure command structure the relationship of social science to public policy is not much of a problem, because the social sciences, aside from their technical vocabularies, are suppressed. The ideology of science is harnessed to the ideology of the state. This is done by celebrating only the "pure" and the "natural" sciences. Applied social sciences may exist, but what does not exist is an analysis of the whole society. To the extent that meaningful data contradict the established order, the social sciences are suspect. Not accidentally, the more exaggerated the totalitarian system, the less available for public inspection is the social scientists' information. The degree to which the development of the social sciences is permitted within a nation operates as a twentieth-century index of freedom. And the extent to which the development of an independent social science is stifled provides a measure of political stagnation. Allowing myself an *ex cathedra* judgment, I do not think anyone can participate in social research and fail to see a high correlation of good social science and a good society.

The evidence provided by the Soviet Union on this score is illustrative. While the research and academic personnel engaged in the "arts, humanities, and social sciences" in the U.S.S.R. continues to grow numerically—from 625,600 in 1956 to 740,400 in 1960—this represents a downward percentile trend compared with the physical and engineering sciences—from 27.9 to 24.0. If this figure is broken down further, it is found that only 3.9 of the scientific personnel are engaged in what would in the West be called the social sciences—and these are gathered in the fields of economics and planning.[1] Undoubtedly, what occurs is a widespread infiltration of social science findings through "alien" fields such as pedagogy, geography, jurisprudence, and even such refined areas as mathematical statistics. More recently, this subterranean approach has been replaced by an opening up of the social sciences to include at least sociology and psychology (the latter has always been available as part of the medical and biological sciences, and now is being thought of as a social science). This indicates a distinct movement in the Soviet Union from totalitarian to authoritarian modalities. That is to say, there is a distinct tendency away from political dominance and surveillance of all scientific products to a political exclusivity that demands relevance rather than conformity in the products of social research.[2]

In a welfare system, in contrast to a command system, the social sciences tend to have exceptionally close ties with policy-oriented sectors of the society. The two are joined functionally by ministries of science, such as those that exist in England, France, and Germany. Policy-makers for their part often think of the social sciences as a rationale required for any projected change considered to be in the social interest. Before a major piece of legislation is introduced into the English Parliament, for example, the likelihood is that a survey has already been conducted, providing a form of social science legitimation. Thus, while investment in social science is relatively smaller in England than in the United States, there is a high payoff for social science information.[3] The social scientist is not only listened to. His advice is fervently sought. Social science has become a recognized aspect of national investment. The welfare system has been a tremendous source for social science growth; and in turn, the social sciences have reinforced the "socialist" tendencies within the societies they operate.

1. See Nicholas DeWitt, *Soviet Professional Manpower; Its Education, Training and Supply* (Washington, D.C.: U.S. National Science Foundation, 1955); and more recently, his essay on the "Reorganization of Science and Research in the U.S.S.R." in *Science and Society*, ed. by Norman Kaplan (Chicago: Rand McNally & Co., 1965), pp. 303–321.

2. Allen Kassof, "American Sociology Through Soviet Eyes," and Talcott Parsons, "An American impression of Sociology in the Soviet Union," *American Sociological Review*, 30, no. 1 (February, 1965): 114–124. A worthwhile collection is contained in Alex Simirenko, *Soviet Sociology* (Chicago: Quadrangle Books, 1966).

3. See Irving L. Horowitz, *The New Sociology* (New York and London: Oxford University Press, 1964), pp. 43–47.

The character of the social science practiced in the welfare system tends to be of a strongly applied nature. England no longer produces the great theories about society; rather it paves the way for practices intended to reshape social policy.[4] Empiricism extends deep into the marrow of the policy orientation. Both the opportunities and the payoff are in such a direction. Furthermore, "pure" social science research involves the study and the evolution of fundamental theories about man, and neither the pragmatism of the twentieth-century British party system nor the empiricism of the educational system places much faith in "theories."

The linkage between the British political and educational systems may have delayed the evolution of an independent social science curriculum at the more traditional places of learning; but when the penetration did take place (by economics in the eighteenth century, administration in the nineteenth century, and political science in the present century) the situation was ready-made for the close cooperation between social science and social policy. And with the defeat of ideological Toryism (based as it was on "classical studies") by the close of World War II, the last shreds of opposition to social science vanished.[5] The impulses of British social science toward welfare projects dovetailed neatly with the welfare projects outlined by the political apparatus. And the mutual suspicions of scientists and policy-makers characteristic of an earlier epoch in British history dissolved into mutual reinforcement and even joint celebration.

In laissez-faire consensus systems, the social sciences are compelled to compete with directly involved policy agencies. For example, in the United States executive policy-makers have traditionally consulted those with training in diplomacy, law, and administration. But until well into the present century little attention was given any of the so-called hard social sciences—psychology, economics, and sociology. Furthermore, not until the establishment of bureaucratic modes of social science performance have the social sciences been granted the kind of hearing they enjoy in the welfare state. The extent to which the laissez-faire system becomes permeated with welfare elements, concerning itself with protecting and caring for the citizenry, to that degree is there a high penetration of the social sciences into the area of government policy.

There appear to be three distinctive factors accounting for the special role of social science in the formation of American policy. They explain not only the significance of social science in policy-making, but the dependence of American social science on policy agencies.

4. A new series of articles on "reshaping social policy" appearing in the English publication *New Society* is indicative of this trend. The articles deal with population pressures, urban design, professional practices, and immigration, all as they relate to England. See *New Society*, 7, nos. 179–181 (March, 1966).

5. For a general outline, see D. S. L. Cardwell, *The Organization of Science in England: A Retrospect* (London: William Heinemann, Ltd., 1957); and for a more specific essay, see Eric Ashby, "Science and Public Policy: Some Institutional Patterns Outside America," in *Science and the University*, ed. by B. R. Keenan (New York and London: Columbia University Press, 1966), pp. 13–26.

First, a strong social reform tendency developed early in opposition to general theories of change and revolution. American social science has been consciously, almost self-consciously, dedicated to issues of practical reform: elimination of poverty, integration of ethnic minorities, immigration and population issues, urban redevelopment schemes, etc. This has led major foundations and philanthropic agencies to lose interest in the direct alleviation of social problems through charity and to invest heavily in indirect means of alleviation: social science programs.

Second, development of a pluralistic educational system made room for many and diverse social scientific activities. This gainful employment in teaching, while it prevented some of the worst excesses of the German university system from being repeated in the United States—chauvinism, nationalism, anti-Semitism—weakened the status system in American higher education. Status tended to be conferred from the outside, especially from federal and private agencies who drew upon educational expertise as the only sources of nonpolitical opinion. This permitted the American social scientist to retain an independence from government no less than the policy-maker could reserve judgment on the worth of the social sciences.

Third, an entrepreneurial spirit developed in American social science to accommodate growing government needs. Bureaucratic organizations served to mediate the claims of educational and political establishments, safeguarding both from detriment or disrepute. Social science middlemen emerged in all forms. Bureaus of social research blossomed at the major universities. Independent, nonuniversity agencies sprang up: RAND Corporation, Institute for Defense Analysis, Aerospace Corporation, Peace Research Institute. Organizations geared to marketing research and national opinion surveys proliferated. These entrepreneurial responses to government needs meant the institutionalization of a buying and selling arrangement. And as is customary in such arrangements, the buyers perform superordinate and the sellers subordinate roles, except in exceptional circumstances.[6] Table 1 indicates the network of private military research agencies and their base of military support.

American society cannot be described exactly as a laissez-faire consensus system. The system of social science evolved in the special circumstances of United States political and economic history. In effect, U.S. political rhetoric remains steeped in consensus, while its economic characteristics have increasingly been subject to welfare elements. This is one central reason for the "schizophrenia" in applied social research.

As an overall characterization it could be said that (1) in a *command society*, policy dictates both the character and the activities of the social sciences. Social science loses control over both the instruments and purposes of research. The

---

6. See Don K. Price, *Government and Science: Their Dynamic Relation in American Democracy* (New York: New York University Press, 1954); and Warren O. Hagstrom, *The Scientific Community* (New York and London: Basic Books, 1965).

Table 1: Private Military Research Agencies

Supported by Military	Contract holdings in millions*
AIR FORCE	
Aerospace Corporation	$76.2
Systems Development Corporation	51.6
Mitre Corporation	34.4
RAND Corporation	11.4
Analytic Services, Inc.	1.3
NAVY	
Applied Physics Laboratory (John Hopkins)	54.9
Franklin Institute (Center for Naval Analyses)	11.5
ARMY	
Research Analysis Corporation	9.3
DEFENSE DEPARTMENT	
Institute for Defense Analysis	2.1
Logistics Management Institute	1.0
CREATED AT SUGGESTION OF MILITARY	
(Major Institutions)	
Lincoln Laboratory (MIT)	49.4
Instrumentation Laboratory (MIT)	47.0

*Net value of prime contract award, fiscal 1964.
Source of Data: Defense Department.

operational aspects become so important with respect to what policy dictates that the social sciences can do little but "plug into" the going political system and hope for enlightened outcomes. To the extent that the sciences do so satisfactorily, they survive. (2) In a *welfare system*, policy and social sciences interact, but without any sense of tension or contradiction between scientific propositions and the therapeutic orientations. The integration is so complete that there is a loss of identity at both the scientific and political poles. Spillover between scientific propositions and therapeutic prescriptions is tremendous; all functions of social science are funneled into a social problems orientation. The result is a decline of interest in the larger analysis of social systems or social forces. (3) In a *laissez-faire system*, the social sciences tend to be independent and autonomous of political policy. However, to the degree that they remain in this pristine condition, they are also weak in power and status. What takes place typically is an exchange system based on a reciprocal transference of information for money. But this reduces the amount of social science autonomy, which leads to a trade-off of high status for maximum power. This in its turn creates a source of inner tension within the social sciences as to the appropriate role of the social scientist in the forging of public policy.

II. Socialization into Secrecy

Until now, we have considered the training of social scientists as a given. Here we must take note of their training as policy consultants or advisors. While most officials in government have a series of checks and balances to guide their behavior, few forms of anticipatory socialization apply to social scientists who advise government agencies. Since such social science advisors are asked for operational guidance on sensitive issues, they are often shielded from the consequences of their policy utterances. The anomaly arises that the more sensitive the policy question, the less subject it is to public scrutiny.

The secrecy that has been maintained about government scientists is practiced elsewhere in Washington only on behalf of CIA agents. As one commentator has recently pointed out: "Not only are the names of some 200 personnel of Special Air Command consultants kept secret, but so are those of other paid scientific advisers to government. Spokesmen for both the Air Force and the Arms Control and Disarmament Agency recently refused to divulge the identity of certain of their scientific advisers on the grounds that to do so would (1) expose them to pressure, (2) ensure that they would receive unwanted mail, and (3) put them under public scrutiny, which was exactly where the did not want to be."[7] Yet, since the purpose of research may have an effect on the judgment of social scientists, why should secrecy be either prized or praised?

The question of secrecy is intimately connected with that of policy because it is a standing assumption of policy-makers never to reveal themselves entirely. No government in the "game" of international politics feels that its policies can be placed on the table for full public review. Therefore operational research done in connection with policy considerations is bound by the canons of privacy. In its most basic form the dilemma is as follows: Social scientists have a "fetish" for publicizing their information. However, policy branches of society have as their "fetish," as their essential method, private documents and privileged information. How does one gain in the game of one-upmanship without privacy, without knowing something that the other side does not know? Therefore, a premium is placed not simply on gaining information but also on maintaining silence about such information. A reversal of premiums and a transvaluation of values arises, leading to extreme tension. What often reduces such tension is the sacrifice of the social sciences, their yielding to considerations of policy.

Social scientists yield on such issues not simply because of a power imbalance between buyer and seller of ideas, but because they prefer a recessive role. Social scientists may enjoy the idea of partaking of a secret order of things. There is something tremendously fascinating about being "in" and not being "out." The cost of this "inside dopester" role may be a heavy one—the institutionalization of a subordinate position. But in being privy to things of secrecy,

7. M. Greenfield, "Science Goes to Washington," in Kaplan, *Science and Society*, pp. 415–429.

Table 2: Federal Research and Development Expenditure, Fiscal 1965 (by Program Area)

Program Area	Est. Expenditure (in millions)
*Space research	$6,700
Military research	5,200
*Medical research	1,300
*Nuclear research	1,200
Agricultural research	179
*Oceanographic research	138
*Meteorological research	108
*Water and transportation research	129
Educational research	24
Vocational rehabilitation research	19
Welfare administration research	7
Other (not allocable)	87
	15,287

*Program estimate by Bureau of Budget. Other items estimated by author.

Source of data: 1965 Federal Budget.

the feeling of powerlessness is largely eliminated; the subordinate role with respect to political authorities may be more than counterbalanced by a superordinate feeling with respect to other social scientists.

One critical factor reinforcing the common acceptance of the norm of secrecy is the allocation of most government research funds for military or semi-military purposes. As Table 2 indicates, approximately 75 per cent of such funds have either a directly military or semi-military basis. Under such circumstances, the real wonder is not the existence of a norm of secrecy, but the relative availability of information.

Social scientists involved with research defined as secret or confidential can easily develop a self-definition of importance derived from their connections rather than from the intrinsic merits of demerits or their work. They come to desire secrecy as much as their superordinates because they want to be shielded from public scrutiny of their work. Being publicly called to account in congressional committee hearings, for example, has a demeaning effect on status. If an economist or political scientist working for the Central Intelligence Agency filed a report to the government so erroneous that it helped pave the way for policy disasters, public availability of the report would reflect negatively on his standing in the academic community. Thus, secrecy is a mutual advantage in the event of failure even more than in successful ventures. In this protected environment, the social science advisory competence becomes an unknown quantity. About the only surety available to the hiring federal agencies is to choose from the elite corps of social scientists and to offer financial rewards high enough to attract such an elite.[8]

The widespread acceptance of the canons of secrecy, no less than the commitment to policy as such, makes it extremely difficult to separate science from patriotism and hence to question the research design itself. The acceptance of the first stage, the right of the government to secrecy, often carries with it acquiescence in the last stage, the necessity for silence on the part of social scientists. The demand for secrecy has its most telling impact on the methodology of the social sciences. Presumably, policy personnel hire or employ social scientists because this group represents objectivity and honesty. The social scientists represent a wall of truth, off which the policy-makers can bounce their premises and practices. The social scientist is thought to provide information that public opinion is not able (or willing) to supply. To some degree, social scientists are hired because they will say things that may be unpopular but nonetheless significant. For example, that the Chinese Communist system is viable and will not collapse is a difficult position to assert unless one is a social science expert. Then such a statement can be made with relative impunity—even before a Senate Foreign Relations Committee hearing.

The norm of secrecy overturns the scientific premise of publicity. Since the terms of research and conditions of work require an initial compromise with the methodology of social science, the lofty purpose of truth acquisition tends to be blunted. The social scientist is placed in a cognitive bind: he is conditioned not to reveal maximum information lest he become victimized by those who employ him, and yet he is employed precisely because of a presumed impartiality. Once the social scientist becomes gingerly and clever, then his value to social science *qua* social science is endangered. But once his scientific acumen interferes with policy, his "usefulness" to the policy-maker may likewise be jeopardized. The social scientist engaged in policy research walks a tightrope, with secrecy as the invisible net should he fall.

Social scientists think they have a good commodity for sale or for hire, and at least one large sector of society shares this estimate. Avid consumers of social science products such as government policy-makers may come into direct competition for services with equally concerned but less affluent consumers of social science. There are people who think highly of social science information and others who think poorly of it. However, even those with a high opinion are not always in a position to pay for social science services. As can be seen in Table 3, funds for research are, for all practical purposes, restricted to government, industry, and university sources.

Given the complex nature of social science activities and their increasing

8. This was clearly done in the case of Project Camelot. The consultants were drawn from the more eminent members of the social science community. See U.S. Congress, House Committee on Foreign Affairs, *Behavioral Sciences and the National Security*, Report No. 4 together with Part IX of *Hearings on Winning the Cold War: The U.S. Ideological Offensive* (Washington, D.C.: U.S. Government Printing Office, 1965). See Ch. 19 of this book.

Table 3: Sources of Funds Used for Research and Development, by Sector, from 1953 to 1962
(millions of dollars)

Year	Total	Federal government	Industry	Colleges and universities	Other nonprofit institutions
1953–54	$5,150	$2,740	$2,240	$130	$40
1954–55	5,620	3,070	2,365	140	45
1955–56	6,390	3,670	2,510	155	55
1956–57	8,670	5,095	3,325	180	70
1957–58	10,100	6,390	3,450	190	70
1958–59	11,130	7,170	3,680	190	90
1959–60	12,680	8,320	4,060	200	100
1960–61	13,890	9,010	4,550	210	120
1961–62	14,740	9,650	4,705	230	155

Source of data: National Science Foundation.

costs—both for human and for machine labor—the government becomes the most widespread buyer. Government policy-makers get the first yield also because they claim a maximum need. Private pressure groups representing corporate interests are the next highest buyer of social science services. The Bureaus of Social Research vaguely attached to universities service most non-federal research needs. The role of foundations and universities is ambiguous. Theoretically they ought to be encouraging pure research, particularly if government agencies encourage applied research. In fact, they are rarely interested in pure research. If anything, they tend to be as concerned with applied problems as the public and business agencies, since they are concerned with justifying their worth to business donors and government agencies. Further, big foundations and major universities are often policy extensions of federal agencies—if not directly, then through special laws and rules governing the taxation of philanthropic agencies and universities. The sources of funds for research tend to be exclusively concentrated in the upper classes. The fact that the President can indirectly participate in the selection process of major foundations indicates the intimacy that exists between federal and private controllers of wealth despite legal niceties. This fusion of government and corporate wealth makes it difficult to bring about a countervailing pluralistic system of power with respect to social science funding.[9]

There is a direct relationship between the ability to pay and a belief in the utility of the social sciences. Who are the high users? The federal government, some state governments, basic industries, marketing industries. Who are the

9. For a defense and an acknowledgment of this, see Paul F. Lazarsfeld, "Reflections on Business," *The American Journal of Sociology*, LXV, no. 1 (July, 1959): 1–26; and for a critique, see Ch. 10 in this book.

low users? Farmer-labor groups, the poor in general, minority groups (with the exception of highly sophisticated groups such as affluent religious organizations that spill over into the high users category). In the main, racial and ethnic groups do not place much value on the uses of social science. Perhaps the use of social science research is itself a suave reflection of wealth. Those who wish to use social science agencies extensively are wealthy enough to afford them; those who disparage social science groups are often rationalizing their own lack of affluence.

The image of social science tends to be far less flattering in the eyes of the poorer classes than in those of the wealthier classes. Ultimately, the social scientists, to the extent that they become involved with policy-making agencies, become committed to an elitist ideology. They come to accept as basic the idea that men who really change things are at the top. Thus, the closer to the top one can get direct access, the more likely will intended changes be brought about.[10]

Two flies can be found in this particular ointment. First, there is slender evidence that information bought and paid for is made the basis of policy in critical times. Indeed, there is just as much evidence for the conclusion that information is used when it suits policy-makers and discarded when it does not "fit" political plans. Second, there is no evidence that the elitist model is uniquely cast to solve problems of social change. The model of elites changing the world is itself controversial. It may be flattering to think that involvement with elites enables one to determine the course of society. But if a Marxian or mass model is used, what happens to the relationship of the policy-maker to the social scientist? The whole situation must then be perceived in terms of social forces. By minimizing any other historically derived model, such as a mass model, the social scientist leaves unexplored variables that ought to be examined and tested for their significance; these variables simply become heuristically manipulated as part of the ongoing ethos of social life.

An aspect of the norm of secrecy often alluded to informally, but rarely publicly, is: How is exact information obtained about potential enemy or alien groups? In situations of relative insularity or isolation, whose judgments concerning the intentions of other nations, races, or groups can be relied upon? The character of the informants no less than the quality of the information itself has become a central problem in decision-making. Nor is this merely a problem for foreign affairs. For example, in estimating the potential for mass violence of American Negroes, how valuable is information supplied by major institutionalized Negro associations? If the leadership of the Urban League is asked about the possibility of mass racial violence, will it provide the same kind of response as the Black Muslims or an opinion survey of the unorganized Negro? The tendency has been to rely upon institutionalized expressions for information concerning "spontaneous" crowd behavior, but reliance upon established organizations may easily distort our vision of a situation. There is a judgmental issue to

10. See Robert Presthus, *Men at the Top: A Study in Community Power* (New York: Oxford University Press, 1964), esp. pp. 3–63.

be settled even before any sampling is undertaken. How serious this can be is reflected in the fact that at the very height of the Negro Revolution, studies of crowd behavior and mass movements in the United States have practically faded from the work done by behavioral scientists.[11]

Even more complicated is the evaluation of foreign affairs. How are the military intentions of Communist China to be estimated? Are studies made in Hong Kong or information supplied by Taiwanese Army officers to be relied upon? Yet, if there is no direct access to the "enemy," whoever it may be at any time, how is exact information to be derived? The alternative to partisan bias would be to accept the rhetoric of the enemy society at face value. However, reading reports of major political and military figures in the enemy society from afar may create an approach akin to inspirational divinations of Biblical passages. Recent examples of multiple and conflicting interpretations abound. Consider the Chinese addresses that have been monitored concerning the politicalization of military cadres in North Vietnam. These remarks have been "interpreted" as indicating Chinese support for the war effort, Chinese distance and even withdrawal from the war effort, and Chinese pleasure (and displeasure) with the National Liberation Front. Interpretation too easily becomes a function of policy perspectives rather than an objective study of foreign power intentions.

The filtering process, based as it is on the secrecy norm, leads to an abuse of what can be considered legitimate scientific inquiry. It minimizes possibilities of empirical and ethnographic surveys. Knowing what the "other side" is doing or planning in the main areas of government policy is absolutely necessary for the establishment of informational parity. But this runs squarely against policy rulings having to do with overseas travel, with definition of the enemy, and sometimes with attitudes toward people considered to be less than human. The needs of policy are difficult to square with the needs of the social sciences. Policy may dictate *de jure* nonrecognition of a foreign power, but it is impossible for the social scientist to accept such policy recommendations as a *de facto* basis for research. He has to find a way of violating non recognition in order to serve in a scholarly capacity.

This unanticipated contradiction between science and policy cannot easily be resolved without redefining the enemy in nonpartisan terms or accepting the idea of partisanship as an institutionalized limit to scientific enquiry. But to do so would require a general redefinition of the role of social science in a democratic culture. What results in situations of high policy stress is low-quality research. Conversely, when there is a low stress situation there can be high-yield information. Democracy is linked to social visibility; hence we know a great deal about England and its society. But England poses no immediate threat, and therefore social scientists working in the area of English affairs are less than vital with respect to policy. The more important the subject the less likely is there to

11. Paul F. Lazarsfeld, "Political Behavior and Public Opinion," in *The Behavioral Sciences Today*, ed. by Bernard Berelson (New York: Basic Books, 1963), p. 187.

be access to critical information. As long as the political situation is defined exclusively in terms of policy needs, the possibility of a social science of operational worth remains seriously impaired.

The proud announcement in the early 1950's of the policy sciences has given way to a profound skepticism of such a concept. Perhaps the notion of a policy science is a contradiction in terms, not previously recognized as such only because of the enormity of federal and commercial needs for exact information in an age when mass participatory democracy has sharply declined. There can never be a policy science from the point of view of the polity, because its needs have to do with sovereignty and with the protection of its citizens even if this involves secrecy, war, and deceitful forms of defense or attack. From the point of view of the social scientist, the same concept of policy science must be challenged because in the final analysis the scientific community can never accept an exclusively therapeutic definition of social life. Social science can never take for granted the things that make for political sovereignty. Perhaps this contradiction is a creative tension. But I am not so optimistic. My own feeling is that this is a degenerative relationship. The negative features implied for both policy and science cancel the pragmatic worth of a concept of policy science.

The value-free doctrine has been examined at too great a length to require additional commentary. Yet there is an aspect of the fact-value issue that deserves deeper analysis here, since it involves the connection of social science to public policy in a direct way. When translated into a personal ideological expression, this fact-value dualism can provide a rationale for selling information to the highest bidder. It can become a way of saying that facts are for public sale, while values are for private sensibilities.

Quite conceivably, the classical disjunction between fact and value may turn out to be a greater problem for distributors of "hard" science than for those who traffic in "soft" science. For if the doctrine of value irrelevance is taken seriously, it becomes a mandate for any values. Hence the complete separation of fact and value can jeopardize tough policy scientists quite thoroughly. Conventionally, advocates of the value-free doctrine have considered it to be a functional instrument safeguarding against any ideological infiltration of the social sciences. However, it is becoming uncomfortably plain that the notion of selling information to the highest bidder is not at all inconsistent with people who have no "higher" values at all, and not only those who refuse to express value preference in their social research.

The more expensive an originating research design turns out to be, the more differential access to the findings is demanded as the price for an initial expenditure of risk capital.[12] The policy sector demand for differential access may take various forms: (1) The policy agency will insist upon a defined period of lead time before release of findings to the public. (2) The results can be made immedi-

---

12. On this question see the contribution by Richard J. Barber, *The Politics of Research* (Washington, D.C.: Public Affairs Press, 1966), pp. 91–108.

ately available only if they are initially cleared by the sponsoring agency so that no information of a "delicate" nature is revealed. (3) This often leads to a more formal situation, in which the publication of an exoteric document is allowed, while a more complete esoteric document serves as a special payoff to the agency. (4) Finally, by insisting that all research done under contract is private, the sponsoring agency settles all "problems" of publication. Often the distinction between "liberal" and "conservative" agencies is made on the basis of data released and has no general political moorings.

None of these four types of processing data represents a classical model of social scientific behavior with respect to publication. But the bureaucratic style has become increasingly generalized. New elements have entered into the policy game even at the level of publication. One sensitive issue, for example, is what constitutes publication. Is a mimeographed report an authentic publication? Reports in such nontypographical form appear regularly, and have peculiar qualities. They are not available for public consumption. They are not copyrighted and hence not subject to public review. Even "official-looking" mimeographed reports released in bound form remain private documents. This raises not only questions of differential access, but of arbitrary limits on access. It is not only who, but how many, people are in a position to read such documents. The norm of secrecy has become so much part of the character of social science publications that the general risks to unlimited diffusion of information have greatly increased.

The issues can be divided into sponsorship problems and ideological problems. At one level, the policy issue is who sponsors the research rather than the character of the research. At the other end of the spectrum, the scientific issue is the goal sought from any given research. More profoundly, as I have already suggested, the issue is the nature of sovereignty and the nature of privacy.

Nations are not often thought to be private entities. Rather we think of them as macroscopic, and publicly available to investigation. However, sovereignty carries with it, if not explicitly then surely implicitly, a notion of restricted public access, that is, privacy. Sovereignty is a statement of the rights of citizens, and such rights impose restrictions upon noncitizens. Therefore, a sovereign, whether in universalistic national form or as a person, has a private side, a private self.

This might best be seen in legal terms of juror performance and jury room wiretapping. From the point of view of social science, the phenomenology of decision-making in a closed setting represents a fascinating problem. How do people interact within "alien" restricted confines? Do the decisions they reach rest upon rational or irrational indicators? What is the character of personal interaction in a jury room? From the point of view of the sovereign, the elements of jury decision-making require secrecy for their realization. The sovereign assumes that people in private interaction, untouched by public pressure, are in a position to make decisions that are more honest and hence more useful than publicly debated decisions. This is an example of competing needs. The political requirement is different from the scientific requirement. Who is right? Would it be right to implant a microphone in a jury room for the sake of social science, running the risk ultimately of destroying the confidence of jurors and potential jurors in a democratic legal system? Or is it right to preserve an irrational kernel of madness that may well be what a jury system is about, simply to maintain the myth of democratic processes?

There is no ready-made answer to this kind of dilemma. But raising this sort of problem gives an indication of the anxieties and disturbances felt by sovereign powers in the realm of foreign area research. For what is being tested by one nation's study of the inner workings of another nation is nothing short of the right to remain private. The justification of such privacy may be quite shaky, based on custom and myth. At the moment, however, the problem is not the *origins* of sovereignty, but rather the *rights* of sovereignty. From this point of view, anxieties concerning foreign area research have to be appreciated, irrespective of social scientific or policy claims.

The sponsoring agent of research may not be as important for the sovereign under scrutiny as for the individuals engaging in a field investigation. The importance of whether sponsorship of foreign area research is under the aegis of the Department of Health, Education, and Welfare or the Department of Defense may dwindle in terms of how such research is perceived by the foreign government. But from either the public or the private viewpoint, visibility of research funds is significant. It may well be that openness of sponsorship is a determining element in how far access to a foreign sovereign may be pushed. To put matters directly: the reaction of the sovereign to an investigatory body in some measure depends on the premises and purposes of the investigatory body. This in turn may require a fresh look at the norm of secrecy—and the understanding that such a norm affects sovereignty as well as science.

III. University Bureaucracies and Value Systems

The social ecology of where various activities are performed leaves an imprint on the nature of the findings. Social scientific activities usually take place within a university context. The university, viewed as a social force, has strong feudalistic elements. Some people mistake this feudal ancestry for humanism, possibly because of the historical distance between our epoch and the founding of the university system nearly 800 years ago. The feudal core of university life is that a stratum of people is employed to engage in activities which may not be practical. They are paid to be nonfunctional. To put matters in a more exact form, the function of a university is to absorb the welter of nonpragmatic activities that go on within any viable society. University activities may or may not relate to the betterment of man, but pragmatic goals do not exhaust the scholarly role as such. This traditional nonfunctionality has begun to crumble under the impact of courses in basket-weaving and jewelry-making on one side, and war-gaming and systems designing on the other. Still, the great thrust of university life in America through the mid-1950's has been to keep the university a place of general theory and statements of fundamentals, to retain the European notion of *universitas*.

Policy-making activities, on the other hand, usually take place in a non-academic or bureaucratic context. Policy as distinct from politics as such is a modern innovation, beginning as a mass enterprise in the industrial era. True, there was a species of policy connected to political classes in ancient or medieval times, where political structure was directly and organically related to class interests. However, policy-making as an autonomous activity, linked to appointment based on expertise, is a twentieth-century phenomenon. The style of policy is anti-feudal. It is based on premises having to do with function, operation, instrumentation, utility—premises converting theory into immediate practice. This differs radically from the traditional university bias toward separation and even suspicion of a ready conversion of theory into action.

The invasion of policy-making into university life, in the form of direct capital expenditures as well as through contractual arrangements for specific purposes, transforms this traditional feudal-industrial dichotomy. Indeed, it undermines even the long-standing ties between university life and the business community that arose earlier in the present century. The information in Table 4—behavioral contracts related to foreign areas—is simply one miniscule indicator of the degree to which the social sciences have furthered an interpenetration of social sciences and policy-formation. The investigators are for the overwhelming part professors, and they are located at major university centers. This serves not only to pragmatize university research projects, but also to supply financial support for graduate instruction, funds for administrative and office personnel, and funds for new and improved buildings and equipment.

The Air Force Office of Scientific Research, the Office of Naval Research, and the Special Operations Research Office of the United States Army each maintain separate funding arms. These are in addition to standard funding agencies such as the National Science Foundation and National Institutes of Health. The development of federal funding to universities has become so extensive and sophisticated that subcontracting is now commonplace. A government agency may provide a coverall grant to the Smithsonian Institution or the Social Science Research Council, which in turn may parcel out the funds for private agencies and individuals. The total amount spent by the Department of Defense establishment alone for one year (1965) came to $27,300,000. Table 5 indicates the distribution of these funds. It is abundantly evident that the disbursements of these funds are usually indirect, through university agencies; and only infrequently direct, through subagencies having direct responsibility to the government. And it is apparent to students of the sociology of science that universities are now faced with the alternatives of either maximizing or holding constant such government allocations of research contracts.

This is a problem not of universities in general, but of social science in particular. To the extent that the social sciences are connected to university styles, to that extent are they concerned with issues beyond those of policy. The growth of bureaucratic mechanisms and institutes to funnel and channelize social science activities, while they have become increasingly important, still do not represent

Table 4: Selected Behavioral Science Contracts Related to Foreign Areas and Foreign Populations *

Title	Location	Description
1963 American Mount Everest Expedition.	Berkeley Institute of Psychological Research	Psychological aspects of stress behavior.
Changing values in Japanese, Americans, and Japanese-Americans.	Institute of Advanced Projects, University of Hawaii	Analysis of how Japanese change their values as they come in contact with American culture.
International conflict (Israel and Egypt).	Stanford University	Analysis of relationship of opinions and writings of decision-makers and the actual actions that took place.
Foreign research symposia.	Social Sciences Research Council	Meetings of American and foreign scholars in Europe in social psychology.
Persuasive communications in the international field.	University of Wisconsin	How foreign nationalities react to various kinds of American communications.
Sociopolitical precursors to insurgency.	Pennsylvania State College	Study of insurgency and causes related to it to determine role Navy plays.
Nationalism and the perception of international crises.	University of Texas	Perceptions that people have of international crises and relating this to the psychology of the persons involved.
Group factors influencing creativity.	University of Illinois	Discovering how a heterogeneous group can establish a common communication system in order to be effective; some of these groups composed of individuals of different language and cultural backgrounds.
Group equilibrium.	Rutgers University	Studies made in U.S. on small-group effectiveness have been replicated in Japan.
Role theory.	University of Missouri	Theory of role structure. Work being done with collaborators in Australia and England.
Cross-cultural investigation of some factors in persuasion and attitude change.	University of Maryland	Structure and mechanics of attitude-change methods; research replicated with Japanese subjects to determine generality of findings.

*Source of data: *Behavioral Sciences and the National Security* (Report No. 4). U.S. Government Printing Office, 1965.

Table 5: *1965 Budgeted Behavioral and Social Sciences Research Funds*
(in thousands of dollars)

| | Military departments | | ARPA* | Total | | |
	(con-tract)	(in-house)	(con-tract)	(con-tract)	(in-house)	Grand Total
Selection and classification	$730	$1,900		$730	$1,900	$2,630
Training and education	4,150	1,480	$60	4,210	1,480	5,690
Job design	300	620		300	620	920
Human performance, engineering, and proficiency management	2,230	2,620	470	2,700	2,620	5,320
Manpower management (assignment, retention, etc.)	520	430		520	430	950
Group effectiveness	1,270		240	1,510		1,510
Psychophysiology and stress	1,650	470		1,650	470	2,120
Support of policy planning and strategic concepts	820		210	1,030		1,030
Studies of foreign countries, counterinsurgency, and unconventional warfare	1,790		3,070	4,860		4,860
Foreign areas information	870		250	1,120		1,120
Psychological operations and weapons	380			380		380
Military assistance and civic action	400			400		400
Decision-making in military operations	110	260		110	260	370
TOTAL	$15,220	$7,780	$4,040	$19,520	$7,780	$27,300
PER CENT	66	34		71	29	

*Advanced Research Projects Agency.

more than a distinct minority of social science staffing in the United States. For the most part teaching remains the core occupation.[13] It is worth considering the degree to which the strain between social scientific activities and policy-making activities ought to be viewed as a conflict of roles between feudal, university-based and modern, state-based institutions. Recognizing the different origins and locales of the distinctive work styles inherent in science and policy

13. See National Register of Scientific and Technical Personnel, National Science Foundation, *Summary of American Science Manpower, 1964* (Washington, D.C.: U.S. Government Printing Office, March, 1966); and Committee on the National Science Foundation Report on the Economics Profession, "The Structure of Economists' Employment and Salaries, 1964," *American Economic Review*, LV, no. 4 (December, 1965), Part 2, Supplement.

will help account for present discrepancies. The strains that exist are not just transient or temporary, not reducible to financial allocations; they are basic differences in the way objects are studied, as well as in what is considered worthy of study.

In examining contract social science research, two problems have to be distinguished: first, the sponsorship involved in any kind of research; and second, the nature and purposes of the research design. Both problems simultaneously involve methodological and moral dimensions. Methodological guidelines can do everything but answer the question: Why study a field? That is why the moral base of social science is directly involved in the nature of the investigatory proceedings.

Let us restrict ourselves to an issue raised, but not resolved, in the previous section of this essay—the issue of sovereignty. Sovereignty is an ultimate politically, but not scientifically. The investigation of another nation is no more and no less legitimate than the study of another person, for the problem of magnitude is not one of morals. It is hard to envision a situation in the immediate future when national studies, so long a part of social science, will vanish. The whole of the nineteenth century was taken up by Europeans studying the United States, from Alexis de Tocqueville to Harriet Martineau. The tradition has persisted into this century. Many of the so-called classics of the social sciences have a national character, including the work of men like Ostrogorskii and Weber. Indeed, anthropologists have made the nation a basic measure. They may have been accused of engaging in unfriendly acts, or in secular missionary roles, but they were not denied access to data.

The question is: Why has this traditional situation of tolerance not prevailed? First, in the past, social scientists were not working for a government. Therefore they were without special interest in bringing to light the private aspects of another sovereignty. Second, the issue of sponsorship has become particularly acute at the present time because to define research in operational terms is necessarily to arouse a considerable amount of fear and trepidation. Operational or instrumental research has a goal beyond the research itself. Such latent political goals elicit fear and even hostility from a "host" sovereign to the social science "vendors." Third, the problem has become acute because sovereigns of superordinate nations are interested not so much in the public side of life in the subordinate nations they study, but in the private side. The subordinate nations are viewed not as objects of disinterested inquiry, but as objects of instrumental or operational worth.

IV. AUTONOMY AND RELEVANCE IN SOCIAL SCIENCE

Let us now turn to the connection that the social scientist should maintain with policy-making bodies. Should the policy-maker continue to be a separate entity with a separate professional identity, or should he be a social scientist in government? Is it the role played or the functions performed that divide policy-maker from social scientist? Before attempting to answer questions of advantages or disadvantages in various relationships of social scientists to policy-making bodies, we ought to look more carefully into the lines of relationships that presently obtain.

Dividing the "world" into four parts—basic social sciences and applied social sciences on one side, executive and legislative branches of government on the other side—reveals interesting relations. The basic social sciences (anthropology, political science, economics, psychology, and sociology) have government connections different from those of the applied social sciences (administrative sciences, education, law, planning, and social work). Let us divide the federal government into the presidential or executive government (White House staff and the cabinet level officials) and the permanent or legislative government (career federal executives, the Congress, and federal judiciary).

The State Department and the Defense Department and the various cabinet level executives are the ones who make the highest use of basic social sciences. The State Department, through its diplomatic functions, has long been associated with political science and anthropology. The White House, for its part, is directly linked to the economics profession through the Council of Economic Advisors. The State of the Union address institutionalizes the relation of the Executive Branch of Government to economics as a social science. The Defense Department, perhaps because its own power is of more recent derivation, relies heavily upon the younger social sciences, especially psychology and, to a somewhat lesser degree, sociology. In sum, the basic social sciences are used primarily by the presidential staff and by the executive branch of government as a whole.

The area of applied social science is more often called upon by the congressional and legislative branches. Education, administrative sciences, social work, and particularly law are in fact areas of professional competence for many congressmen themselves. Thus the legislative relationship to applied social science fields is not only utilitarian but organic. The pragmatic base of enacting legislation having to do with changing relations between men insures the legislators' continuing demand for applied researches.

The gap between applied and basic models of social science that obtains in most American universities is paralleled by lines of influence in the government.[14] Policy-making cannot be considered a unified science or a unified role. Quite the contrary, the tendency is for policy-making groups within the executive branch to be related to the social sciences differently than are policy-making bodies within the congressional sphere. While it is true that definitions of "basic" and "applied" social sciences vary, there is enough consistency to reveal this differential policy pattern.

14. The judiciary itself makes little direct use of social science findings. If it employs such findings at all, it is through the law journals and periodicals relating to the legal profession. Insofar as social science permeates law journals, to that degree the judiciary reacts to trends in social science. This may be one factor in the length of time it takes for judicial decision concerning Negro-white relations. The access system between the judiciary and social sciences is often so blocked that important social science issues escape the attention of the judiciary for a longer span than for any other federal group.

What then are the supposed advantages of fusing social science and social policy? The basic advantage is said to be a higher sense of responsibility for the social sciences and a greater degree of training for policy-oriented personnel. This has, at any rate, been the classical rationale for a tighter linkage between policy-making and social science.

What has prevented this amalgamation from occurring is not simple negligence or sloth. On the contrary, to judge by the amount of federal funds dedicated to bringing about such a union—de facto if not de jure—the wonder is how slight the steps toward amalgamation have been. The reason is that it is quite impossible to think of therapeutics as being the same as science. In order to get a fusion of social science and policy, there would have to be a complete disruption of the present notion of social science as sharply different from reform therapy. While applied social science may be the expression of practical reason in the twentieth century, an applied social science cannot dictate the character of social science findings. The notion of basic science requires a distinct separation of its functions and those of policy-making. That high level policy implies a recognition of this distinction can be seen by the extensive use the executive departments make of "basic" findings and theories. On the other hand, the more practical the level of policy-making (legislative activities are typical), the more closely linked they are to applied researches. The realities of the situation are such that the utility of the social sciences to policy-making bodies depend upon some maintenance of the separation of the social sciences from the policy situation.

Essential to understanding the present dilemmas about the relationship of science to policy are the radically different conceptions which government officials and social scientists have of that relationship. What concerns social scientists is not only making available the most important findings for "intelligence" needs, but the methods by which the policy process gets put into motion and the results of the study of policy for general scientific theory. What concerns government policy-makers is not so much social science but social engineering. The ready-to-hand bureaucratic research institutions set up at major universities and in the giant corporations provide both the institutional support and the ideological props with which to pursue these engineering "systems" ends with great vigor.[15]

The government in the present period has sought to resolve its staffing problems in key agencies and committees by attracting people whose conception of social science extends to construction but not to criticism. In contrast to the types of men solicited for marginal advisory roles, decision-makers have been chosen from the fields of business administration and urban planning rather than from the "hard" social sciences.

The "constructive" policy-science approach was actually begun in the administration of Herbert Hoover and continued at an accelerated rate by Franklin

15. See Robert Boguslaw, The New Utopians: A Study of System Design and Social Change (Englewood Cliffs, N.J.: Prentice-Hall, 1965).

Delano Roosevelt. Hoover had a deep engineering commitment. In fact, his image of the Presidency often bordered on that of the great engineer, the social engineer. The President's Research Committee on Social Trends (1930–1932), which Hoover created, inaugurated the difficult relationships between social science and social policy that have now come to plague the American policy. The degree to which this early effort was a mutually felt need is reflected in the fact that the Social Science Research Council, with its support stemming from the Rockefeller-dominated Spelman Fund, underwrote the President's Research Committee on Social Trends. The demands of social science professionalization coincided with the crisis in the American economy—a crisis profound enough to generate demands from within the polity to seek out support even from previously ignored, if not feared, intellectual currents.

Given the enormous significance of the "generation of the thirties" in founding relations between public officials and social scientists, it might be instructive to single out three important intellectual figures who assisted in the creation of these relations: Charles Merriam, Luther Gulick, and Louis Brownlow. Merriam, a founder of the American Political Science Association and of the Social Science Research Council, was the only one of the three who qualified as an academic figure. Even he had stronger ties to government officials, regional planners, and managers than to other social scientists. Brownlow was Merriam's closest associate at the University of Chicago; his main contribution was as Director of the Public Administration Clearing House. He was, in effect, the chief manager of the nation's city managers. Brownlow had been a city manager in Washington, D.C., Knoxville (Tenn.), and Petersburg (Va.) long before he came to join Merriam at Chicago. Gulick was a different kettle of fish. Like the Dulles, Kennan, and Davies families, he came out of the milieu of the American (Congregational) Foreign Mission Society. (John Foster Dulles was, in fact, an aide to Gulick's father.) He entered government planning service not by way of the social sciences but through the auspices of the New York Bureau of Municipal Research, which also had the support of large capital (the Harriman banking interests).

These were the men who made up the Committee on Administrative Management under Franklin Delano Roosevelt and under Herbert Hoover. They provided government officials with an early indication of what was to become the dominant "policy-making style," i.e., an unconcern with politics, or at least a strict division between politics as a mass activity (with which the policy-making social scientists were unconcerned) and policy as an elite activity (with which they were intimately concerned).[16]

Their highest achievement was to draft the Executive Reorganization Act of

16. See Barry Dean Karl, *Executive Reorganization and Reform in the New Deal: The Genesis of Administrative Management, 1900–1939* (Cambridge: Harvard University Press, 1963). I would like to acknowledge the suggestions offered by Thomas M. Hill on the critical importance of the New Deal period in establishing the present relationships between the behavioral sciences and government policy-making echelons.

1939, which foreshadowed many of the changes that took place in the postwar executive regimes of Truman, Eisenhower, and Kennedy. The Council of Economic Advisors was, for instance, an early fruit of this reorganization plan. This in turn led to the Council of Scientific Advisors. The men who established the institutional and organizational patterns relating social science to social policy were by training and inclination engineers, managers, and planners. When they did link up to a social science, it was invariably to political science—a field which in its successful attempt at rapid professionalization chose alignment with federal interests, rather than criticism of such interests, as its high road to success.

The dominant view of the relationship of social science to social policy was, consequently, that social science should fulfill an ancillary function to social engineering—no less, but certainly no more. The policy-makers sought to answer the question "knowledge for what?" in a pragmatic and direct way: Harold Lasswell sought to answer Robert Lynd's defiant stance by asserting the need of knowledge for augmentation and operationalization of federal policies in the areas of health, welfare, and war. During the period between 1930 and 1945, the growth of social science organizations was fused to their increasing acceptance of a professional ideology. This combination of organizational advancement in the social sciences and ideological commitment to the political system served to cement the relations with policy-making branches of government by removing the last vestiges of ideological mistrust.

These new developments deeply affected the autonomous character and growth of the social sciences. Standards of methodological precision were raised, a wider set of people from diverse class and ethnic backgrounds began to permeate the social sciences, and professionalism itself served both to unite and to distinguish between the tasks confronting social science and those of government. The very growth of social science work styles that were both accessible and amenable to policy-makers also served to raise anew the doubts as to the worth of such a fusion.[17]

This brings us face to face with the relationship of autonomy to involvement. This issue is especially significant in light of the large number of government contracts and policy-making demands upon the time, energies, and capabilities of social scientists. This is not simply a contrast of citizen responsibility and professional roles, but a question of the nature of the discipline itself—over and beyond the way in which the social scientist perceives institutional affiliations. The autonomy of the social sciences was rarely doubted until the present. The same cannot be said for the autonomy of policy-making sectors of government. Since the latter are openly involved in operational research, they make slender pretenses towards autonomy.

17. See S. M. Lipset and Mildred A. Schwartz, "The Politics of Professionals," in *Professionalization*, ed. by H. W. Vollmer and D. L. Mills (Englewood Cliffs, N.J.: Prentice-Hall, 1966), pp. 299–309; and Irving L. Horowitz, "Professionalism and Disciplinarianism," *Philosophy of Science*, 31, no. 3 (July, 1964): 275–281.

The problem now arises on two fronts in the federally supported research situation. What are the lines of independence, and what are the lines of responsibility from the "vendors" to the "funding agency"? The autonomy of a social science is directly linked to the very existence of each field. The most powerful argument for the maintenance of a distinction between public policy and social science is that without such a distinction the very concept is severely jeopardized. Admitting the risk of inviting dilettantism or "idle speculation," to transform all research into command performances is far riskier. There is no science that does not have an element of autonomous growth. Indeed, a great deal of time and energy in any social science is spent arguing and worrying, not about the social world in general, but about people occupying critical roles or command positions in the world of social science. Nor is such self-reflection and constant autoexamination to be lightly dismissed, since it helps to explain precisely the sorts of heuristic activities in the functioning of a scientific theory that provide operational worth to begin with. In other words, the autonomous realm is not incidental either to the formation of the social scientist or to that which makes him truly scientific in his behavior.

The great failing of a policy science approach is that it has not recognized that the price of rapid professionalization and integration is high. By raising the banner of "the policy sciences of democracy" this approach minimizes the autonomous and critical aspects of social scientific development.[18] Without this autonomic aspect to science, one cannot really speak either of a profession or of an occupation. There are standards in a social science, and levels of performance within each science, that link its practitioners together apart from their actions or reactions toward policy questions. When a breakdown of autonomy occurs, when policy questions or ideological requirements prevail, the deterioration in the quality of the social science is a certain consequence. Policy places a premium on involvement and influence; science places a premium on investigation and ideas. The issue is not so much what is studied, or even the way an inquiry is conducted, but the auspices and the purposes of a study.

Finally, the relationship of social science to public policy as a civic issue reflects first and foremost the belief in the efficacy and the feasibility of scientific activities in social life. It is no longer either fashionable or particularly profound to ask: Are the social sciences really sciences? This is a naive question, a meaningless question. The efficacy of social science is firmly established. Were this not the case, the issues herein dealt with would never have arisen in the first place. But precisely at that point in scientific history where efficacy is established beyond any doubt in the minds of both policy personnel and social scientists, the question of the aims of social science loom large. This issue of purpose was not raised when the social sciences were really little else than a species of literature or *belles lettres*.

18. See, for example, Harold D. Lasswell, "The Policy Orientation," in *The Policy Sciences*, ed. by Daniel Lerner and Harold D. Lasswell (Stanford, Calif.: Stanford University Press, 1951), pp. 3–15.

When an individual pontificates about the nature of the world or the nature of man in society, one man's platitudes may be another man's poison. But when someone offers a plan for redesigning the world, and proceeds to do so in a more or less anticipated way, he can be ridiculed and reviled, but not easily ignored. The recognition of this has been so widespread that the value demands upon the social sciences have become central, with decisions as to the performance of the science becoming directly linked to the goals set for the society.

What we witness in the present generation, from the point of view of the social sciences, is the break-up of the functionalist ideology with its value-free orientation. Because the peculiar autonomous aspects of each social science generate a special internal history, the break-up occurs differently in each discipline.[19]

From the point of view of policy-makers, the break-up of the old way of doing things has been equally profound. Perhaps the largest shock that they have undergone is the recognition that there is probably no such animal as a policy scientist. There has been no definition of a policy-maker that can legitimate his role as a social scientist—basic or applied. Policy-makers in one agency have slender connection with policy-makers in other branches of government. Increasingly, the policy-maker is being confronted with the fact that he is not so much an applied social scientist as he is a representative of the State Department or a representative of Health, Education, and Welfare. In other words, what defines his role is not the policy-making activities but rather the requirements of the agency for which he works. In effect, what he is engaged in is ideology, not policy.[20] Therefore, unless one is willing to speak of the science of ideology, which is a contradiction in terms, it is not possible to legitimately deal with the social sciences exclusively from a policy point of view.

The social sciences are challenged and tested as never before by their involvements with policy organs. This association increases the chances for meaningful research and knowledge that scientists may acquire about the workings of the world. It also makes possible the corruption of social science on a scale hitherto unimagined, through the submerging of tasks of inquiry into contract fulfillments. The drive shaft of government agencies' demands upon social scientists is ideological; and yet the larger need of such agencies is, as never before, a wider understanding of the shape of societies around the world. Perhaps the main problem comes right down to the relation of policy to science, a common challenge to social scientists and policy-makers that must, however, be answered in separate and distinct ways.

19. N. J. Demerath, III, and R. A. Peterson, eds., System, Change and Conflict: Functionalists and Their Critics (New York: Free Press, 1967).

20. See Irving L. Horowitz, "The Life and Death of Project Camelot," Ch. 19 in this book; and Kalman H. Silvert, "American Academic Ethics and Social Research Abroad: The Lesson of Project Camelot," in American Universities Field Staff Reports (West Coast South American Series), XII, no. 3 (July, 1965).

19. *The Life and Death of Project Camelot*

IN JUNE OF 1965—in the midst of the crisis over the Dominican Republic—the United States Ambassador to Chile sent an urgent and angry cable to the State Department. Ambassador Ralph Dungan was confronted with a growing outburst of anti-Americanism from Chilean newspapers and intellectuals. Further, left-wing members of the Chilean Senate had accused the United States of espionage.

The anti-American attacks that agitated Dungan had no direct connection with sending U.S. troops to Santo Domingo. Their target was a mysterious and cloudy American research program called Project Camelot.

Dungan wanted to know from the State Department what Project Camelot was all about. Further, whatever Camelot was, he wanted it stopped because it was fast becoming a *cause célèbre* in Chile (as it soon would throughout capitals of Latin America and in Washington), and Dungan had not been told anything about it—even though it was sponsored by the U.S. Army and involved the

This study was a field examination of perhaps the most important single government contract over issued to social scientists, Project Camelot. The paper goes through the origins and cancellation of the project, the career profiles of the men involved, and the methodological and moral issues introduced, or at least highlighted, by the project. Since its original publication, it has been reprinted in ten anthologies and translated into three foreign languages; which indicates the continued interest in the implications of the project both domestically and abroad, particularly Latin America. First published in *Trans-Action*, 3, no. 1 (November–December, 1965); reprinted by permission.

tinderbox subjects of counterrevolution and counterinsurgency in Latin America.

Within a few weeks Project Camelot created repercussions from Capitol Hill to the White House. Senator J. William Fulbright, chairman of the Senate Foreign Relations Committee, registered his personal concern about such projects as Camelot because of their "reactionary, backward-looking policy opposed to change. Implicit in Camelot, as in the concept of 'counterinsurgency,' is an assumption that revolutionary movements are dangerous to the interest of the United States and that the United States must be prepared to assist, if not actually to participate in, measures to repress them."

By mid-June the State Department and Defense Department—which had created and funded Camelot—were in open contention over the project and over the jurisdiction each department should have over certain foreign policy operations.

On July 8, Project Camelot was killed by Defense Secretary Robert McNamara's office which has a veto power over the military budget. The decision had been made under the President's direction.

On that same day, the director of Camelot's parent body, the Special Operations Research Organization, told a Congressional committee that the research project on revolution and counterinsurgency had taken its name from King Arthur's mythical domain because "It connotes the right sort of things—development of a stable society with peace and justice for all." Whatever Camelot's outcome, there should be no mistaking the deep sincerity behind this appeal for an applied social science pertinent to current policy.

However, Camelot left a horizon of disarray in its wake: an open dispute between State and Defense; fuel for the anti-American fires in Latin America; a cut in U.S. Army research appropriations. In addition, serious and perhaps ominous implications for social science research, bordering on censorship, have been raised by the heated reaction of the executive branch of government.

GLOBAL COUNTERINSURGENCY

What was Project Camelot? Basically, it was a project for measuring and forecasting the causes of revolutions and insurgency in underdeveloped areas of the world. It also aimed to find ways of eliminating the causes, or coping with the revolutions and insurgencies. Camelot was sponsored by the U.S. Army on a $4-6,000,000 contract, spaced out over three to four years, with the Special Operations Research Organization (SORO). This agency is nominally under the aegis of American University in Washington, D.C., and does a variety of research for the Army. This includes making analytical surveys of foreign areas; keeping up-to-date information on the military, political, and social complexes of those areas; and maintaining a "rapid response" file for getting immediate information, upon Army request, on any situation deemed militarily important.

Latin America was the first area chosen for concentrated study, but countries on Camelot's four-year list included some in Asia, Africa, and Europe. In a working paper issued on December 5, 1964, at the request of the Office of the Chief of Research and Development, Department of the Army, it was recommended that "comparative historical studies" be made in these countries:

Latin America: Argentina, Bolivia, Brazil, Colombia, Cuba, Dominican Republic, El Salvador, Guatemala, Mexico, Paraguay, Peru, Venezuela.

Middle East: Egypt, Iran, Turkey.

Far East: Korea, Indonesia, Malaysia, Thailand.

Others: France, Greece, Nigeria.

"Survey research and other field studies" were recommended for Bolivia, Colombia, Ecuador, Paraguay, Peru, Venezuela, Iran, and Thailand. Preliminary consideration was also being given to a study of the separatist movement in French Canada. It, too, had a code name: Project Revolt.

In a recruiting letter sent to selected scholars all over the world at the end of 1964, Project Camelot's aims were defined as a study to "make it possible to predict and influence politically significant aspects of social change in the developing nations of the world." This would include devising procedures for "assessing the potential for internal war within national societies" and "identify-[ing] with increased degrees of confidence, those actions which a government might take a relieve conditions which are assessed as giving rise to a potential for internal war." The letter further stated:

The U.S. Army has an important mission in the positive and constructive aspects of nation-building in less developed countries as well as a responsibility to assist friendly governments in dealing with active insurgency problems.

Such activities by the U.S. Army were described as "insurgency prophylaxis" rather than the "sometimes misleading label of counterinsurgency."

Project Camelot was conceived in late 1963 by a group of high-ranking Army officers connected with the Army Research Office of the Department of Defense. They were concerned about new types of warfare springing up around the world. Revolutions in Cuba and Yemen and insurgency movements in Vietnam and the Congo were a far cry from the battles of World War II and also different from the envisioned—and planned for—apocalypse of nuclear war. For the first time in modern warfare, military establishments were not in a position to use the immense arsenals at their disposal—but were, instead, compelled by force of a geopolitical stalemate to increasingly engage in primitive forms of armed combat. The questions of moment for the Army were: Why can't the "hardware" be used? And what alternatives can social science "software" provide?

A well-known Latin American area specialist, Rex Hopper, was chosen as director of Project Camelot. Hopper was a professor of sociology and chairman of the department at Brooklyn College. He had been to Latin America many times over a thirty-year span on research projects and lecture tours, including some under government sponsorship. He was highly recommended for the position by his professional associates in Washington and elsewhere. Hopper had a long-standing interest in problems of revolution and saw in this multi-million dollar contract the possible realization of a lifelong scientific ambition.

The Chilean Debacle

How did this social science research project create a foreign policy furore? And, at another level, how did such high intentions result in so disastrous an outcome?

The answers involve a network spreading from a professor of anthropology at the University of Pittsburgh, to a professor of sociology at the University of Oslo, and to yet a third professor of sociology at the University of Chile in Santiago. The "showdown" took place in Chile, first within the confines of the university, next on the floor of the Chilean Senate, then in the popular press of Santiago, and finally, behind U.S. embassy walls.

It was ironic that Chile was the scene of wild newspaper tales of spying and academic outrage at scholars being recruited for "spying missions." For the working papers of Project Camelot stipulated as a criterion for study that a country "should show promise of high pay-offs in terms of the kinds of data required." Chile did not meet these requirements—it is not on the preliminary list of nations specified as prospects.

How then did Chile become involved in Project Camelot's affairs? The answer requires consideration of the position of Hugo G. Nutini, assistant professor of anthropology at Pittsburgh, citizen of the United States and former citizen of Chile. His presence in Santiago as a self-identified Camelot representative triggered the climactic chain of events.

Nutini, who inquired about an appointment in Camelot's beginning stages, never was given a regular Camelot appointment. Because he was planning a trip to Chile in April—on other academic business—he was asked to prepare a report concerning possibilities of cooperation from Chilean scholars. In general, it was the kind of survey which has mild results and a modest honorarium attached to it (Nutini was offered $750). But Nutini had an obviously different notion of his role. Despite the limitations and precautions that Rex Hopper placed on his trip, especially Hopper's insistence on its informal nature, Nutini managed to convey the impression of being an official of Project Camelot with the authority to make proposals to prospective Chilean participants. Here was an opportunity to link the country of his birth with the country of his choice.

At about the same time, Johan Galtung, a Norwegian sociologist famous for his research on conflict and conflict resolution in underdeveloped areas, especially in Latin America, entered the picture. Galtung, who was in Chile at the time and associated with the Latin American Faculty of Social Science (FLACSO), received an invitation to participate in a Camelot planning conference scheduled in Washington, D.C., in August, 1965. The fee to social scientists attending the conference would be $2,000 for four weeks. Galtung turned down the invitation. He gave several reasons. He could not accept the role of the U.S. Army as a sponsoring agent in a study of counterinsurgency. He could not accept the notion of the Army as an agency of national development; he saw the Army as managing conflict and even promoting conflict. Finally, he could not accept the asymmetry of the project—he found it difficult to understand why there would be studies of counterinsurgency in Latin America, but no studies of "counter-intervention" (conditions under which Latin American nations might intervene in the affairs of the United States). Galtung was also deeply concerned about the possibility of European scholars being frozen out of Latin American studies by an inundation of sociologists from the United States. Furthermore, he expressed fears that the scale of Camelot honoraria would completely destroy the social science labor market in Latin America.

Galtung had spoken to others in Oslo, Santiago, and throughout Latin America about the project, and he had shown the memorandum of December, 1964, to many of his colleagues.

Soon after Nutini arrived in Santiago, he had a conference with Vice-Chancellor Alvaro Bunster of the University of Chile to discuss the character of Project Camelot. Their second meeting, arranged by the vice-chancellor, was also attended by Professor Eduardo Fuenzalida, a sociologist. After a half-hour of exposition by Nutini, Fuenzalida asked him pointblank to specify the ultimate aims of the project, its sponsors, and its military implications. Before Nutini could reply, Professor Fuenzalida, apparently with some drama, pulled a copy of the December 4 circular letter from his briefcase and read a prepared Spanish translation. Simultaneously, the authorities at FLASCO turned over the matter to their associates in the Chilean Senate and in the left-wing Chilean press.

In Washington, under the political pressures of State Department officials and Congressional reaction, Project Camelot was halted in midstream, or more precisely, before it ever really got under way. When the ambassador's communication reached Washington, there was already considerable official ferment about Project Camelot. Senators Fulbright, Morse, and McCarthy soon asked for hearings by the Senate Foreign Relations Committee. Only an agreement between Secretary of Defense McNamara and Secretary of State Rusk to settle their differences on future overseas research projects forestalled Senate action. But in the House of Representatives, a hearing was conducted by the Foreign Affairs Committee on July 8. The SORO director, Theodore Vallance, was questioned by committee members on the worth of Camelot and the matter of military intrusion into foreign policy areas.

That morning, even before Vallance was sworn in as a witness—and without his knowledge—the Defense Department issued a terse announcement terminating Project Camelot. President Johnson had decided the issue in favor of the State Department. In a memo to Secretary Rusk on August 5, the President stipulated that "no government sponsorship of foreign area research should be undertaken which in the judgment of the Secretary of State would adversely affect United States foreign relations."

The State Department has recently established machinery to screen and judge all federally financed research projects overseas. The policy and research consequences of the presidential directive will be discussed later.

What effect will the cancellation of Camelot have on the continuing rivalry between Defense and State departments for primacy in foreign policy? How will government sponsorship of future social science research be affected? And was Project Camelot a scholarly protective cover for U.S. Army Planning—or a legitimate research operation on a valid research subject independent of sponsorship?

Let us begin with a collective self-portrait of Camelot as the social scientists who directed the projects perceived it. There seems to be general consensus on seven points.

First, the men who went to work for Camelot felt the need for a large-scale, "big picture" project in social science. They wanted to create a sociology of contemporary relevance which would not suffer from the parochial narrowness of vision to which their own professional backgrounds had generally conditioned them. Most of the men viewed Camelot as a bona fide opportunity to do fundamental research with relatively unlimited funds at their disposal. (No social science project had ever before had up to $6,000,000 available.) Under such optimal conditions, these scholars tended not to look a gift horse in the mouth. As one of them put it, there was no desire to inquire too deeply as to the source of the funds or the ultimate purpose of the project.

Second, most social scientists affiliated with Camelot felt that there was actually more freedom to do fundamental research under military sponsorship than at a university or college. One man noted that during the 1950's there was far more freedom to do fundamental research in the RAND Corporation (a private research organization doing work for the air force under contract) than on any campus in America. Indeed, once the protective covering of RAND was adopted, it was almost viewed as a society of Platonist elites or "knowers" permitted to search for truth on behalf of the powerful. In a neoplatonic definition of their situation, the Camelot men hoped that their ideas would be taken seriously by the wielders of power (although, conversely, they were convinced that the armed forces would not accept their preliminary recommendations).

Third, many of the Camelot associates felt distinctly uncomfortable with military sponsorship, especially given the present United States military posture. But their reaction to this discomfort was that "the Army has to be educated." This view was sometimes cast in Freudian terms: the Army's bent toward violence ought to be sublimated. Underlying this theme was the notion of the armed forces as an agency for potential social good—the discipline and the order embodied by an army could be channeled into the process of economic and social development in the United States as well as in Latin America.

Fourth, there was a profound conviction in the perfectability of mankind; particularly in the possibility of the military establishment performing a major role in the general process of growth. They sought to correct the intellectual paternalism and parochialism under which Pentagon generals, State Department diplomats, and Defense Department planners seemed to operate.

Fifth, a major long-range purpose of Camelot, at least for some of its policy-makers, was to prevent another revolutionary holocaust on a grand scale, such as occurred in Cuba. At the very least, there was a shared belief that *Pax Americana* was severely threatened and its future could be bolstered.

Sixth, none of them viewed their role on the project as spying for the United States government, or for anyone else.

Seventh, the men on Project Camelot felt that they made heavy sacrifices for social science. Their personal and professional risks were much higher than those taken by university academics. Government work, while well-compensated, remains professionally marginal. It can be terminated abruptly (as indeed was the case), and its project directors are subject to a public scrutiny not customary behind the walls of ivy.

In the main, there was perhaps a keener desire on the part of the directing members of Camelot not to "sell out" than there is among social scientists with regular academic appointments. This concern with the ethics of social science research seemed to be due largely to daily confrontation of the problems of betrayal, treason, secrecy, and abuse of data, in a critical situation. In contrast, even though a university position may be created by federally sponsored research, the connection with policy matters is often too remote to cause any *crise de conscience*.

THE INSIDERS' REPORT

Were the men on Camelot critical of any aspects of the project?

Some had doubts from the outset about the character of the work they would be doing, and about the conditions under which it would be done. It was pointed out, for example, that the U.S. Army tends to exercise a far more stringent intellectual control of research findings than does the U.S. Air Force. As evidence for this, it was stated that SORO generally had fewer "free-wheeling" aspects to its research designs than did RAND (the Air Force-supported research organization). One critic inside SORO went so far as to say that he knew of no SORO research that had a "playful" or unregimented quality, such as one finds at RAND (where, for example, computers are used to plan invasions but also to play chess). One staff member said that "the self-conscious seriousness gets to you after a while." "It was all grim stuff," said another.

Another line of criticism was that pressures on the "reformers" (as the men engaged in Camelot research spoke of themselves) to come up with ideas were much stronger than the pressures on the military to actually bring off any policy changes recommended. The social scientists were expected to be social reformers, while the military adjutants were expected to be conservative. It was further felt that the relationship between sponsors and researchers was not one of equals, but rather one of superordinate military needs and subordinate academic roles. On the other hand, some officials were impressed by the disinterestedness of the military, and thought that, far from exercising undue influence, the Army personnel were loath to offer opinions.

Another objection was that if one had to work on policy matters—if research is to have international ramifications—it might better be conducted under conventional State Department sponsorship. "After all," one man said, "they are at least nominally committed to civilian political norms." In other words, there was a considerable reluctance to believe that the Defense Department, despite its superior organization, greater financial affluence, and executive influence, would actually improve upon State Department styles of work, or accept recommendations at variance with Pentagon policies.

There seemed to be few, if any, expressions of disrespect for the intrinsic merit of the work contemplated by Camelot, or of disdain for policy-oriented work in general. The scholars engaged in the Camelot effort used two distinct vocabularies. The various Camelot documents reveal a military vocabulary provided with an array of military justifications; often followed (within the same document) by a social science vocabulary offering social science justifications and rationalizations. The dilemma in the Camelot literature from the preliminary report issued in August, 1964, until the more advanced document issued in April, 1965, is the same: an incomplete amalgamation of the military and sociological vocabularies. (At an early date the project had the code name SPEARPOINT.)

POLICY CONFLICTS OVER CAMELOT

The directors of SORO are concerned that the cancellation of Camelot might mean the end of SORO as well as a wholesale slash of research funds. For while over $1,000,000 was allotted to Camelot each year, the annual budget of SORO, its parent organization, is a good deal less. Although no such action has taken place, SORO's future is being examined. For example, the Senate and House Appropriations Committee blocked a move by the Army to transfer unused Camelot funds to SORO.

However, the end of Project Camelot does not necessarily imply the end of the Special Operations Research Office, nor does it imply an end to research designs that are similar in character to Project Camelot. In fact, the termination of the contract does not even imply an intellectual change of heart on the part of the originating sponsors or key figures of the project.

One of the characteristics of Project Camelot was the number of antagonistic forces it set in motion on grounds of strategy and timing rather than from what may be called considerations of scientific principles.

The State Department grounded its opposition to Camelot on the basis of the ultimate authority it has in the area of foreign affairs. There is no published report showing serious criticism of the projected research itself.

Congressional opposition seemed to be generated by a concern not to rock any foreign alliances, especially in Latin America. Again, there was no statement about the project's scientific or intellectual grounds.

A third group of skeptics, academic social scientists, generally thought that Project Camelot, and studies of the processes of revolution and war in general, were better left in the control of major university centers and, in this way, kept free of direct military supervision.

The Army, creator of the project, did nothing to contradict McNamara's order cancelling Project Camelot. Army influentials not only felt that they had to execute the Defense Department's orders, but they are traditionally dubious of the value of "software" research to support "hardware" systems.

Let us take a closer look at each of these groups which voiced opposition to Project Camelot. A number of issues did not so much hinge upon, as swim about, Project Camelot. In particular, the "jurisdictional" dispute between Defense and State loomed largest.

State vs. Defense

In substance, the debate between the Defense Department and the State Department is not unlike that between electricians and bricklayers in the construction of a new apartment house. What "union" is responsible for which processes? Less generously, the issue is: Who controls what? At the policy level, Camelot was a tool tossed about in a larger power struggle, which has been going on in government circles since the end of World War II, when the Defense Department emerged as a competitor for honors as the most powerful bureau of the administrative branch of government.

In some sense, the divisions between Defense and State are outcomes of the rise of ambiguous conflicts such as Korea and Vietnam, in contrast to the more precise and diplomatically controlled "classical" world wars. What are the lines dividing political policy from military posture? Who is the most important representative of the United States abroad: the ambassador or the military attaché in charge of the military mission? When soldiers from foreign lands are sent to the United States for political orientation, should such orientation be within the province of the State Department or the Defense Department? When undercover activities are conducted, should the direction of such activities belong to military or political authorities? Each of these is a strategic question with little pragmatic or historic precedent. Each of these was entwined in the Project Camelot explosion.

It should be plain therefore that the State Department was not simply responding to the recommendations of Chilean left-wingers in urging the cancellation of Camelot. It merely employed the Chilean hostility to "interventionist" projects as an opportunity to redefine the balance of forces and power with the Defense Department. What is clear from this resistance to such projects is not so much a defense of the sovereignty of the nations where ambassadors are stationed, as it is a contention that conventional political channels are sufficient to yield the information desired or deemed necessary.

Congress

In the main, congressional reaction seems to be that Project Camelot was bad because it rocked the diplomatic boat in a sensitive area. Underlying most congressional criticisms is the plain fact that most congressmen are more sympathetic to State Department control of foreign affairs than they are to Defense

Department control. In other words, despite military-sponsored world junkets, National Guard and State Guard pressures from the home state, and military training in the backgrounds of many congressmen, the sentiment for political rather than military control is greater. In addition, there is a mounting suspicion in Congress of varying kinds of behavioral science research stemming from hearings into such matters as wire-tapping, uses of lie detectors, and truth-in-packaging.

Social Scientists

One reason for the violent response to Project Camelot, especially among Latin American scholars, is its sponsorship by the Department of Defense. The fact is that Latin Americans have become quite accustomed to State Department involvements in the internal affairs of various nations. The Defense Department is a newcomer, a dangerous one, inside the Latin American orbit. The train of thought connected to its activities is in terms of international warfare, spying missions, military manipulations, etc. The State Department, for its part, is often a consultative party to shifts in government, and has played an enormous part in either fending off or bringing about coups d'etat. This State Department role has by now been accepted and even taken for granted. Not so the Defense Department's role. But it is interesting to conjecture on how matter-of-factly Camelot might have been accepted if it had had State Department sponsorship.

Social scientists in the United States have, for the most part, been publicly silent on the matter of Camelot. The reasons for this are not hard to find. First, many "giants of the field" are involved in government contract work in one capacity or another. And few souls are in a position to tamper with the gods. Second, most information on Project Camelot has thus far been of a newspaper variety; and professional men are not in a habit of criticizing colleagues on the basis of such information. Third, many social scientists doubtless see nothing wrong or immoral in the Project Camelot designs. They are therefore more likely to be either confused or angered at the Latin American response than at the directors of Project Camelot. (At the time of the blowup, Camelot people spoke about the "Chilean mess" rather than the "Camelot mess.")

The directors of Project Camelot did not "classify" research materials, so that there would be no stigma of secrecy. They also tried to hire, and even hired away from academic positions, people well known and respected for their independence of mind. The difficulty is that even though the stigma of secrecy was formally erased, it remained in the attitudes of many of the employees and would-be employees of Project Camelot. They unfortunately thought in terms of secrecy, clearance, missions, and the rest of the professional nonsense that so powerfully afflicts the Washington scientific as well as political ambience.

Further, it is apparent that Project Camelot had much greater difficulty hiring a full-time staff of high professional competence, than in getting part-time, summertime, weekend, and sundry assistance. Few established figures in academic life were willing to surrender the advantages of their positions for the risks of the project.

One of the cloudiest aspects of Project Camelot is the role of American University. Its actual supervision of the contract appears to have begun and ended with the 25 per cent overhead on those parts of the contract that a university receives on most federal grants. Thus, while there can be no question as to the "concern and disappointment" of President Hurst R. Anderson of the American University over the demise of Project Camelot, the reasons for this regret do not seem to extend beyond the formal and the financial. No official at American University appears to have been willing to make any statement of responsibility, support, chagrin, opposition, or anything else related to the project. The issues are indeed momentous, and must be faced by all universities at which government-sponsored research is conducted: the amount of control a university has over contract work; the role of university officials in the distribution of funds from grants; the relationships that ought to be established once a grant is issued. There is also a major question concerning project directors: Are they members of the faculty, and, if so, do they have necessary teaching responsibilities and opportunities for tenure as do other faculty members?

The difficulty with American University is that it seems to be remarkably unlike other universities in its permissiveness. The Special Operations Research Office received neither guidance nor support from university officials. From the outset, there seems to have been a "gentleman's agreement" not to inquire or interfere in Project Camelot, but simply to serve as some sort of camouflage. If American University were genuinely autonomous it might have been able to lend highly supportive aid to Project Camelot during the crisis months. As it is, American University maintained an official silence which preserved it from more congressional or executive criticism. This points up some serious flaws in its administrative and financial policies.

The relationship of Camelot to SORO represented a similarly muddled organizational picture. The director of Project Camelot was nominally autonomous and in charge of an organization surpassing in size and importance the overall SORO operation. Yet at the critical point the organizational blueprint served to protect SORO and sacrifice what nominally was its limb. That Camelot happened to be a vital organ may have hurt, especially when Congress blocked the transfer of unused Camelot funds to SORO.

Military
Military reaction to the cancellation of Camelot varied. It should be borne in mind that expenditures on Camelot were minimal in the Army's overall budget, and that most military leaders are skeptical to begin with about the worth of social science research. So there was no open protest about the demise of Camelot. Those officers who have a positive attitude toward social science materials, or are themselves trained in the social sciences, were dismayed. Some had hoped to find "software" alternatives to the "hardware systems" approach applied by the Secretary of Defense to every military-political contingency. These officers saw the attack on Camelot as a double attack—on their role as officers and on their professional standards. But the Army was so clearly treading in new waters that

it could scarcely jeopardize the entire structure of military research to preserve one project. This very inability or impotence to preserve Camelot—a situation threatening to other governmental contracts with social scientists—no doubt impressed many armed forces officers.

The claim is made by the Camelot staff (and various military aides) that the critics of the project played into the hands of those sections of the military predisposed to veto any social science recommendations. Then why did the military offer such a huge support to a social science project to begin with? Because $6,000,000 is actually a trifling sum for the Army in an age of a multibillion dollar military establishment. The amount is significantly more important for the social sciences, where such contract awards remain relatively scarce. Thus, there were different perspectives of the importance of Camelot: an Army view which considered the contract as one of several forms of "software" investment; a social science perception of Project Camelot as the equivalent of the Manhattan Project.

WAS PROJECT CAMELOT WORKABLE?

While most public opposition to Project Camelot focused on its strategy and timing, a considerable amount of private opposition centered on more basic, though theoretical, questions: Was Camelot scientifically feasible and ethically correct? No public document or statement contested the possibility that, given the successful completion of the data-gathering, Camelot could have, indeed, established basic criteria for measuring the level and potential for internal war in a given nation. Thus, by never challenging the feasibility of the work, the political critics of Project Camelot were providing backhanded compliments to the efficacy of the project.

But much more than political considerations are involved. It is clear that some of the most critical problems presented by Project Camelot are scientific. Although for an extensive analysis of Camelot, the reader would, in fairness, have to be familiar with all its documents, salient general criticisms can be made without a full reading.

The research design of Camelot was from the outset plagued by ambiguities. It was never quite settled whether the purpose was to study counterinsurgency possibilities, or the revolutionary process. Similarly, it was difficult to determine whether it was to be a study of comparative social structures, a set of case studies of single nations "in depth," or a study of social structure with particular emphasis on the military. In addition, there was a lack of treatment of what indicators were to be used, and whether a given social system in Nation A could be as stable in Nation B.

In one Camelot document there is a general critique of social science for failing to deal with social conflict and social control. While this in itself is admirable, the tenor and context of Camelot's documents make it plain that a "stable society" is considered the norm no less than the desired outcome. The "breakdown of social order" is spoken of accusatively. Stabilizing agencies in developing areas are presumed to be absent. There is no critique of U.S. Army policy in developing areas because the Army is presumed to be a stabilizing agency. The research formulations always assume the legitimacy of Army tasks—"if the U.S. Army is to perform effectively its parts in the U.S. mission of counter-insurgency it must recognize that insurgency represents a breakdown of social order. . . ." But such a proposition has never been doubted—by Army officials or anyone else. The issue is whether such breakdowns are in the nature of the existing system or a product of conspiratorial movements.

The use of hygienic language disguises the antirevolutionary assumptions under a cloud of power-puff declarations. For example, studies of Paraguay are recommended "because trends in this situation [the Stroessner regime] may also render it 'unique' when analyzed in terms of the transition from 'dictatorship' to political stability." But to speak about changes from dictatorship to stability is an obvious ruse. In this case, it is a tactic to disguise the fact that Paraguay is one of the most vicious, undemocratic (and like most dictatorships, stable) societies in the Western Hemisphere.

These typify the sort of hygienic sociological premises that do not have scientific purposes. They illustrate the confusion of commitments within Project Camelot. Indeed, the very absence of emotive words such as "revolutionary masses," "communism," "socialism," and "capitalism" only serves to intensify the discomfort one must feel on examination of the documents—since the abstract vocabularly disguises, rather than resolves, the problems of international revolu-tion. To have used clearly political rather than military language would not "justify" governmental support. Furthermore, shabby assumptions of academic conventionalism replaced innovative orientations. By adopting a systems approach, the problematic, open-ended aspects of the study of revolutions were largely omitted; and the design of the study became an oppressive curb on the study of the problems inspected.

This points up a critical implication for Camelot (as well as other projects). The importance of the subject being researched does not per se determine the importance of the project. A sociology of large-scale relevance and reference is all to the good. It is important that scholars be willing to risk something of their shaky reputations in helping resolve major world social problems. But it is no less urgent that in the process of addressing major problems, the autonomous character of the social science disciplines—their own criteria of worthwhile scholarship—should not be abandoned. Project Camelot lost sight of this "autonomous" social science character.

It never seemed to occur to its personnel to inquire into the desirability for successful revolution. This is just as solid a line of inquiry as the one stressed—the conditions under which revolutionary movements will be able to overthrow a government. Furthermore, they seem not to have thought about inquiring into the role of the United States in these countries. This points up the lack of symmetry. The problem should have been phrased to include the study of "us" as well as "them." It is not possible to make a decent analysis of a situation unless one takes into account the role of all the different people and groups involved in it; and there was no room in the design for such contingency analysis.

In discussing the policy impact on a social science research project, we should not overlook the difference between "contract" work and "grants." Project Camelot commenced with the U.S. Army; that is to say, it was initiated for a practical purpose determined by the client. This differs markedly from the typical academic grant in that its sponsorship had "built-in" ends. The scholar usually *seeks* a grant; in this case the donor, the Army, promoted its own aims. In some measure, the hostility for Project Camelot may be an unconscious reflection of this distinction—a dim feeling that there was something "non-academic," and certainly not disinterested, about Project Camelot, irrespective of the quality of the scholars associated with it.

THE ETHICS OF POLICY RESEARCH

The issue of "scientific rights" versus "social myths" is perennial. Some maintain that the scientist ought not penetrate beyond legally or morally sanctioned limits, and others argue that such limits cannot exist for science. In treading on the sensitive issue of national sovereignty, Project Camelot reflects the generalized dilemma. In deference to intelligent researchers, in recognition of them as scholars, they should have been invited by Camelot to air their misgivings and qualms about government (and especially Army-sponsored) research—to declare their moral conscience. Instead, they were mistakenly approached as skillful, useful, potential employees of a higher body, subject to an authority higher than their scientific calling.

What is central is not the political motives of the sponsor, for social scientists were not being enlisted in an intelligence system for "spying" purposes. But given their professional standing, their great sense of intellectual honor and pride, they could not be "employed" without proper deference for their stature. Professional authority should have prevailed from beginning to end with complete command of the right to thrash out the moral and political dilemmas as researchers saw them. The Army, however respectful and protective of free expression, was "hiring help" and not openly and honestly submitting a problem to the higher professional and scientific authority of social science.

The propriety of the Army to define and delimit all questions, which Camelot should have had a right to examine, was never placed in doubt. This is a tragic precedent; it reflects the arrogance of a consumer of intellectual merchandise. And this relationship of inequality corrupted the lines of authority and profoundly limited the autonomy of the social scientists involved. It became clear that the social scientist savant was not so much functioning as an applied social scientist as he was supplying information to a powerful client.

The question of who sponsors research is not nearly so decisive as the question of ultimate use of such information. The sponsorship of a project, whether by the United States Army or the Boy Scouts of America, is by itself neither good nor bad. Sponsorship is good or bad only insofar as the intended outcomes can be predetermined and the parameters of those intended outcomes tailored to the sponsor's expectations. Those social scientists critical of the project never really denied its freedom and independence, but questioned instead the purpose and character of its intended results.

It would be a gross oversimplification, if not an out right error, to assume that the theoretical problems of Project Camelot derive from any reactionary character of the project designers. The director went far and wide to select a group of men for the advisory board, the core planning group, the summer study group, and the various conference groupings, who in fact were more liberal in their orientations than any random sampling of the sociological profession would likely turn up.

However, in nearly every page of the various working papers, there are assertions that clearly derive from American military policy objectives rather than scientific method. The steady assumption that internal warfare is damaging disregards the possibility that a government may not be in a position to take actions either to relieve or improve mass conditions, or that such actions as are contemplated may be more concerned with reducing conflict than with improving conditions. The added statements about the United States Army and its "important mission in the positive and constructive aspects of nation building . . ." assume the reality of such a function in an utterly unquestioning and unconvincing form. The first rule of the scientific game is not to make assumptions about friends and enemies in such a way as to promote the use of different criteria for the former and the latter.

The story of Project Camelot was not a confrontation of good versus evil. Obviously, not all men behaved with equal fidelity or with equal civility. Some men were weaker than others, some more callous, and some more stupid. But all of this is extrinsic to the heart of the problem of Camelot: what are and are not the legitimate functions of a scientist?

In conclusion, two important points must be clearly kept in mind and clearly apart. First, Project Camelot was intellectually and, from my own perspective, ideologically unsound. However, and more significantly, Camelot was not cancelled because of its faulty intellectual approaches. Instead, its cancellation came as an act of government censorship, and an expression of the contempt for social science so prevalent among those who need it most. Thus it was political expedience, rather than its lack of scientific merit, that led to the demise of Camelot because it threatened to rock State Department relations with Latin America.

Second, giving the State Department the right to screen and approve government-funded social science research projects on other countries, as the President has ordered, is a supreme act of censorship. Among the agencies that grant funds for such research are the National Institutes of Mental Health, the National Science Foundation, the National Aeronautics and Space Agency, and the Office of Education. Why should the State Department have veto power over the scientific pursuits of men and projects funded by these and other agencies in order to satisfy the policy needs—or policy failures—of the moment? President Johnson's directive is a gross violation of the autonomous nature of science.

We must be careful not to allow social science projects with which we may vociferously disagree on political and ideological grounds to be decimated or dismantled by government fiat. Across the ideological divide is a common social science understanding that the contemporary expression of reason in politics today is applied social science, and that the cancellation of Camelot, however pleasing it may be on political grounds to advocates of a civilian solution to Latin American affairs, represents a decisive setback for social science research.

PROJECT CAMELOT: A RETROSPECTIVE EVALUATION

As in all major events, the passage of time does not so much diminish interests as it alters perspectives. Issues have arisen that will occupy and preoccupy the attention of social scientists and policy-makers for years to come. Here we can only allude to some of the new perspectives that have emerged in the wake of Project Camelot.

We shall now concentrate on three points—each of which has come up quite frequently in correspondence and conversations on Project Camelot. These may not be the central issues for the public at large, but they certainly appear to be central for the social science community.

First, a big issue is whether the social scientist should work for the government (or at least for certain agencies within the government). In our terms, this is the conflict between "selling out" on one side and "copping out" on the other. This conflict can only be resolved by a firm concept of *autonomy*—both organizational and ideological. In a world of power, it seems to be more sober to develop countervailing modalities of power than to huff and puff at the walls of the national sovereignty. At this level, the trouble has been that social science organizations too often are used as clearinghouses for "trustworthy"scholars, while these same organizations make far too few demands upon federal agencies. At times, it appears as if the leadership of social scientific organizations still does not believe that the successes of the social sciences are real. Having been reared in a period of relative deprivation for the social sciences, the social scientists view all funds as big and all projects as wonderful. Perhaps if we were to realize that the social sciences are no longer at the stage of primitive accumulation, we might be able to resolve this dilemma of selling out versus copping out.

Second, some critics of Camelot are vigorous in affirming the right of the State Department to censor projects of a social science nature. They say that the problem is not one of substance but of subjects; that is, who is in charge of these programs? I believe this to be an irrelevant consideration. The need of the moment is not for more liberal-minded censors (although it may be for more liberal attitudes in general) but for an end to censorship as such, benign or malignant. To paraphrase a thought from the late Bernard Shaw: censorship, mild or severe, is severe. The problems presented in the design of Project Camelot cannot be resolve by presidential fiat or administrative edict but only by the constant checking and cross-checking that define the methods of social science research.

Third, other critics of Camelot wish to place a moratorium on social science work for or under federal sponsorship. It is my view that a less drastic, but perhaps far more effective, way of gaining respect for the social sciences would be an across-the-board change in the format of the higher arts of grantmanship:

a. The need for more grants (scientifically initated research) and fewer contracts (agency-initiated research).

b. The need for a financial pool arrangement; that is, on every grant received there should be a portion set aside (preferably under the supervision of either the university or the social science institute processing grants) for *free research* unconnected with the grant—and disbursed without regard to either the disburser or the recipient of the grant.

c. The need for more emphasis on individuals and less on collectivities. The great big grants given to teams may have so many dysfunctional by-products (the creation of new bureaucratic substructures, the mediocrity of the finished product, etc.) that it may be time for the social science agencies themselves to begin researching the shortcomings in team efforts (as in the past they did for individual efforts) and request, even demand, of federal and private agencies more concern and attention to the needs of the individual scholar.

Equation of policy research with applied social science in general is perhaps summed up by the word "instrumental." The assumption of those who argue on heuristic grounds appears to be as follows: *If all research conducted by scholars for the government is operational research and is subject to some form of control, then any research done for the government is subject to control.* We should deny the premise and therefore the logic of the conclusion as well. The somber implication that work done for the government is something other than scholarship raises doubts as to the credibility of social science research in area studies. Precisely this recourse to operational definitions of government-sponsored work may stimulate, rather than curb, subterfuge in assignment of funds and create a broad-scale suspicion (among Latin Americans at least) that even university-based research is not necessarily liberated from government-determined operational needs.

It is perfectly fair to expect that the division of federal agencies responsible for sensitive work be made as crystal clear as possible and with a minimum of embarrassment to our own personnel—researchers and diplomats alike. It is also the responsibility of the State Department to conduct foreign affairs in a way that will neither discredit our own people nor outrage the people of the host countries. It is also fair to expect the State Department to prevent the kind of executive agency rivalries that would lead to chaos and competition rather than useful information. But the terms of the presidential mandate under which the review board has been set up are frighteningly extensive. They are likely to inhibit not only the operational research represented by Camelot but also the kind of independent research—let us say, on the consequences of United States intervention in the Dominican Republic—that may be either noninstrumental or downright counterinstrumental in character.

The problem with Project Camelot is not exclusively political but methodological as well. The identification of revolution and radical social change with a social pathology is the final proof, if such were necessary, that the functionalist credo of order, stability, pattern maintenance, stress management, and so forth does indeed reveal strong conservative drives. However, a cautious note should be added: The fact that certain functionalists and systems designers employ their method for conservative goals does not mean that all functional or structural social scientists are conservative—or for that matter, that the goals of Project Camelot created a need for such a strict methodology. Examination of the documents shows that there is scant evidence of a direct linkage between functional analysis and ideological faith. Some men connected to the Project even revealed a somewhat Marxian methodological preference.

If Project Camelot has served to focus the attention of social science on the acute problems of the interconnections between organization and research, ideology and science, then its "unanticipated consequences" will have by far outweighed the discomforts and even the agonies of the present moment.

Clearly, Project Camelot, by raising in the sharpest way the question of the *credibility* of American social science precisely at that point in time when the problem of data reliability seems to have been resolved, is an issue of paramount significance. The coming of age of American social science has been a painful experience. But could it have been otherwise?

20. *Federally Sponsored Overseas Research: A Dilemma for Social Science*

MICHIGAN STATE UNIVERSITY (MSU) has been politically newsworthy, at least in a negative sense, only twice. The first time was the famous famine month in which salaries were withheld from university employees, including the faculty, because there was no money in the state treasury. The second time was more recent. A connection between the Central Intelligence Agency (CIA) and MSU has been brought to light, threatening to rock academia more profoundly than any single event since the rise and fall of Project Camelot. To be sure, the recent "scandal" affected university affairs more intimately, since it took place on the campus of a large university and with the collusion of wide administrative and professorial sectors, whereas Project Camelot was a direct government contract of autonomous characters—although there, too, American University of Washington, D.C., acted as a clearinghouse and broker for the study of counterinsurgency in the developing world.

In the 1966 MSU catalogue, President John A. Hannah indicated that "most

This study seeks to explain the general attitudes and responses of professional sources of opposition to federally sponsored policy research. It focuses specifically on the interrelationship between a single university and a specific government agency. It is aimed to shed light on problems of data reliability and policy credibility. First published, in a slightly abbreviated version, in *The Bulletin of the Atomic Scientists*, 22, no. 7 (September, 1966).

appropriately in these times Michigan State has a strong commitment in the international arena." The strength of this commitment is attested to and gauged by three editors of *Ramparts*, the liberal Catholic magazine published on the West Coast. Warren Hinckle, Stanley Sheinbaum, and Robert Scheer wrote an article for the April, 1966, issue on the MSU-CIA linkage that received front-page national coverage. Indeed, an anomaly of the magazine article is why it took so long for a press and editorial explosion to occur. In a report by Robert Scheer, published in 1965, and prepared for the Center for the Study of Demo-cratic Institutions—*How the United States Got Involved in Vietnam*—the same allegations and charges were made.

Several reasons suggest themselves: (1) the escalation of the war in Vietnam raised the news value of the original story of how the CIA was brought into MSU affairs. (2) The steady revelation of the sizable portion of the American professoriat in government activities, in such institutions as MIT and American University, has pushed to the forefront questions about the policy commitments of social scientists—both in theory and in application. (3) Finally, and not to be underestimated, is the power of a mass media publication such as *Ramparts* in contrast to a "scholarly" report.

There have been no substantive denials of the 1965 report or the 1966 exposé. True enough, James H. Denison, assistant to President Hannah, denied that his boss was the son of an Iowa chicken farmer and that police cars occupy excessive amounts of campus parking facilities. But the significant charges stand.

President Hannah's own belated "defense of the university" in April, 1966, scarcely shed light on the charges raised. His statement concerned mainly peripheral matters: the "public service" role of the university, the patriotic res-ponse to government requests, the "training and advisory" roles of the professors, the absence of "luxurious living," the "positive accomplishments" registered by the MSU-CIA project in the "public administration" field, and, finally, the counter-accusation that the *Ramparts* article was "an amazingly brazen, and regrettably successful, promotion scheme." Even if a president of a major uni-versity is not called upon to make self-critical remarks for public consumption, he could easily have made public the contractual arrangements which the univer-sity had worked out with the CIA. In this way, the public might judge for itself the truth or falsity of the more extravagant claims. As matters stand, the major and uncontested points seem to be as follows:

1. CIA personnel were hired by the university to help train Vietnam's police forces from 1955 until at least 1962.

2. Despite early denials, there is a concession from university officials that the university was fully aware of the presence of the CIA officials. This is seconded by statements made public by Lyman Kirkpatrick, former director of the CIA police training program in South Vietnam.

3. Art Brandstatter, head of the MSU School of Police Administration and an ex-colonel in the Military Police, began training Ngo Dinh Diem's palace guard.

4. Wesley Fishel, professor of political science, went to work for the Diem

government in 1954 as an advisor on government reorganization; two years later he became head of the MSU project.

5. MSU President, John Hannah, a leading state Republican, was urged by then Vice-President Richard Nixon to participate in the project—which officially was to be part of the International Cooperation Administration program of aid to underdeveloped countries. According to Professor Charles Killingsworth, former chairman of the Economics Department, this project was taken on reluctantly.

6. Ralph Smuckler, also a political science professor at MSU, who took over from Fishel, granted the essential correctness of the allegations, and indicated that the amount of money allocated the university from government sources was "only $5,354,352.75 in seven years."

7. Toward the later years of the grant, especially between 1957 and 1959, the CIA took a more active role. Not only were they involved in training secret police for the South Vietnam regime, but also took over the task of organizing Civic Action teams while functioning as "police administration specialists" for the university.

8. MSU had, as a matter of routine, advised the South Vietnamese on what hardware they would need. It was even established that MSU staff members bought a certain number of weapons on their own, although the number is in doubt.

Professor Fishel has accused the authors of the *Ramparts* article of a lack of expertise, a lack of honesty, and of being outspoken advocates of the Vietcong. But Fishel's own prognosis and predictions on Vietnam are quite remarkable independent of his allegations. As late as 1959, he asserted that the Diem regime "speaks the language of democracy"; that Vietnam is "one Asian area where communism has been rolled back, and rolled back without war"; that "there is little likelihood of a revolution against the regime"; and, finally, that religious issues may be important in European and American politics, but not among the Vietnamese.

In contrast to these statements, a conference directed by the same Professor Fishel produced an article on the International Voluntary Services (IVS), a "private organization" with clear State Department support, which included the following paragraph: "During the later days of Diem's regime, Vietnamese student and youth organizations were strictly controlled. The government regulated student elections and secret police infiltrated student and youth groups. The Directorate for Youth and Sports organized the Republican Youth as a political support group for the government; failure to join usually meant imprisonment. The Diem government was despised by the students for these activities, and the barrier of mutual distrust between the government and students erected at that time still remains a serious political problem today." The pattern of conflict and competition between the State Department and the CIA manifests itself. The additional irony is that the recruitment of American college students into IVS was encouraged by college officials and professors who earlier had performed vital roles in the maintenance of the Diem regime.

Rather than stress such anomalies, however, I should like to deal with the probable future of such projects—particularly the triple-pronged opposition that is beginning to emerge against those professors who substitute therapeutics for science, operations for application.

The foremost fact about the MSU-CIA project is its basis in therapeutics. It has little to do with either pure or applied social science. It has much to do with the manufacture and salvation of a policy, not with the clarification of the basis of action. This distinction between manipulation and clarification, operations and activities, prevents any meaningful fusion of policy and science. The marriage came to nothing precisely because it demanded unification of entities that are different both in kind and in purpose. The "policy sciences" demanded, as the cost of being politically relevant, a price few social scientists could afford to pay—those who would become members of the "new breed" had to transform themselves into operational guides for policy-making and decision-making, separating themselves from chances of success, from historic circumstances, and from worthiness of the objects pursued. Perhaps this helps to explain why the linkage of policy to science is no closer now than it was twenty years ago.

THE OPPOSITION

First to oppose any enlargement of the MSU-CIA type of project will be the conservative "Establishment" sectors of various social science disciplines themselves. Psychology, sociology, economics, and political science have spent between thirty and fifty years insistently and consistently asserting demands for autonomy and professional standards of social science work. The MSU-CIA project violates the drive toward autonomy—away from operational requirements and toward professional insularity.

The thrust toward policy definitions of social science, even of police activities in the name of social science, moves counter to this search for an autonomous base of operations. Such a drive is perceived by the leaders of each social science as a matter of self-interest rather than moral outrage against federal intrusion into scholarly activities. The drive within the social sciences has been toward professionalism, since this protects not only the mystique of a discipline, but each individual covered by the operations of the closed society. The MSU-CIA project represents an overt challenge to political science as a profession, since it replaces the standards of the closed group (the scientific community) with that of the total society (the governing elite).

Opposition by Establishment sectors of the social sciences to MSU-CIA types of projects will be further insured since many of the men engaging in such projects are themselves professionally marginal. Their career profiles are often marked by administrative rather than intellectual success. Or, not infrequently, they are men in a hurry to rectify past ideological misdemeanors. In organizational terms, many of the men engaged in shadow government work have continued to be professionally marginal in most social sciences. They are as a rule locked out of positions of professional power, and thus removed from the norms of the Establishment factions within each social science organization. They bear little or no loyalty to the university itself and often have low stakes in their professional on-campus activities. Political mobility serves as a way into powerful circles, and at the same time serves as a status payment for services rendered.

This new breed of social scientists—in the universities and in such places as RAND Corporation, Special Operations Research Office, Systems Development Corporation, and others—has become the keeper of the entrepreneurial keys to the policy sciences. By means of support from federal agencies, a new force in professorial power emerged to challenge such Establishment sources of funding as the Ford Foundation, the Russell Sage Foundation, the Social Science Research Council, and the Rockefeller Foundation.

The stage has been set for a conflict between old and new forms of social science financial props—a conflict which is, in some measure, rooted in the general federal competition between "old" agencies of power such as the State Department and "new" agencies of power such as the Defense Department. The aristocracy of the various social science professions has begun to explode vigorously against this new trend toward policy roles for professors. The motivational as well as the organizational reasons for the extent of this negative response are rooted in something short of pure principles. Clearly the policy-anchored intellectuals offer a serious threat to the hegemony of the professional intellectuals. This threat is not exclusively in financial terms; more impressively, there is a basis for fearing the kinds of dual allegiances which have historically been anathema to professional societies—particularly less secure ones such as political science, which tend to insist upon exclusive and intensive allegiance as a price of admission to the elite.

A danger in the reaction to the MSU-CIA project is that an extreme professionalism may very well stifle free research in unsanctioned areas. These policy intellectuals may be inadvertently the primary agents for the most severe restrictions placed on social science researchers. Social scientists can ill afford extreme internal censorship. The auto-censorship that may result from any extreme push toward the professional regulation of social research may turn out to foster greater problems for social scientists than the revelations that there are policy intellectuals in our midst. It is simpler to isolate a few individuals now than to regulate an entire profession. And it is easier to provide more funds for more social scientists than to create a government regulatory agency.

How are these policy intellectuals to be regulated? How is undue rigidity in a social science field to be avoided? The problem of throwing out the baby with the bath water will become increasingly evident in months and years to come, as "revelations" of other policy involvements on the part of social scientists are brought to light. Young scholars in particular will be compelled to make a needless reification: politics or professionalism, or, perhaps more excruciating, relevance without science or science that is irrelevant.

Much opposition to the MSU-CIA sort of project may emanate from conservative sectors within university administration affairs. Long displeased by the incredible network of mini-empires built by men within departments of social science, this latest incursion into the policy sciences by such "interdisciplinary" programs as the Office of International Programs may unleash a powerful effort at greater supervision and control of social science projects in the future.

The notion that any department or program at a university could achieve a degree of autonomy that would allow it to negotiate directly with a government bureau and enable it to build an edifice on campus independent of the established network of administrative controls flies in the face of university administration as such. The whole mythology of a university is tied to the traditional performance of certain roles which are nonfunctional in character. To destroy such roles, whether illusory or real, to make the university into a military training ground, would in effect enlist the university in a crusade that it cannot enter without admitting its self-destruction as a place of objective learning. President Nathan M. Pusey of Harvard has never fallen prey to this kind of easy funding—not because he is radical or liberal, and not because of Harvard's private wealth, but because he is a medievalist and recognizes the threat that government sponsorship with strings poses for the autonomy of that university.

Vital research remains a political necessity. But this must be broadly construed and individually determined. From reevaluations of the pre-Socratics to mighty questions of survival, vital research is not considered merely "useful" research. Vitality is determined by breadth of scope, quality of mind, and relevance to "eternal" human problems. It is ironic that "pure" research unconcerned with heuristics should have come down to the level of useful research unconcerned with purity. This should persuade us anew that great intellectual range and humanely based inquiry are the underlying points of vital research. The excessive utilitarianism of modern education is rapidly breeding intellectual salesmen peddling wares and touting their usefulness in the name of vitality. And it is possible to detect in the MIT refusal of further contract work for the CIA a more vigorous role by university officials than has previously been the case.

The third source of opposition to the MSU-CIA type of project, and the one that could be the most effective, is the federal government itself. Large sections of the policy-linked community fully appreciate the dangers of substituting patriotism for facts. Middle-echelon personnel are especially concerned with getting humane as well as plausible programs under way. Being a nation without a popular opposition, where we thrive on consensus and opinion polls, somebody somewhere has to be responsible for providing accurate information to government planners. The help of academic social scientists to this undertaking has fallen short.

If every possible source of opposition to national policy is systematically eliminated, the basis of opposition and the basis of reality will also be eliminated. There are men in government work who know this. Recently a top State Department official informed me that the most horrible thing for his research staff is to read opinions by academics that cater to what they *imagine* to be the desired opinions of the State Department. Therefore, instead of forming a cor-rective against zealous error, policy intellectuals take the lead in reinforcing established dogmas, thus frustrating possible lines of political change. The constant expressions of disappointment in academic performance expressed by government personnel seem largely based on the perception that academic social scientists are more concerned with placating current policies than in reformulating them.

Intellectuals have always been enlisted in special work during war. But during World War II the nation was united. Now it is not. Despite the fact that this is a reasonable basis of opposition to the policy mind, something is at stake that is not subjective or a matter of personal opinions. No matter what purposes are served by a contract given to any professorial team, secrecy in awarding, administering, or dividing funds violates the scrupulous integrity that must prevail if the dangers and risks of academic involvement with any government agency are to be offset. This is true whatever the wartime situation, no matter who the "enemy," no matter what arm of government is involved. The uses of social science by a body of men must be open to the view of the whole profession. In this way we may distinguish political usage from scientific findings every step of the way.

It is unconscionable to take or use monies "out of sight," to justify any uses of it as a private matter. The hidden, invisible character of the case at MSU is the product of either shame or fear that criticism of such involvement is unanswerable. In either case, the one point which the university professoriat and administration ought never to agree to or tolerate is secrecy in findings, in the uses of findings, in sources of funding for their discovery, or in personnel connected with them. The atomic scientists have protested secrecy in scientific exchange for a long time, because of, first, its absurdity given the current state of knowledge; second, the dangers of increased error; and third, decreased freedom of movement and thought for the individual scientist. Informed at the outset of the social effects of secrecy in research, we cannot find acceptable the "hidden project," which is not in the tradition of scientific, but rather of political practice. It certainly does not emanate from anything intrinsic to applied scientific work.

OBJECTIVE SOCIAL SCIENCE

It would be misleading and false to assume that only a question of personal and public ethics is involved in the MSU-CIA affair. Above all, the question of social science itself is involved. It is precisely in times of stress and under terms of duress that the worth of a science is fully tested. There is the same need for an objective social science when a political consensus exists, as during World War II, as during periods of conflicting values. Perhaps the social sciences are not yet in a position to make war less attractive, less subject to popular passions. Had the social sciences been as powerful in the 1941 period as now, perhaps the Nisei would not have been brutally detained in concentration camps for potential disloyalty. Perhaps the portrayal of Japanese as apes and monkeys could have been avoided, thus making the unleashing of atomic war less probable. There are many aspects of a war that deserve a critical and searing light—by-products no less than essential features. The total mobilization of a society is at the very least a dangerous act. What can perhaps lessen such dangers is the retention of elementary distinctions between science and policy, especially during wartime stress.

There is no need to accept the militarization of social science as the price of relevance. The notion of an applied social science is a meaningful alternative to ivory-tower and irrelevant forms of research; but no less is it an alternative to bestiality. The notion of application should not be viewed as an alternative to social science, but as an enlargement of social science. The purpose of science is clarification, not manipulation; and the purpose of applied science is the widest dissemination of scientific information, so that reason can command the decisions of the masses. The view that applied social science is the same as militarization of social science is a violation both of common sense and of the history of science and technology.

The Problems of Application

The notion of application in the social sciences presents its practitioners with grave issues. At an earlier epoch this was scarcely a problem, since the imprecision of the social sciences made any exact attribution to its findings difficult to ascertain. But the physical sciences have provided us with the meaningful guidelines. When, as a result of applied expertise, an atom bomb of devastating potential was manufactured, the physical and engineering sciences demonstrated their vast social capabilities. But, as D. F. Fleming and Gar Alpervitz have suggested, it was only after the post-Roosevelt American political leadership decided to use the atom bomb as a "demonstration effect" against the Soviet Union, as well as to put a quick end to the war against the Japanese, that the physical scientists became both aware of the problems they had introduced and alarmed at their own traditional political ineptidude. The quarter-century struggle between physical scientists and political elite for preeminence in the policy-making field is hardly resolved in favor of the scientists—but at least scientists from Oppenheimer to Teller recognize the political necessity, no less than the moral right, for scientists to perform roles as agents of clarification.

Will that lead to default in the applied fields? Hardly. There is no lack of application of basic knowledge in the physical sciences as a result of the consensus of most physicists against the use of nuclear weapons; so too, there need be no lack of application of basic findings in social sciences. But the conditions of application must be made clear. Obviously, they were not in the MSU-CIA project. The need is for open visible research, for competence rather than cops in determining meaningful research tasks. The need is for applied information to be based upon the most advanced research and theory, and not to fly in the face of evidence.

Practically speaking, social scientists directly engaged in foreign area research have the most to lose by an indifferent attitude about the form in which government contracts for social science are awarded to universities. If universities begin to behave as adjuncts to policy, we will have gone a long way toward the sort of relationship between social science and public policy that obtains in the totalitarian states: a relationship of government commands and scientific obedience to those commands. The creative tensions that have traditionally characterized the connections between science and policy will have dissolved in a final paroxysm of mutual reinforcement and mutual celebration. And at that point, the question will be the life and death of social science, rather than the life and death of any single misanthropic project.

The dilemma for social science in America, raised to new heights by the MSU-CIA project, is simple but devastating: at the very moment when the social sciences are becoming capable of resolving their traditional problem of data *reliability*, they are faced with the pressing problem of *credibility* of the social scientists. The plight of the basic social sciences is that after a half-century of more or less successful separation of public policy and personal ethics from the operations of their fields, macroscopic considerations have come back to plague them with a shattering impact that has redivided people and redefined professions. Each and every practicing social scientist must answer anew: Is he a member of a human science or of an anti-human science?

21. *Social Science "Fiction" and the Americanization of Conflict*

COMMONLY ACCEPTED political folklore has it that fascism failed to become respectable in the United States because of its inability, at least during the ascendant period of Nazi Germany and Fascist Italy, to evolve a form that could connect up with mass American experience. The rapid crumbling after Pearl Harbor of the largest social movement in which fascists took part in pre–World War II life, namely, the America First Committee, indicates how difficult it was for fascism to gain an indigenous foothold within the American system. Now, after Vietnam, whether as a result of ideology as such becoming Americanized, or of American society becoming more susceptible to ideological interpretations of its own history and destiny, fascism has been raised to a unique position of intellectual respectability. The preeminence in American society of an intensive militarization no longer permits either disregard or contempt for the fascist frame of reference—which is, after all, the perfect organizational counterpart of military determinism. The essential value, then, of *Report from Iron Mountain* (New York: Dial Press, 1967) is that in its sophistication it represents something meaningful despite hints of inauthenticity. It is a frame of

This study is an examination of an alleged federal report prepared by a group of social science notables, and geared to explain why United States policy must be pegged to a permanent war system. The analysis attempts to show how the distinction between fact and fiction in federal reports has tended to increase over time, due to the legitimation provided by social scientists and by the inflexible foreign policy positions taken in recent years. First published in *The Bulletin of the Atomic Scientists*, 24, no. 3 (March, 1968).

reference too immediately within our common experiences to be ignored by intellectuals.

I

Report from Iron Mountain is the title given to a Report of the Special Study Group of a major, anonymous, and probably even spurious organization, supposedly governmental in sponsorship, which was set up in 1963 to determine "accurately and realistically" the nature of the problems that would confront the United States if and when a condition of stable peace should be achieved. The task of this commission was supposed to have been to draft a program dealing with this extraordinary "contingency." We are told by the publisher's introduction that the commission must have been of the highest order for high-ranking men to commit themselves to it without question; that it worked regularly for more than two and one-half years; that the meetings took place at an underground nuclear hideout used by large commercial firms as an emergency storage vault; that the meeting place for the group was "located near the town of Hudson" in "Iron Mountain." Presumably the sessions were in fact held in New York state, and have only symbolic reference to Herman Kahn's Hudson Institute.

The *Report* reached the publishing firm of Dial Press ostensibly via "John Doe, a Conference participant," who brought it to the attention of Leonard C. Lewin, a free-lance writer, because "John Doe" felt the need for its widest dissemination among the American public. "Doe"—who may well be Lewin's alter ego—was convinced that dissemination was important not because he disagreed with the findings (he indicates his own endorsement of the major findings), but because he believed in the value of disclosure before the general public. If the document in question is legitimate, the publishers of the volume deserve substantial praise for incurring the possibilities of harassment and anguish in the future; if it is a hoax, then praise is due to the author for carrying off the show.

Before turning to the *Report* itself, it is important to examine the manifest reasons for prior failure to make the *Report* public. First, while the Special Study Group was not sworn to secrecy, the group nevertheless operated within the norm of secrecy—what is termed "confidentiality" by such units—a common-place in quasi-legitimate enterprises. Second, there was a belief that release of the document would raise fear and misunderstanding, such as that created by other reports such as the Moynihan Report and Humphrey's Subcommittee on Disarmament, which seemed to lend credence to the Marxist view that war production was the basis of success for American capitalism (perish the thought!). A third possibility, not mentioned, is that the sponsoring agency or contractor that commissioned the Study Group prohibited publication of the *Report* under the name of the men who prepared it. This would explain the reluctance of "John Doe" to identify himself—especially if in doing so, the other identities might be betrayed. Of course, the simplest and most evident explanation is that the document is a hoax.

The following speculations are predicated on the belief that this *Report* is important—whether or not it is "authentic." Thus, I will take refuge in Vaihinger's "As/If" formula, and treat the *Report* as real in that I believe it will have real consequences—much like Richard Rovere's report on the American Establishment.

The American context of mid-1963 must be recalled to see how urgent it appeared for major branches of the armed forces, the Defense Department, and even the executive offices to work out the contours for a Warless World. It was a period in which the thawing out of the Cold War reached a high point, and a period in which it seemed highly likely that test-ban treaties on the uses of nuclear devices would lead to a general and complete disarmament. Paradoxically, what lends *credibility* to the *Report* is this obvious concern and reflection of this 1963 context; what detracts from its value is its oblivious insensitivity to the 1966 context of guerrilla warfare, revolution in the Third World, and the deadlocks in the armaments control negotiations in Geneva.

And if the general context of this *Report* is credible, so too is the internal content. That is to say, special study groups are continually being formed on an *ad hoc* "privileged information" basis. There were such groups formed after the assassination of President Kennedy for the purpose of studying where breakdowns in communications between federal agencies take place. There are such groups studying technological needs of American industry in a Space Age. There are groups studying and recommending expenditure priorities in times of crisis. Therefore, whether the document in question is a hoax or not, the content and context in which it was produced give it high credibility. It is so persuasive that one may consider it a legitimate viewpoint of a legitimate group of men observing the present American condition.

The unnerving aspect of *Report from Iron Mountain* is that one could cull from it the thoughts of many respectable war-gamers. This fact, while frightening, is strangely reassuring: frightening in the sense that the implications of the *Report* could reflect on current policy-making, reassuring in that we are in fact dealing with a sophisticated document professing a genuine concern for peace.

Despite their professed intent, however, the conditions for peace considered are slightly less unthinkable than the unthinkable itself. If the *Report* can be viewed as a United States summation of the current international situation, it not only elicits support for a system of permanent terror as the stabilizer of present world order, but poses this as the only possible response to military struggle. And the scope of this stabilization process is not merely national. It would extend a fascistic peace around the world to comprise a global system.

The global nature of *Report from Iron Mountain* is the first truly intellectual response from a kind of extreme Right, on a scale and on a level hitherto reserved for the kinds of oracular wisdom usually issued from the international Left. Possibly, the document is an internally created myth—through one of the special working groups of the Department of Defense. Take, for example, the "Directorate of Doctrine, Concepts and Objectives" of the Department of the

Air Force. According to the most recent Directory of Government Resources on Foreign Affairs Research (a most fascinating library item in its own right), this United States counterpart to Soviet bureaucracy "contracts out a limited number of studies dealing with international relations to support and improve long-range military planning." It is also pointed out that "the completed studies, although generally unclassified, are for the Air Force and other governmental agencies' use and not ordinarily available to private individuals." Then too, the study might have been prepared under the auspices of the Weapons Systems Evaluation Group, which was functioning in high gear in 1963, housed as a matter of fact in the Pentagon and responsible directly to the Joint Chiefs of Staff. This relatively autonomous unit was absorbed by the larger cover organization IDA (Institute for Defense Analysis) in 1965, which may help explain the relative intellectual atrophy which seems to grip the final report issued. These study groups are merely noted to account for the labyrinthian nature of federally sponsored "behavioral research," and hence the obvious difficulty in even tracking down the mythic source of *Report from Iron Mountain*.

Speculation does not end with the question of agency sponsorship. Questions arise as to actual or potential participants. From the footnote references to the German language materials, for example, one must conclude that at least one member of the panel was conversant in the German language. This raises the possibility of men like Hans Speier or Paul Keckesmeti being involved in the group. Then the frequent allusions to the necessity of a "war system" for the maintenance of technological innovation strike very close to the kind of speculation engaged in over the years by Edward Teller and his coterie of advisors. The emphasis on violence, gaming, and conflict strategies for resolving problems raises the possibility that men like Oskar Morgenstern and Bernhard G. Bechhoefer were present at these meetings. The sort of economic analysis given, with a scarcely veiled attack on welfare economies, raises the possibilities that the dean of conservative economists, Milton Friedman, or someone of a lesser stature, like Henry Hazlitt, may have had a hand in the creation of these documents. In sum, one can easily think of ten times the fifteen men announced as being responsible for the *Report from Iron Mountain*; which perhaps makes it all the easier to accept the fact that it is the work of an individual.

If a fairly representative sample of men can be drawn up who might have had a hand in *Report from Iron Mountain*, there are also some strong indications that social scientists had a minimal role in its preparation. First, the document is made to read as if it were drawn up by defense intellectuals who are so deep in the mire of their heuristic craft that they are either unaware of or unable to use the main conceptual tools of present-day sociology or economics. Second, the strange references to the German writings of Gumplowicz and Fischer indicate an atrophied vision of conflict theory that is alien to the current spirit of the social sciences. Third, there are literary devices common to policy intellectuals but alien to academic social scientists. We are referred to "informed persons in this country" and "among thoughtful men," but never given exact references—an appeal to authority unthinkable to social scientists, but quite common to engineers of the soul.

Fourth, a tabulation of footnotes indicates that the *Report* contains little that one would call general modern social science. Four government or semi-government reports are cited. Four speeches of public officials. Seven general circulation monthly or weekly periodicals. Four references to defense literature (all to either Herman Kahn or Hudson Institute monographs). Seven classics or near-classics of European thought. Two references to social science disarmament works (both from Benoit and Boulding). Five references to the movies and newspapers. One reference each to mathematics and simulation, social science outside the disarmament field, and one unpublished dissertation. This final point decisively serves to indicate that the person or group drawing up the *Report* was marginal to social science, and mainliner only in fiction.

II

What we are confronted with, then, in *Report from Iron Mountain* is not an idiosyncratic document, not a document representing the excremental vision of a *lumpenproletariat*, but rather a major document in American intellectual life, probably prepared by a marginal intellectual(s). And if, with some justification, government sources might declare their disregard for its findings, at the same time the position outlined in the *Report* has clearly been more vital on the policy-making front than any other coherent body of ideology or agencies. This fact makes the importance of the *Report* hinge not on its authenticity, but rather on how far the blueprints outlined have already been, or are now in the process of being, operationalized.

What makes this document unique is not only the content, but the single-minded methodology that underwrites the approach. The absence of any doubts made manifest in the written *Report*, the instinctualist assumptions concerning the nature of human society and its many parts, the didactic flavor in its deductive reasonings, the taking for granted of empirical problems: all of this has a disconcerting element that cannot be overlooked in appraising the significance of this *Report*.

This single-mindedness is, however, the undoing of the document. It comes apart; it becomes a hoax precisely because it fails to withstand any empirical challenges—or even to appreciate where such challenges might emanate from. The *Report* has none of the elements of self-consciousness to perceive the inner strains and weaknesses of the political theory underwriting the various strategies being advocated. In fact, it could be argued that the very insistence on anonymity as a prerequisite to the "group's" unhindered pursuit of its objectives makes a serious dent not only in normal scientific procedures concerning freedom of information, but in its potential for being widely accepted as true.

Despite the great emphasis on the economic factors of war and peace, and even a bow in the direction of the importance of culture and technology, the most intriguing aspect of the *Report* is its psychology. Underneath the institutional and organizational analysis lies a powerful disposition toward an instinct-displacement theory of psychology. This provides a framework for a notion of peace as a set of "surrogates" and "displacements" for military violence. Violence is the constant of human nature in the profile drawn by the *Report*. It can only be displaced rather than destroyed, changed in direction rather than in substance. There is the assumption that in order to be rid of the "war system" one needs a surrogate for armed violence as such. The instinctual theories from James to Freud underlying this are too obvious to need amplification. As in the Jamesian scheme, one needs moral equivalents or nonmilitary equivalents for the military system. But the possibility that something other than instinct theory operates in human relations, or that something other than a displacement effect is required to explain different forms of human behavior, is never taken into consideration, or at least never expressed, in the *Report*. The possibility, then, of real change in human emotions is left out of the reckoning. This instinctualism serves the "study group" well at the level of heuristics, since it becomes a way to justify precisely the kinds of political myths and ethnic antagonisms which play such an important part in the displacement of what they have termed the war system. A stable peace must replace nothing less than this war system, which may be transformed into something more horrible than any of the past wars Americans have fought.

A related and equally unexamined premise of *Report from Iron Mountain* is the faith in the leader principle. Not only is there an abstract reliance upon a Paretan theory of elites, but more precisely a faith in presidentialism: the rationality of one supreme man. The spurious "letter of transmittal" to the group expresses the hope that its recommendations will bring on subsequent presidential action in this area. Part of the context of "realism" is bypassing any regular constitutional or democratic frameworks within the American government. This is made plain in its blueprints for a new War/Peace Agency, which would have the latent purpose of counteracting the work of the Arms Control and Disarmament Agency.

We propose the establishment, under executive order of the President, of a permanent War/Peace Research Agency, empowered and mandated to execute the programs described in (2) and (3) below. This agency (a) will be provided with nonaccountable funds sufficient to implement its responsibilities and decisions at its own discretion, and (b) will have authority to preempt and utilize, without restriction, any and all facilities of the executive branch of the government in pursuit of its objectives. It will be organized along the lines of the National Security Council, except that none of its governing, executive, or operating personnel will hold other public office or governmental responsibility.

In essence this document is naively asking the President to transfer his authority to run the country to the way the "group" sees fit. Nothing in the government approaches the autonomy they purportedly insist upon, except the CIA or the FBI.

It is not only an appeal to the President in terms of executive power, but rather an appeal to the President as Commander-in-Chief of the armed forces that shines forth as the essential basis for this kind of policy framework. Rationality in the system proceeds downward from a superior Being, superior in situation and in reason; therefore the appeal is made to the President. By making this direct appeal, by insisting on executive attention, the "group" also seeks to create a basis for its own organizational semi-autonomy, separate and apart from any other limiting agencies of government. The very notion of a directorate that "will be provided with nonaccountable funds sufficient to implement" its chores, and that "will have authority to preempt and utilize" without any restrictions facilities of the executive branches of government indicates the reliance on a model made operational by both the Federal Bureau of Investigation and the Central Intelligence Agency. Its self-declared rights to withhold information on its activities from anyone other than the President entails a style of politics that mockingly reflects a breakdown in the traditional "checks and balances" of American society.

The main type of expertise exhibited in the "group" report is in the area of macroeconomics. This is made clear in the central question it raises: What can be expected if peace comes? What should we be prepared to do about it? What are the real functions of war in modern society? Posing issues in this way calls forth economic responses. Here, as in general, there is an almost pleased acceptance of the fact that America operates in terms of Kenneth Boulding's "world war industry," in which approximately one-tenth of the national output is in the military sphere, and approximately 55 to 60 per cent of the federal budget is spent on military hardware.

The question then becomes: What would general disarmament do to the economic system? What would scrapping of highly developed occupational specialties in the economy do to postwar social adjustment? Here there is a strong anti-Galbraithian sentiment (not unlike that exhibited by the Left) that there is a limit to the power of social welfare devices to influence fundamental economic forces. The *Report* admits that Keynesian devices can provide new incentives in the economy, but denies that they can in themselves transform the production of a billion dollars worth of missiles a year to its equivalent in food, clothing, prefabricated housing, and television sets. The key is that commodity production reflects economic health; it does not motivate economic growth. Because of this, the group considers phasing out certain kinds of military spending with specific forms of substitute spending that would not in any way alter the character of the economy. But this in turn is said to rest on a recognition that not the economy, but the military, determines the American social structure, and therefore it is military need that has to determine the character of economic production. This is made plain when the *Report* speaks of military waste as being exercised entirely outside the framework of supply and demand, and thus providing the only critically large segment of the total economy subject to complete and arbitrary federal control.

. . . It must be remembered that up to now all proposed social-welfare expenditures have had to be measured *within* the war economy, not as a replacement for it. The old slogan about a battleship or an ICBM costing as much as x hospitals or y schools or z homes takes on a very different meaning if there are to be no more battleships or ICBM's. . . . Here is the basic weakness of the social-welfare surrogate. On the short-term basis, a maximum program of this sort could replace a normal military spending program, provided it was designed, like the military model, to be subject to arbitrary control.

The fact that war production is wasteful is precisely what enables the economy to be harnessed to the military system. What has to be maintained is the progressive nature of the war production system, without a progression to a military utilization that would collapse the entire American social order. This would be done through substitutes for war in the form of production for external necessities, such as potential threats from other planets or other peoples, which could, ostensibly, only be met through technological innovation and through continued waste in the productive mechanism.

While the kind of economic theorizing done is ingenious, it rests on presumptuous considerations that are not in fact intrinsic to sound economic policies or analysis. First, the relationship between economic necessity and economic luxury remains unclear in the *Report*, as in fact it is in real-life situations; yet it serves as the touchstone for its neo-fascist planning. The notion of waste is itself ambiguous, extrinsic to modern economic consideration of the nature or health of the economy. It may be true that there is considerable waste in military production, but one might just as well argue the notion of waste in secondary commodity production. Thus, the ascetic concept of waste neither helps overcome problems in the American economy, nor provides a model for any one type of spending in the future.

While it is correct to note that there are noneconomic factors which prevent an easy transformation of the American economy from a war basis to a peace basis, the existence of these obstacles in no way demonstrates the metaphysical need for a permanent war footing to the economy. It may simply point up the enormity of the challenge. Further, the options outlined in the *Report*—continued military expenditure or space expenditure—omits two central facts: first, space expenditures are already part of the military spending network. As a matter of fact, they are nearly equal to the amount of money spent for direct military purposes, *i.e.*, space expenditures are *now* approximately at the same level as direct military expenditures. Second, a whole cluster of solutions to economic problems built around the relationship of the United States and other advanced economies with the underdeveloped economies is left unexamined. The ability of these underdeveloped economies to absorb at least the amounts of monies now expended on war—what might be termed a Galbraithian option—is not considered by the drafters of the *Report*. They do not really take seriously the possibility of any structural change in the American economy that would enable it to survive while at the same time change its form in order to address itself to the problem of the widening gap between wealthy and impoverished nations.

The entire area of underdevelopment is simply left out of the reckoning by the *Report*. Their elite predilections were such as to lead them to consider only the most powerful and the most advanced societies as part of the global social system. Perhaps they consider violence so intrinsic to human life that underdeveloped nations are viewed as a simple extension of the major centers of a war system.

The *Report* further implies that perpetual scarcity can be dealt with only by organized violence. Thus scarcity and violence *explain* progress. Not only does this fail to match the historical case in explaining technological growth, but it also does not consider the extent to which increasing abundance becomes a new factor providing new motivation for human action. Can abundance be managed by a "war system"? Has technocracy, in fact, been so linked to conflict that any other options are ruled out? There is nowhere in the document an analysis of what would in fact happen if peace were introduced and events were allowed to take their normal course. We do not really know what the dangers are that the *Report* is designed to avoid, since there is no effort at proof of what those dangers would be. Instead, the argument is simplistic: (a) we have always had war; (b) if we give up something we have always had, things will probably become worse; and therefore (c) we have to find a substitute. But the argument that war is essential because it is historical represents a genetic fallacy, an assertion rather than a demonstration of inevitabilities.

Directly related to this economic assessment is a judgment on the nature of technology. The *Report* repeatedly asserts that the only way an advanced society can hope to achieve technological innovation is through the war system. The claim is made that society does not and will not accept the desire for knowledge unless it is connected to war. In point of fact, scientific discovery may or may not be used for warfare. By all research reports, it is an independent variable. To attach a premium to the world war industry system because it stimulates scientific invention is as faulty a notion as the fossilized belief that a slowdown or rollback of technology would increase the chances for world peace. This kind of martial defense of modernization is a false option to the Luddite spirit of traditionalism. Many technological achievements have not been tied to the war economy in causally clear sequence. Peacetime technology oftentimes gets converted to wartime uses. The airplane was invented for strictly peacetime commercial purposes. Only as a result of two world wars were its noncommercial uses made vital.

The same situation obtained for inventions such as tractors and threshers, which were invented for advancing agricultural economy. Only as a result of the war system were tanks seen as a possible military spin-off from the tractor invention. These examples can be multiplied indefinitely. For our purposes it is important to see that *Report from Iron Mountain* took for granted a causal sequence in technology which by no means offers an empirical warrant for the permanent war system.

Despite the supposed existence of hundreds of supporting empirical documents (which are not referred to, and which are perhaps only hundreds of simulation runs), what is surprising is that no significant evidence is cited in the summary *Report*. There is a lack of statistical information; there is a lack of stated options to the position adopted.

The need to manufacture a mythic basis for social order and social cohesion is so taken for granted that the science of sociology finds itself reduced to the social control of social deviance. We are told that:

". . . in the permanent absence of war, new institutions must be developed that will effectively control the socially destructive segments of societies. . . ."

This contrasts with what is well known in the literature of social change and development: on the one hand, a certain amount of deviance is not only advantageous but absolutely necessary in order to stimulate industrial innovation. On the other hand, rational perception of a given order is essential in keeping it just. But in the *Report* there is a devastatingly amateurish lumping together of disorganization and deviance, and assumptions that essentially nonrational needs must be given priority. It is proposed that the Selective Service System be used as a cultural upgrading for the poor, and as a form of social discipline for deviance. The precedents of the Civilian Conservation Corps and the National Recovery Administration Acts under the New Deal are plucked out to illustrate past uses of quasi-military units in order to prevent deviant behavior and to smash any form of political opposition at this group level. The younger and more dangerous elements of society are those who are potentially hostile to the political order. They have in the past been kept under control by the Selective Service System. The extension of this latent function is considered an absolutely necessary one, and quite feasible once it is clearly determined that there is an enemy waiting to destroy our civilization, that this enemy can function within the nation as well as in directly military contexts.

The general militarization of society *precisely because of international peace* is urged. The mystification of the world by polarizing the population into friends and enemies is insisted upon as the price of peace and nationhood. The introduction of even the "blood sacrifice" is considered necessary in order to maintain the vestigial earnest and the phylogenetic martial spirit of the society. The capability and willingness of a society to make war, its willingness to have its citizens kill and be killed, becomes evidence for the ultimate worth of society per se.

An illuminating aspect of the *Report* is its faith in a nineteenth-century anthropology that does not shrink from the implications of the theory of human sacrifice and the blood myth as the basis of social cohesion. While the *Report* treads lightly in this area, it does tread. There is nothing "satirical" about its understatements. It makes a most illuminating distinction between economic exploitation of a traditional variety and the stimulation of ethnic enemies of this mythic variety. The *Report* speaks of Negroes in the United States and South Africa as suffering from a traditional economic exploitation; but what the *Report* has in mind (and this is made clear only in the footnotes, not in the text) is what was called in Nazi Germany an "ethnic repression directed to specific sociological ends." When one tries to fill in the missing blanks and comes up with ethnic enemies, it becomes painfully apparent that if "natural slavery" finds a place for Negroes in a peace system, then sentimental or ethnic slavery may find, once again, a place for Jews as well—all the more, given the time-honored custom that could legitimize such a solution. And then, do we exterminate enemies? By guns or eugenics in a final "comprehensive program of applied eugenics"? Or do we breed them to perpetuate the needed racial balance? The *Report* does not make clear whether we have the task of controlling the master-slave ratio or "improving" the whole species. The difference is not small. For what is involved is an appeal to tradition in contrast to an appeal to mass murder.

This renewed interest in eugenics corresponds more or less precisely with the end of an era of Jewish celebration in America, and with the rise of polarization not only of pro-Negro and anti-Negro sentiments, but also, even within the Left and within the militant Negroes, of powerful scapegoat feelings, anti-Semitic feelings against the Jews. Once again, the *Report* is prophetic: there is a possibility of an ethnic enemy quite apart from the traditional economically downtrodden. The fact that the *Report* alludes to this, however gingerly, should certainly lead to a considerable amount of pause as to who the "chosen" of the American future will in fact be.

A favorite pastime of fascist theories has always been social ecology; what starts as "social ecology" inevitably turns into eugenics or the study of the selective propagation and disposal of the human race. The impact of eugenics has an important reflection in the literature of American Nazism from the times of Alexis Carrell, as it had under Alfred Rosenberg in Germany. The *Report* displays a strong spillover in this direction. It is pointed out that man's ability to increase his productivity of the essentials of physical life underscores the need for protection against overabundance. It is suggested that there are "regressive effects of medical advances." The rate of population growth is considered too expensive, whereas modern methods of mass destruction are inefficient because they have failed to keep pace with the population growth. Under such circumstances the recommendations made are as clear as they are perhaps implausible; namely, universal contraception, with the birth, continuation, and maintenance of the species controlled by artificial insemination, or the permitted procreation of selected people. This would be worked out by a selection of vital indicators of health. It would not be allowed to occur through randomized sexual activity. From birth control we are led to scientific maintenance of the balance of birth and death rates.

"A uniquely human system of population control must insure the survival, if not necessarily the improvement of the species, in terms of its relation to environmental supply."

Along with a comprehensive program of applied eugenics, there is to be an even more comprehensive program of sociological controlled functions; the leading function of which is to be slavery. The group flatly claims that in "a technologically modern and conceptually euphemized form, slavery may prove a more efficient and flexible institution" than it has ever proven in past centuries. And in the absence of any program of ecological control or programmed eugenics, which can only come about once peace is guaranteed, slavery might well turn into that peculiar institution which is the next best thing; namely, the separation of masters from menials, or perhaps of officers from enlisted men. This is because war formerly served the need to establish a proper relation between conquered and conquerer. But in a "peaceful" epoch, a reversion to slavery may be required in order to satisfy this drive under conditions of peace.

III

It is obviously difficult to resist the temptation of arguing with specific points in the *Report*. There are many phases of the program that require discussion and analysis, and aspects of the *Report* that in fact may indicate a need for a general overhaul of just what it is that Americans want out of a peaceful world. The *Report* has something for everybody—"humanists" included. There is an outlandish appeal for decorative aesthetics on anthropological grounds; weird claims that the Department of Defense is stockpiling birds in the expectation that insect life will overrun the earth after an atomic attack unless there is a sufficient supply of predatory birds on hand to offset this tendency. These and other points would certainly prove normal bedtime reading for those who take seriously their social science fiction.

Lost are the halcyon days of the period from 1960 through 1963. Many of the war-gamers went into a virtual eclipse during the 1964–1967 period. The sorts of arguments which shocked an earlier generation of scholars (such as those set forth by Kahn, Brodie, Iklé, et al.) have become so absorbed into the general consensus that the shocking has been turned into the commonplace. What was once distinctive has become part of the American operational code book. Indeed, with the rise of guerrilla warfare, micromilitary problems have returned and global-military ideologists have been eclipsed. However, the American intellectual community has always exhibited an insatiable need for distinctiveness, not only as a response to the special role of intellect, but more to the point, the special role of intellectuals in a policy environment. In the new context of this *Report* the war-gamers have become peace-gamers. *Report from Iron Mountain*—hoax or otherwise—is the first major result of the transformation of the war game into the peace game.

The peace envisioned and advocated by this anonymous "group" of scholars has in fact turned into something more nightmarish than the original premises on which global destruction in this decade were predicated. For peace is seen as coming, indeed if it is to come at all, only through the widespread use of quasi-fascist techniques. These include human slavery, political mythology, the widespread use of eugenics, and many cultural indicators used to characterize the fascist way of "life." The paradox drawn for us that must be faced is that the war game is allowed in an *open society*, while the peace game involves a *closed society*. The possibility that war and fascism may be related in the same way that peace and democracy can be related is dismissed by the group as being naive. Perhaps the most disturbing part of this *Report* is that the concept of democracy is left to rot as something irrelevant to policy formation rather than something that needs to be done away with in open combat.

The essence of *Report from Iron Mountain* is that for the first time we have an appropriately pathological American response to Maoist slogans, to the concept that social change is made by looking down the barrel of a gun. If Hegel could be turned upside down by Marx, and if Marx could be turned inside out by Pareto, there is no reason to doubt that Mao Tse-Tung could be turned upside down in order to create a "meaningful" form of social explanation of current American life. (Whether this trick could be carried out by Lewin is another matter.) This explanation of the war system in fact stares down the critique of the international Left by accepting the basic premises of that critique; namely, that America has become a military society. The search for the deterministic variable is over; its resolution is expressed in armed might. We are bluntly told that it is incorrect to think of war as an institution subordinate to the social system it is believed to serve. Rather, it is the other way around. The true magnitude of the present situation, the present turn in American life, is that the military system is itself the key defining variable in the social system. The military organization of life defines the present social system, and this condition is without precedent except perhaps in a few simple preindustrialized societies. This *Report* can be viewed as farcical only in that it assumes with equanimity the most hideous prima facie charges against American society. The person or group responsible for this *Report* scandalizes us by pointing out what we all know—that wars are not caused by international conflicts of interest; rather that the proper logical sequence compels us to state the premise the other way around—namely, that war-making societies require international conflict. But to be told the obvious is often necessary—particularly when what is prima facie truth is also prima facie hideous.

If this social science fantasy is to be believed, what fascism has in store for us is in fact a *world of peace*. This is the first time—that I know of, at least—that fascism has been correlated with the peace system. The European tradition of fascism has always been framed in terms of the values of activism, war, and violence, and ultimately guns rather than butter. The thousand years of peace spoken of by Hitler was always to be a consequence of *Pax Germanica*, requiring a hundred years of war to set it up. It was to be a consequence of a general military conquest of the world. In this *Report*, a fascist program for peace is presented for the first time as part of an already operating quasi-official network, as a thing already in motion and being innovatively Americanized. And only in the form of a program for world peace could it possibly be accepted within an American context. That this challenge has been so fancifully—and, I might add, at times brilliantly—met, should occasion all of us to think carefully about the kind of peace we want; and about what kind of peace would perhaps be in the offing if the war in Vietnam were terminated at any given time in the foreseeable future. To paraphrase the critics of Herman Kahn several years ago: Will the living envy the dead in the wake of an atomic bomb explosion? Will the devotees of peace envy the advocates of war in this world concocted by fascist utopians? These are questions not only for writers of social science fiction, but for social science as such. Mr. Lewin once edited a *Treasury of Political Humor*; he has now added to his fame by preparing this Treasury of Political Tragedy.

22. *Social Indicators and Social Policies*

THE FOLLOWING QUESTIONS form the core of any serious discussion of the worth of social indicators and a council of social advisors: (1) Can a useful national social accounting system be established? Will collection of such data assist us in determining specific national social objectives? It is possible to design a set of reliable social indicators? (2) How can we insure against violations of individual rights of privacy, given the nature of the data to be gathered? What safeguards might be written into this legislation to prevent the manipulation or use of such data in a manner not intended by the framers? (3) What role might state and local governments play in formulating, implementing, and participating in creating a national social policy? (4) Should data collection be a state, regional, or national responsibility?

These four questions and the many items within each, can be satisfactorily resolved only *after* a Council of Social Advisors is established, that is, only when some kind of social accounting for the nation is operationalized. Too often there is an anxiety ritual on the part of both political men and social scientists to resolve questions a priori, in such a way as to assure passage of legislation and at the same time reinforce the social science community as to the worth of a pro-

First presented as a statement before the United States Senate Committee on Government Operations, Subcommittee on Government Research, Washington, D.C., in June, 1967. The statement attempts to indicate the social scientific advantages of a federally sponsored council of social advisors, and at the same time points out the implicit dangers involved in the social indicators movement. Publication of the Senate Hearings are pending.

posed piece of legislation. But unless we are candid at this particular juncture, we can dampen the long-run enthusiasm on the part of legislators, and weaken the resolve of social scientists who already are profoundly nervous concerning their involvement with the government in the aftermath of various scandals and ineptitudes that have occurred during the past several years.

Many of the answers that we are searching for in common depend on the boldness of vision which would enable us to develop flexible legislative guidelines so as to resolve real problems in the social world, rather than pronouncements that seek to anticipate all problems of the future, and to unofficially resolve problems which exist at this time only within the narrow bureaucratic confines of policy-makers and social scientists.

The four questions outlined above can be separated into two different varieties of fundamental issues. One cluster of questions asks: Just what good for the American people would be served by the passage of the Full Opportunity and Social Accounting Act? And the second, another entirely different cluster of questions, is related to how this legislation would affect the methodology and procedures of two sets of people: policy-makers at state and local as well as national levels; and social scientists willing and able to participate in the formation of national social policy.

The first question raised is the most significant, since it addresses itself to the American public. We shall examine these questions in rotation, and take up the procedural issues in context.

On the question: Can a useful National Social Accounting system be established? We shall first outline what we mean by an accounting system. Generally, what this signifies is a credit and debit ratio enabling us to tell what the profits or the losses of any given enterprise are. Usually when dealing with profits, losses, and cost-effectiveness systems, we are speaking of arithmetic transformations of real wealth rather than qualitative indicators. In the case of a social accounting system it may not always be possible to work with arithmetic indicators. We may be compelled to work with qualitative data—systematic, but not arithmetic. Therefore the measurement of profit and loss might be considerably more value-laden or at least give the appearance of being more value-laden than would an economic accounting system.

To design a set of reliable social indicators to improve "program evaluation" is by no means impossible. Yet, since we are dealing with qualitative as well as quantitative inputs, this design is noticeably more complex than cost-effectiveness analysis in areas such as military procurements. I shall illustrate this point by reference to the field of mental health. At a purely quantitative level, we might say that often the prescription for mental health is the number of mental institutions available in the nation and in each community handling those people designated by psychiatrists as mentally ill. We find that we are usually led to solutions based on a notion of bigger and better mental institutions, when clearly this is not what is meant by improving the mental health of the citizenry. A true definition of mental health might be the number of mental institutions that become transformed into educational agencies or preventive medical labora-tories, rather than the simple multiplication of institutions for the treatment of those designated as mentally ill or retarded. In other words, to develop a reliable set of social indicators means to have a fairly undistorted notion of what Ameri-can national social objectives are. If a national social objective is greater mental health, then the reliable social indicators may be a *decline* rather than an increase in the quantity of institutional facilities available for servicing the "mentally ill."

In order to present the complexity of the situation, and to introduce an imme-diate methodological challenge posed by social auditing, I shall examine the definition of such an amorphous concept as "neurosis." On one hand, there exists the diverse work of men like Henry, Srole, and Opler, who are inclined to include large population clusters in the category of neurotic, while on the other end of the measurement spectrum there are scholars like Thomas Szasz, who tend to dismiss the notion of mental illness, or who at the very most would have a fraction of one per cent placed in the category of mentally ill. A series of measures can be developed in which some psychiatrists will consider ninety per cent of the American population as mentally deficient in one sense or another, while at the other end are scholars who conceive of less than one per cent of the American population as mentally ill.

Nor is this an isolated example. The field of alcoholism is strewn with the debris of therapeutically demonstrated theories that define all forms of drinking as latent (if not actual) forms of alcoholism, and insist that treatment centers consider the mild social drinker along with the habitual drinker in a broad cor-rective process. It may well be that a less severe and inclusive definition of alcoholism is required, rather than a wider use of alcoholic elimination centers. Indeed, it could be argued that therapy is easier when the definition of alcoholism does not include every sort of drinker.

Under such circumstances, the question of developing reliable social indicators is not separable in any way from determining specific national social objectives. Unless the value component in the thinking of the social scientist as well as in the demands of the society is fully realized and met, what we will have in the Full Opportunity and Social Accounting Act is a highly mechanistic approach whereby larger amounts of services for certain kinds of illnesses, and for certain kinds of maladjusted situations, are equated with full opportunity or with mental or physical health.

Penetrating this issue at its deepest level, we are confronted with the pheno-menon of the totally controlled society in which there is a perfect correlation between social deviance and alienation on one hand, and social integration and full participation in social affairs on the other. It is a curious anomaly, but one that we must take very seriously, that those societies, such as contemporary China, which insist most loudly upon their absence of social deviance and mental illness, frequently are those with a very high totalitarian impulse to regulate *all* forms of marginality. Indeed, the situation became reduced to its bare mechanical nexus during the Nazi epoch in Germany, when deviants and misfits were simply done away with hygienically in order to retain the imagined purity and full integration of the society. The total liquidation of deviant behavior, or the presumed absence of mental illness in a modern society, is by no means an indication of the general health of that society. It may simply be an indication of the general backwardness and widespread network of social controls. Legislation such as the Full Opportunity and Social Accounting Act would do well to guard against the possibility of taking a eugenic point of view as to what constitutes mental health, or a stringent therapeutic view of the normative features of American life. In other words, while this legislation could provide a major social accounting system, it must be careful not to encourage a framework which has so rigidified its normative assumptions that the very realization of the goals of this legislation would betray its lofty purposes.

The second large question: How can we insure against the violation of individual rights of privacy, given the intimate nature of the data to be gathered? is becoming a central federal issue. The most important safeguard in this connection is *publicity*. To insure individual rights of privacy we must guarantee the widest sort of publicity on those who use the data. Public opinion, through its lawmakers and judiciary, must make perfectly plain the licit rather than illicit importance of gathering the information. As for exact methodological safeguards, the legislation should include provisos for making public all exchanges of information between agencies of government. Therefore, if one branch of government, let us say, Health, Education and Welfare, or any of its subdivisions, like the Social Security Administration, is to turn over information to another branch of government, say, the Finance Department, or more specifically, the Bureau of Taxation, then transference of information must be solicited from the Council of Social Advisors. The legislation should include provisos whereby individuals would have to grant their personal permission before any information is turned over. Finally, even after the transference of data, the information must be returned to the original files, so that there is no general system whereby a single agency develops a superior cross-check file system over any other agency.

That there will be arbitrary manipulation of an enlarged data bank, that there will be abuses of privacy, we can have no doubt. There are already abuses, and certainly these will not dissolve. Yet the very existence of a Social Accounting Act might provide a channel, an agency, through which these abuses can be properly reviewed. At present we do not have any overall review board because we do not have a Full Opportunity and Social Accounting Act and, more basically, because the citizenry has not yet fully realized that there is a problem.

If the data gathered can be generalized, universalized, so much the better. The more information gathered can be linked to general stratification, ecological, and demographic variables, the fewer will be the abuses of privacy; to the extent that information can be extrapolated from individual survey data sheets, to this degree interagency requests for data can be handled in universalistic rather than in particularistic manner. An essential task of the Council of Social Advisors is to develop universalistic parameters, so that the information that is exchanged concerns not individual behavior, but rather aggregate data. In this way, a considerable amount of protection can be provided to individuals that is not now insured because of the absence of any rigorous universal standard or agency regulation for the dissemination and display of information.

The Full Opportunity and Social Accounting Act by no means should exclude the role of state and local government in formulating, implementing, and even participating in national policy. The very existence of a social accounting system could point up the need for further analytic tools to describe and disseminate intervening variables or independent variables that have pertinence at local, state, or community-wide levels. Social indicators would yield a good rough approximation of optimal and minimal standards for American community life. They would by no means replace the need for further data at microscopic levels. Rather, they could serve to provide a universalistic basis for asking the right questions.

This can work both ways: the national accounting system would depend on information gathered in every city and town in America to handle questions such as racial violence. If a data bank of the social accounting can be set up as a kind of a Dewey decimal system, such as any library uses, rather than as a strict balance sheet reckoning, those advocating a social accounting system would have a far stronger analogy to operate with than any now extant. This systematic division of labor can be broken down into ten large problem categories: race conflict, drugs and alcoholism, mental health, urban redevelopment, marriage and divorce, population control, poverty, arms control and disarmament, ethnic and religious friction, class transformation and bureaucratization. Each of these can then be subdivided into all sorts of subcategories; and within the subcategories, individual items of local and specialized interest can be isolated for further examination.

One might divide the area of mental health in this kind of way: the general category would be *mental illness*. The specific task of the social accounting system would be to develop statistical information on (a) numbers of people hospitalized and institutionalized; (b) numbers of mental institutions set up for the treatment of certain kinds of illnesses; and (c) the numbers of people who are rehabilitated annually, *i.e.*, made effective in terms of work activities; (d) the amount of recidivism involved in mental health care centers. The local government could plug directly into this by asking a series of questions relating to (a) services provided for mental illness in general hospitals; (b) types of professional personnel available in both hospitals and outpatient clinics for the treatment of mental illness; (c) variations in the definition of mental illness among different hospitals or different practicing psychiatrists, and so forth.

The difficulty in a social accounting network would arise not so much in plugging in state, local, and regional governments to national indicators, but rather in developing categories that can give some sort of worthwhile approximation of the social state of the nation as a whole. Only then can you have a tight fit between various sectors of society—so that the data at one level may become instrumental in stimulating findings at another level. The problem lies in developing broad categories that are useful at all levels, acceptable to all forms of social science, and not simply the somewhat contrived problem of state versus national control over social indicators. It might well be that the struggle between state or national control over the data shrivels in comparison with the struggle between maximizing personality or institutional variables.

This brings us to the last question—should data collection be a state, regional, or national responsibility? As has been indicated above, it may be that the question itself reveals a timid reading of American history in terms of national versus state lines of authority. Information, that is, scientific knowledge, is not the private property of any single level or sector of society. It can be generated within bureaucratic institutional settings; or it can be generated within two-person laboratory (or analytic) settings. Knowledge can be generated from the top down or from the bottom up. What we have to bear continually in mind is that the knowledge explosion is not a question of state, regional, or national responsibility. From a legislative viewpoint, the harnessing of this knowledge into a series of social indicators has to do with providing essential information to those sectors of society that until the present time have been either unable or unwilling to make use of basic social science services because they have not been exposed to basic social science inputs in their decision-making.

As I have discussed elsewhere,[1] there is a powerful tendency of the wealthy sectors in American society, particularly industry and government, to be high users of social science, while the impoverished sectors of society—racial minorities, voluntary organizations, ethnic and religious groups, etc., make little if any use of social science information.

The ultimate purpose of the kind of social accounting for the nation that we are here considering would be to provide a great equalizer. Social accounting must be transformed into social opportunity. This legislation should allow all sectors of society to dip into a common pool of knowledge, so that the present esoteric-exoteric dualism, which is in reality a split between the more and the less affluent sectors of society, finally can be dissolved. This is the paramount question to be faced—and not whether data collection should be conducted at a state or a national level. Once a piece of social welfare legislation such as we are considering gets under way, this kind of parochial consideration will become academic. The more significant consideration will be how to operationalize the widest possible use of social science data among all sectors of American society with the least possible negative effects.

The challenges of the full opportunity act are manifold and grave. The passage of this legislation imposes a challenge on the legislators themselves. Once the social indicators are defined, there is an implicit obligation that they be used. This legislation should serve to minimize the present gap between the availability of knowledge and congressional action based on such knowledge.

---

1. Irving Louis Horowitz, "Social Science and Public Policy: An Examination of the Political Foundations of Modern Research," Ch. 18 in this volume.

The greatest responsibility is to determine how social indicators might be employed in the areas of foreign affairs. For example, there is strong evidence to suggest that the conventional bombing policies toward North Vietnam have become thoroughly dysfunctional, serving to reinforce rather than to smash the social cohesion of the opposition. Had we made use in the decision-making stages of available indicators in this area of conventional bombing—and I have in mind especially the *United States Strategic Bombing Survey* made after World War II, and the *United States Air Force Operations in the Korean Conflict* studies— then we might have been spared one more exercise in futility. Also, if the social indicators had been in full use, then we could have called upon the pre-World War II experiences recorded in the Maxwell Air Force Base survey, *Civilian Morale under Aerial Bombardment, 1914–1939.*

While this legislation may provide a useful tool for policy-making, it must be viewed as more than that—as a set of guidelines that should be examined not only in areas of relative nonbelligerence, but also in those aspects of American decision-making that come closest to the more intimate problems faced by the American public at the level of international conflict.

To think of social indicators as a piece of domestic legislation, to ignore the international ramification of social science inputs, would do a disservice to the purposes of the proposed legislation.

II

It is important for all those who support social science legislation to realize the limited nature of what is entailed. One gets the impression in listening to critics of the social indicators legislation that it has a necessary and almost infinite spill over into the realm of policy decision-making. As a matter of fact, this legislation is but a modest beginning toward the federal use of already available information. So far would such a Council of Social Advisors be from being a policy-making branch of the government that were it to become a problem, we would already presume a considerable amount of information worth making policy on.

What is posed by this kind of legislation at this level are a series of questions: Who gathers information? Who transmits information? Who uses information? Finally, who affects information at the level of policy? They do not involve anything like an overall transformation of government, such as might be implied by a systems design of planning, programming, and budgeting. The Council of Social Advisors would provide a way in which those qualitative aspects of American life can be explored and transmitted from the social scientist to the executive, legislative, and judicial branches of government, and back again to the American people as a whole.

Social auditing and a social council constitute a piece of populist legislation, not unlike Medicare and Social Security. The ultimate concern is the health, welfare, and peace of the American people. The question is too readily made into a matter of whether social scientists are to become respectful servants of power or whether they can retain their integrity. The presumption is that social scientists have an unsullied integrity to begin with and that they lose their virginity by association. Even the harshest critics do not make assumptions about the social scientists' integrity—either as being there to begin with, or as being corrupted by association with governmental agencies. But even were that the case, the question of real moment is what the proposed legislation would mean for 200 million Americans and not just what it means for 8,500 fellows and active members of the American Sociological Association and their spiritual purity. That is the basis of any significant legislative action. Whatever their personal purposes in supporting such legislation, congressmen are officials elected by vast numbers. This legislation has to be perceived, in that sense, as a contribution to that public. What does the Council of Economic Advisors do for the American people? Basically, it supplies an annual presidential message, usually in January, telling the American people about the position in which the economy is. It tells the American people what the credit and debit situation is internationally for American currency; it tells the American people in what way funds have been allocated in previous years and what recommendations have been put forth for reallocation of funds in this and subsequent years; it gives Americans a means of measuring goods and values.

The purpose of the social indicators is to give the American public a corollary theory for the quality of life. Indicators will not say how much money has been allocated for mental hospitals; but they might say, if the indicator were refined enough (and admittedly there are methodological problems here) how many fewer people this year than last year have been committed to mental insitutions. Or it might tell them to change *forms* of rehabilitation in the area of mental health. It might not tell them that the gross national budget is 55 per cent given over to warfare, but it would tell them, on the other hand, the social consequences of that war. It would tell them what the risks are, what the human costs are, and ultimately of the possibilities of peace and what steps have been made to gain that peace. It would be a form whereby many of the informational agencies of the United States government would at the very least be able to have some kind of cohesiveness and present a unified picture of the qualitative indicators of what the American style is in any given year.

The first main criticism—that economic indicators are relatively hard (although there are not a few economists who might even doubt that) and the social indicators are relatively soft—takes a highly prejudicial view of the relationship of qualitative to quantitative inputs in the decision-making process. What we find continually among social scientists, and especially among *nouveau riche* sociologists, is a worry over the reduction of quality into quantity. The definition of the good becomes "the hard," of the bad becomes "the soft." Any substantial effort to use qualitative information becomes, by definition, futile— things over which we have no control, things about which we are really not very clear anyhow. But even if we leave all of that aside, what is so astonishing is that one can take men like Friedman and other established, reputable economists, and they will argue identically about the Council of Economic Advisors, and economic indicators, and the presidential economic message in exactly the same way as the discussion has gone on concerning the social indicators and the Council of Social Advisors: Why should any one group of men be involved to the exclusion of others? Can they be trusted? Do we have enough hard information? Are not indicators ambiguous and confusing? Can we really entrust any social scientist to become a servant of power without at the same time losing his autonomy?

All of these issues worry the Council of Economic Advisors and were being discussed in the late 1930's. They became burning issues of the thirties. It was economists like C. Wesley Mitchell and Gardner Means who finally prevailed, who in effect indicated that the Council of Economic Advisors would neither solve the problems of economic science nor lead to a further degeneracy of that science, but only enable the economists to have information that they did not then have, and sources of financing the requests for information which up to the time of the formation of the Council of Economic Advisors were not legitimated. In short, with respect to point one, what is involved is a legitimation process. Social scientists would be legitimated in their requests and demands for certain kinds of information that they cannot yet get funding for. The legislators would legitimize and justify their use of information (and it should be pointed out that they already are inundated with floods of information; the question is its quality).

The legitimation process for the legislative and the executive branches would enable them to set policy based on a body of *bona fide* information. Policy makers must make decisions. The question is now, as always, on the basis of what information? At present there is no compelling force to use reason in the process of relying on this information. A serious problem is whether legislators will really use such information, or abuse it. Or (as is more likely), will they use it selectively? Needless to say, this problem cannot be liquidated by a Council of Social Advisors any more than Republican economic philosophy can be liquidated by the Council of Economic Advisors. It can put a great deal of pressure on various branches of government to maximize their uses of the best kind of information, something which they can now completely disregard at their will —and as a matter of fact, they do.

My own evaluation of the United States government is involved here, and that evaluation runs to this: We live in a country which can best be described as genteel tyranny. By that I mean that we have a benevolent but concentrated system which harms very few people, which does not go out of its way to hurt anybody it can avoid hurting. On the other hand, it can no longer gain legitimation simply through mass appeal as in the nineteenth century. That is to say, it cannot rely and has not relied too much upon *vox populi*. To whom, then, is that government especially responsive and responsible? That is where the issue becomes an issue of elites. Social scientists as an elite group have certainly not only responsibilities, but also the obligation to prevent the worst possible outcomes from occurring in a situation which at best is a difficult and even a nasty one. Under such circumstances, the source of legitimation for certain kinds of policy may very well be the social scientist. This may even lead to the restoration of a wider use of better norms and to a rejuvenation, a renewed energy in the popular masses, who would then be in better position to exercise not only their franchise but effective control over government. Their use of social science information would become legitimate for the first time, and the importance of that information would become known to vast numbers of people for the first time. At present there is a highly selective body of users of that information. The people who buy and sell this information are simply not the people of the United States as a whole.

The purposes of this legislation, therefore, are infinitely more democratic than almost any other kind of legislation now being recommended; since in effect it says, the people will decide. Admittedly, there are some elements of a utopian fantasy here. The democratic ethos has its limits. Yet it can be utilized, despite its limits, in a selective, perhaps even conservative way, as a form of organizational elitism such as is represented by an American Sociology Association or an American Psychological Association or the kind of private organization which is recommended should be tapped into widely. In that connection I call to the readers' attention that the very thing scholars say private agencies should be doing—namely, collecting information—has been done over the last thirty years by the National Register, which is part of the United States government, and manpower evaluations are so costly that they cannot be handled by any but a federal agency. To ask that manpower evaluations be the first order of business for private sources of funding is a retrograde recommendation. We already have a National Register performing this function, and it is a federal register at the same time.

I shall now turn to a second major issue: What are the social indicators on which advice would have to be given? Here I find myself very much in tune with what the critics maintain. We have a set of indicators that are now likely to lead to the formation of policy. Yet the shabby informational situation with respect to decisions and policies on the aged, racial problems and the Negroes' plight, and the demographic underreporting in the census could be improved. But we do not get these kinds of recommendations. Instead we are merely told of the Herculean nature of the task. The implicit assumption is that if anybody else ever found out how shabby the information really is, not only will it be unusable, but we may be laughed at. Therefore, it is safer to remain the way we are now, even with the shabby inputs. Hopefully, through private effort and the initiative of individual scholars, both of which have failed miserably in the fifty years of sociological history, we will eventually be calling upon these groups to bail out of these problems. By use of an attitude survey, we might find that you can establish rates of mental illness up to 90 per cent. But if you use a structural criterion—for example, the number of man-hours lost on a job—in defining mental illness, one might well conclude with a mental illness rate that falls below one per cent. What kind of data are we going to use? The data that tell us that 90 per cent of the people in the United States of America are mad, or data that tell us that less than one per cent of the American people are mad? The appeal to the American Sociological Association to do this kind of work is not only mistaken, but even has misanthropic implications, since the assumption is that this kind of body is somehow a humane agency interested in the general welfare.

Finally, I wish to express my own basic misgivings. But rather than use the term "integrity" as they do, I prefer to speak of academic autonomy as it relates to social science self-respect and self-development. Social science needs autonomy, freedom of inquiry being its most vital outcome. Any incursion upon that autonomy in the name of Big Sociology, or Important Sociology, or even to serve government operations, would constitute a direct assault on the very nature and the very basis of the social science itself. Given that, I certainly support the idea, not so much of academic integrity, because I think that is a separate, general question related to the nature of the university, but rather as a matter of the need for social science autonomy.

How does one go about protecting autonomy? Where have the incursions on autonomy been most clearly exhibited in the past? Here the question of academic autonomy is oftentimes used not so much as a defense of the integrity or autonomy of the field, but rather as a preserver of the parochialism of the field at any given moment, as a defense of the established body of wisdom in that field against any incursion upon it. The real assault upon scientific integrity, upon intellectual autonomy, rarely has come from without. It always comes from within the profession. The most reactionary groups are always those groups protecting established knowledge. They are most concerned about the prevention of genuine autonomous development and the maintenance of a system, a network of ideas; so that, for instance, functionalism in sociology survived twenty years after it had been absolutely emasculated by the philosophy of science. The problem of integrity is rarely if ever a problem from without, but rather a problem from within sociology. Therefore the further assertion that a Council of Social Advisors would somehow represent an incursion upon that autonomy would be hard to demonstrate, even in connection with other groups such as the Council of Economic Advisors. I do not, for example, notice a breakdown in the moral fiber of American economists at this point. The economic members of the social science community are not crying shamefacedly because of the Council of Economic Advisors. Quite the contrary: a certain amount of respect has accrued to them precisely because of their linkage to policy questions. This same kind of respect would be directed at sociologists if they should dare a similar venture.

Beyond that point is a major issue: How ought social science information be validated? Is it always to be legitimized by professional peers, or can there be appeals to outside sources of legitimacy? For example, there are many members of the sociological community who gain legitimation by the fact that there is a student radical movement. There are members of the social science community who gain legitimation in market terms of the volume of their book sales. There are members of the social science community who gain legitimation by "executive means," that is, the number of boards they sit on in connection with grants. There are members of the profession who are legitimized by their editorial advice and services. In other words, integrity and autonomy do not constitute a simple question of having a committee of peers approve work done in order to have it published in approved journals; rather, it is a widespread network of activities. What the call for social indicators represents is a call for further expanding the autonomous activities of social science to the area of government. This, too, becomes one more source of legitimation of the activities, behavior, and beliefs of the social scientists. The people who need this kind of legislation the most are precisely those who are not protected by the rubric of a confining professional society, whether that be a medical association or a sociological association.

The risk of capitulation is vital, and always present. There are right now many servants of power who are social scientists, but what should be appreciated is that the purpose of this legislation is not to drag more social scientists into government work, but to give those social scientists who are not in government work a role in the shaping of the national policy, and to prevent those social scientists in places like the CIA and the FBI from knuckling under. A strong line of connection between the academic community and the political processes, which does not now exist, could have a preventive function. It is for that reason, to expand the political relationships of the social scientist, and to commit the government of the United States to a more rational policy both domestically and in foreign policy, that I feel that this kind of legislation is desirable.

23. *Social Science Yogis and Military Commissars*

THE BONDS BETWEEN the government and the universities are . . . an arrangement of convenience, providing the government with politically usable knowledge and the university with badly needed funds." The speaker of these words, Senator J. William Fulbright, went on to warn that such alliances may endanger the universities, may bring about "the surrender of independence, the neglect of teaching, and the distortion of scholarship." Many other distinguished Americans are worried by the growing number of alliances between the military and the university.

I. THE SETTING

Instead of the expected disclaimers and denials from university officials, however, in recent months these men—from both the administrative and academic sides—have rushed to take up any slack in doing secret research on campus, asking that the number of projects they are already handling be increased. Arwin A. Dougal, assistant director of the Pentagon's office for research and engineering, has indicated that while some major universities are gravely concerned about academic

This study assesses recent trends in the relationship between the social sciences and national policy agencies. Using a case study method, similar to that employed in the examination of Project Camelot, the *Report of the Panel on Defense Social and Behavioral Sciences* is evaluated for its implications for present and future tendencies and trends in federally supported social science research. First published in *Trans-Action*, 5, no. 6 (May, 1968); reprinted by permission.

340

research for military ends, most universities realize how important "classified research" is to the national security. Indeed, Dougal has said that many professors involved in secret research actually try to retain their security clearances when their projects are completed. Rather than disengaging themselves, they, like many university leaders, are eager to participate to an even greater extent.

Symptomatic of the ever-tightening bond between the military and the social scientist is a "confidential" 53-page document entitled *Report of the Panel on Defense Social and Behavioral Sciences*. It was the offspring of a summer, 1967, meeting, in Williamstown, Mass., of members of the Defense Science Board of the National Academy of Sciences. This board is the highest-ranking science advisory group of the Defense Department. The meeting's purpose: to discuss which social-science research could be of most use to the Department of Defense (DoD).

The *Report of the Panel on Defense Social and Behavioral Sciences* throws a good deal of light on current relations between the national government and the social sciences. Unlike Project Camelot, the abortive academic-military project to investigate counterinsurgency potentials in the Third World (see Ch. 19), this Report was not inspired by government contractual requests. It is the work of leading social scientists who have been closely connected with federal research. Unlike *Report from Iron Mountain* (see Ch. 21), this Report can hardly be described as a humanistic hoax. The authors are known, the purpose of the Report explicit, and the consequences clearly appreciated by all concerned. What we have in this Report is a collective statement by eminent social scientists, a statement that can easily be read as the ominous conversion of social science into a service industry of the Pentagon.

Most of the scholars who prepared this Report have one striking similarity— they have powerful and simultaneous academic and government linkages. They move casually and easily from university to federal affiliation—and back again to the university.

Gene M. Lyons, who is executive secretary of the Advisory Committee on Government Programs in the Behavioral Sciences of the National Research Council (affiliated with the National Academy of Sciences), is also a professor at Dartmouth College. (He maintains, however, that he attended only one day of the meeting, and as an observer only.)

Peter Dorner, functioning through the Executive Office of the President on the Council of Economic Advisers, is also a professor of economics at the Land Tenure Center of the University of Wisconsin.

Eugene Webb, listed as a professor at Stanford University, is now serving a term as a member of the Institute for Defense Analysis, specifically, its science and technology division.

The panel's chairman, S. Rains Wallace, the exception, is president of the American Institutes of Research, a nonprofit organization that does research under contract for government agencies, including the Defense Department.

Other panel members—Harold Guetzkow of Northwestern University;

Michael Pearce of the RAND Corporation; anthropologist A. Kimball Romney of Harvard University; and Roger Russell, formerly of Indiana University and now Vice-Chancellor for Academic Affairs at the University of California (Irvine)—also shift back and forth between the polity and the academy. It is plain, then, that these men have penetrated the political world more deeply than members of past project-dominated research activities.

In addition to this similarity, nearly all of these social scientists have had overseas experience and are intimately connected with federal use of social science for foreign-area research. Yet, as in the case of Camelot, this common experience does not seem to produce any strong ideological unanimity. The men range from relatively conservative political theorists to avowed pacifists. This underscores the fact that patriotism and professional purpose tend to supersede the political viewpoints or credos these men may adhere to.

II. The Report

The Report itself closely follows the memorandum John S. Foster, Jr., director of Defense Research and Engineering of the Department of Defense, issued to the chairman of the panel. Foster's marching orders to the panel members requested that they consider basically four topics: (1) "high-payoff" areas in research and development—"areas of social and behavioral science research in which it would be reasonable to expect great payoffs over the next three to ten years"; (2) research to solve manpower problems; (3) project THEMIS, a DoD project for upgrading the scientific and engineering capabilities of various academic institutions so they can do better research for the Defense Department; and finally (4), broad-ranging government-university relationships.

Before commenting on the Report, let me provide a summary statement of what its findings and recommendations are.

To begin with, the Report urges increased effort and funding for research on manpower, in all its aspects; for research on organization studies; for research on decision-making; for increasing the understanding of problems in foreign areas; and for research on man and his physical environment.

Under "Manpower," we read, among other things:

In order to make full use of the opportunities provided by Project 100,000 [to make soldiers out of rehabilitated juvenile delinquents] both for the military and for the national economy, we recommend that fully adequate funds be invested to cover all aspects of the military and subsequent civilian experience of the individuals involved.

Under "Organization Studies":

Research on style of leadership and improved methods of training for leadership should be revitalized.

Under "Decision-Making":

Techniques for the improvement of items which might assist in forecasting alliances, neutralities, hostile activities, etc., and for use in tactical decision-making need to be expanded, applied, and tested in the real world.

Under "Understanding of Operational Problems in Foreign Areas":

Despite the difficulties attendant upon research in foreign areas, it must be explicitly recognized that the missions of the DoD cannot be successfully performed in the absence of information on (a) sociocultural patterns in various areas including beliefs, values, motivations, etc.; (b) the social organization of troops, including political, religious, and economic; (c) the effect of change and innovation upon sociocultural patterns and socio-cultural organization of groups; (d) study and evaluation of action programs initiated by U.S. or foreign agencies in underdeveloped countries.

Solid, precise, comparative, and current empirical data developed in a programmatic rather than diffuse and opportunistic fashion are urgently needed for many areas of the world. This goal should be pursued by: (a) multidisciplinary research teams; (b) series of field studies in relevant countries; (c) strong representation of quantitative and analytic skills; (d) a broad empirical data base.

Under "Man and His Physical Environment":

Continuing and additional research are needed on the effect of special physical and psychological environments upon performance and on possibilities for the enhancement of performance through a better understanding of man's sensory and motor output mechanisms, the development of artificial systems which will aid performance, and the search for drugs or foods which may enhance it.

Under "Methodology":

We recommend increased emphasis upon research in behavioral-science methodology. While this is basic to all of the areas listed above, it needs to be recognized as worthy of investment in its own right. The systematic observation of the many quasi-experimental situations which occur in everyday military activities must be made possible if we are to learn from experience. We recommend that a capability be established in one or more suitable in-house laboratories to address the question of how the logistical problems of such observation can be solved.

On "Government-University Relations":

There is disagreement concerning the involvement of first-rate academic groups in behavioral science research relevant to long-term DoD needs. The task statement implies that DoD has not been successful in enlisting the interest and service of an eminent group of behavioral scientists in most of the areas relevant to it. This panel does not concur. We therefore recommend that the [National Academy of Sciences] Panel on Behavioral and Social Sciences be asked to address this problem and to determine whether, in fact, an acceptable proportion of first-rate academic workers are involved in DoD behavioral science research.

More high-quality scientists could probably be interested in DoD problems if DoD would more frequently state its research needs in terms which are meaningful to the investigator rather than to the military. . . . Publicity concerning the distinguished behavioral scientists who have long-term commitments to the DoD should be disseminated as a way of reassuring younger scientists and improving our research image.

III. The Panelists

Why did these distinguished social scientists accept the assignment from the Department of Defense? Most of them seemed particularly intrigued by the chance to address important issues. They view the work done by the DoD in such areas as racially segregated housing, or the rehabilitation of juvenile delinquents through military participation, as fascinating illustrations of how social science can settle social issues. It is curious how this thirst for the application of social science led the panelists to ignore the prima facie fact that the DoD is in the defense business, and that therefore it inevitably tends to assign high priority to military potential and effectiveness. Further, the question of what is important is continually linked to matters of relevance to the DoD. In this way, the question of professional autonomy is transformed into one of patriotic responsibility.

In general, the idealism of social scientists participating in DoD-sponsored research stems from their profound belief in the correctability of federal shortcomings, as well as in the perfectibility of society through the use of social science. Despite the obviousness of the point, what these social scientists forget is that the federal government as well as its agencies is limited by historical and geopolitical circumstances. It is committed to managing cumbersome, overgrown committee and data-gathering agencies. It is committed to a status quo merely for the sake of rational functioning. It can only tinker with innovating ideas. Thus federal agencies will limit investigation simply to what is immediately useful—not out of choice, but of necessity.

The social scientist often imagines he is a policy formulator, an innovating designer. Because of the cumbersome operations of government, he will be frustrated in realizing this self-image and be reduced to one more instrumental agent. His designing mentality, his strain toward perfecting, will appear unrealistic in the light of what he can do. He gets caught up in theoryless applications to immediacy, surrenders the value of confronting men with an image of what *can be*, and simply accepts what others declare *must be*. Thus, what the social scientist knows comes down to what the Defense Department under present circumstances can use.

Although the initiative for this Report came from the social scientists, the DoD provided the structure and direction of its content. To a remarkable degree, the study group accepted DoD premises.

For example, the two major assumptions that influenced its thinking are stated baldly. First, since the DoD's job now embraces new responsibilities, its proper role becomes as much to wage "peacefare" as warfare. Peacefare is spelled out as pacification of total populations, as well as having a role in the ideological battle between East and West. Toward such ends, it is maintained, social science can play a vital part.

Nowhere in the document is the possibility considered that the DoD ought not to be in many of these activities—that perhaps the division of labor has placed too great an emphasis upon this one agency of government at the expense of all others. Nor is it anywhere made clear that educational and antipoverty programs similar to those the Defense Department is engaged in are already under way in other branches of government—that DoD activities might be duplicating and needlessly multiplying the efforts of HEW (Health, Education and Welfare) or NSF (National Science Foundation).

The second explicit assumption the group makes is that hardware alone will not win modern wars: Manpower is needed, too. Here the panelists see social science as providing data on the dynamics of cultural change and a framework for the needs and attitudes of other people.

But here, too, there is a remarkable absence of any consideration of the sort of "manpower" deployed in foreign environments or of the differing responses of overseas peoples to such manpower. The foreign role of the U.S. Defense Department is simply taken as a given, a datum to be exploited for the display of social science information. In this sense, U.S. difficulties with foreign military activities can be interpreted as a mere misunderstanding of the nature of a problem. Expertise and objectivity can then be called upon where a policy design is lacking or failing. Thus even the DoD can mask policy shortcomings behind the fact of a previously inadequate supply of data. In this way, the credibility gap gets concerted into a mechanical informational gap—which is exactly what is done in the Report. All efforts, in other words, are bent on maximizing social science participation rather than on minimizing international conflict.

Still a third assumption of the panel participants—one that is not acknowledged—is that their professional autonomy will not be seriously jeopardized by the very fact of their dependence upon the DoD. Indeed, many scholars seem to have abandoned their primary research interests for secondary ones that can be funded. And the main responsibility for this shift lies not with the DoD but with the social science professions and the scholarly community at large.

As one panel member ironically noted in response to my questionnaire, the position of the DoD is an unhappy reflection of university demands that individual scholars and university presidents pay for expanding university overhead and enlarged graduate programs—rather than of any insistence by federal agencies that the nature of social science be transformed. Another panel member indicated that, whatever dishonor may exist in the present relationships between social science and the DoD, the main charge would have to be leveled at the professoriat, rather than at the funding agencies. And while this assignment of priorities in terms of who is responsible for the present era of ill will and mistrust can be easily overdone and lead to a form of higher apologetics in which there is mutual accusation by the social scientists and government policy-makers, it does seem clear that the simplistic idea that the evil government corrupts the good social scientist is not only an exaggeration but, more often, a deliberate misrepresentation.

IV. The Findings

Reexamining the specific findings of the first section of the Report, "High-Payoff Research in Development Areas," leaves no doubt that the panelists mean by "high payoff" those potential rewards to be netted by the DoD, rather than advantages to be gained by social scientists. This is made explicit in the section on "Manpower," in which the main issues are contended to concern problems of improving the performance of soldiers equipped with high-level technology. It is in this connection that the panelists heartily approve of Project 100,000. Although (with the exception of two panelists) there is a special cloudiness as to the nature of Project 100,000, the panelists have no doubt that the employment of delinquents in this fashion makes the best use of marginal manpower for a "tremendous payoff" for the future efficiency of the defense establishment.

A number of the Report's recommendations amount to little more than the repetition of basic organizational shibboleths. But even at this level, special problems seem to arise. There is confusion in the minds of the panelists, or at least throughout the Report that they prepared, about what constitutes internal DoD functions as opposed to general military functions. The phrase "military establishment" functions as an umbrella disguising this ambiguity. Not only is the relationship between a civilian-led DoD and a "military establishment" unresolved, but beyond that, the panelists appear willing to discount the organizational intermingling of the DoD with other governmental agencies—such as the Census Bureau, the Department of Labor, and the Department of Health, Education, and Welfare.

This leads to a tacit acceptance of DoD organizational colonialism. Not only is the Defense Department urged to be on the lookout for other agencies' collecting similar data and doing similar sorts of analyses, but an explicit request is included that the DoD exert a special effort to use the work of outside agencies. On behalf of "cooperation," there exists the risk of invasion of privacy, and other dangers encountered when any single department functions as a total system incorporating the findings of other subunits.

The Report contends that those parts of the armed services responsible for developing basic knowledge about decision-making have done their work well. Interestingly, no illustrative examples are given. Moreover, the military and civilian personnel who provide support for decision-making within the military establishment are said to have a rare opportunity to contribute to this steadily improving use of sound decision-making models for areas like material procurement for front-line battle medical services. Nothing is said about the nature of the conflict to be resolved, or the values employed in such decisions.

While several members of the panel, in response to the questionnaire of mine, indicated that they held this Report to be an indirect resolution of problems raised by Project Camelot, the formulations used in this Report are similar to those used in the Camelot study concerning overseas research.

The Report states: "Comparative organizational work should not be done only when in civilian groups such as large-scale building and construction consortia and worldwide airlines systems, but also within foreign military establishments." In Project Camelot, the same desire for military information was paramount. Curiously, no attention is given to whether, in fact, this is a high-payoff research area; or if it is, how this work is to be done without threatening the sovereignty of other nations. In other words, although the Report superficially is dedicated to the principle of maximum use of social science, this principle is not brought into play at the critical point. The ambiguities and doubts raised by previous DoD incursions into the area of foreign social research remain intact and are in no way even partially resolved.

The panelists are dedicated to the principle of high-payoff research, but appear to be disquietingly convinced that this is equivalent to whatever the members of the panel themselves are doing, or whatever their professional specialties are. Thus a high-payoff research area becomes the study of isolation upon individual and group behavior; or the area of simulation of field experiences that the military may encounter; or the study of behavior under conditions of ionizing radiation. It is not incidental that in each instance the panelists themselves have been largely engaged in such kinds of work. One is left with the distinct impression that a larger number of panelists would have yielded only a larger number of "high-payoff" areas, rather than an integrated framework of needs. This leads to a general suspicion that the Report is much more self-serving than a simple review of its propositions indicates.

The references to methodology again raise the specter of Camelot, since it is evident that no general methodology is demonstrated in the Report itself and no genuine innovations are formulated for future methodological directions. There is no discussion of the kind of methodology likely to yield meaningful prediction. Instead, the DoD is simply notified of the correctness of its own biases. We are told that "predictive indicators of a conflict or revolutionary overthrow are examples of the type of data which can gain from control applications." No illustrations of the success of such predictors is given. The purpose turns out to be not so much prediction as control of revolutionary outbreaks. This, then, constitutes the core methodological message of the Report.

V. Project Themis

As for Project THEMIS, designed to upgrade scientific and engineering performances at colleges and universities for the benefit of the Defense Department, the project titles at the institutions already selected do not furnish enough information to assess the actual nature of the research. A proposal of more than $1.1 million for research into "chemical compounds containing highly electronegative elements" was turned down by the dean of faculties at Portland (Ore.) State College. Said he: "I know what the proposal was talking about. It could very easily be interpreted as a proposal involving biological warfare." The proposal could be construed as "committing the university to biological warfare."

Among the universities now contracted for Project THEMIS work is the University of Utah, with the project title "Chemistry of Combustion." Newspaper accounts during the summer of 1967 indicated clearly that this project was aimed at improving missile fuels. Additional illustrations could be given, but the point is clear: Project THEMIS is what it claims to be, a program to involve universities in research useful to the Defense Department.

The panelists assure us that "DoD has been singularly successful at enlisting the interest and services of an eminent group of behavioral scientists in most of the areas relevant to it." They go on to say that, indeed, "the management of behavioral science research in the military department should be complimented for long-term success in building the image of DoD as a good and challenging environment in which to do both basic and applied research." No names are cited to indicate that there are eminent clusters of behavioral scientists working in the DoD. Nor is there an indication whether "the eminent men" connected with DoD are in fact remotely connected as part-time consultants (like the panelists themselves) or intimately connected with basic work for the government. And even though Foster's letter indicates that there is a problem of recruitment and government-university relations, the panel simply dismisses this as insignificant. Yet members go on to note that the Defense Department image is perhaps more tarnished than they would like to think; that, for example, the Civil Service Commission discriminates against the behavioral scientist with respect to appointments, and that it is hard to persuade behavioral scientists that the DoD provides a supportive environment for them. Despite the censure of the Civil Service Commission, it is claimed that the DoD has not been as attractive and as successful in social science recruitment as we were earlier led to believe.

More damaging, perhaps, is the allegation of the panelists that quality control of research at universities is not in any way superior to that exercised within other research sources, such as the DoD. They tend to see "quality control" as something unrelated to university autonomy and its implications for objectivity. Lest there be any ambiguity on this point, they go on to indicate in an extraordinary series of unsupported allegations that the difficulty is not one of social science autonomy versus the political requirements of any agency of government, but rather one of bad public relations—which is in turn mostly blamed on "Representatives of Civilian Professional Organizations" who lack a clear picture of DoD requirements and yet testify before congressional committees, which in turn are backed up by social and behavioral scientists who regard such DoD activities as a threat to academic freedom and scientific integrity, and who "are usually ignorant of the work actually being performed under DoD's aegis."

The specific committee hearings referred to are nowhere indicated. Certainly, the various hearings on such proposed measures as a national social science foundation, or on social accounting, do exhibit the highest amount of professional integrity and concern. It might be that Defense Department intellectuals are concerned precisely over the nonpolicy research features of such proposed legislation.

Finally, the panelists offer a gentle slap on the wrist to defense research managers who allegedly lack the time to address themselves to these kinds of problems. In short and in sum, the Report ignores questions having to do with social science autonomy as if these were products of misperceptions to be resolved by good will and better public relations between the DoD and the Academy. That such conclusions should be reached by a set of panelists, half of whom are highly placed in academic life, indicates the degree to which closing the gap between the academy and the polity has paradoxically broken down the political capabilities of social science by weakening its autonomous basis.

The panelists have enough firmness of mind to make two unsolicited comments. But the nature of the comments reveals the flabbiness that results from the tendency of social scientists to conceive of their sciences as service activities rather than as scientific activities. They urge, first, that more work be done in the area of potential high-payoff fields of investigation that might have been overlooked in their own Report, given the short time they had available in preparing it. They further urge the establishment of a continuous group with time to examine other areas in greater depth and to discuss them more deliberately, so that high-payoff areas can be teased out and presented for cost considerations. In other words, the unsolicited comments suggests mechanisms for improving these kinds of recommendations and making them permanent. They do not consider whether the nature of social science requirements might be unfit for the bureaucratic specifications of Foster's originating letter.

VI. Advise and Dissent

In some ways, the very tension between social scientists and policy-makers provides each group with a reality test against which basic ideas could be formulated about policy issues. But the very demand for a coalescence of the two, whether in the name of "significant" research or as a straight patriotic obligation, has the effect of corrupting social science and impoverishing policy options.

The question that the Report raises with terrible forcefulness is not so much one of the relationship between pure and applied research, but of what the character of application is to be. Applied research is clearly here to stay and is probably the most forceful, singular novel element in American social science as contrasted with its European background. What is at stake, however, is a highly refined concept of application that removes theoretical considerations of the character and balance of social forces and private interests from the purview of application. The design of the future replaces the analysis of the present in our "new utopian" world.

The panelists simply do not entertain the possibility that the social world is a behavioral "field" in which decisions have to be made between political goals as well as means. Reports cannot "depoliticalize" social action to such an extent that consequences do not follow and implicit choices are not favored. Innovation without a political goal simply assumes that operations leading to a change from one state to another is a value. The Report does not raise, much less favor, significant political changes in the operations of the DoD; and its innovative efforts are circumscribed to improving rather than to changing. However, efficiency is a limited use of applicability because it assumes rather than tests the adequacy of the social system.

The era of good feelings between the federal government and social science, which characterized the period between the outbreak of World War II and extended through the assassination of President John F. Kennedy no longer exists. In its place seems to be the era of tight money. The future of "nonprofit" research corporations tied to the DoD is being severely impeded from both sides. Schools such as the University of Pennsylvania, the University of California, and Princeton have taken a hard look at academic involvement in classified research for the Pentagon. Princeton, with its huge stake in international relations programming, is even considering cancelling its sponsorship of a key research arm, the Institute for Defense Analysis. On the other side, many of the "hard" engineering types have continued to press their doubts as to the usefulness of software research. And this barrage of criticism finds welcome support among high military officers who would just as soon cancel social science projects as carry out their implications.

With respect to the panelists, it must be said that a number of them have indicated their own doubts about the Report. One of the participants has correctly pointed out that the Report has not yet been accepted by the DoD, nor have the findings or the recommendations been endorsed by the National Academy of Science. Another member claimed that his main reason for accepting the invitation to serve on the panel was to argue against the Defense Department's involving universities in operations such as Project Camelot. He went on to point out that his mission was unsuccessful, since he obviously did not influence the other panelists.

A third panelist points out that the Camelot type of issue was not, to his recollection at least, a criterion in any discussion of the topics. Yet he strongly disclaims his own participation as well as membership in the National Academy of Science Advisory Committee on Government Programs in the Behavioral Sciences. He also indicates that his panel had nothing but an administrative connection with the National Academy of Science, and he, too, seems to indicate that he had an ancillary advisory role rather than an integrated preparatory role.

Trying to gauge the accuracy with which the final Report represented a true consensus of the panelists proved most difficult. While most panelists, with hedging qualifications, agreed that the Report reflected an accurate appraisal of their own views, the question of the actual write-up of the document brought forth a far from consistent response. One panelist claims that "all members contributed to the basic draft of the Report. Each assumed responsibility for composing a section, all of which were then reviewed by the panel as a whole." Another panelist declared his participation only "as an observer," and that he was not involved in any final write-up. Yet a third panelist disclaimed any connection with the preparation of the Report.

A final, and still different, version was stated as follows: "The report was written by members of the committee and the overall editing and bringing-together responsibility was undertaken by Rains Wallace. One or two members of the committee were assigned to specific topics and drafts were prepared at Williamstown. These went to Wallace, who organized them, did some editing, and sent them back to us. Each person responded and the final version was then prepared by Wallace." In other words, the actual authorship of a document that was released "in confidence" over the names of some of America's most distinguished social scientists is either the work of all and the responsibility of none, or perhaps—as is more likely the case—the work of one or two people and the responsibility of all.

VII. FAR *vs.* DoD

The Department of Defense is the most sought-after and frequently found sponsor of social science research. And the DoD is sought and found by the social scientists, not, as is often imagined, the other way around. Customarily, military men provide only grudging acceptance of any need for behavioral research.

There are four distinct reasons why the DoD is sponsoring more and more social science research.

First, money. In fiscal 1968, Congressional appropriations for research and development amounted to the monumental sum of $14,971.4 million. Of this, an incredible $13,243.0 million, or about 85 per cent, was distributed among three agencies whose primary concern is the military system: the Atomic Energy Commission, the National Aeronautics and Space Administration, and the DoD. The figure for the DoD alone was $6680.0 million. This means that a *single* federal agency commanded nearly two-fifths of the government research dollar. So it is easy to see why so much effort and energy is expended by social scientists trying to capture some of the monies the DoD can experiment with. As bees flock to honey, men flock to money—particularly in an era when costly data-processing and data-gathering strain the conventional sources of financing.

Second, the protection that research has when done for the DoD. I am referring to the blanket and indiscriminate way in which Congressional appropriations are made for both basic and applied research. Policy-linked social scientists operate under an umbrella of the secrecy established by the DoD's research agencies. Reasons of security ward off harassment by congressional committees. Attacks over supposed misallocation of funds and resources—undergone by the National Institutes of Health at the hands of the committee headed by Rep. L. H. Fountain of North Carolina—are spared those academics with Defense Department funding.

This dispensation is strikingly illustrated by the fact that DoD allocations for research and development are not itemized the way allocations are for Health, Education, and Welfare. This auditing cover allows for even more experimenting in DoD spending than its already swollen funds might indicate. Such a *carte blanche* situation probably places far less strain on social scientists than would be the case if they worked for other agencies. In the world of research, power provides the illusion of freedom.

Third, the relatively blank-check Congressional approach to DoD funds, and the security umbrella of the auditing system, provide social scientists with un-limited resources. DoD allocations are not broken down into subagencies, nor are any of their specialized activities or services checked, unlike the usual scrutiny directed at other agencies.

That this fact has not gone entirely unnoticed is shown by the Congressional demand that as of 1968 the DoD be called to account on an appropriations budget.

Fourth, the DoD's connection with the "national security"—which protects the DoD and those who work for it—offers great temptations to social researchers interested in the "big news." It enables the DoD not only to outspend such agencies as the National Science Foundation in university-based activities, but also to penetrate areas of non-Defense research that are central only to the social science researcher. Programs to support juvenile-delinquency research (Project 100,000) and others to upgrade academic institutions (Project THEMIS) are sponsored by the DoD rather than by the Office of Economic Opportunity—and not simply because of their disproportionate funds. Just as important is the legitimation that the DoD can provide for policy-oriented researchers in sensi-tive areas.

These are the main reasons why many social science researchers are now enlisting the support of the DoD in their activities—despite the negative publicity surrounding Project Camelot and other such fallen angels.

The issuance, even in semiprivate form, of the *Report on Defense Social and Behavioral Sciences* reveals the existence of a wide gap between the thinking of the two chief departments involved in sensitive research and in research in foreign areas—namely, the Department of Defense and the Department of State. Indeed, the issuance of this Report is likely to exacerbate the feelings of high officials in the State Department that the Defense Department position represents an encroachment upon rather than an enhancement of the present situation.

The memorandum issued in December, 1967, by the Department of State's Foreign Area Research Coordination group (FAR), in which it set forth foreign-area research guidelines, represents a direct rebuke or, at the very least, a serious challenge to the orientation that the Report of the Defense Science Board represents. It is a high point in the federal recognition that real problems do exist.

The FAR Report is broken into two different sections with seven propositions in each section. First, under "Guidelines for Research Contract Relations Between Government and Universities," the following are used:

(1) The government has the responsibility for avoiding actions that would call into question the integrity of American academic institutions as centers of independent teaching and research.

(2) Government research support should always be acknowledged by sponsor, university, and researcher.

(3) Government-supported contract research should in process and results ideally be unclassified, but given the practical needs of the nation in the modern world, some portion may be subject to classification. In this case the balance between making work public or classified should lean whenever possible toward making it public.

(4) Agencies should encourage open publication of contract research results.

(5) Government agencies that contract with university researchers should consider designing their projects so as to advance knowledge as well as to meet the immediate policy or action needs.

(6) Government agencies have the obligation of informing the potential researcher of the needs that the research should help meet and of any special conditions associated with the research contract, and generally of the agency's expectations concerning the research and the researcher.

(7) The government should continue to seek research of the highest possible quality in its contract program.

A second set of seven recommendations is listed under "Guidelines for the Conduct of Foreign Area Research under Government Contract," and these too bear very directly on the panel Report and do so most critically and tellingly.

(1) The government should take special steps to insure that the parties with which it contracts have the highest qualifications for carrying out research overseas.

(2) The government should work to avert or minimize adverse foreign reactions to its contract research programs conducted overseas.

(3) When a project involves research abroad, it is particularly important that both the supporting agency and the researcher openly acknowledge the auspices and financing of research projects.

(4) The government should under certain circumstances ascertain that the research is acceptable to the host government before proceeding on the research.

(5) The government should encourage cooperation with foreign scholars in its contract research program.

(6) Government agencies should continue to coordinate their foreign-area research programs to eliminate duplication and overloading of any one geo-grahical area.

(7) Government agencies should cooperate with academic associations on problems of foreign-area research.

This set of recommendations (with allowances made for the circumstance of their issuance) unquestionably represents the most enlightened position yet taken by a federal agency on the question of the relationship between social science and practical politics. These sets of recommendations not only stand as ethical criteria for the federal government's relationship to social scientists, but—even more decisively—represent a rebuke to precisely the sort of militarization of social science implicit in the panel Report. The reassertion by a major federal policy-making agency of the worth to the government of social science autonomy represented the first significant recognition by a federal agency that Project Camelot was the consequence, not the cause, of the present strains in social science—federal bureaucracy relationships.

Name Index

Adler, Franz, 211
Adorno, T. W., 20, 89
Albert, Ethel M., 130, 145, 147
Alpert, Harry, 38
Alpervitz, Gar, 312
Anderson, Hurst R., 297
Aron, Raymond, 74
Asch, Solomon E., 101
Ashby, Eric, 265
Axelrod, Sidney, 23

Bachoffen, Johann J., 38, 63
Bacon, Francis, 71
Baldwin, James, 182
Barber, Bernard, 160
Barber, Richard J., 274
Barnard, Chester I., 11, 163
Barnes, Harry Elmer, 138
Barr, Stringfellow, 160, 161
Barth, Karl, 106
Bartlett, F. H., 34
Barzun, Jacques, 133
Beauvoir, Simone de, 187
Becker, Ernest, 176
Becker, Howard, 40
Becker, Howard S., 45, 84, 100, 109, 110, 111, 138, 184, 187, 199
Bechhoefer, Barnhard G., 317
Bell, Daniel, 13, 70, 248
Bellamy, Edward, 78
Bendix, Reinhard, 39, 203
Benedict, Ruth, 23, 43, 44, 182, 183, 184
Benoit, Emile, 318
Bensman, Joseph, 196, 199

Berelson, Bernard, 9, 44, 75, 101, 160, 273
Berger, Bennett M., 203, 236
Bernard, Jessie, 109
Bierstedt, Robert, 44, 165, 229
Black, Harold, 116
Black, Max, 5, 190
Blumer, Herbert, 88, 250
Boas, Franz, 47, 48, 54
Bogardus, Emory S., 231
Boguslaw, Robert, 282
Boorstin, Daniel, 106, 216
Boran, Behice, 42
Boulding, Kenneth, 318, 320
Bowman, C. C., 42
Braithwaite, Richard Bevan, 31, 237
Brandstatter, Art, 306
Bredemeir, H. C., 73
Breed, Warren, 229
Brodbeck, May, 23
Brodie, Bernard, 325
Broom, Leonard, 4, 5, 7, 66, 101, 133, 216
Brown, Norman O., 34
Brotz, Howard, 239
Brownlow, Louis, 283
Buber, Martin, 106
Bukharin, Nikolai, 19
Bunster, Alvaro, 291
Burgess, Ernest, 88
Burke, Kenneth, 187

Calverton, V. F., 42
Campanella, Tomasso, 71
Campbell, Angus, 112
Cannan, Edwin, 33

Caplow, Theodore, 165, 206
Cardwell, D. S. L., 265
Carr, E. H., 223
Carrel, Alexis, 240, 241, 324
Castro, Fidel, 222
Catlin, G. E. C., 39
Chambliss, Rollin, 33
Chapin, Stuart, 231
Chinoy, Ely, 4
Christie, Richard, 72
Clarke, Alfred C., 83
Clemence, R. V., 236
Clinard, Marshall B., 174
Cloward, Richard A., 114
Cohen, Robert S., 28
Cole, G. D. H., 20
Cole, William E., 81
Comte, Auguste, 32, 33, 200
Cooley, Charles H., 41, 187
Coser, Lewis A., 10, 31, 103, 109, 242, 243
Cottrell, Leonard S., Jr., 4, 5, 7, 66, 101, 132, 216
Cousin, Victor, 36
Cray, Ed, 122

Dahlke, H. Otto, 40
Dahrendorf, Ralf, 51, 215, 239
D'Alembert, Jean le, 205
Darwin, Charles, 134
Davie, M. R., 245
Davis, James A., 198
Davis, Kingsley, 206, 236, 244, 245, 246, 247
DeGre, Gerard L., 28
Demerath, N. J. III, 3, 286
Denney, Reuel, 14
Denison, James H., 306
Deutscher, Isaac, 69, 223
Dewey, John, 6, 43, 187, 192, 198, 202, 242
DeWitt, Nicholas, 264
Diderot, Denis, 28
Diem, Ngo Dinh, 306
Dilthey, Wilhelm, 34
Dinitz, Simon, 83
Dorner, Peter, 341
Dougal, Arwin A., 340, 341
Dubnow, Simon, 106
DuBois, W. E. B., 115
Dulles, John Foster, 283
Duncan, Hugh Dalziel, 188, 189
Dungan, Ralph, 287
Durkheim, Emile, 4, 36, 37, 38, 39, 40, 41, 54, 63, 190, 192, 194, 242, 243
Dynes, Russell R., 83

Eckstein, Harry, 116
Edel, Abraham, 28, 183, 184, 237
Edel, May, 183, 184
Einstein, Albert, 135

Eisenhower, Dwight D., 284
Eisenstadt, S. W., 86
Elliot, Mabel, 230
Elman, Richard M., 114
Engels, Friedrich, 6, 63
Etzioni, Amitai, 60
Evan, William M., 229
Evans, Rowland, 121

Fairseruis, Walter A., Jr., 46
Fanon, Franz, 115
Farber, Marvin, 32, 40, 67
Fascell, Dante B., 251
Feigl, Herbert, 23
Feldman, Arnold S., 229
Ferracuti, Franco, 114
Ferris, Abbott L., 130
Festinger, Leon, 229
Feuer, Lewis S., 6, 104
Feuerbach, Ludwig, 102, 103, 106
Finch, H. A., 36
Firth, Raymond, 47, 53, 59, 184
Fischer, J. L., 317
Fischel, Wesley, 306, 307
Fleming, D. F., 312
Foster, John S., Jr., 342, 348, 349
Fountain, L. H., 351
Frank, Lawrence K., 14, 86
Frank, Philipp G., 28, 34
Frankel, Charles, 74
Frazier, E. Franklin, 134
Frenkel-Brunswik, Else, 34, 89
Freud, Sigmund, 25, 34, 35, 39, 118, 190, 222, 226, 319
Friedman, Milton, 317, 335
Fromm, Erich, 26, 103, 225
Fuenzalida, Eduardo, 291
Fulbright, J. William, 288, 291, 340

Galtung, Johan, 290, 291
Gamow, George, 135
Gardner, Burleigh B., 228
Germani, Gino, 22
Gerth, H. H., 36, 39, 41, 188, 192, 193, 222, 223, 226, 227
Giddings, Franklin H., 42
Giedeon, S., 135
Gilmore, Susan, 118
Ginsberg, Morris, 28, 38
Gittler, J. B., 23
Glazer, Nathan, 14
Goffman, Erving, 100, 184, 187, 206, 224, 225, 227
Goode, William J., 44
Gordon, C. Wayne, 135
Gouldner, Alvin W., 10, 130, 132, 197, 222, 230
Gowin, D. B., 129

Gray, David J., 215
Grazia, Alfred de, 133
Green, Arnold W., 4
Greenfield, M., 268
Greer, Scott, 229
Griswold, A. Whitney, 154
Gross, Llewellyn, 51, 66, 132, 165, 190, 203, 230, 237
Gross, Neal, 4
Guetzkow, Harold, 341
Gulick, Luther, 283
Gumplowicz, Ludwig, 6, 317
Gurvitch, George, 35

Habenstein, Robert W., 215
Hagstrom, Warren O., 266
Hammond, Philip E., 196, 198
Hannah, John A., 305, 306, 307
Harriman, W. A., 283
Harrington, Michael, 134, 206
Hatt, Paul K., 44
Hayek, F. A. von, 69
Hazlitt, Henry, 317
Hegel, George W. F., 20, 102, 103, 326
Heisenberg, Werner, 228
Hempel, Carl G., 51, 237
Henderson, J. J., 189
Henry, Jules, 135, 330
Herskovitz, Melville J., 54
Hertzler, J. O., 4
Hilgard, Ernest P., 162
Hill, Thomas M., 283
Hinckle, Warren, 306
Hirsch, Walter, 196
Hitler, Adolph, 326
Hobbes, Thomas, 6, 20, 125
Hobhouse, Lionel, 43, 243
Hogbin, H. Ian, 59
Hoebel, E. Adamson, 62
Homans, George C., 165
Hoover, Herbert, 282, 283
Hopper, Janis Harris, 134
Hopper, Rex, 126, 289, 290
Horowitz, Irving L., 31, 39, 56, 67, 75, 107, 112, 116, 119, 126, 131, 132, 134, 151, 187, 190, 193, 199, 200, 216, 238, 239, 243, 264, 284, 286, 333
Horton, Paul B., 81, 82
Howard, George Elliott, 231
Hughes, Everett C., 195, 199, 215
Hull, Clark L., 226
Hume, David, 40
Humphrey, Hubert, 315
Huszar, George B. de, 140
Huxley, Aldous, 68, 78, 104
Huxley, Thomas H., 134, 135

Iklé, Fred Charles, 325
Ishino, Iwao, 83

Jahoda, Marie, 72
James, William, 140, 168, 192, 319
Janowitz, Morris, 9, 14, 75
Johnson, H. M., 66, 71
Johnson, Lyndon B., 291, 302
Jordan, Nehemiah, 228

Kahn, Herman, 45, 315, 318, 325, 327
Kant, Immanuel, 40, 223
Kaplan, Norman, 264, 268
Kardiner, Abram, 23
Karl, Barry Dean, 283
Kassof, Allen, 264
Kecskemeti, Paul, 28, 41, 317
Keenan, B. R., 265
Keller, A. G., 245
Kelman, Herbert C., 86
Kelsen, Hans, 20
Kennan, George F., 283
Kennedy, John F., 122, 284, 316, 350
Keniston, Kenneth, 71
Key, V. O., 112
Keynes, John M., 236
Kierkegaard, Sören, 195, 196
Killingsworth, Charles, 307
Kimball, Solon T., 145, 147
King, Martin Luther, 122
Kirkpatrick, Lyman, 306
Kluckhohn, Clyde, 23, 183
Koffka, K., 226
Kolb, William L., 239
Kolodny, Ralph L., 228
Kosa, John, 211
Knight, Frank H., 41
Kroeber, A. L., 47, 166

Labedz, L., 19
Labes, Marvin J., 116
Lang, Gladys E., 7, 8, 123
Lang, Kurt, 7, 8, 123
Laquer, W. Z., 19
Larrabee, Eric, 25
Larsen, Otto N., 44
Lasker, Gabriel W., 130, 145, 147
Lasswell, Harold D., 9, 20, 21, 24, 75, 162, 284, 285
Lazarsfeld, Paul, 20, 149, 150, 162, 163, 165, 200, 202, 207, 238, 271, 273
Lee, Alfred McClung, 82, 204, 230
Lee, Dorothy, 135
Lee, Elizabeth Briant, 82
Lemert, Edwin M., 110, 113
Lenin, V. I., 78
Lenzen, Victor F., 22
Lerner, Daniel, 14, 162, 285
Leslie, Gerald R., 81, 82
Levinson, D. J., 89
Lévy-Bruhl, Lucien, 38, 49, 62

Lewin, Leonard C., 315, 326, 327
Lewis, Oscar, 61, 177, 178, 179, 180, 181, 182
Lichtheim, George, 19
Lieberson, Stanley, 115
Liebowitz, Martin, 108
Lipset, Seymour M., 5, 6, 11, 13, 46, 73, 112, 116, 236, 248, 284
Litwak, Eugene, 8
Lowie, Robert H., 41, 179
Lowry, Ritchie, 229
Lubell, Samuel, 112
Lundberg, George A., 44
Lynd, Robert S., 32, 201, 202, 231, 284
Lynton, R. P., 23
Lyons, Gene M., 341

McCarthy, Eugene, 291
McDonagh, Edward C., 81
Macdonald, Dwight, 106
McGee, Reece J., 165, 206
Machiavelli, Nicolo, 188
MacIver Robert M., 42, 43, 44
MacKenzie, Norman, 164, 204
McNamara, Robert S., 288, 291, 295
Madge, John, 189
Malin, Irving, 106
Malinowski, Bronislaw, 31, 37, 46, 47, 48, 49, 50, 51, 52, 53, 54, 55, 56, 57, 58, 59, 60, 61, 62, 63, 64, 242, 243, 244, 246
Mandelbaum, David C., 130, 145, 147
Mandelbaum, Maurice, 28
Manheim, Ernest, 28
Manheim, Karl, 17, 18, 27, 28, 40, 41, 43, 66, 68, 70, 72, 73, 74, 77, 235
Mao Tse-Tung, 326
Marcuse, Herbert, 24, 26, 34, 216, 225, 226
Marshall, Alfred, 190
Marsilius of Padua, 6
Martindale, Don, 189
Martineau, Harriet, 32, 280
Marx, Karl, 5, 6, 19, 20, 33, 34, 35, 39, 43, 73, 102, 103, 104, 105, 106, 118, 123, 143, 171, 188, 192, 193, 222, 235, 326
Mason, Ward S., 148
Mauss, Marcel, 62
Mayo, Elton, 163, 228
Mead, George Herbert, 43, 198, 222, 223, 226
Mead, Margaret, 57, 182, 184, 187
Means, Gerdner, 336
Medalia, Nahum Z., 148
Merriam, Charles, 283
Merton, Robert K., 4, 5, 7, 10, 12, 20, 50, 66, 75, 83, 101, 132, 157, 165, 186, 190, 191, 192, 193, 194, 195, 196, 197, 206, 216, 228, 237, 238, 241
Meyersohn, Rolf, 25

Michels, Roberto, 10, 20, 24, 72, 119, 155
Mill, John Stuart, 243
Miller, Charles H., 81
Miller, Michael V., 118
Miller, S. M., 222, 228, 230
Mills, C. Wright, 20, 36, 39, 41, 66, 105, 112, 134, 160, 161, 171, 186, 187, 188, 192, 193, 194, 195, 196, 200, 206, 216, 220, 222, 223, 226, 227
Mills, D. L., 284
Mises, Ludwig von, 69
Mitchell, C. Wesley, 336
Moore, Wilbert E., 165, 229, 245
Moravia, Alberto, 105, 106
More, Thomas, 71
Morgan, Lewis H., 49, 63
Morgan, Thomas, 206
Morgenstern, Oskar, 317
Morris, Charles, 198
Morse, Wayne, 291
Mosca, Daetano, 6
Muensterberger, Warner, 23
Murdock, George Peter, 56, 57
Murray, H. A., 23

Nadel, S. F., 31, 53, 57
Nagel, Ernest, 51, 201, 237, 246
Nettler, Gwynn, 66, 107, 108
Neumann, Franz L., 24
Neurath, Otto, 23
Neuwirth, Gertrud, 189
Newcomb, Theodore, 4, 7, 224
Newfield, Jack, 119
Newman, Donald J., 229
Nisbet, Robert, A., 83
Nixon, Richard, 307
Novak, Robert, 121
Nutini, Hugo G., 290, 291

Oakley, Kenneth P., 48
Ogburn, William F., 42, 44
Opler, Marvin K., 330
Oppenheimer, Robert J., 260, 312
Ornstein, M., 205
Orwell, George, 39, 68, 69, 78, 104
Osbourne, R., 34
Ostrogorskii, M. Y., 280

Packard, Vance, 206
Padmore, George, 115
Pareto, Vilfredo, 20, 190, 194, 326
Park, Margaret, 184, 187
Park, Robert E., 7, 88, 177, 199, 231
Parsons, Talcott, 5, 10, 12, 20, 41, 47, 66, 67, 186, 188, 189, 190, 191, 192, 194, 196, 206, 264
Pearce, Michael, 342
Peirce, Charles S., 23, 25

Peterson, Richard A., 3, 286
Pittman, David J., 229
Plekhanov, G. V., 19
Podhoretz, Norman, 182
Popper, Karl R., 23
Presthus, Robert, 272
Price, Don K., 266
Proudhon, Pierre Joseph, 33
Pusey, Nathan M., 310

Radcliffe-Brown, A. R., 50, 61, 243
Radin, Paul, 179
Rainwater, Lee, 100
Reckless, Walter, 88, 199
Record, Wilson, 150
Redfield, Margaret Park, 176
Redfield, Robert, 47, 62, 166, 176, 177, 179, 182, 183, 184
Reeve, H., 7
Reichenbach, Hans, 28
Reiley, Alan C., 11
Rein, Martin, 203, 204
Reissman, Leonard, 136
Richter, Melvin, 242
Riesman, David, 14, 106, 134, 198, 206, 228
Rivers, W. H. R., 63
Robbins, Richard, 229
Robson, William A., 162, 204
Rochefoucauld, François, 225
Rockefeller, Nelson, 283
Rodman, Hyman, 228
Romney, A. Kimball, 342
Roosevelt, Franklin Delano, 282–283
Rosenberg, Alfred, 324
Rosenberg, Bernard, 25, 31, 103, 238, 243
Ross, Ralph, 229
Rousseau, Jean-Jacques, 20, 188
Rovere, Richard, 316
Rusk, Dean, 291
Russell, Roger, 342

Saint-Simon, Claude Henri, 143
Sanford, R. N., 89
Santayana, George, 78
Sargent, Stansfeld S., 23
Sartre, Jean Paul, 187
Savio, Mario, 119
Schaff, Adam, 104
Schattschneider, E. E., 126
Schatzman, Leonard, 124
Scheer, Robert, 306
Scheler, Max, 31, 40, 41, 67, 73
Schelling, Thomas C., 45
Schlesinger, Rudolf, 20
Schmoller, Gustav, 36
Schneider, David M., 23
Schneider, Herbert W., 32
Schrag, C. C., 44

Schumpeter, Joseph, 236
Schwartz, Mildred A., 284
Scott, Jerome F., 23
Scott, Marvin B., 107
Seeman, Melvin, 103, 107
Selznick, Philip, 4, 11
Shapiro, Golbert, 203
Shapiro, H. L., 56
Shaw, George Bernard, 302
Sheinbaum, Stanley, 306
Sherwood, Clarence C., 229
Shils, Edward A., 36, 41, 72
Sibley, Elbridge, 130, 151, 204
Silvert, Kalman H., 286
Simirenko, Alex, 264
Simmel, Georg, 5, 6, 13, 72
Simon, Rita James, 229
Simpson, George, 242
Simpson, Jon E., 81
Sjoberg, Gideon, 8, 196
Skinner, B. F., 224, 225, 226
Smelser, Neil J., 46, 236
Smith, Adam, 32, 33, 63, 243
Smith, Marian W., 23
Smuckler, Ralph, 307
Solari, Aldo, 116
Solotaroff, Theodore, 145, 161
Sorel, Georges, 20, 43, 72, 75
Sorokin, Pitirim, 192, 196
Speier, Hans, 317
Spence, Larry D., 118
Spencer, Herbert, 35, 50, 235, 248
Spengler, Oswald, 143
Spindler, George D., 135
Spinoza, Benedict, 186
Spivack, Sydney S., 150
Spranger, Edward, 77
Srole, Leo, 330
Stahl, H. H., 36
Stalin, Joseph, 85
Stark, Werner, 18
Stein, Herman D., 219
Stein, Maurice E., 104, 196, 199, 211, 217
Steiner, Gary A., 101
Stephenson, R. M., 73
Stouffer, Samuel, 196, 202
Strauss, Anselm, 100, 124
Streib, Gordon, 229
Sumner, William Graham, 42, 86, 245
Sussman, Marvin, 197
Swain, Joseph W., 242
Szasz, Thomas S., 184, 330

Tarde, Gabriel, 54
Tawney, R. H., 240, 241, 245
Teller, Edward, 260, 312, 317
Thielens, Wagner, 165
Thompson, Hunter S., 122, 124

Tillich, Paul, 106
Tocqueville, Alexis de, 6, 7, 143, 280
Toennies, Ferdinand, 228
Townsend, Peter, 164, 204
Toynbee, Arnold J., 143
Truman, Harry S, 284
Tumin, Melvin, 59, 245
Turner, William W., 120
Tylor, Edward, 47, 48

Vaihinger, Hans, 316
Vallence, Theodore, 291
Veblen, Thorstein, 19, 24, 187, 192, 198
Vidich, Arthur J., 104, 196, 199, 211, 217
Vollmer, H. W., 284

Wakefield, Dan, 206
Wallace, S. Rains, 341, 351
Ward, Lester F., 41
Warner, Lloyd W., 187, 188
Watson, Jeanne, 198
Webb, Eugene, 341
Weber, Alfred, 17
Weber, Max, 10, 19, 24, 36, 37, 38, 39, 40,
   41, 44, 47, 60, 72, 73, 143, 155, 186–194,
   199, 222, 227, 247, 248, 280
Weitling, W. C., 78

Westfall, Richard W., 205
White, David Manning, 25, 238
White, F. R., 71
White, Howard B., 14, 15
Whitehead, A. N., 195, 196
Whyte, William H., 134
Wiese, Leopold von, 45
Williams, Robin M. J., 165, 190
Wilson, Logan, 160
Wirth, Louis, 41, 43, 88, 199
Wolfgang, Marvin E., 114
Wolff, Kurt H., 5, 66, 165, 242
Wrong, Dennis H., 207

X, Malcolm, 115, 122

Yablonsky, Lewis, 111
Young, Michael, 68

Zamyatin, Evgennii, 68, 104
Zetterberg, Hans L., 131, 172, 173, 167, 168,
   169, 170, 171
Zilsel, Edgar, 18, 23
Zilsel, Paul R., 220
Znaniecki, Florian, 66
Zollschan, G. K., 196

Subject Index

Acquisitive Society (The), 240
Alienation, 101–107
  culturalist approach, 106–107
  definitions of, 102–103
  and ideology, 103–104, 106
  and marginality, 106–107
  meanings of, 103–107
  philosophical school of, 102–103
  psychological school of, 103–104
  and religion, 106–107
  school of, 225–226
  sociological school of, 104–106
  and stratification, 105–106
AMERICAN SOCIOLOGY:
  educational orientations, 161–162
  empiricism in, 159–160, 164–166, 198–202, 204
  professionalization, 164–168
  recruitment, 160–161
  sociology of, 159–166
  sponsorship, 163–164
  status striving, 162–163
  value neutrality in, 41–45, 164–166
  and the Weberian tradition, 186–194
  See also Sociology; Social science
American University, and Project Camelot, 297
Anthropology, and functionalism, 58–62; methodological underdevelopment of, 175
Applied sociology, 227–232
  character of, 349–351
  problems, 312–313
  vs. pure sociology, 83–87, 227, 229

  and social problems, 87–92, 95–100
Applied Sociology: Opportunities and Problems, 222, 227–232
Armed Forces (United States), reactions to Project Camelot, 297–298; and social science research, 292–295, 299; and the universities, 340
Autonomy, in social science, 280–286

Bureaucracy, university, 276–280; Weberian theory of, 10

Capitalism, and Marxism, 5–6
Central Intelligence Agency (CIA), and Michigan State University (MSU), 305–313
Character and Social Structure, 222–227
Chicago school of sociology; *see* Midwest tradition in sociology
Chile, and Project Camelot, 290–291
Civil disobedience, 114–117; and social deviance, 114–117
Command social system, and social science, 264, 266–267
Conflict, 3–16
  and deviant behavior, 110–112
  programming of, 16
  and social control, 112
  study of, 182–183
  theory, 6–16
Congress of the United States, and the legislative uses of social science, 257–259, 295–296

361

Consensus, 3–16
  and deviant behavior, 108–112
  and functionalism, 3–4
  and laissez-faire, 10
  meanings of, 4
  theory, 4–16
Control, and deviant behavior, 112, 125, 330–331
  and marginality, 330–331
  and social problems, 92
  and the state, 125
  See also Repression
Cooperation, 3–16; theory of, 15–16
Corporate structure, 13–14
Council of Economic Advisors, 335–336, 338; criticisms of, 335–336
Council of Social Advisors, 328–329
Counterinsurgency, and Project Camelot, 288–290
Crime, economic explanation of, 87
  nonutilitarian, 87
  and social problems, 87–92
  theories on, 87–90
Culture, and alienation, 106–107
  change, 57
  meaning of in functionalist theory, 48–55
  of poverty, 178–182; see also La Vida
  preliterate; see Preliterate cultures and functionalism

Decentralization, of policy research, 255–256
Defense Department (United States), and social science research, 294–296, 344–354; vs. State Department, 295–296, 352
Descriptivism vs. prescriptivism, 13, 28, 37, 235–249
Deviance, 12
  conflict model of, 110–112
  consensus welfare model of, 108–109
  legitimation of, 112
  political, 112–117, 125
  and political marginality, 108–126
  and rehabilitation, 108–109
  and social control, 112–114, 125, 330–331
  and social problems, 109–110
  and therapy, 108–109
  and violence, 120–122
Double interchange paradigm, 67–68
Dysfunction, and social problems, 84–87
  See also Function

East Coast tradition in sociology, 189–192
Empiricism, in American sociology, 159–160, 164–166, 198–202, 204
  as ideology, 159–160, 164–166
  and positivism, 198–202
  and pragmatism, 198–202

Ethics, of policy research, 300–302; scientific study of, 183–184
  See also Sociology of knowledge, and a sociology of ethics
Ethnography, 224–225
Experimentalism, 224

Fascism, in American society, 314–315, 324–327
Foreign policy (United States), 251–261
  and science, 256–257
  and secrecy, 256–257
  and social science, 262–286
Full Opportunity and Social Accounting Act, 329–339; and individual privacy, 331–332; purposes of, 337
Function, and social systems, 84–87
  See also Dysfunction
Functionalism, 46–64
  and anthropology, 58–62
  institutions, 52–55
  magic, 51–52
  meaning of culture, 48–55
  principles of, 50–51
  religion, 54, 244–245
  science, 54
  social change, 55–58
  and social problems, 84–87
  and social stratification, 245–246
  suicide, 51
  and value neutrality, 30–31, 235–249
Funding; see Sponsorship

Game theory, 225
Government (United States), and the universities, 340; uses of basic research, 252–253
Grants, and contracts, 257; and a National Social Science Foundation, 257

IDEOLOGY:
  and alienation, 103–104, 106
  definition of, 72–74
  of empiricism, 159–160, 164–166
  end of, 13
  individual, 67–68
  of occupationalism, 203–210, 214–220
  of professionalism, 200–210, 214–220
  and propaganda, 74–76
  social, 67–68
  theory of, 66–72
  vs. utopia, 66–68, 71–72
Indicators, of alcoholism, 330
  of mental health, 329–330
  purpose of, 335
  and social policies, 328–339
Institutions, and functionalism, 52–55

Laissez-faire social system, and social science, 265

Latin American Faculty of Social Science (FLACSO), and Project Camelot, 290–291

La Vida, 177–182

Legitimation, of deviance, 112; of social science information, 338–339

Magic, and functionalism, 51–52

MARGINALITY:
  and alienation, 106–107, 330–331
  in applied sociology, 228
  and the antisociologist, 211–220
  and deviant values, 123–126
  political, 108–126, 330–331
  and social control, 330–331
  in social theory, 197–220
  and the unsociologist, 211–220

Mental health, social indicators of, 329–330, 332, 335; social policies on, 329–330, 332, 335

Michigan State University (MSU), and the Central Intelligence Agency (CIA), 305–313

Midwest tradition in sociology, and the Weberian tradition, 186–189

National Science Foundation (NSF), 251–261

National Social Science Foundation (NSSF), 251–261; and grants, 257

Objectivity, in the physical sciences, 35–36; in the social sciences, 35–36

Occupationalism, and professionalism, 203–210, 214–220; as a sociological ideology, 203–210, 214–220

Parsonian school, 10; and the Weberian tradition, 188–190

Policies, on alcoholism, 330; on mental health, 329–330, 332, 335; and social indicators, 328–339

Policy-making, and social science, 262–304, 308, 311–313, 349–351

Political science, and economics, 24–25; and ideology, 24–25

Politics, and deviance, 112–114, 125; and marginality, 120–122; and sociology, 108–126

Positivism; *see* Empiricism, and positivism

Pragmatism; *see* Empiricism, and pragmatism

Prejudice, racial, 182

Preliterate cultures, and functionalism, 52

Professionalism, and occupationalism, 203–210, 214–220; as a sociological ideology, 200–210, 214–220

Professionalization, 200–203; in American sociology, 164–168

Project Themis, 347–349
  See also Report of the Panel on Defense Social and Behavioral Sciences

Psychoanalysis, and Marxism, 34–35; and the sociology of knowledge, 25–27; and value neutrality, 34–36, 40

Pure sociology, *vs.* applied sociology, 83–87, 227, 229
  See also Social theory

Race, prejudice, 182

RAND, 292–293

Recruitment, in American sociology, 160–161

Rehabilitation, and deviance, 108–109

Relevance, in social science, 280–286

Religion, and alienation, 106–107; and functionalism, 54

Report from Iron Mountain, 314–327

Report of the Panel on Defense Social and Behavioral Sciences, 340–354
  challenge to, 352–354
  and the Defense Department, 344–354
  findings, 346–347
  panelists, 341–342, 344–346, 349–351
  Project Themis, 347–349

Repression, and political deviance, 113–114, 330–331; and social deviance, 113–114, 330–331
  See also Control

Research, basic, 251–252; interdisciplinary, 175–177, 183–185; policy, 251–304

Rule, Caesaristic, 5

Science, and functionalism, 54
  and policy, 256–257, 308
  and secrecy, 256–257, 268–276
  and therapy, 83–87

Secrecy, 256–257; and social science, 26–8 276

Social change, 7, 12
  and cultural change, 57
  and functionalism, 55–58
  and social problems, 94–95

Social disorganization, 12–13

Social problems, 80–100
  and crime, 87–92
  definitions of, 81–82
  and deviant behavior, 108–109
  and functionalism, 84–87
  and political action, 113–114
  problem of, 83–87
  resolutions of, 86
  and social change, 94–95
  and social control, 92
  and social dysfunction, 84–87
  and social practice, 87–92, 95–100
  and social systems, 92–95

theory of, 80–87, 89, 91
and therapy, 83–87
the welfare model, 108–109

SOCIAL SCIENCE:
autonomy, 280–286, 302, 308, 338
and the command social system, 264, 266–267
and the laissez-faire consensus social system, 265, 267
legislative uses of, 257–259
and military sponsorship, 292
objectivity, 35–36
and public policy, 262–304, 308, 311–313, 349–351
and relevance, 280–286
and secrecy, 268–276
and the welfare social system, 264–265, 267
See also American sociology; Sociology
Social scientists, response to the MSU-CIA affair, 308–311; response to Project Camelot, 296–297
Social systems, and social function, 84–87; and social problems, 92–95
Social theory, and mainliners vs. marginals, 197–220
and social practice, 83–87, 227, 229
and social problems, 80–87, 89, 91
See also Pure sociology
Social Theory and Social Practice, 167–173
SOCIOLOGY:
American; see American sociology
of American sociology, 159–166
in college, 138–144, 155–156
of education, 129, 139
graduate training in, 144–155
in high school, 135–138, 155
learning, 129–158
and politics, 108–126
social role of, 158
stratification in, 130–131
students, 131
teaching, 129–158
of values, 165–166
See also American sociology; Social science
SOCIOLOGY OF KNOWLEDGE:
aims of, 17–20, 29
criticisms of, 17–19
historical perspectives of, 27
and ideology, 17–19, 66–67
and political science, 20–21
and psychology, 21–22, 25–27
roles of, 23–24, 27–28
and science, 23
and social science, 23
and a sociology of ethics, 28

Special Operations Research Organization (SORO), 288, 291, 293–294, 297
Sponsorship, 300–301
in American sociology, 163–164
Defense Department, 294
military, 292
State Department, 294
State (the), and social control, 125
State Department (United States), vs. Defense Department, 295–296, 352; Foreign Area Research Coordination (FAR), 352–354; and social science research, 294–296
Status, in American sociology, 162–163
Stratification, and alienation, 105–106; and functionalism, 245–246; in sociology, 130–131
Subordination; see Superordination vs. subordination
Subsidization; see Sponsorship
Suicide, and functionalism, 51
Superordination vs. subordination, 5; and consensus theory, 10–11; and the policy-maker/sociologist relation, 170–173
SYSTEMS:
counterideological, 71–72
counterutopian, 68–69
ethical, 183–184
ideological, 68–69
utopian, 71–72

Therapy, and deviance, 108–109; and science, 83–87; and social problems, 83–87

Universities, and the government of the United States, 340; and value systems, 276–280
Utopia, constellations, 76–78; constructs, 78–79; vs. ideology, 66–68, 71–72

VALUE NEUTRALITY:
in American social science, 41–45, 164–166
and empiricism, 36–40, 164–166
and Freudianism, 34–36, 40
and functionalism, 30–31, 235–249
and Marxism, 33–36, 40
and positivism, 33, 35–36
and social metaphysics, 40–41
and utilitarianism, 33, 35–36
Values, deviant, 123–126; social science of, 165–166, 183–184; and university bureaucracies, 276–280
Violence, and deviance, 120–122

Weberian tradition, and American sociology, 186–194; and the Midwest tradition, 186–189; and the Parsonian school, 188–190

Welfare, and deviance, 108–109; state, 124

West Coast tradition in sociology, 189